Law and Evolutionary Biology

Publisher:

GRUTER INSTITUTE
FOR LAW AND BEHAVIORAL RESEARCH

Law
&
Evolutionary
Biology

Selected Essays in Honor of

Margaret Gruter

on her 80th Birthday

Lawrence A. Frolik, Editor

with

Wolfgang Fikentscher and Gerti Dieker

Published by
GRUTER INSTITUTE FOR LAW AND BEHAVIORAL RESEARCH
158 Goya Road
Portola Valley, California 94028

Printed in the United State of America

Library of Congress Cataloging-in-Publication Data

ISBN 0-9669673-1-3

Table Of Contents

LAWRENCE A. FROLIK
Foreword   i

MONIKA GRUTER MORHENN
Prologue   iii

SUSAN LOW BLOCH
Birthday Letter   1

PAUL BOHANNAN
One Anthropologist's Gratitude to the Gruter Institute   3

TIMOTHY H. GOLDSMITH
Evolutionary Psychology and Heuristic Opportunity   15

MICHAEL T. McGUIRE
Evolutionary Theory and the Limits of Law   27

ROBERT TRIVERS
How I wrote: The Evolution of Reciprocal Altruism   37

KATHLEEN WERMKE
No Language But a Cry   57

Kingsley R. BROWNE
Law, Biology, Sex, and Politics   73

ROBERT D. COOTER
Mongolia: Avoiding Tragedy in the World's Largest Common   87

E. DONALD ELLIOTT
Evolutionary Models in Law: Pros and Cons   111

WOLFGANG FIKENTSCHER
Law Related Education, Moral Development,
and the Sense of Justice   127

ROBERT FRANK
Regulating Sexual Behavior; Richard Posner's *Sex and Reason* 149

LAWRENCE A. FROLIK
Biology and the Undue Influence Doctrine 169

OLIVER GOODENOUGH
The Nature of Business: Bringing the Insights of Biologically
Informed Behavioral Science to Business and the Law 181

HERBERT HELMRICH
Der evolutionären Entwicklung von Werten auf der
Spur – Ein Werkstattbericht 193

HAGEN HOF
Rules of Respect 243

RAIMUND JAKOB
Legal Procedure as a Place of Aggression 257

OWEN JONES
Law, Emotions and Behavioral Biology 269

ADELHEID KUHNE and MARTIN USTERI
The Correlation Between Psychology and Law – A Few
Considerations and Comments on Research and Practice
from the Point of View of Legal Psychology and Jurisprudence 281

MICHAEL LEHMANN
Evolution in Biology, Economics and Law 297

THOMAS T.M. MÖLLERS
A Call for Consideration of Human Modes of Behavior
When Promoting Environmentally Correct Behavior by
Means of Information and Force of Law 315

William H. Rodgers
Epilogue:
Margaret Gruter: A Creative Force for Improvement in Law 351

List of Authors 357

Publications by Margaret Gruter 361

Foreword

I am pleased to have the singular honor of acting as the primary editor for this extraordinary collection of essays that celebrate Margaret Gruter on her 80th birthday. These essays represent two of the most salient accomplishments of a remarkably talented woman. First, the essays exemplify Margaret's appreciation of the symbiotic intellectual relationship between what others might think of as quite diverse disciplines: biology and law. The world has many great thinkers, but only a few great synthesizers. Margaret is one of those rare individuals able to look beyond traditional categories and so perceived the critical links between biology and law. As a result, she almost single handedly demonstrated how a new field of intellectual inquiry - what many now refer to as evolutionary psychology - could be used to illuminate and understand law and legal institutions. Years from now, when law school courses in Law and Biology become commonplace, the antecedent of those courses will be identified as Margaret's pioneering writings and her unflagging efforts to introduce law professors, judges and lawyers to the relevance and even the necessity of understanding our biological roots.

These essays are written by some of the finest scholars in America and Germany. This is no accident. For the second great accomplishment of Margaret was her insistence that lawyers be introduced to biology by leading scientists, and in turn that the scientists be exposed to leading legal scholars and jurists. Margaret has no patience for mediocrity. Whenever she has organized and sponsored conferences, institutes, articles and talks, only the best has been good enough. Consequently, her efforts have created a secure intellectual foundation for this interdisciplinary undertaking.

On a personal level, I owe Margaret deepest thanks for introducing me to ideas and insights that have truly made the world anew. My effort in soliciting and editing these essays represents my appreciation to her for all she has done for me both intellectually and personally. I am proud to call her my friend and mentor.

Lawrence A. Frolik
Editor

Prologue

This book celebrates the achievements of a woman who has built a bridge connecting law with the behavioral sciences, a pioneering and novel task. Through her multifarious talents in scholarly inquiry, business acumen, and most pronouncedly her unceasing drive, Margaret Gruter has succeeded in bringing a wealth of insights from the behavioral sciences to the law.

Beginning with the premise that law, at its most basic, attempts to regulate human behavior, Margaret Gruter set on a mission to bridge the gap between law and the findings from the behavioral sciences. If law seeks to affect human behavior, then it makes sense to understand what motivates and causes people to behave in certain ways. To what degree can law affect human behavior? The law is benefited, for example, by an understanding of what behavioral predispositions are built into our species by our evolutionary past, even if we may choose to use law to counteract these predispositions.

In search of a forum in which to pursue these ideas, Margaret Gruter founded the Gruter Institute for Law and Behavioral Research in 1981. The Gruter Institute has fostered multi-disciplinary research to make lawyers, legal scholars and judges more aware of scientific knowledge. Insights from fields such as neurobiology, genetics, game theory, ethology, and new reproductive science are just a small sampling of the wealth of information which can better serve to inform jurists about what to expect in human behavior. That developing and communicating such insights is not a simple task is clear. Indeed, the complexity of the task of informing the social sciences about human behavior is unsurprising when looking back at the *a priori* questions of human behavior, law, and ethics which have confronted and confounded philosophers such as Aristotle, Kant and Nietzsche, to name but a few.

A non-profit foundation, the Gruter Institute is organized around a group of research fellows comprised of some of the finest scientists and educators from the United States and Europe. Since its founding, the Gruter Institute has conducted over 50 conferences and seminars, produced more than 50 publications, and introduced scores of law professors and judges to the relationship between law and biology. Workshops, symposia and project teams are targeted at addressing the ever-increasing number of new theories and applications. Recently budding projects include the implications of behavior on comparative, international arbitration and dispute resolution; and the new genetics and reproduction: the legal response. Margaret Gruter's extraordinary leadership in these projects is unparalleled.

Perhaps most remarkable, however, is that throughout her heralded academic career, Margaret Gruter has never ceased to flourish in her role as wife, mother, and as I can say with unrivaled good fortune, as a grandmother. In between fostering novel ideas and projects, publishing numerous books and articles, and organizing conferences, there is never a time when she is not there to gather the family for a sumptuous meal, or to hold a wise ear to the tales of our lives. Indeed, during the many years in which I have worked with her on various Gruter Institute endeavors and been supported by her guidance in my own career in law, I have often found myself looking on with awe as she seemingly effortlessly masters the skills that so many of us seek to achieve.

Fittingly, it is this woman of such unique drive and myriad abilities who has pioneered the bridging of the gap between law and the behavioral sciences. The most exciting part of this endeavor is – as the articles in this Festschrift show – that the inquiry has just begun.

Monika Gruter Morhenn

February 1, 1999

HAPPY EIGHTIETH BIRTHDAY!!!

Dear Margaret,

Happy, happy birthday to a great lady, scholar, pioneer, and most importantly a great friend. As you know, I've been immersed in trying to protect the Constitution during the roller coaster ride involving the impeachment battle between the President and the Congress this past year. Hence, I have not had time to write a lengthy scholarly article on evolutionary biology. But I must say that after witnessing and, in fact, participating in the constitutional crisis that has embroiled the country for the last thirteen months, I have several evolutionary observations that I want to share with you.

– The actions of the House of Representatives in launching this partisan impeachment process demonstrates the power of testosterone and males fighting for dominance.

– The President's misbehavior demonstrates the strength of the same forces even more dramatically. His perseverance under the relentless attack by the independent counsel and the House of Representatives reveals the power of persistence and compartmentalization, a new concept we should investigate to see if it exists in other primates.

1

– The public's rational and thoughtful reaction both to the President's behavior and to Congress's impeachment process indicates the wisdom of the people not caught up in the political partisanship of those fighting for dominance.

– The framers of the Constitution designed a good structural system, making sure that the more thoughtful, less politically vulnerable Senate has the final word on impeachment, and then only if two-thirds of the Senators agree. The experience demonstrates how important structure and process are.

It is too early at the time of this writing to know how this saga will end. But I hope that the constitutional structure designed in 1781 proves to be as wise as I now think it is and allows us to escape this misadventure with a strong country that is not devastated by nasty factions and brutal sexual witch-hunts. To go back to Hobbe's state of nature would be too big a price for our country to pay for Mr. Clinton's errant behavior.*

Margaret, I hope that as you read this, you are enjoying your birthday and the accolades of all of us who have learned from you and profited so immensely from your wisdom, experience, and many valuable conferences.

Much love,

Susan Low Bloch

* Please forgive my hyperbole. I have not enjoyed watching this constitutional crisis run on with no one in control...

One Anthropologist's Gratitude to the Gruter Institute

Paul Bohannan*

One of the most gratifying activities of my professional life has been a long-term association with the Gruter Institute and its founder, Margaret Gruter. It began on Christmas eve of 1980. Dr. Gruter called me, apologized for the date, said she knew my writings on African law, and wanted to talk to me. I asked her to come over.

Dr. Gruter had a commitment from the Goethe Institute in support of a conference on Law and Biology. However, that commitment was contingent on her finding university sponsorship for the conference. I was, at that time, teaching at the University of California, Santa Barbara. UCSB had just taken over Robert Hutchins' old Institute for the Study of Democratic Institutions and had hired Dr. James Miller to be its Director. I had been on the committee (composed partly of UCSB faculty and partly of directors of the Institute) that was charged with integrating the Institute into the University without undermining the reputation and goals of the Institute and without flying in the face of University regulations.

* Professor Emeritus of Anthropology and Law, University of Southern California, Los Angeles.

3

At the time Dr. Gruter called, I was interested in both legal anthropology and the new developments then taking place in primatology, in which biological anthropologists were playing an important role. Only five years before, in 1975, E. O. Wilson's Sociobiology had been published. Many of its ideas had been around for some time, but organizing them according to the premises of genetics was daring. The dust had not yet settled. I was convinced of two things: that Dr. Wilson did not know enough about culture (he has since fixed that), and that some—indeed, most—of the negative reactions by cultural anthropologists grew from ignorance.

Dr. Gruter, who holds a law degree from Heidelberg and another from Stanford, was very well read in ethology in general and primatology in particular. She convinced me of something I had never even thought of: that if ethology, the social sciences and law could learn to talk to one another, all would be better off.

As a result of that meeting, I went to James Miller with the idea that the Hutchins Institute and UCSB should supply the institutional requirement that the Goethe Institute had made a proviso of Gruter's conference. Miller, being a systems theorist, was not in the least shocked by the idea that fields as ostensibly separate as biology and law might well have a lot to learn from one another. He was, indeed, convinced that systems theory itself could do the job.

The result was the first Monterey Dunes Conference, held in September of 1981. It was attended by scholars from Germany, Japan, England, Canada and the United States. It lasted three days. And it was wildly—no other adverb will do—successful. The Gruter Institute had been well and truly launched. Not only did we all learn a lot at that conference, not only did we all have a good time, but we were all convinced that we were on the edge of something important (for all that we were leery of being misunderstood).

On a personal note, I was pleased when Margaret asked me to join her in editing the re-written papers.

Since that first conference, the Gruter Institute has sponsored many conferences (all with international casts), expanding our knowledge of both law and biology, in several countries. It has opened several branch offices in American and in German universities.

Although I still feel closely associated with the Gruter Institute, I am no longer active in it. Because I am therefore both inside it and outside it (and because I have no startling new ideas on the topic of law and biology), the rest of this short paper is focussed on two points about which the Gruter Institute has made a tremendous difference.

First, the scholars of the Institute have underscored the fact that human beings remain animals in spite of the fact that language and other cultural assets allow them to expand their animal capacities in ways that seem, on the surface, to be nonanimal. Culture has vastly expanded the animal capacities of human beings, but it has not done away with any of them.

Second, the Gruter Institute has shown time and again that the culture in which a person was reared and educated cannot, without comparative data from other species and other cultures, provide an adequate basis for theorizing about the "human" condition.[1]

The Gruter Institute's consideration of the Baby M case makes the point clearly. A woman made a contract to be artificially inseminated (in exchange for a fee), then hand the child over to the sperm-donor and his infertile wife. After the birth of the baby, she found it difficult to live up to the terms of the contract—she sued to keep the baby. The Gruter Institute pointed out the need for courts to consider the infra-cultural, animal dimension of parenthood—the physical and mental states of the mother—when it makes decisions about the legal "disposal" of children of surrogate mothers. It explored the issue of what the infra-cultural, biologically

---

1 A prime example of this error was Alfred Kinsey's calling his 1948 book *Sexual Behavior of the Human Male*, when what he was really talking about were middle-Western, American, upper-middle class, white males.

determined dimensions of parenthood may be, and conditions under which courts might legitimately consider them to over ride or mitigate contract.

Second is a problem I have long been concerned with. Theories of jurisprudence should be informed by insights from many cultures as well as from many intellectual disciplines. When I was a graduate student at Oxford University, I attended a series of lectures by Max Gluckman on African law—particularly the law of the Barotse or Lozi people of what was then Northern Rhodesia (the lectures were given before this material was published[2]). When I began my own field research, among the Tiv of Nigeria in 1949, I discovered that if I was to report what the people of that society considered important, I had to go to meetings in which elders settled disputes—about wives and bridewealth, about the boundaries of fields, about debts, about crimes considered too picayune (or too esoteric) to involve the British administration. At those sessions, Tiv elders (who were appointed officials of, and paid a pittance by, the colonial government) acted as judges. British administrative officers called these meetings "courts."

However, I soon learned that there were two kinds of meetings, both called jir by Tiv: those courts sponsored by the British colonial government, and another kind of meeting in which the elders acted not in their roles as government servants, but rather as "repairers of the land." To make a distinction in English which Tiv did not make, I came to call the second type of meeting by the old English term "moots," because those meetings in some ways resembled the moots held in medieval Britain. Tiv moots handled disputes and problems that British culture and European ideas found unsuitable to their definitions of law and court. Tiv exchange marriage had been declared illegal by the British colonial administration in 1928 on the grounds that it was so complicated the British could never understand it (I once saw this statement written, in approximately those words, in a government file). Obviously, Tiv ideas on the

---

2 Gluckman, Max, The Judicial Process among the Barotse of Northern Rhodesia. Manchester: Manchester University Press, 1955.

subject were not expunged or even changed by a mere change in the law made by colonial administrative officials without consulting them.   However, the British colonial officers considered such marriages "illegal." Thus disputes about them could not (they said) be brought to government courts.   That did not mean, of course, that Tiv did not consider them important or that disputes that arose around them did not have to be settled.

The other kind of cases heard by these moots was what those same British government officials called "witchcraft cases."   The official government position was that witchcraft does not exist. The administration could not, the officials said, admit that it did by allowing disputes concerning it into the officially recognized courts. They added that you cannot settle witchcraft disputes in a court of law because there could be no facts. To deal with those disputes, Tiv met and considered them—not exactly behind the colonial government's back, but certainly without its blessing.

As I attended more and more courts and moots, and as I began to understand what Tiv were doing and why, I made what was for me an important discovery: to even try to force Tiv ideas into European legal categories did serious damage to the Tiv ideas. I thought that the Tiv ideas were important—not only to Tiv but to students of legal anthropology and jurisprudence. I still think so. By putting the Tiv ideas clearly, the victories of <u>Western</u> law could be seen in a new context, as cultural victories rather than merely the human way to proceed. At the same time, Tiv victories, dealing with much the same kind of situations, could also be acknowledged. That is to say, you can legitimately and profitably do it <u>that</u> way too!

The legal system is a great victory for any civilization. That does <u>not</u> mean that any one of those systems can provide an adequate theoretical framework for considering all legal systems in all societies at all periods of history. To translate the legal activities and ideas of many people in the world into a Western framework often takes a lot of twisting of the original ideas.

My dealing with the problem as I did had an unintended result. It put me in direct conflict with the ideas of Max Gluckman. I admired Max; I liked him and was grateful for the help he had given me on several occasions. Max stuck to his grounds; so did I. I think it is to his credit, and mine, that this "Gluckman-Bohannan controversy" did not undermine our admiration or our friendship.

Gluckman's position, as I read it, was that law and jurisprudence were a set of propositions that were not only known, but were "true." These truths had been set forth in Roman-Dutch law, the common law, and other Western systems. Nobody I know has ever denied that those legal systems are great cultural achievements. But for me, that was not the issue. The issue was whether one could use the particular categories and connections developed in those legal systems as the basis for analyzing alien legal systems that shared no history with them and had developed quite different answers to quite similar problems.

When I questioned his point, Max told me and said in print that if I believed <u>that</u>, I was being solipsistic—that is, that the legal ideas of each society would have no way of influencing one another or of being compared and fitted into a larger-scale system of thought. I asked him, both personally and in print, how he, a magnificent ethnographer, could abandon his ethnographic perspective when he turned to comparison.

In 1966, at a conference at Burg Wartenstein in Austria, Laura Nader brought Max and me together in hopes that we could "work out" our differences. Neither of us would take the bait. We publicly agreed to disagree on this point.

After that conference, I wrote a small piece that was included in the volume of that conference that Laura Nader edited.[3] My point was a simple one. You first learn the distinctions and practices (and the premises that underlie both) of as many different legal systems as possible—including, of course, the ones that underlie our own practices. That is, indeed, the province of legal anthropology. You

---

3 "Ethnography and Comparison in Legal Anthropology" in Law and Culture in Society. Laura Nader, editor, Chicago: Aldine Publishing Company, 1969.

are then in a position to be fully aware when you compare one system to another. As an example, in the Tiv language, there are two words that are antonyms of their word that can fairly sensibly be translated lie (although their word has different implications than ours). One of those "truths" means "what actually happened." The other means "what should have happened, and would have happened if people had behaved correctly." In Tiv conviction and courtesy, people should be given the benefit of the doubt. It is antisocial and wrong, they claim, to use the first term if the second term will do. When Tiv, in court, acted on these cultural principles, the British first called them "liars" and then generalized the proposition by saying that all Tiv were terrible liars.

The difficulty, obviously, was in the British premises and values a they examined a Tiv situation they did not fully understand. Understanding such differences in vocabulary and values in different cultures is, surely, the best way yet discovered to get to the premises that underlie your own values—values that may be out-of-awareness and are hence unquestioned. It is not, however, always easy to do.

Long after Max's death, I still think that this part of his work was misguided. However, his view is far easier for people who lack cross-cultural experience to accept—especially lawyers, because Max was skillfully writing in their language, and did not in any way make it necessary for them to re-examine the ideas that underlie their own practices. It is my own conviction that the very fact of examining these ideas is instructive about the over-all nature of law, and the subtlety with which culture-bound premises can lead to cross-cultural misunderstanding.

"Law and biology" means that you learn the facts of biology not only about your own, but about all, species. A precise equivalent is that you learn the "facts" of legal activity not only from your own culture and its history, but from all cultures, including those that have solved pan-human problems in quite different ways. It means speaking as well as one can for all living beings—and all members of the human species—by creating a mode of understanding that does not short-change any of them.

Being an ethnographer means that you have to understand not only the culture of the people you are studying, but also your own culture. The ideas and "prejudices" you bring to your study turn out to be "just another ethnography." If you look at them that way, they twist ideas far less than if you look at your own as the standard by which to judge all others. You have to learn to see the ways of your own culture, no matter how effective or how beautiful they are, as just one way to do it, whatever "it" may be. There are other ways to do pretty much the same thing—and some of them are also efficient and beautiful.

It is in this variety of ways that the importance of ethnography emerges. Social theory, if it is to be optimally effective, cannot be based on the experience of any single people or a set of closely related peoples ("the Europeans") any more than the topic of society can be exhausted by limiting oneself to human societies.

Being a student of jurisprudence includes exploring the many ways human beings have learned to resolve human disputes. Like all other human culture, systems of law have limits in historical time and cultural space. I thought—and still think—that there were Tiv ideas that were just as relevant to European law as European legal ideas were relevant to Tiv law. Both sets of ideas work—in the right context. To consider one to be "true" and the other either primitive or irrelevant is to flaunt—and be done in by—one's ethnocentric biases and limitations.

My position was—and is—that any global "theory" of law has to take all these distinctions and insights into account, and not short-change any one of them by reducing it to some other. That means considering the common law or the Napoleonic code in its ethnographic context and as a source of valuable ideas, but not promoting it to the level of a framework for social theory applicable to all human examples. The requirement is that judicial theory be enlarged to accommodate ideas from many sources.

Just here is where Margaret Gruter and the Gruter Institute are important. Margaret saw that the discoveries of ethologists and primatologists were relevant to any legal system (as well as to any theory of law), and that any legal system that does not take the biological foundation of humanity into account must necessarily be out of touch with the human beings to whom it applies. Genetically derived information underlies cultural information—and law is an important dimension of culture. Margaret saw that ethnographic and historical information is essential to everyone—including lawyers—if they are to expand the limits of their own species, their own times, their own training, and their own cultural viewpoints.

At the time Margaret called me that Christmas of 1980, most cultural anthropologists (too often inadequately informed) had ganged up against sociobiology. They saw the problem in terms of either/or: if anybody made a claim for biology, they assumed that person was denying the importance of culture. Today we know, of course, that both biology and culture—and some wonderful mixture of the two—underlie all human behavior. The two are not to be forced into an either/or situation—and neither must be forgotten. At that time, most lawyers, understandably enough, were informed only in the principles of their own codes and their own legal system. We now know that expanding their base makes them better lawyers.

We have come a long way since Christmas of 1980. That first Monterey Dunes conference set the tone: there is a biological foundation to human behavior, including law, that the culture (including legal culture) has to understand and accommodate. The 1984 conference on "Ostracism: a Social and Biological Phenomenon"[4] made deep inroads into the cross-cultural point as well as into the biological point.

The task of the Gruter Institute is clear: it is to make all of us, including lawyers and social scientists and biologists, "think bigger" about the ideas we take for granted.

---

4. Gruter, Margaret and Roger D. Masters, editors, Ostracism: A Social and BiologicalPhenomenon. Elsevier. Ethology and Sociobiology, 7, iii, 1986.

Because there is so much cultural variation and so many social contexts in the modern world, law is sometimes thrust (by lawyers, legislators or the general public) into areas beyond its traditional depth. American law—indeed, law of many developed nations— has, for example, a tendency to put everything into an adversarial context. In many contexts that is suitable—but in some it is a distraction or worse. Some legal systems, in some places and times, have adjusted to this point. We are beginning to understand that in family law, for example, turning family members into adversaries and then determining that one is right and the other therefore wrong, just to arrive at a surface resolution of their disputes, is not only counterproductive but socially damaging. When American divorce—especially when young children are involved—is handed to the law (there are several ways to cope with divorce that have nothing whatever to do with law), consideration of biological dimensions and of comparative methods is essential. If, at divorce, you pit one parent against the other, you not only drive them farther apart, you may make it next to impossible for them to focus on their basic parental responsibilities. California's 1970 divorce law (later adopted by most other states) did away with the need for grounds for divorce—divorcing couples no longer had to lie under oath. At the same time, the new law created social problems that had not been foreseen and have not yet been solved. Most importantly, we still have to find a good way to deal with parental responsibility in the absence of an intact family. Merely condemning divorce or making it difficult to get will not solve this problem—in a long history, it never has.

The point—and this is why the work of the Gruter Institute is so important—is that the achievements of law, if they are to work, must be in accord with both the biological and the social/cultural dimensions of human nature. Some of those dimensions lie far deeper than the capacity of law-makers, as law-makers, can reach. It is <u>never</u> adequate to fill in the gaps of ignorance with personal opinion or folklore. Yet, that is almost inevitable in the absence of knowledge. The Gruter Institute has exposed a lot of such ignorance, and provided a lot of knowledge to fuel alternatives. Its work is only just beginning.

So—thanks, Margaret. The wisdom and energy (not to mention money) you have put into all this have created a magnificent monument not only to scholarship but to both the world of legal affairs and to "human" affairs. Your work and that of the Institute stands. And I'm <u>very</u> glad to be counted among your many friends!

Evolutionary Psychology and Heuristic Opportunity

Timothy H. Goldsmith*

I am honored to salute Margaret Gruter on the occasion of her 80th birthday. She has had a prescient view of the importance of evolutionary theory in understanding the mysteries of human nature, and she has played a unique role in casting a net, if not yet a spell, over the legal profession, drawing together scholars from different disciplines, and generating stimulating and productive dialogue. It has been my great privilege to be present on a number of these occasions. The following short essay is offered in her honor and in the spirit of reaching an ever-widening audience with the message that she has worked so hard to deliver.

---

* Professor of Biology, Department of Molecular, Cellular, and Developmental Biology, Yale University

* * *

As a teacher I am regularly faced with a paradox. Biological evolution, with its centerpiece natural selection, has fashioned our world. Evolution has not only brought forth life in all of its spectacular diversity, it has also shaped major features of our physical environment. Yet when we contemplate our human nature, we remain enthralled by explanations that lack historical connections. We are just starting to wrestle with deep knowledge of ourselves in ways that incorporate evolutionary understanding.

The historian of science Robert Siegfried (1998) has recently drawn attention to the powerful role that the heuristic nature of evolutionary theory played in generating "vast new areas for investigation not previously perceived." In this respect, evolutionary theory contrasts with more traditional concepts of nature that reflect "providential design." Evolution is heuristic in suggesting relationships that can be explored iteratively with successive refinement, whereas explanations that do not invoke the history of life offer no such opportunity. The idea is not new. Charles Darwin put the case clearly:

> ". . . when we regard every production of nature as one which has had a history; when we contemplate every complex structure and instinct as the summing up of many contrivances, and each useful to the possessor . . . when we thus view each organic being, how far more interesting, I speak from experience, will the study of natural history become!

> A grand and almost untrodden field of inquiry will be opened, on the causes and laws of variation, on correlation of growth, on the effects of use and disuse, on the direct action of external condition, and so forth." (Darwin, 1859, pp 485-486)

Evolutionary psychology, as a subset of Darwinian theory, offers the same opportunity. It recognizes that evolution has made us, and it thus encourages us to think about the origins of human nature in historical terms. Although evolutionary theory provides a powerful framework to organize and test hypotheses, as in all accounts of history, reconstruction is frequently difficult. Consequently we must utilize every source of information that we can find. But because evolution is a very broad subject drawing on the physical and social sciences as well as biology, there is no shortage of avenues to explore.

The emerging field of evolutionary psychology not only provides a framework for organizing current knowledge, it can also point the way to new and important questions. As Siegfried has said (with notable understatement), "[evolution] can provide additional perspective on today's debates."

Evolution, however, also provides the uninitiated with a babble of confusion. There is not another subject in science so poorly understood by so many who are nevertheless so willing to speak with such grand assurance. The result lapses effortlessly into caricature. Natalie Angier (1999), who writes about biology for the New York Times, has recently offered a useful example with a popular article on evolutionary psychology entitled "Men, Women, Sex and Darwin." It illustrates how simple it is to make mischief with the false dichotomy, the imperfectly understood example, and indifference to empirical evidence. There is no sense of the heuristic, for ". . . when it comes to human nature, 'universal laws' are meant to be broken." In short, the article provides a convenient vehicle for clarifying a number of popular misconceptions.

Theory and reality

Angier's theme is illustrated with four cartoons, each stating a proposition as a theory and the author's refutation as fact:

Theory: Women prefer older men with high status.

Reality: Maybe it's just a matter of space. Who can breath in the presence of a handsome young ego?

Theory: Even financially successful women want a rich man.
Reality: Women need a man's money because they'll never make as much.

Theory: Women go for the virile alpha male.
Reality: Even some female baboons prefer the nice, little guys.

Theory: Women's sex drive is lower than men's.
Reality: Laws and customs everywhere aim at curbing the female libido.

Before proceeding, we need to expose this rhetorical ploy in which theory is contrasted with reality. Is theory the opposite of reality? Is theory simply a casual idea waiting to be knocked aside by a fact? These may be common, everyday meanings, but the central goal of science is to create broadly encompassing explanations—theories—that make sense of masses of observation and experiment. Kinetic theory, cell theory, and evolutionary theory are important examples. The suggestion that reality (fact) is the antithesis of theory is a stratagem currently used by religious creationists in political efforts to keep evolution from being taught in science classrooms. "Evolution is just a theory, not fact," they insist. Consequently, it is disquieting to find this confusion so prominent in the work of a professional science writer.

We will come back to this dichotomous labeling shortly, but first, some background. What has the study of evolution taught us about mating systems? The related concepts (read theories) of sexual selection (Darwin, 1871) and parental investment (Trivers, 1972) are not primarily addressed to human behavior. They have much broader significance, and evolutionary psychology examines the degree to which pan-cultural features of human mating practices can be understood in terms of these more general biological principles.

Sexual selection is the result of competition among members of one sex for reproductive access to members of the opposite sex, and when present it is usually (but not always) a feature of males. Males become larger than females, or showier (e.g., with bright plumage), or noisier, or equipped with weapons such as antlers or large incisors. Humans have experienced a modest amount of sexual selection. For example, on average men are larger and stronger than women.

The concept of parental investment has proved very useful in understanding why species differ in the amount of sexual selection that has occurred. Reproduction can be so demanding that it limits lifetime reproductive success. For example, because internal gestation and lactation of female mammals represent a large parental investment, the number of offspring a female is able to produce is consequently limited. Sperm, by contrast, are cheap. In principle there is virtually no limit to the number of females a male mammal can inseminate. Female mammals therefore characteristically become a limiting reproductive resource for which males compete. When the competition is great, there are more losers than winners among the males, males have greater variation in mating success than females, and the mating system is frequently polygynous. Humans are unusual mammals in that males generally make a significant parental investment. Human mating systems vary between monogamy and a mixture of monogamy and polygyny (Daly and Wilson, 1983). Polyandry is rare and occurs in particular ecological conditions.

Sexual selection and differential parental investment are thus components of evolutionary theory that help us to understand the origins of a variety of animal mating systems. One of the interests of evolutionary psychologists has been to examine human mating systems in the light of evolutionary theory. With this background, we return to the first two of the "theories" of the Angier article, only to see that neither is a theory in the sense of being an explanation. Each contains a statement of reality based on empirical research. The data come from a variety of sources including surveys done in 37 different cultures from around the world (Buss, 1989, 1999).

Women prefer to marry men who are a few years older than they are. The average preference is 3.4 years and varies in different cultures from 2.2 to 4.9 years. Preference and practice are similar: the average age difference at marriage is about 3 years. The wishes of women are, on average, consistent with the wishes of men, who seek to marry younger women.

What is the basis for women's preference? Evolutionary social theory suggests conditions in which a male's resources are essential to the female. Resources are frequently important in species where male parental investment is required to rear offspring successfully, as in many species of birds. Females of such species select mates on the basis of the male's demonstrated ability to hold territory, build nests, or construct a bower.

Historically the interdependence of men and women is complex, involving divisions of labor and role. Men almost certainly provided protection, both individually and in the group. From the perspective of women, this is a resource that is made more reliable by long-term male commitment. Human females also seem to have become more dependent on males for animal protein than is the case for any other species that hunts. As societies specialized, men assumed control of other resources, making women more dependent.

Not surprisingly, women value resources in a potential mate about twice as highly as do men, independent of geographic location, technological development of society, race, religion, politics, or any other factor. Is this empirical finding related to women's documented preference for somewhat older men? The latter preference seems to reflect the probability that such men will have greater status and access to resources. As described below, however, other considerations are also important in female choice (Buss, 1999).

Theory and reality are now further turned on their head. Angier's "reality" is not empirically based description. The notion—"Maybe it's just a matter of space. Who can breath in the presence of a handsome young ego?"—is really hypothesis, a possible explanation, albeit somewhat frivolously stated, for the observation that women prefer older men. As explanation, though, it is not inconsistent with an evolved psychology that looks to find in males the signs of maturity that can come with success and status.

Success and status are clearly not the only important criteria that women employ, for otherwise the preferred age difference would be larger than it is. Young women also have other mate preferences that are more likely to be present in younger men. One of the hallmarks of evolutionary adaptations is that there are inevitably compromises. Similarly, any complex behavior with evolutionary roots is likely to have multiple proximate causes.

The hypothesis that wealthy or powerful women might not value resources in a mate as highly as other women because they do not need additional wealth has been tested, and it fails (reviewed in Buss, 1999). Women seek economically successful mates regardless of their own personal wealth. The explanation cannot be that women make an objective assessment of financial *need*, because the phenomenon is observed in well-paid Western professional women (Buss, 1989) and in at least one culture where women hold the major economic power (Ardener, Ardener, & Warmington, 1960). Angier's explanation (labeled "reality") is not easily consistent with these facts and is colored by recent Western cultural values concerning sexual equality in the workplace. The evidence suggests that relative wealth of mates may be more important to women than absolute wealth. This would be consistent with an evolved psychology that enhances the acquisition of resources by seeking them in a mate (i.e., "marrying up"). It could also involve a wish not to compromise the self-esteem of the man. The two are not necessarily alternatives.

Contingency and choice

Are women interested in "the virile alpha male?" In general, women are interested in taller men, men that are strong and athletic, and who show signs of leadership. These features of a partner were likely valuable through human evolutionary history when men could provide women with physical protection from other men. But in addition to physical appearance and resources, there are many other things about a potential mate that interest women: a readiness to commit to one partner, an interest in and willingness to invest in children, generosity, affection, ambition, interests similar to the woman's, a compatible personality, and even similar physical attributes. All of these features are important to long-term bonds and therefore to reproductive success, but how a woman weighs them may be very individualistic and depend on circumstances. (This intricacy is a core tenet of evolutionary psychology, but Angier would have us believe that only primatologists and evolutionary psychologists who are women understand it!) For example, young women exploring a short-term relationship or approaching marriage for the first time may give more weight to physical appearance, whereas women entering a second marriage are likely to be more interested in those traits of character that indicate commitment (reviewed in Buss, 1999).

Angier's "reality" is that "even some female baboons prefer nice little guys." One might add that some female baboons also trade sex for protection (Smuts, 1985). The problem is not that "when it comes to human nature, 'universal laws' are meant to be broken." The task is to identify correctly the centrally important factors that enable meaningful generalizations about nature. The name of the evolutionary game is reproductive success. Humans clearly have multiple, contingent strategies for achieving this end, and one strategy is not disproved by pointing to another that is practiced at another time, under other circumstances, or by another individual. It is hardly necessary to invoke the behavior of baboons to make this point.

It takes two to tango

Is women's sex drive lower than men's? That proposition actually conceals a more complex reality (Geary, 1998). David Buss (1999, pg 315) puts it this way:

"Men sometimes seek sexual access with a minimum of investment. Men often guard their resources and are extraordinarily choosy about who they invest those resources in. They are 'resource coy' and often preserve their investment for long-term mates. Because women often pursue a long-term sexual strategy they often seek to obtain investment, or signals of investment, before consenting to sex. Yet the investment that women covet is precisely the investment that men most vigorously guard. The sexual access that men seek is precisely the resource that women are so selective about giving."

Sexual selection and parental investment make sense of this conflict. Men and women have evolved somewhat different strategies to achieve reproductive success. Although both can be very selective in their long-term strategies of mate selection and marriage, men bear fewer potential costs (at least historically) in pursuing a less discriminating short-term strategy. Or to put it another way, men are more inclined to seek more partners, more frequently, and with less concern with long-term investment. Yet for every man who finds a partner of the moment without resorting to force, there is a willing woman, a condition that had to exist for male psychology to evolve as it has. Women, too, can pursue their own reproductive interests with short-term relationships, but there is nevertheless an asymmetry between the sexes. Male inclination provides the economic incentive for the world's oldest profession.

In this example Angier's "reality" is on the mark, but it raises the question *why* "laws and customs everywhere aim at curbing the female libido." The general answer is that males that make a substantial parental investment are genetic losers if they unwittingly invest in offspring that are not their own. In species with internal fertilization males frequently guard their mates to prevent insemination by another male. In human cultures concern about paternity takes many forms: male sexual jealousy (focussed on the possibility that the woman has been inseminated by another man), desire that brides be virgins, veiling and sequestering unmarried women, and genital mutilation of young girls to eliminate pleasure in intercourse. Controls of women have likely been amplified since the invention of agriculture 10,000-12,000 years ago, and the creation of centralized, stratified societies in which men could control resources that women need for survival. A subordinate role of women in the patriarchal, pastoral cultures of the Middle East of 2,000 years ago is reflected today in traditions of the more conservative branches of Christian, Jewish, and Muslim religions.

Evolution and mind

Evolutionary arguments can seem detached from conscious perceptions. The unhappy wife who has an affair with her tennis instructor or the guy who is hankering to get in bed with the new office receptionist are not thinking about maximizing their lifetime reproductive success. Each is responding to complex motivations that evolved in the service of reproduction but employ a variety of proximate modes for their satisfaction. People seek relationships in which they are valued, and people seek pleasure in sex. Evolutionary theory shows us *why.*

The single most important cultural influence on human sexual behavior has been the recent technological capacity of women to exert control over their own reproduction. In our society, women also have increasing opportunity for economic independence. The combined impact on marriage patterns, family structures, and even military service (Browne, 1999) may become large, but how our evolved psychology ultimately accommodates to these important cultural changes—or *vice versa*—remains to be seen.

Summary

Evolutionary psychology, like its parent discipline evolution, offers a heuristic path to understanding human nature. Concepts such as sexual selection and parental investment suggest interpretations of human behavior that can be tested and refined by further study. Like providential interpretations of nature, explanations of psychological norms that draw on pop understanding of evolution, political belief, or personal whim lead nowhere. Those who interpret science for a general readership, and the media that employ them, have a special responsibility to inform themselves.

References

Angier, N. Men, Women, Sex and Darwin. The New York Times. Feb. 21, 1999: Magazine (Section 6): 48-53.

Ardener, E.W., Ardener, S.G. & Warmington, W.A. (1960). Plantation and Village in the Cameroons. London: Oxford University Press.

Browne, K.R. (1999). Women at War: An Evolutionary Analysis. George Mason Law Review (in press).

Buss, D.M. (1989). Sex differences in human mate preferences: Evolutionary hypotheses tested in 37 cultures. Behavioral and Brain Sciences, 12, 1-49.

Buss, D.M. (1999). Evolutionary Psychology: The New Science of Mind. Needham Heights, MA: Allyn & Bacon.

Daly, M. & Wilson, M. (1983). Sex, Evolution, and Behavior, 2nd ed. Belmont, CA: Wadsworth Publishing Co.

Darwin, C. (1871). The Descent of Man and Selection in Relation to Sex. London: Murray.

Darwin, C. (1859, 1964). On the Origin of Species. A Facsimile of the First Edition. Cambridge, MA: Harvard University Press.

Geary, D.C. (1998). Male, Female: The Evolution of Human Sex Differences. Washington, DC: The American Psychological Association.

Siegfreid, R. (1998). Evolution as a Heuristic. Reports of the National Center for Science Education, 18, 20-21.

Smuts, B.B. (1985). Sex and Friendship in Baboons. New York, NY: Aldine de Gruyter.

Trivers, R. (1972). Parental investment and sexual selection. In B. Campbell (ed.), Sexual Selection and the Descent of Man: 1871-1971 (pp. 136-179). Chicago: Aldine.

Evolutionary Theory and the Limits of Law

Michael T. McGuire*

Writing a chapter to celebrate Margaret Gruter's accomplishments is a thoroughly enjoyable undertaking. Margaret's far-ranging mind, her inquiries into the biological foundations of law, and her untiring devotion to law-related education have benefited not only those who have had the privilege of knowing and working with her, but also those who have experienced the influence of her ideas and educational efforts.

INTRODUCTION

The invitation to contribute to this book has given me the opportunity to explore a seldom-discussed idea, yet one that I believe can inform both the practical and theoretical sides of law.

* Professor, Neuropsychiatric Institute School of Medicine University of California, Los Angeles

The idea can be put as a question: Is social ostracism a more effective means of regulating behavior than enumerated behavioral rules by legislative decree?

The chapter begins with a brief review of selected evolutionary contributions to our understanding of law and law-related behavior. It then turns to a discussion of interactions between group size and behavior with an emphasis on the manipulation and regulation of behavior through social and legal means. The chapter ends with a discussion of the limits of law.

BACKGROUND

Inquiries into how evolutionary theory can inform our understanding of law and law-related behavior have led to numerous insights about both the effectiveness and ineffectiveness of laws. For example, laws that conflict with individual self-interest (e.g., laws restricting sexual behavior), constrain individuals from investing time and resources in kin (e.g., anti-nepotism laws), or forbid certain associations among persons with similar interests (e.g., meetings among individuals with similar religious or political views), are unlikely to regulate behavior in ways intended by those writing such laws. Conversely, laws that facilitate self-interest and kin investment, allow for a wide range of associations among individuals with different values and preferences, and enhance survival are likely to be successful. A sampling of these inquires can be found in <u>Law and the Mind</u> (Gruter, 1993), Fikentscher and McGuire (1997), and Grady and McGuire (1998). The basic idea underpinning each of these inquiries is that human beings have evolved such that they are strongly motivated to act in some ways (e.g., invest in kin) but not others (e.g., purposely endanger one's self). Taken as a whole, these insights illuminate the relationship between the degree to which members of a society follow laws and the degree to which laws are concordant with evolutionary principles.

SOCIAL OSTRACISM AS A BEHAVIOR REGULATOR

Personal experiences will be used to open this discussion.

Four times in my life I have built homes, twice in urban areas, twice in remote rural locations. For both of the urban homes, detailed contracts were developed with builders which included not only specifics about the homes, but also a variety of protections such as contractors' bonds and insurance for accidents and possible defaults. Contracts were signed and in some cases notarized. Insurance coverage was verified, and so on. For both of the urban homes the final products were faulty, points on which the contractors and I did not agree. When I demanded that the terms of the contracts be fulfilled, the contractors and subcontractors argued among themselves about who was responsible for rectifying the situations. The arguments did not lead to resolutions. A series of costly legal actions followed and eventually the homes were completed according to specifications.

For both of the rural homes, formal contracts were never written. All arrangements with the contractors and subcontractors were made by verbal agreement, handshake, and a few scribbled notes. As with the urban homes, the final products did not meet the specifications. In both instances, the contractors and subcontractors corrected their mistakes without argument and without legal costs.

How might these outcomes be explained? Part of the answer can be found in looking at the potential social and legal consequences for not fulfilling contracts in urban and rural communities.

In rural environments, contractors and subcontractors do not like to work with individuals that fail to carry out their contractual obligations. Rural communities have the option of socially ostracizing individuals that fail to meet their contractual agreements where the same option is usually ineffectual in urban communities. In rural settings, information about which individuals do not fulfill their contractual agreements travels through the community almost as rapidly as e-mail travels from one part of the world to another. For those who fail to honor contractual agreements, there are fewer invitations to participate in new jobs, fewer social events to which one is invited, and fewer easy lines of credit. In effect, whatever the potential legal consequences, the social and economic consequences of social ostracism are precise, immediate, and measurable.

Of course, all rural settings are not exactly as I have described them. Often there are two classes of individuals, the economically privileged and everyone else, and the potential consequences of not fulfilling contractual arrangements are greater for the contractor who dissatisfies the privileged. There are also factors that foster the spread of information. People in rural settings process far more local information than people in urban settings, and they mold it to fit social values and functional options. Local newspapers carry minimal national and international news, and they often print local reports of arrests and trials (the "police blotter"). Further, legal remedies are often public, and in small communities, this fact may compound problems by tearing at the heart of how the community views itself. If legal remedies are pursued, their outcomes often closely mirror social nonlegislated (not necessarily illegal) outcomes. Rural settings are primarily functional settings where work, values, and priorities reflect either the agricultural or the pastoral traditions. The fact that, compared to urban settings, God, mother and American values are generally taken more seriously also has consequences, namely stricter and more precisely defined behavior rules. Unlike cities, which are often dynamic and volatile (and pride themselves on these characteristics), rural settings are more likely to be cautious about shifts in values, new ideas, and new migrants to their community when their personal histories are unknown.

In urban settings, a contractor may socially ostracize a subcontractor who fails to honor contractual agreements. However, this may have minimal social or economic consequences. There are usually hundreds of other contractors with whom a subcontractor can work. Moreover, when contractors and subcontractors are unable to resolve who is responsible for contractual deficiencies, seeking legal resolutions is often prohibitive because of time and cost. Similar points apply to individuals that have engaged contractors. The time and financial costs of pursuing legal remedies for the nonfulfillment of contracts are often sufficient to discourage such actions. In short, compared to the rural setting, the social and economic consequences of contract failures are ambiguous, seldom immediate, and frequently difficult to measure.

Social memory is also a factor. In urban settings, memory is short. Contractors can declare bankruptcy today and start their business anew tomorrow with a different company name, and few in the city will know about such events. Not so in the country, where the histories of individuals often linger for generations.

EVOLUTIONARY BIOLOGY, CHEATERS, AND SOCIAL OSTRACISM

In the vocabulary of evolutionary biology, persons who fail to fulfill contractual agreements are often referred to as "cheaters" or "defectors." They are characterized in such terms because of a common ingredient in their behavior. They adopt a strategy of maximizing their benefits and minimizing their costs without regard for those with whom they interact.

Evolutionary biologists view many cheaters and deceivers as enacting evolved strategies rather than as innocent victims of adverse upbringing (the usual social explanation for such behavior). An evolved strategy is one that has been favored by natural selection and is influenced genetically. The evidence supporting the evolved strategy interpretation is compelling and recently reviewed in detail by Mealy (1997).

Why might natural selection favor deceptive or cheating behavior? The evolutionary answer is straightforward. In a population in which there are no deceivers or cheaters, and thus where individuals minimally guard against the possibility of deception or cheating (lowered threshold), a single cheater joining the population will be able to cheat and deceive with minimal chances of being detected. Conversely, a society composed primarily of cheaters and deceivers will require literally every member of the society, including new members, to be cautious about the possibility of cheaters (elevated threshold). Like most things that have an evolutionary basis, a compromise evolves, and this would appear to be the case for that subset of cheaters that cheat because of genetic influence. They are present but their numbers are limited.

To argue that there are genetic predispositions for deceptive and cheating behavior is not to say that there are not experiences and situations that in some instances make individuals more or less likely to become cheaters. Often, these influences are significant. There is evidence suggesting that adverse upbringing environments increase the probability of cheating and deception among individuals that are moderately predisposed to cheat. There is also evidence that certain individuals learn to cheat and deceive as part of a survival strategy (e.g., when individuals are chronically hungry). In the former instance, the environment contributes to the expression of moderate genetic tendencies. In the latter, the tendencies may not be present, but survival may require that one adopt a strategy of deception and cheating. Moreover, even those with the strongest tendencies to cheat do not do so all of the time. Rather, they tend to pick their moments. Thus, the range of cheaters in most societies can differ significantly as well as fluctuate over time.

Cheaters and defectors are present in rural environments just as they are present in urban environments. But the fact that they are present in both locations should not obscure the evolutionary points being discussed here, points which can contribute to our understanding of why contract-by-handshake in rural settings is often the more effective way of assuring that a contract will be fulfilled compared to more formal legal arrangements of written contracts that prevail in the city. In rural settings, there are forces that constrain cheating and deceptive behavior, and this is where social ostracism returns to the analysis.

Why is social ostracism such a powerful mechanism for molding and regulating behavior? The answer is relatively straightforward.

Homo sapiens is a social species. Few individuals are capable of remaining sane and surviving without membership in a group or without receiving reassurance and assistance from members of their group. Individuals join groups in part to assure that there are others on which they can rely for help, for reassurance, for special economic opportunities, for loans when they are broke, for advice, for somatic pleasures, and so forth.

Group membership and reciprocal helping relationships do not occur over night. Time and effort are required, which means that people must know each other over a relatively long period and interact frequently. It is necessary to test others' trustworthiness, as in instances where one initiates the first step in a helping relationship and waits to find out if the receiver of the help reciprocates. Group membership and mutual trust are achieved after many encounters, many instances of helping and sharing, and the incremental development of trust. As trust of others develops, the need for caution in relationships declines. Worry about defending oneself against possible cheaters becomes less important. In effect, one's "defensive guard" is down and one is more susceptible to deception and cheating by others. Said another way, the threshold for cheating is lowered in rural settings and, as a consequence, news about cheating and deceiving travels quickly in such communities.

Social ostracism is a highly effective means of regulating behavior when groups are small, when individuals are known to each other, and when there are immediate and measurable social and economic consequences for deception. Generally, social ostracism is effective in groups that have fewer than 150 members, a characterization that would apply to contractors and subcontractors in a large percentage of rural settings. Among such groups, everyone knows each other. Group members talk frequently. There are established ways of solving problems and conflicts. Those who defect can be easily and rapidly detected and information about defections can be transmitted rapidly. Those defectors whose actions have adverse consequences for the group are often treated harshly. And although there may be formal or legislated rules, they usually are of minimal importance relative to customs and the performance expectations that develop as a result of interpersonal histories.

There are of course many negative features to social ostracism. Individuals can be ostracized unfairly. Local biases can make life intolerable for law-abiding individuals and families because of their color or religious beliefs. Those who have defected in the past may have a difficult time changing social perceptions compared to defections in urban settings. Social ostracism, thus, is a double-edged edged sword. It is also a functional system that is as unlikely to disappear as cheating.

THE LIMITS OF LAW

The idea that I have tried to address in the preceding discussion is that of social ostracism as a means of regulating behavior. One may like or dislike the idea that social ostracism is an effective means of behavioral regulation, but liking or disliking is not an issue addressed in this chapter. What is at issue is whether enumerated laws without concordant social norms are likely to be effective or, that social norms without enumerated laws are likely to be fair.

What the examples above suggest is that there are a series of complex tradeoffs for self-defined rule-of-law societies. On one hand, social ostracism, while highly effective, can also be abusive. On the other hand, laws without social reinforcement are unlikely to be effective. Thus, a balance between laws that are largely concordant with evolutionary behavioral tendencies and that are reinforced by social consequences for non law-following behavior would seem the most effective. While the development and enforcement of laws can be endorsed in many instances, the use of laws as substitutes for social settings in which there are well understood and potentially costly consequences for defections limits the possibility that individuals will engage in legal behavior. Would a greater percentage of contracts be fulfilled in rural settings if somehow it was mandatory that formal contracts had to be written in addition to handshaking among participants? It seems doubtful. A possible counter argument was mentioned earlier, namely, laws that facilitate self-interest and kin investment, allow for a wide range of associations among individuals with different preferences, or enhance survival might be successful irrespective of social norms. However, crafting such laws is easier to advocate than to carry out successfully, largely because individuals differ genetically, differ in the intensity of their motivations, and differ in their preferences.

Acknowledgements

My thanks to Nancy Brown, Michael Cogan, and Mary O'Byrne who provided constructive comments on earlier versions of this chapter.

References

Fikentscher, W. and McGuire, M.T. (1994) A four-function theory of biology for law. Rechtstheorie, 25:291-309.

Grady, M.F. and McGuire, M.T. (1997) A theory of the origin of natural law. Journal of Contemparary Legal Issues, 8:87-130.

Gruter, M. (1991) Law and the Mind. Newberry Park. Sage.

Mealy, L. (1996) The sociobiology of sociopathy: An integrated evolutionary model. Behavioral Brain Sciences, 18:523-599.

How I Wrote:
"The Evolution of
Reciprocal Altruism"

Robert Trivers*

[This material is adapted from *Classic Papers of Robert Trivers* to be published by Oxford University Press. It is meant to introduce the reader to: Trivers, R.L. 1971. *The Evolution of Reciprocal Altruism,* Quarterly Review of Biology 46:35-57.]

It was the spring semester of 1969, and the population geneticist Richard Lewontin had come to Harvard to deliver a talk on a new methodology that promised to revolutionize the field of population genetics. Lewontin was then at nearly the height of his powers and 250 people, myself included, were crammed into a lecture hall to hear his eagerly anticipated talk. It was my devout wish that the organism himself would fall flat on his face.

The reason for this is that I had just been introduced to him by E.O. Wilson, Harvard's fabulous social insect man, at the tea

* Professor of Anthropology and Biological Sciences, Rutgers University, New Brunswick, NJ.

preceding his talk. Lewontin had, at once, proceeded to dump on me, a mere first-year graduate student. In the previous fall I had written a very negative paper attacking the work of two theoretical ecologists, Robert MacArthur and Richard Levins, and Lewontin was a personal friend of Levins at the University of Chicago. A fellow graduate student had carried the manuscript to a conference and allowed someone to make a xerox copy, and like a true pathogen it had spread rapidly around the globe. I even received a glowing letter from a well-known Australian ecologist. When I realized the manuscript had gone public I sent copies to MacArthur and Levins. MacArthur wrote a very nice letter in return; Levins did not deign to reply. Lewontin began by saying. "Oh yes, you're the fellow that wrote that wrong-headed paper on MacArthur and Levins," and dismissed it in a few sentences. He pointed to some equations on the board which he had apparently shown off to Ed Wilson and told me that one of my criticisms was easily handled if you used these equations. As Ed Wilson squinted myopically toward the board (and with only one good eye at that!), I thought I could see at a glance that Lewontin had merely complexified the problem— thereby hiding the error more deeply—but that the same problem remained in his formulation as in the work of Levins himself. I have learned in life that my memory of behavior that I regard as odious is always more negative than the behavior itself, but in any case Lewontin had a somewhat arrogant and condescending style and his treatment of me, I later learned, was by no means out of character. I took an immediate dislike to him.

Ernst Mayr, Harvard's venerated evolutionary biologist (all sub-fields) introduced Lewontin, and I remember Lewontin thanked "Ernst" for his introduction, which drew an almost audible gasp from the audience, who had not hitherto heard Professor Mayr referred to in public by his first name only. Lewontin then went on to deliver a masterful talk. He began by describing a problem that he said lay at the heart of evolutionary biology, namely, the degree of genetic variation present in natural populations. There were two competing schools of thought: one, that there was lots of variation, the other that there was very little. Each view had important implications for other matters. He then described a hopeless methodological conundrum, one method biased to an unknown degree in one direction, and the alternative methodology biased to an unknown degree in the opposite. Enter from stage left Lewontin and Hubby with their new methodology, gel electrophoresis. This methodology allowed a large number of loci to be sampled relatively easily for genetic variants at each locus. He described the methodology, and then gave the first wave of results which clearly supported one school of thought: there was lots of genetic variation in natural populations. He then, as I remember it, presented a second wave of data which showed parallel geographical patterns of variation in closely related species, thus suggesting the ongoing action of natural selection (since random forces, acting independently, should not produce <u>parallel</u> distributions).

Some people claim that at the end of the lecture he shot his chalk twenty feet into the air and caught it in his suit pocket, but if this occurred I did not see it. The point is that he put on quite a show, both in content and in presentation. I remember halfway through the lecture feeling some intense internal pain. This organism—odious cretin though he was—was not about to fall on his face. This contradiction led me to some soul-searching about my paper on MacArthur and Levins. I realized that the paper was entirely negative, that is, I had nothing positive with which to replace their incorrect views but had, at best, only a bagful of <u>their</u> errors. While this is not without its use in science, its long-term value is strictly limited, for the criticism will soon sink out of sight along with the views it criticizes. Did I have anything positive to say on the subject of theoretical ecology? I knew at once that I did not. To make progress in this area you needed mathematical skills and discipline that I was not about to develop, and you would also benefit greatly from twenty or thirty years of running around in the woods. That is, if you could combine intuition and real knowledge of nature with the kind of mathematics required to handle complex interactions, then perhaps you could make some headway. I decided, in the space of a few minutes, not to try to publish this attack nor to do any more work along those lines.

What positive thoughts did I have? Two immediately came to mind. One was reciprocal altruism—you scratch my back and I'll scratch yours—as an evolutionary problem. And the other was what became parental investment and sexual selection. I had been watching pigeons for some time and knew that male pigeons practiced the same type of double standard and had the same kind of attendant psychological problems (or at least behavioral ones) as did men. This suggested some novel thoughts about the evolution of sex differences. I decided, at once, to concentrate on both of these problems and to tackle reciprocal altruism first, because the solution to that problem was more straightforward, but to continue my pigeon observations and associated thoughts.

I left Lewontin's talk, as I remember it, in high good spirits, a burden lifted from my shoulders and my eyes firmly set on the prize ahead. For one thing, it was such a relief to kiss mathematical ecology good-bye! It was a small burden then, but one that could easily have grown with time. I wonder how many academics happen to get into areas they neither really enjoy nor are particularly suited for, yet stay in those areas for many years. At the same time, by turning to what I really cared about and throwing the same kind of energy and effort into it as I had thrown into attacking MacArthur and Levins, I would really have something to show for my time.

It later often seemed ironic to me that Lewontin should have helped put me so firmly on a path that he came to detest so much himself. He was to return to Harvard as a full professor when I was an assistant professor, and he was to be chairman of Organismic and Evolutionary Biology when I came up for tenure. During that bitter dispute, I heard by the grapevine that he had disparaged me to one group of students as an "intellectual opportunist." Of course, I was an intellectual opportunist! What else made sense in this short life? The inability of biologists to think clearly on matters of social behavior and evolution for over a hundred years had left a series of important problems untackled. And it was a wonderful opportunity, especially if you had some social insight and interests (my rough analog to twenty years in the woods). The area was so underdeveloped you hardly needed mathematics. Logic plus fractions would get you through most situations!

I had started to focus on reciprocal altruism largely because of the wonderful work of W. D. Hamilton on kinship and social behavior. Hamilton had shown that you could define a variable degree of relatedness (or coefficient of relatedness) to others which would have a strong effect on selection acting on social behavior between related individuals. In particular, an individual could sacrifice personal reproductive success (or fitness, as it was usually called then), and still be favored by natural selection as long as this benefitted relatives such that, when the benefit was devalued by the degree of relatedness, the resulting number was still larger than the cost suffered.

Hamilton did something else in his famous 1964 paper which was deceptively simple, namely, he defined the four major categories of social interaction in terms of their effects on the reproductive success of the two individuals involved in a social interaction. So "altruistic" behavior was behavior that caused a loss to the actor and a benefit to the recipient where these were defined in terms of effects on their reproductive success. Selfish behavior was the reverse, while in cooperative behavior both parties benefitted, and in spiteful behavior neither benefitted and each suffered a cost. This four-fold classification of behavior, or social traits more broadly, had the benefit of immediately stating how natural selection was acting on the interaction from the standpoint of each of the two individuals.

This was a use of language which social scientists and others were to detest. When they were aroused in full antipathy towards "sociobiology" you often read that this was a perversion of language. True altruism had to refer to pure internal motivations or other-directed internal motivations without thought or concern for self. To an evolutionist, this seemed absurd. You begin with the <u>effect</u> of behavior on actors and recipients, you deal with the problem of internal motivation, which is a secondary problem, afterwards. If you made this point, by the way, to some of these nay-sayers, they would often argue back that, if that were the case, then Hamilton at the very least should have chosen words that had no connotations in everyday language. This was also a very short-sighted view. In the extreme case, I suppose, Hamilton could have called the behaviors x, y, w, and z, so as to avoid any but alphabetical connotations. But this, of course, meant that you would always have to be translating those symbols into some verbal system that made sense to you before you could think clearly. Incidentally, when the great sociobiology controversy did roll forth I soon came to see that the real function of these counter-arguments was to slow down your work, and if possible, stop it cold. If you start with motivation you have given up the evolutionary analysis at the outset. If you are forced to use arbitrary symbols, progress will be slowed for no good reason. Even the invitation to argue with them seemed to me to benefit them by wasting your time!

In any case, once you've conceptualized certain behavior or traits as "altruistic" yet could show they exist in nature, then you immediately have a problem, and a severe one in classic Darwinian theory, because natural selection acting on the actor should be removing genes that tend to induce altruistic acts in those possessing them. The phrase "a gene for altruism" was also later subject to bitter attack. How could a single gene cause altruism? etc. etc. And again, the primary function of this objection was to make it very difficult for people to talk and think who wanted to make the analysis in question. Lewontin, incidentally, who was one of those who raised this and related objections, I always felt fought sociobiology tooth and nail, because he had committed himself already to an alternative system of social interpretation, Marxist or pseudo-Marxist, and he would rather keep his evolutionary theory for population genetics and the kinds of problems he tackled in his office, while retaining Marxist thinking for handling social interactions. In any case, by simply calling certain behaviors and acts altruistic and defining them the way he did, Hamilton brought into clear focus the problem involved. In his own kinship theory he solved many such cases in nature while at the same time producing much deeper implications as well.

When I came into biology originally at age twenty-two, never having had a course in biology and knowing next to nothing about animal behavior, my knowledge was almost entirely restricted to our own species. In our own species it was obvious, as adults, that though kinship was a very important factor—blood being thicker than water—it could not explain all phenomena. We had strong positive feelings towards friends and we were willing to act altruistically toward them and toward others. Kinship could not explain this. What could?

Well, reciprocity, in some form, could obviously do the trick— that is, you scratch my back and I'll scratch yours—but reciprocity required some thinking to get the argument right. When we are each scratching each other's backs we are simultaneously trading benefits and suffering costs. That does not create much of an evolutionary problem, but what about when we act nicely toward an individual and the return benefit, if any, must come later? This raised some interesting evolutionary problems. So, I saw that what, in the human species, was obviously a major area of life, including deep and complex emotions which involved altruism, was not explained by Hamilton's theory, and required some new explanation. Note that the use of the term altruism helped immediately in thinking about reciprocity or reciprocal altruism. Reciprocity, after all, can be negative—reciprocal spite—as Frans deWaal is fond of emphasizing. Anthropologists, I soon learned, were fond of talking about "reciprocity," but by using that term they usually bypassed the theoretical problem at once. They were even able to dream up formulations where parental care was an example of "reciprocity" between the generations, because the offspring would later invest parental care in its own offspring.

So, one day I sat down and wrote out a short manuscript on the evolution of reciprocal altruism. I began with the evolutionary problem and tried to formulate the matter mathematically. I remember I had a locus with genes that affected altruism but I realized that I had better have a second locus in the other individual directing the return effort so that my analysis would not become confused with kinship complications at that same locus. So, in any case, I wrote out a short, and I might add, feeble "mathematical-genetic" section. I had two examples in mind from nature, neither of which, in fact, was a good example of reciprocal altruism though both were good examples of "return effect altruism." That is, you act altruistic and a return benefit reaches you but not because another individual chooses to reciprocate your original altruism.

The first example was cleaning symbioses in fish. I used to read very widely in those days, and I remember seeing an advertisement for a book entitled, "The Biology of the Mouth." I thought to myself, who wouldn't want to understand the biology of the mouth? and I sent off for my copy. I was thoroughly disappointed in most of the articles, which gave you no evolutionary understanding or overview of the mouth, but dealt only with problems related to dentistry. One chapter, though, caught my eye, a chapter on cleaning symbioses in the ocean. These are symbioses in which a member of one species, the cleaner species, cleans the body and sometimes the mouth of a member of the host species of ecto-parasites. Both parties benefit instantaneously. That is, with each bite, the cleaner gets a meal and the host loses one ecto-parasite, and evolution had clearly favored warm interactions between the two. But, in the article, I read of behavior not so easily explained. In some cases, when a cleaner is cleaning the inside of a host fish's mouth, the host will spot a predator on itself, and instead of (as I imagine I would have done) simply swallowing the cleaner and getting the hell out of there, the host closed its mouth and then opened it—as a warning to the cleaner to depart—and then took off running itself. Ahhh, here was a delay requiring explanation. Was there a return benefit? I did indeed gather evidence that the hosts often return to the same cleaners and that they probably benefit from doing so, and therefore, a concern for the welfare of the life of the cleaner, even at some cost to your own life, may pay its way. The individuals involved were members of different species, so kinship could be ruled out.

The second problem from nature was warning cries in birds. In many, many, species of birds, individuals who spot a predator give an alarm call, which warns other individuals of a predator at some presumed cost, however small, to the individual giving the warning call. Indeed, Peter Marler had written a beautiful little paper, showing that the sound characteristics of warning calls were very different than those of territorial calls in a couple of species of birds. The latter had a wide frequency variation while the warning calls tended to be pure tone. Wide frequency variation permits listeners to locate, easily and quickly, the direction from which the sound is coming, while pure tones are almost vantriloquil. So, it was nice for the bird that its warning call did not reveal much about its location while its territorial assertion call did. But, from an evolutionary standpoint, those pure tones had to evolve. They had to begin as calls with frequency variation. So that beautiful pure-tone picture that Marler published connoted to me so many dead birds to get to that pure pitch. That was indirect evidence of cost.

Now, there was no bar in principle to explaining all of bird calls as kin-directed. On the other hand, nothing was known about the kin structure of any bird species, so there was no direct evidence in favor of this interpretation. How might one explain bird calls in my system? The obvious would be reciprocal altruism itself: I warn you when I spot the predator, you warn me when you spot the predator, and we both show a net gain over time. The problem with this though, was that I thought it was a hopeless system to police, so to speak. How are you going to discriminate against the cheater? To put it in human terms, you can imagine a bird spotting a predator late, almost being eaten itself, and then going to its neighbor Fred, and saying, "Why the hell didn't you warn me?" Fred throws up his wings and says, "I was as surprised as you, brother!" All I could see selection doing was silencing the birds throughout their range. There was no way to identify cheaters, no way to punish them, except not calling yourself when the shoe was on the other foot, as you imagined it, and thus birds would fall silent.

But, there were plenty of opportunities for return-effect altruism to explain warning calls. I knew from my teacher, William Drury, that predators had been shown, in some cases, to form specific search images, in which experience killing one member of a species greatly increased their chance of spotting and killing other members of the same species. Imagine a highly cryptic, i.e. camouflaged moth, resting against the bark of a tree. You overlook many, but when you spot the first one as edible food and consume it, you become aware of their existence and rapidly learn characteristics to discriminate them from bark, and start cleaning up on moths resting on bark. In short, my neighbor not getting eaten might decrease the chance of a predator learning useful things when it turned to attack me, but some small familiarity with predator-prey interactions in animals immediately suggested more direct possibilities. When predators are sneaking up on prey and are spotted, and a warning cry is subsequently issued, and everyone dashes to safety, the predators often move then to some other area where they have not yet been spotted. So, warning your neighbor that a predator is nearby may be the quickest way to get the predator to move on elsewhere. Incidentally a mistake that is easy to make, and some are very attracted to it, is that you would like to have your neighbor eaten because that increases your relative fitness, or reproductive success. However, your relative reproductive success is really calculated across the entire species or a very large interbreeding section of it, and thus, the diminution of one life is trivial, in terms of your overall relative fitness.

So, I tried to think through as many ways as I could that were plausible, of natural selection favoring alarm calls in birds through return effects. Since there was no direct evidence on any of these possibilities, my thinking at least had the virtue of generating alternative explanations to the kinship logic.

I then wrote, if I remember correctly, a very short few pages on human reciprocal altruism with no evidence cited, nor research results discussed.

I Meet W.D.

A little bit after this, perhaps in the fall of 1969, W.D. Hamilton himself came to Harvard to lecture and I had the opportunity to meet him. He was coming from a "Man and Beast" symposium at the Smithsonian in Washington where he had presented some of his latest thinking, which I believe was the same talk he gave us. There were perhaps eighty or ninety people, almost filling a lecture hall, most of us with eager anticipation. Hamilton got up and gave one of the worst lectures, as a lecture, that I had until that moment heard. There was an emeritus Harvard professor who occasionally used to give a lecture, widely appreciated, on how to give a poor lecture. W.D. did not need any teaching in this regard and has generated some wonderful tricks of his own. I say this as a man who loves W.D. but his early troubles in this regard were sometimes very funny. For one thing, he lectured for a full fifty-five minutes without yet getting to the point. It was abstruse, technical, he often had his back to us while he was writing things on the board, you had difficulty hearing his voice, you did not get any overview of where he was going nor why he was going there. When he realized that he was five minutes overtime, and still had not gotten to the point, nor indeed very near it, he looked down at Ed Wilson, his host, and asked him if he could have some more time, perhaps ten or fifteen minutes. Of course, Professor Wilson granted him some more time but he also made a rolling, "lets-try-to-speed-this-up" motion with his arms. Hamilton then called for slides. The room went dark and there was a rumble and a roaring sound and some students were nearly trampled as about 90% of the audience took this opportunity to exit the room for some fresh air.

I remember walking home from the lecture with Ernst Mayr, both of us shaking our heads. It was obvious that the man was brilliant, a deep thinker, and his every thought well worth attending to, but whoaa, was he bad in public! Hamilton was not unaware of this problem and once told a class we taught together that after hearing his lectures many students would doubt that he understood even his own ideas! By the way, he has improved considerably in the intervening years, but he still shows the touch of a true master, that is the ability to innovate new ways of lecturing poorly. I invited him to lecture to law professors in Squaw Valley, as a guest of Margaret Gruter's Institute for the Study of Law and Behavioral Sciences, and there he introduced a new trick that I had not seen before. He showed a number of interesting but complex slides. He had a hand-held microphone but no pointer, so he used the microphone as a pointer. Often all you would hear him say was, "Here, as you can see . . ." and then the microphone would point to various parts of the slide, while his mouth continued to move. Then you might hear again, "And then in the next slide . . ." and then once again you would not hear anything about the slide, though you could see Dr. Hamilton pointing to various places in it with his microphone!

Later, I got the chance to meet him in person. Mary Jane West Eberhard, the celebrated student of wasps, was, I believe, a postdoc at the time with Wilson, and she held a small party for him. I brought along the little paper that I had written on reciprocal altruism to give him to read and I think he expressed interest in meeting me (that he had heard I had been thinking about this or something like that). He was a shy man; very quiet spoken. You often had to lean into him to catch what he was saying. He had a kind of horsey-looking face, as he would describe it to others, for example, when he was meeting someone new at the train station. I remember thinking, at some point in my relationship with Bill, that if the argument ever became physical the contest I would least like to be engaged in against Hamilton was a shoving contest. I felt he would dig in his heels, that you would be unable to move him, and that he would lean forward and shove you slowly and stubbornly to wherever he wanted to get you.

Some time thereafter I received a letter from W.D. and I remembered liking, indeed, the gentle tone with which he dealt with my efforts. He encouraged me to continue. He could see why I had chosen separate loci for actor and recipient, but he suggested (without telling me that my mathematical attempts were littered with errors as they were) that it would be, perhaps better, to delete the "maths," as he called it, from the paper. I only half followed his advice. I deleted the separate loci but tried to expand the "maths" and of course introduced new errors in the process. For example, I make assertions about the evolution of reciprocal altruism genes which, in fact, apply only when the gene for altruism is exactly 50% in frequency. This is not a very helpful formulation from an evolutionary standpoint. The evolutionary problem is to get a gene that begins at low frequency to a high frequency. And what is happening at the 50/50 mark is usually an irrelevancy. But I was very much trying to mimic, however feebly, Hamilton's kind of thinking itself, that is, try, if at all possible, to get the formulation down to the level of genes so as to be more sure that you have got the argument right, and so as to give a quantitative form to it if possible. Hamilton also pointed out that my two non-human examples were not actually examples of reciprocal altruism, and suggested that I rename the paper, "The evolution of return effect altruism." This I was not about to do, though later I wished I had taken this opportunity to stress the difference between the two categories.

Human Reciprocal Altruism

The key to the paper besides its evolutionary approach is the section on human reciprocal altruism. Could I reorganize facts about human psychology around this new argument in a coherent and interesting way? If so, there would be immediate pay-off for the argumentation itself. This required that I become familiar with a literature from social psychology that I knew nothing about. Naturally, I sought out short-cuts. I saw that in the Harvard catalog a man was teaching a course on moral behavior and from the description in the catalog, this sounded about exactly right. So I said to myself that I would humble myself and take the entire course (as an auditor of course) in order to learn this material, and at the end of the semester I should have the human section in hand, or at least be ready to write it. I attended, I believe, only two lectures.

The problem with the course was that the teacher seemed to think it was immoral to teach a course on morality without first canvassing all the students to find out what they wanted to know about the subject. This was not what I wanted. I wanted someone to lay out a subject matter for me so that I could reinterpret it as I wished. However, I noted that his graduate teaching assistant, Dennis Krebs (now a Professor of Psychology at the Simon Fraser University), was cited on the reading list as having written a review, soon to be published, of the literature on altruistic behavior. Ahh, this was perfect! As a graduate student of the professor you could take it for granted that his review was going to be very thorough and very likely better than the professor himself might have done. I could skip the lectures entirely and simply read that man's paper, assuming he was willing to provide a copy. I went to Mr. Krebs and he very kindly provided me with a copy. I never saw the class nor its professor again.

On the other hand, I did not immediately digest Krebs' paper either. It was written in a different language and I was required to master that language before I could understand exactly what he was saying. I read around in the paper to try to familiarize myself with the kinds of evidence that was available. One thing that amused me, right off the bat, was that social psychologists called altruistic behavior "pro-social behavior." Now that seemed immediately somewhat ill-defined, and I soon learned how it came about. Social scientists were already writing about anti-social behavior. Indeed, this provided justification for some of their monetary support. They would help us handle "juvenile delinquency" or "criminality" or other also somewhat misleading terms, and the pro-socialists' claim to utility was that they were dealing with the other side of the coin—the neglected positive side of life—pro-social behavior. From the perspective of evolutionary language, or indeed everyday language, this seemed like hopeless gibberish. Social is easily opposed to solitary, so social interaction is one involving more than one organism. I can be fighting you and it is a social interaction. Am I pro-social if I am in favor of fights? An anti-social individual might be a hermit, but anti-social was being used to refer to someone whose behavior was bad for others, as the author saw it, and ought best to be curbed. Again, defining categories of behavior in this way seemed like a hopeless way to proceed if you were interested in building up a solid scientific approach to human behavior. There were, of course, other linguistic hurdles I had to overcome. Krebs had organized his paper along conventional distinctions within that discipline. For example, there were immediate precipitating variables where you were more, or less, likely to give a dollar to a beggar if snot was coming out of his nose. There were personality variables in the potential prosocialists. There were situational variables that might affect the tendency. And, of course, all this research was guided by the goal of increasing pro-social behavior, though not really understanding it, certainly not at any deep level, but desiring to increase its occurrence in society. What was missing, of course, was exactly what was missing from the discipline itself, and that was, any functional understanding of the behaviors that they were talking about. Why did it make sense for the organism to do it? This was, of course, what evolutionary biology, and myself in particular, were set to provide. So, all I had to do was master the literature cited by Krebs, and then reorganize it appropriately.

This sounded easier, perhaps, than it was, at least for me, and the more I comprehended Krebs' paper, the more I dreaded having to study the works that he was citing. They would be written in a bizarre language and I was afraid to learn too much about the actual methodologies used. I read a few of the papers and then decided to take another short-cut and write the section based on Krebs' review. I piously told myself that I would, of course, read all the papers whose citations I would be lifting from Krebs' review, as by good scientific and academic procedure I should, but in fact I never did.

I remember I was visiting my parents' home in the Midwest for two or three weeks, and had decided to take this opportunity to write the human section. I was depressed the first week and lay around doing little more than sleeping. Then I roused myself and said, you have two boring weeks ahead of you, however you slice it, so you might as well do this work which has to be done anyway. I spread out the few papers I had actually copied, reread Krebs' account, and simply reorganized the information around obvious psychological categories, like sympathy, gratitude and moralistic aggression.

How to Write a Classic Paper

In retrospect, I think my paper on reciprocal altruism can be used to illustrate how one might go about writing a classic paper. Here is my recipe:

1 – Pick an important topic.
2 – Try to do a little sustained thinking on the topic, always keeping close to the task at hand.
3 – Generalize outward from your chosen topic.
4 – Write in the language of your discipline but, of course, try to do so simply and clearly.
5 – If at all possible, reorganize existing evidence around your theory.

Pick an important topic. This is perhaps easier said than done because, of course, you must pick an important topic on which progress can be made. But it still seems remarkable to me how often people bypass what are more important subjects to work on less important ones. Constructing a scientific understanding of human psychology and social behavior is an important task and within that subject reciprocal altruism was, to me, an important topic when I began work on it. The very fact that so many strong emotions could be associated, in humans, with friendship, with helping others, with guarding against being cheated, said to me that it was an important topic in human psychology. There was no reason, in advance, to believe that it would not be an important topic in at least some other species, certainly closely related monkeys and apes, but very likely other species as well.

Do some sustained thinking. To me this is easier than it sounds. There are no great intellectual gymnastics in my paper. I am not proving Fermat's Last Theorem, nor generating Goedel's Proof. I am only trying to think simply and clearly on an interesting and important subject. I was amazed when I went into academic work—and it still baffles me today—why so many people take the first available path off their main argument into trivia-land. The sustained thinking must always be directed back to the key subject itself. I suppose it is easier, at first, to write a section on the semantics of discussing altruism, or sometimes to review previous failed efforts in considerable detail if these failed efforts are in front of you and easy to interpret. But this is all a waste of energy and effort. It diverts you from your main task. Get to the point and stick to the point. When I sent the paper to M. L. Roonwal, the great Indian student of termites and locusts (whom I had met on a very memorably ten-day monkey viewing visit with Irv DeVore), he praised the paper for its "intellectual architecture." And I thought the phrase was very apt. I had constructed the paper much as you might build a house, with roughly the same kinds of mental operations required. Nothing brilliant or flashy, just the steady construction of a series of arguments and facts regarding reciprocal altruisms.

Generalize outward. In most of my papers I took the opposite road that biologists usually take, or in any case, are usually accused of, which is arguing from a knowledge of animals to suppositions about humans. I usually begin with humans and then try to generalize outward so as to include as many other species, and phenomena, as I can. In this case, I took pains to formulate the argument with as few assumptions as possible. These only appear later as limitations. For example, both Charles Darwin and George C. Williams, very respectable minds both, had a few words to say on human reciprocal altruism, but each presupposed that its appearance would require the kind of intellectual talents that we know exist in our species: to recognize individuals, to remember past interactions, to alter behavior appropriately, etc. What this does is limit the argument to human beings in advance and in a way that is completely unnecessary. It seemed to me obviously preferable to avoid any such limitation until absolutely forced to accept it, but in this case also, easily argued against. The mental processes they cite could easily evolve <u>after</u> the fact. If you could just get a little bit of reciprocal altruism going, selection pressures to spot cheaters, to reward especially good fellow altruists, etc. ought easily to evolve.

<u>Write in the language of your discipline, but simply and clearly</u>. I was trying to make an evolutionary argument within the field of evolutionary biology. You need to satisfy the criteria of your discipline to be accepted or noticed. Of course, as I have admitted, I dressed up a pseudo mathematical genetical section to look as if I was using the concepts and language of my discipline more than I was, but I am convinced that had the later material, on humans for example, been written without any citations or references, it would easily have been neglected. So, even though the literature that was cited was a good bit weaker than I would have liked, I think it was important for the seriousness with which people took the paper. Alas, it had very little effect, quite opposite to my supposition, on social psychology itself. I naively imagined that social psychologists would be delighted to see that their work could be given much more interest and meaning when put in an evolutionary framework, and that they would immediately see new ways of doing their work that would prove more fruitful than the paths that they were taking. For example, let us assume you show, as they did, that if the other person resembles you more, you are more likely to act nicely towards that person. As an evolutionist you immediately wonder whether this is because of kin selection, in which case the organism is unconsciously measuring a degree of relatedness, or whether it might be due to a reciprocal mechanism in which the likelihood of exchanging benefits was more likely with closer resemblance. Yet this immediately raises another question, since reciprocal altruism between individuals who are complementary in characteristics may give greater value in some contexts than when they are similar. Pursuing this line of thought would suggest experiments or observations that discriminated these possibilities as well. Nothing

like this has, in fact, happened. I know of no social psychologists who have altered their work because of my paper (I would be very happy to hear of any), and have been very disappointed to discover that the only new work done is by people who first start with an evolutionary interest and then turn to trying to do something social psychological.

The virtues of writing simply and clearly should be obvious, certainly from the standpoint of the recipient, but attempting to do so has virtues for the writer as well since it repeatedly forces you to think through your subject clearly and well. I was very fortunate at Harvard, in having several professors who were excellent critical readers. The most useful from my standpoint was Irven DeVore, the famous Harvard "baboon man" and anthropologist. Irv was, and is, a superb stylist, and through five or six rewrites of the paper, he would continually improve the presentation. Similarly my advisor, Ernest Williams, would continually force me to tighten the argument and clarify the presentation. Incidentally, when I brought Professor Williams the sixth draft of the paper I remember saying to him, "Is it finished Dr. Williams? Is it finished?" There was a small pause and then Ernest looked at me and said, "A paper is <u>never</u> finished, Bob, it is only abandoned." He then told me that he thought that this paper was ready to be abandoned.

All those drafts that the paper was put through reaped a rich reward when the paper was actually published. There was an immediate, large, and very welcome response. I began to receive reprint requests, in the mail, mostly from the U.S. but, in fact, from all over the world. It gave me immense pleasure, especially to receive the foreign reprint requests, to know that my thinking would be studied in countries around the world. I had ordered six hundred reprints (this was in the days before whole-scale xeroxing of papers), and soon enough they were all exhausted. I was especially gratified at the number of reprint requests that came from Soviet bloc or communist countries because, of course, there was otherwise so little exchange across the so-called Iron Curtain. After a while, it struck me that their socialist ideology and emphasis on the possibility of naturally cooperative behavior among humans would make this an interesting topic for them, and perhaps, even one that was socially acceptable to pursue. I also learned that in their literature, Peter Kropotkin was an early pioneer whom they would have expected me to cite.

<u>Try to reorganize or reinterpret existing information</u>. Many, many theoretical papers in biology and elsewhere fail to show, at the end of the paper, that there is anything out there in the real world to which the argumentation just given actually applies. It applies in principle, of course, but they are unable to reinterpret any existing information. A typical effort might pick an important topic, do some sustained mathematical thinking on some part of the problem, usually misrepresented as being central to the problem, and then derive results which not only cannot immediately be tested against reality, but which would require an awful lot of work to do so. The value of the work, of course, depends upon how restrictive the initial assumptions are. If the initial assumptions are highly restrictive, then even if your mathematics is correct, you have solved a highly specialized problem and it may be of very marginal interest to test whether your statements are true which, in turn, may require very detailed and difficult measurements. Of course, if you have modelled something central to a problem and your results are not easy to test, that is another matter.

In my case, I think the last section gave life to the paper in a very important way because it showed, in principle, that the simple argument given could reinterpret information gathered in social psychology and give us a deeper understanding of similar kinds of facts known from our day-to-day experience.

No Language but a Cry

Kathleen Wermke*

The acquisition of language and its associated communication skills is probably the most difficult and complex developmental task for a child. This is true even accepting Steven Pinker's description of language as an "instinct," which is "no more a cultural invention than is upright posture." (Pinker 1995, p. 18) Language, according to Pinker, "develops in the child spontaneously, without conscious effort or formal instruction, is deployed without awareness of its underlying logic." (p. 18) Given this background and the importance of vocal communication to humans, the ability to develop language must at some level be robust and resilient even in extreme conditions. Children in a wide variety of settings achieve that skill. Only in cases of certain brain disorders or of a development under extreme social deprivation is the language acquisition process severely disturbed.

---

* Institute of Anthropology, Medical Faculty, Humboldt-University, Berlin, Germany

From history we know of a variety of cases of children deliberately raised in conditions of extreme isolation and deprivation. Often cited are the experiments of the old Egyptian pharaoh, P.sammetichos, the Holy Roman Emperor Frederik II and King James IV of Scotland in order to discover the most ancient languages (Larcher 1844, Itard 1965, Campbell/Grieve 1982, Skuse 1988). All children showed not only a retardation concerning their prespeech or language abilities, but showed an extreme retardation of all their communicative behavior and social capabilities. Also well-known is the case of Caspar Hauser, who was discovered in a street in Nuremberg (Bavaria) in 1828 (Stumpfe 1969, Leonhard 1970, Simon 1978, Thierauf 1993). Having spent about 16 years of his life in a dark cramped cell with no human company, he was without comprehensible language or social skills.

From different descriptions, recent cases of extreme social deprivation of children and their dramatic effects are also known (Curtiss et al. 1974, Zetterström 1984, Skuse 1988, Pinker 1995). One of the most tragic cases of extreme deprivation is the development of "Genie," a girl discovered in 1970 at the age of thirteen (Curtiss et al. 1974). With respect to language acquisition, Genie's speech abilities after several years of treatment support the theory of "critical periods" for language development (Lenneberg 1967, Pinker 1995).

The appearance of language in children is often defined by reference to the first meaningful words at about 12 months. But already much earlier, indeed with the very first cries, infants start prespeech development as an important stage of early language acquisition. This occurs in the form of various morphological and functional maturation processes of structures and mechanisms underlying sound production.

The theory of "critical periods" for language development is supported also by phenomena observable during these prespeech developmental processes (Mende/Wermke 1992, Wermke/Mende 1992, Mende et al. 1994, Wermke/Mende 1994): refinement of laryngeal coordination during the first weeks of life and the step-by-step addition of upper pharyngeal and oral controls provide several elementary abilities (modules) used much later in speech. From the very first vocal utterances of an infant (cries), these modules are "trained" for its use later in speech. The term "trained" refers to instinctive learning by doing and does not stand for conscious application. A "training" directed to speech acquisition during the first weeks and months of life is an important prerequisite, especially for the expression of non-linguistic elements of adult speech. For instance, this is true for the modulation of the fundamental frequency of the cry sounds over a large frequency scale, the scale of very rapid fluctuations of muscle tremor up to intonation patterns as macrodynamic elements of vocal expression. In cases of certain neuromuscular disorders, the mentioned developmental steps are not observable. This is related to later retardation concerning language performances. The theory of "critical phases" within prespeech development is also supported by observations of children with cleft lips and palate. Missing essential "training" phases during the first months of life caused by cleft palates might reduce later speech abilities in spite of perfect operation techniques.

Also on the perceptual site, important developmental changes are observable during the first year of life. Prespeech perceptual development is the first stage of language processing. For instance, Weissenborn/Höhle (1998) investigating perceptual abilities in infants found that during the first six months, the child becomes increasingly sensitive to the prosodic properties of the target language. During the second half of the first year of life, phonotactic and morphosyntactic information becomes accessible to the child. It is well-known, from long-time observations in children frequently suffering from Otitis media, that hearing disorders delay or disturb the process of language acquisition.

A co-development of performances of prespeech production and perception provides a biological basis for language acquisition, but has to be embedded in an age-adequate caregiving. Environmental deficits in terms of inadequate parenting can cause tremendous disorders of the early child development. Observations that have been made on children whose environmental deprivation resulted from an upbringing in neglectful and unstimulating institutions (e.g. orphanages) support this view. Those children were late in smiling, in handling toys and in their differential response to people. Their vocal and verbal development were often severely delayed (for example Brodbeck/Irwin 1946, Provence/Lipton 1962, Fisichelli 1950, Bishop/Mogford 1988).

During the last decades, a lot of research work in the field of human ethology, anthropology and developmental psychology yielded new insights in the importance of age-adequate social interaction processes between a mother and her child for a normal development of the child (e.g. Goldberg 1982, Korner/Grobstein 1976, Hassenstein 1987, Van de Rijt-Plooij/Plooij 1988, Esser et al. 1989, Jorg et al. 1994, Papousek/Papousek 1983, Spangler/Grossmann 1993, Papousek et al. 1996, Siegmund et al. 1996, Lykken 1997). A long phylogenetic adaptation process enables that the mother and her new-born baby are apriori tuned to each other ("biological attachment theory" Bowlby (1958,1969), Ainsworth (1969)).

Even very young infants are able to give cues to their mothers that affect the mother's behavior towards the infant. A variety of signals support the early interaction. For instance, crying is very important in the development of early infant-mother attachment from an ethological perspective as proximity-promoting behavior (Bowlby 1969). As an example: picking up, cuddling and holding a baby upright on the shoulder is not only the most effective strategy of mothers in terminating crying of her baby, but also a universal strategy, enabling eye contact, smiling, talking etc. (Korner/Grobstein 1976, Lester/Zeskind 1982). So crying not only promotes physical survival, but may also help to establish a relationship that guarantees social interaction (Goldberg 1982, Lester/Zeskind 1982).

Attachment-promoting behavior can also be based on visual signals or in the case of eye contact and smiling. Visual signals are complemented in their efficiency by certain facial and body characteristics of the infant which engender nursing behavior ("Kindchenschema" Konrad Lorenz 1943).

Mothers are extremely responsive to such signals in their infants (Robson/Moss 1970, Eibl-Eibesfeldt 1986, Hassenstein 1987) and have difficulty feeling positive towards their infants if they are missing (Fraiberg 1974, 1975). The importance of those signals is expressed in the following observation:

> "As observers we were initially puzzled and concerned by the amount of bouncing, jiggling, tickling and nuzzling that all of our parents, without exception, engaged in with the babies. In several cases we judged the amount of such stimulations as excessive by any standards . . . The parents' own need for the response smile, which is normally guaranteed with the sighted child at this age, led them to these alternative routes in which a smile could be evoked with a high degree of reliability." (Fraiberg 1975:231)

While normal prespeech interactions involve visual as well as acoustical communication, several investigations support the higher importance of acoustical stimuli compared to visual stimuli (e.g. Adamson et al. 1977, Als et al. 1980, Tronick 1979, Landau/Gleitman 1985, Andersen et al. 1984). I will not contribute to this discussion here, but focus on a doubtless powerful signal used within the early mother-child interaction, the infant cry.

The infant cry is a powerful social stimulus and serves as a distress signal to the caregiver. Along with other attachment behavior the cry evolves to promote proximity to the mother, serving as a salient and powerful trigger of parenting behavior. Crying serves two basic functions: alerting a social ally (caregiver) mediated by signaling "helplessness" as well as expressing "protest."

An assessment of these two messages (Todt 1988) by adult listeners were found to vary with particular signal parameters. "Shrillness" and noise bands were decoded as "protest," while tonal patterns extended over time were interpreted as "helplessness." Typical changes in sound characteristics in cases of neurosensory impairments or developmental retardation enforce those sound features which are interpreted as aversiveness ("protest"): higher fundamental frequency, sudden frequency shifts, noise bands.

During the long evolution of primates, the rising complexity of social interactions, the importance of acoustic signals for co-operation, and necessary information about internal states within groups of individuals led to improved performance of differentiation for producing sounds and perceiving them (Mende/Wermke 1988). Within this process the infant cry also developed certain physical characteristics in a way that the cry became a very effective alarm signal, a "Biosiren." The infant cry has typical alerting sound characteristics and a high penetrative force because of its frequency modulation content and its harmonic character (high harmonic-to-noise ratio).

With the help of these sound features, the cry works as an effective emergency signal. On the other hand, the cry can also become a releaser of negative emotions and reactions of a destructive nature (e.g. rejection). The significance of crying in this respect is well-described by several authors (e.g. Parke/Collmer 1975, Michelsson/Rinne 1987, Lester/Zeskind 1982, Volkin 1987, Wilkes 1987). A cry that is perceived as particularly annoying or grating may exceed the caregiver's capacity to respond with an appropriate caregiving behavior. So crying, especially excessive crying may under certain conditions, evoke responses of extreme hostility, rejection or abuse. Crying is one of the major perceived precipitants of abuse for infants (Murray 1979, Wiessbluth 1984, Kirkland 1985, Gray 1987, Wilkes 1987, Baildam et al. 1995).

The effects of infant crying on adult responses have been reported in a series of studies by Frodi et al. (1978) in an attempt to determine some of the antecedents of child abuse. More arousal was elicited by crying in general compared with visual signals, with the cry of the premature infant eliciting greater arousal and more negative emotions than the term infant cry. The strongest negative emotional ratings were found in the combination of the face and the cry of the premature infant. In a further study of abusive mothers, a crying infant elicited greater arousal and more negative emotional ratings by the abusers than by the controls. Abusing mothers show greater tendency to label young infants cries as "angry" than nonabusing control mothers. Among the population of failure-to-thrive, abused and adopted infants, low birthweight, small-for-gestation-age and handicapped babies are over-represented.

The research literature about maltreatment and violence against children is characterized by convincing evidence that excessive, persistent but even more often abnormal crying is the main trigger of maltreatment and violence against the child. According to this there exists a "high-risk-for-abuse" population (Gil 1970, Light 1974, Lester/Zeskind 1982, Michelsson/Rinne 1987, Bax 1985 , Frodi/Lamb 1980, Wilkes 1987, Wermke 1997).

In ratings of perceived sound qualities adults, regardless of child care experience, rated the high-risk infant cries (e.g. premature infants, low birthweight and small-for-gestation-age babies) as more "urgent, grating, sick, arousing, discomforting, aversive, and distressing." (Lester/Zeskind 1982:166) This matches the fact that low birthweight (Parker/Collmer 1975) and small-for-gestation-age babies are over-represented in the population of failure-to-thrive (Weston et al. 1993), abused, and adopted infants (Gil 1970, Light 1974).

Indeed the sound characteristics of cries of premature babies are different from cries of term-born healthy babies (Wasz-Höckert et al. 1968, Michelsson 1971, Lester/Boukydis 1985, Wermke 1987, Wermke et al. 1988). Premature babies often cry at a higher fundamental frequency and have much more noise bands within their sounds. Both characteristics could be seen as enforcing the alerting function of the cry because of the special needs of these infants. At the same time they carry a tremendous potential for releasing aversiveness and violence. On the perception side, those high-pitched, shrill sounds are very difficult to tolerate, and if excessively uttered may violate the limits of an often already stressed caregiver.

This leads to questions about the significance of the cry and the kinds of messages and meanings that are encoded in the cry, as well as the importance within the context of the development of infant-caregiver interaction. Fundamental investigations are necessary to decide whether or not differences in caregiving may affect frequency patterns of cries and which parenting strategies are able to reduce "violence-releasing features" of cry signals.

Early mother-child interaction is based on social signals which have been highly tuned through a long evolutionary adaptation process. The phylogenetically-acquired mechanisms enable and support these interactions immediately after birth. They help to establish a strong attachment between infant and mother. Characteristics of both infant and mother help shape and ultimately determine their interaction. In handling her baby, mothers do not need explicit instructions. Based on pre-programmed patterns, mothers act using strategies relevant to the child's age ("intuitive parenting" Papousek et al. 1996). Under certain conditions these mechanisms can become "mistuned" or counterproductive. During their interactions, the mother as well as the child develop special expectations and concepts of how the behavior of the other should be in the next moment. If there exists a (non-verbal) misunderstanding or a bad tuning between mother and child, neither will fulfill the mutual expectations and hence cannot react adequately. The relationship is stressed and reflected as a burden (Hassenstein 1987). This vicious circle is described above, explaining the changes of acoustical cry features in the case of CNS disorders and the perceptive effects on listeners.

There is another aspect to be mentioned in this framework. Most of the information material on child development for young mothers supports wrong expectations and put mothers under pressure to succeed, particularly because of the propagation of age-related normative values for several physical and mental performances of the child (normative values for the motor development, for "normal" sleep and feeding rhythms, for prespeech and language performances). The prevailing opinion is that growth and development are processes that reach a new stage step by step on the scale of progress during ontogenesis. This is not incorrect, but ignores the existence of "regression phases" and developmental crisis regularly occurring after reaching a certain developmental stage (van de Rijt/Plooij 1988,1992,1994, Wermke/Mende 1990, 1994).

Among the variety of textbooks for young mothers there is hardly any which informs mothers about normal "regression phases" and explains the changes of child behavior occurring during this time (more frequent crying, sleeping and eating disturbances, demand for more body contact). Being uninformed about those normal changes, mothers expect behavior patterns which the child might not be able to produce at the moment. Hence the mothers feel helpless, inadequate, depressed, anxious and finally angry or aggressive.

From an ethological perspective, a successful treatment of the child depends on treatment of the mother/parent-child interaction. Parents, especially parents of premature, retarded or handicapped children, should know the trigger-function of biological signals. This seems to be at least one method of preventing certain kinds of violence. We cannot abrogate our phylogenetic gifts in the case we find them no longer helpful or even counterproductive, but we can use cultural means to cope with them. Taking in account that an abused child not only suffers physical pain, but may also face delays in such socially important areas of functioning as language, motor development, and social skills, this becomes even more important. These long-term effects should be taken into account in assessing legal consequences for the actions of these individuals.

66 Kathleen Wermke

References

Adamson, L., Als, H., Tronick, E., Brazelton, T.B. (1977): The development of social reciprocity between a sighted infant and her blind parents. Journal of the American Academy of Child Psychiatry, 16:194-207

Andersen, E., Dunlea, A., Kekelis, L. (1984): Blind children's language: resolving some differences. J. Child Lang. 11:645-664

Ainsworth, M.D.S. (1969): Object Relations, Dependency and Attachment: A Theoretical Review of the Infant-Mother Relationship. Child development 40:969-1025

Als, H., Tronick, E., Brazelton, T.B. (1980): Affective reciprocity and the development of autonomy: The study of a blind infant. Journal of the American Academy of Child Psychiatry, 19:22-40

Baildam, E.M., Hillier, V.F., Ward, B.S., Bannister, R.P., Bamford, F.N., Moore, W.M.O. (1995): Duration and pattern of crying in the first year of life. Developmental Medicine and Child Neurology, 37, 345-353

Bax, M. (1985): Crying: A Clinical Overview. In: B.M. Lester & C.F.Z. Boukydis (eds.) (1985): Infant crying. Theoretical and Research Perspectives. New York: Plenum Press

Bishop, D. & Mogford, K. (1988): Language development in exceptional circumstances. Churchill Livingstone, Edinburgh/London/Melbourne and New York

Bowlby, J. (1958): The Nature of the Child's Tie to His Mother. International Journal of Psycho-Analysis, 39:350-373, zit. in Eibl-Eibesfeldt (1986:238)

Bowlby, J. (1969): Attachment and loss. In: Masud, M. u. Khan, R. (eds.): Attachment 1. London Hogarth Press, The Int. Psycho-Analytical Library, No. 79

Brodbeck, A.J., Irwin, O.C. (1946): The speech behaviour of infants without families. Child Develop., 17, 145

Campbell, R.N. & Grieve R. (1982): Royal investigations of the origin of language. Historiographia Linguistica IX:1/2, pp. 43-74

Curtiss S. Fromkin, V., Krashens, S., Rigler, D. & Rigler, M. (1974): The linguistic development of Genie. Language 50, pp. 528-555

Eibl-Eibesfeldt, I. (1986): Die Biologie des menschlichen Verhaltens. 2.,überarbeitete Aufl., Piper München, Zürich

Esser, G., Scheven, A., Petrova, A., Laucht, M., Schmidt, M.H. (1989): The Mannheim Rating Scale for the Assessment of Mother-Child Interaction in Infancy. Z-Kinder-Jugendpsychiatr. 17(4), pp. 185-193

Fisichelli, R.M. (1950): A study of prelinguistic speech development of institutionalized infants. unpublished Ph.D. Dissertation, Fordham University, cited in Hirsch de, K.: A Review of Early Language Development. Dev. Med and Child Neurol. vol. 12, No. 1 (1970), pp. 87-97

Fraiberg, S. (1974): Blind infants and their mothers: An examination of the sign system. In M. Lewis & L.A. Rosenblum (eds.): The effect of the infant on its caregiver (pp. 215-232). New York: Wiley

Fraiberg, S. (1975): The development of Human Attachments in Infants Blind from Birth. Merrill-Palmer Quarterly 21:315-334, zit. in Eibl-Eibesfeldt (1986:260)

Frodi, A.M., Lamb, M.E., Leavitt, L.A., Donovan, W.L., Neff, C. & Sherry, D. (1978): Father's and mother's responses to the faces and cries of normal and premature infants. Developmental Psychology 14:490-498

Frodi, A.M. & Lamb, M.E. (1980): Child abuser's responses to infant smiles and cries. Child development 51:238-241

Gil, D.G. (1970): Violence against children. Journal of Marriage and the family 33:637-657

Goldberg, S. (1982): Some biological aspects of early parent-infant interaction. In: Moore, S.G. & C. R. Cooper (eds.): The young child: Reviews of research. Washington, D.C.: National Association for the Education of Young Children, zit. in Lester/Zeskind (1982)

Gray, P. (1987): Crying Baby. How to cope. London: Wisebuy

Hassenstein, B. (1987): Verhaltensbiologie des Kindes. 4., überarbeitete und erweiterte Aufl., Piper München, Zürich

Itard, J. (1965): Victor, das Wildkind von Aveyron. Rotapfel-Verlag Zürich & Stuttgart

Jorg, M., Dinter, R., Rose, F., Villalba-Yantorno, P., Esser, G., Schmidt, M., Laucht, M. (1994): Category system for microanalysis of early mother-child interaction. Z. Kinder Jugendpsychiatr. 22(2), pp. 97-106

Kirkland, J. (1985): Crying Babies: Helping families cope. London: Croom Helm.

Korner, A.F. & Grobstein, R. (1976): Individual differences at birth: Implications for mother-infant relationship and later development. Journal of the American Academy of Child Psychiatry 6:676-690

Landau, B., Gleitman, L. (1985): Language and Experience: Evidence from the Blind Child. Cambridge, Mass.: MIT Press

Larcher L. (1844): Comments on the history of Herodotus, Bd. 1, Sp. 199

Lenneberg, E. (1967): Biological Foundations of Language. New York: Wiley

Leonhard K. (1970): Kaspar Hauser und das moderne Wissen über Hospitalismus. Confin. Psychiatr. 13(3):213-229

Lester, B.M. & Zeskind, P.S. (1982): A Biobehavioral Perspective on Crying in Early Infancy. In: Fitzgerald/Lester/Yogman (eds.): Theory and Research in Behavioral Pediatrics, Vol. 1: Plenum Publishing Corporation: pp. 133-180

Lester, B.M. & Boukydis, C.F.Z. (eds.) (1985): Infant crying. Theoretical and Research Perspectives. New York: Plenum Press

Light, R. (1974): Abused and neglected children in America: A study of alternative policies. Harvard Educational Review 43:556-598

Lykken, D.T. (1997): Incompetent parenting: Its causes and cures. Child Psychiatry Hum. Dev. 27(3), pp. 129-137

Lorenz, K. (1943): Die angeborenen Formen möglicher Erfahrung. Zeitschrift für Tierpsychologie 5:235-409

Mende, W. & Wermke, K. (1988): Evolution und Ontogenese des auditiv-vokalen Systems. Wiss. Z. HUB, 37:299-304

Mende, W., Wermke, K. (1992): Über die Strategie der Komposition komplexer Laute aus einfachen Schrei-und Nichtschreilauten während der frühen Sprachontogenese. Wiss. Z. HUB, R. Medizin 41, Heft 2:31-39

Mende, W., Wermke, K., Schindler, S., Wilzopolski, K. & Hoeck, S. (1990): Variability of the cry melody and the melody spectrum as indicators for certain CNS disorders. Early Child Development and Care 65:95-107

Mende, W., Wermke, K., Ruppert, R., Borschberg, H. (1994): Evolution of sound spectra of prespeech vocalizations of twins during the first year. Genetic Epidemiology of Twins and Twinning—An International Symposium, Course Book, P 31

Michelsson, K. (1971): Cry analyses of symptomless low birth weight neonates and of asphyxiated newborn infants. Acta Paediatrica Scandinavica, 116 Suppl. 216:1-45

Michelsson, K. & Rinne, A. (1987): Cry research—where do we stand now? In: Kirkland J. (ed.) Cry reports—Special Issue 1987: Palmerston North, N.Z.: Massey University Press p. 1-5

Murray, A.D. (1979): Infant Crying as an Elicitor of Parental Behavior: An Examination of Two Models. Psychological Bulletin, vol. 86, no. 1:191-215

Papousek, H., Papousek, M. (1983): Biological basis of social interactions: implications of research for an understanding of behavioural deviance. J. Child Psychol. Psychiatry 24(1), pp. 117-129

Papousek, H., Papousek, M., Rothaug, M. (1996): A Cross-Cultural View of the Beginning of Human Communication and its Medical Significance. In: Gottscvhalk-Batschkus, Ch.

E. & Schuler, J. (eds.) Ethnomedical Perspectives on Early Childhood. Curara Special Volume 9:301-311

Parke, R.D. & Collmer, D.A. (1975): Child abuse: An interdisciplinary analysis. In: E.M. Hetherington (ed.): Rev. of Child Development Res., vol. 5. Chicago: University of Chicago Press

Pinker, St. (1995): The language instinct. Harper Perennial, 494 pp.

Provence, S., Lipton, R. (1962): Infants in Institutions. New York: International University Press cited in Hirsch de, K.: A Review of Early Language Development. Dev. Med and Child Neurol. vol. 12, No. 1, (1970), pp. 87-97

Robson, K.S. & Moss, H.A. (1970): Patterns and determinants of maternal attachment. Journal of Pediatrics 77:976-985

Siegmund, R., Schiefenhövel, W. & Tittel, M. (1996): Time Patterns in Infants—Activity, Rest and Mother-Child Interactions in Crosscultural Comparison. In: Gottschalk-Batschkus, Ch.E. & Schuler J. (eds.): Ethnomedical Perspectives on Early Childhood. Journal for Ethnomedicine, Special Volume 9, pp. 293-301

Simon, N. (1978): Kaspar Hauser's recovery and autopsy: a perspective on neurological and sociological requirements for language development. J. Autism. Child Schizophr. 8(2), pp. 209-217

Skuse, D.H. (1988): Extreme deprivation in early childhood. pp. 29-45. In: Bishop, D. & Mogford, K. (1988): Language development in exceptional circumstances. Churchill Livingstone, Edinburgh/London/Melbourne and New York

Spangler, G. & Grossmann, K.E. (1993): Biobehavioral organization in securely and insecurely attached infants. Child Dev. 64(5), pp. 1439-1450

Stumpfe, K.D. (1969): Der Fall Kasper Hauser. Prax. Kinderpsychol. Kinderpsychiatr. 18(8), pp. 292-299

Thierauf, P. (1993): Kaspar Hauser—individuelle pathologische Beobachtungen basierend auf Autopsie befunden. Pathologe 14(2), pp. 120-122

Todt, D. (1988): Serial Calling as a Mediator of Interaction Processes: Crying in Primates. In: Primate Vocal Communication, edited by Todt/Goedeking/Symmes, Springer-Verlag Berlin Heidelberg

Tronick, E. (1979): Infant Communicative Intent: The Infant's Reference to Social Interaction. pp. 5-16. In: Stark, R.E. (ed.) Language Behavior in Infancy and Early Childhood. Proceedings of a Pediatric Round Table held at the Santa Barbara Biltmore Hotel, Santa Barbara, California, October 10-13, 1979

Van de Rijt-Plooij, H.H. & Plooij F.X. (1988): Mother-infant relations, conflict, stress and illness among free-ranging chimpanzees. Dev. Med. Child Neurol. 30(3), 306-315

Van de Rijt, H. & Plooij, F. (1992): Infantile Regressions: Disorganization and the Onset of Transition Periods. Journal of Reproductive and Infant Psychology, vol. 10:129-149

Van de Rijt, H. & Plooij, F. (1994): Oje, ich wachse! Mosaik Verlag München

Volkin, J.I. (1987): Mother-child interaction in abusive, distressed, and normal families. Dissertation, University of Pittsburgh

Wasz-Höckert, O., Lind, J., Vuorenkoski, V., Partanen, T. & Valanne, E. (1968): The Infant Cry. A Spectrographic and Auditory Analysis. Clinics in Developmental Medicine 29. Lavenham, Suffolk:Spastics International Medical Publications

Weissenborn, J. & Höhle, B. (1998): Discovering Grammar. To appear in: Friederici, A. & Menzel, R. (eds.) Learning: Rule Extraction and Repreentation. Berlin: de Gruyter, 1998

Wermke, K. (1987): Begründung und Nachweis der Eignung des Säuglingsschreis als Indikator für zentralnervöse Funktionsstörungen des Neugeborenen—Fallstudien unter Einsatz eines speziellen Computerverfahrens. Thesis. Berlin: Humboldt-University

Wermke, K. Mende, W., Grauel, L., Wilsopolski, K., Schmucker, U. & Schröder, G. (1988): The significance and determination of pitch in newborn cries and the melody spectrum as a measure of fundamental frequency variability. In: Kirkland, J. (ed.) Cry Reports—Special Issue 1987. Palmerston North, N.Z.: Massey University Press

Wermke, K., Mende, W. (1992) Sprache beginnt mit dem ersten Schrei. Spectrum der Wissenschaften, Dezember 1992, 115-118

Wermke, K., Mende, W. (1994) Ontogenetic development of infant cry- and non-cry vocalizations as early stages of speech abilities. Proceedings of the third congress of the International Clinical Phonetics and Linguistics Association, 9.-11.8.1993, Helsinki/Finnland, S. 181-189

Wermke (1997) The infant cry—a Biosiren expressing the need for relief of distress, but also a trigger for violence against the child. In: Gruter M. & Rehbinder M. (Hrsg.) Gewalt in der Kleingruppe und das Recht. Schriften zur Rechtspsycholgie, Band 3-Bern: Stämpfli, pp. 237-250

Weston, J.A., Colloton, M., Halsey, S., Covington, S., Gibert, J., Sorrentino-Kelly, L., & Renoud, S.S. (1993): A legacy of violence in nonorganic failure to thrive. Child-Abuse-Negl. Nov-Dec; 17(6):709-714

Wiessbluth, M. (1984): Crybabies. London: Futura

Wilkes, J.C. (1987): Maternal response to infant cries: An analogue study of bidirectional influences in child abuse. Dissertation, California School of Professional Psychology—San Diego

Zetterström, R. (1984) Responses of Children to Hospitalization. Acta Paediatr Scand 73:289-295

Law, Biology, Sex, and Politics

Kingsley R. Browne*

The intertwining of law and biology that Margaret Gruter has been tirelessly advocating for three decades shows increasing signs of acceptance. More and more legal academics are incorporating biological insights into both their scholarship and their teaching. It is far too soon, however, to declare victory, because explicit consideration of behavioral biology by judges and other policy makers continues to be rare indeed. Moreover, because much of the biological learning implicates matters about which many people feel passionately – what is the nature of humans? of men? of women? – political objections will continue to loom large.

One of the most robust findings of human behavioral biology involves differences between the sexes.[1] Average differences exist between the sexes in a whole host of temperamental, cognitive, and reproductive domains, and for many of these differences plausible

---

* Professor, Wayne State University Law School.
E-mail: kingsley.browne@wayne.edu.
1 See generally David C. Geary, Male, Female: The Evolution of Human Sex Differences (1998).

and coherent evolutionary explanations have been provided. Moreover, many of these differences affect outcomes that are at the core of much public policy discussion, such as the glass ceiling, the gender gap in compensation, differential occupational representation of the sexes,[2] as well as such evils as rape[3] and sexual harassment.[4]

The law must rest on an accurate understanding of the nature of – and differences between – males and females if it is to be an effective instrument of our collective will. Ironically, until approximately the time that Margaret Gruter began her work on law and biology, the law in many ways reflected the longstanding assumption of most people that males and females differ substantially and that there was nothing presumptively illogical or immoral in the law's making distinctions based upon sex in certain circumstances. Of course, most laws did not make such distinctions; overwhelmingly, laws applied to males and females alike. But in a few areas, the differences between the sexes that seemed "natural" were recognized in law. Many of these laws were designed to protect women, such as laws obliging a husband to support his wife or prohibiting employers from working women for overly long hours.

Beginning largely in the 1960s and 1970s, with the advent of certain strains of feminism, the notion that there were "natural" differences between the sexes that might legitimately be recognized in law came under increasing challenge.[5] Laws that were designed to protect women came to be viewed – accurately in some cases – as a means to disadvantage women, to infantilize them by suggesting that they needed the same sorts of special protection that children do. If a woman did not want the special protection of the

---

2 See generally Kingsley Browne, Divided Labours: An Evolutionary View of Women at Work (1998); Kingsley R. Browne, Sex and Temperament in Modern Society: A Darwinian View of the Glass Ceiling and the Gender Gap, 37 Ariz. L. Rev. 971 (1995) [hereinafter Sex and Temperament].

3 Owen Jones, An Evolutionary Analysis of Rape, ___ Cal. L. Rev. ___ (1999).

4 Kingsley R. Browne, An Evolutionary Perspective on Sexual Harassment: Seeking Roots in Biology Rather than Ideology, J. Contemp. Leg. Issues 5 (1997).

5 See, e.g., Ruth B. Ginsburg, Sexual Equality Under the Fourteenth and Equal Rights Amendments, 1979 Wash. U.L.Q. 161.

laws, the argument went – if , for example, she wanted to earn more money by working the night shift in a factory – then she should have the same right to compete for the position as a man. This individual-rights view struck a receptive chord in a people philosophically dedicated to individual liberty. The argument that a woman should have the right to choose her occupation and to be judged as an individual without regard to sex is indeed an appealing one, and one that can be justified even in the face of substantial average differences between the sexes in job-relevant traits.

Makers of law and policy did not stop with their judgment that women should be allowed to compete for jobs in which they are interested, however. They went an additional giant step that ultimately rests upon an empirical judgment that turns out to be wrong. They decided that not only should women be *allowed* to make the same choices as men, but also that, left to pursue their own preferences, women would actually *choose* the same as men. Therefore, when the average woman's career path or compensation diverges from that of men, for example, discrimination by employers or the greater society is judged responsible.

Without fully understanding it, those who predict that women and men will make the same choices because they have the same preferences are implicitly resting their argument on what has been called the "Standard Social Sciences Model" (the "SSSM"). According to this model, humans have no essential nature and the only "real" difference between men and women is in reproductive function and (although some contest even this[6]) in physical strength. This model views human behavior as overwhelmingly a product of social conditioning, and it considers observed temperamental and behavioral sex differences to be products of differential conditioning.

The SSSM exalts humans to a position unique in the animal kingdom. Adherents of that model readily attribute an inherent "nature" to all other animals. A dog raised in a group of

---

6 See Anne Fausto-Sterling, Myths of Gender: Biological Theories About Women and Men 148-49(2d Ed. 1992).

chimpanzees will never attempt to swing from the trees, and no one expects it to. Human behavior, on the other hand, is viewed not as a product of human nature but of social programming. In other words, man is the maker of man. More precisely, humans are the makers of males and females, for just as there is no essential human nature, there is, under this view, even more emphatically no "male nature" and "female nature."

The extreme behaviorism of John Watson[7] – whose famous assertion "that there is no such thing as inheritance of capacity, talent, temperament, mental constitution and characteristics" but rather that these traits "depend on training that goes on mainly in the cradle" – has been largely abandoned by modern psychology. However, its legacy persists in other social sciences that are influential to policy makers. As a result, suggestions that individual or group differences have a biological origin tend to be met with extreme skepticism, and apparently many would still concur with anthropologist George Murdock's later-repudiated statement that the science of culture is "independent of the laws of biology and psychology."[8]

The findings of modern evolutionary biology and psychology render the assumptions of the SSSM wildly implausible. The centrality of mating and reproduction to evolutionary success, coupled with the differential investment of mammalian males and females in offspring, makes behavioral identity of the sexes highly improbable. Just as cows and bulls, mares and stallions, and hens and roosters exhibit consistent differences in behavior, so do women and men.

The architects of sexual equality tended to assume that lifting restrictions on women in the workplace would result in parity with men because men and women inherently have identical desires and capacities. When women have not reached parity once formal discrimination is eliminated, hidden discrimination is assumed to be

---

7 John B. Watson, Behaviorism 74-75 (1925).
8 George P. Murdock, The Science of Culture, 34 Am. Anthro. 200 (1932). But see George P. Murdock, Anthropology's Mythology, Proceedings of the Royal Anthropological Institute of Great Britain and Ireland for 1971 17-24 (1972).

the culprit. If hidden discrimination can be disproved, then other, informal, barriers, such as sexist attitudes of others, are assumed to be the culprit. If direct external forces must finally (and reluctantly) be abandoned because the path that women's lives have taken must be attributed to their own choices, then their choice becomes a "choice" that is a consequence of their internalization of "patriarchal" notions about the proper role of the sexes.[9] While the causal attribution may shift over time, what does not change is the persistent invocation of causes other than differences between men's and women's inherent predispositions. This persistence is hardly surprising coming, as it often does, from people who reject the entire notion that people *have* "inherent predispositions."

The disappointment of the "integrationists" – those who believe that parity of representation of men and women in all positions is a goal both appropriate and achievable – is a predictable consequence of their erroneous view of human nature. For reasons having substantial roots in evolutionary biology, men and women differ in fundamental ways that have significant workplace implications. Well-known stereotypes of men as more competitive, more driven toward seeking status and resources, and more inclined to take risks than women, and stereotypes of women as more nurturing, more risk averse, less greedy, and less single-minded than men are true as generalizations and have an underlying biological basis. Those individuals, whether male or female, who are inclined toward competition, risk-taking, and status-seeking are more likely to reach the pinnacle of career success than those who are not.

Important average cognitive differences also exist between the sexes.[10] Men outperform women on a number of measures of spatial ability and in mathematical reasoning, while women outperform men on tests of object location memory, mathematical calculation, and verbal fluency. Men outperform women at

---

9   See generally Joan Williams, Gender Wars: Selfless Women in the Republic of Choice, 66 N.Y.U. L. Rev. 1559 (1991).

10   See generally Doreen Kimura, Sex and Cognition (1999).

targeting tasks, such as throwing a ball at a moving target, while women have superior fine motor skills. Differential demands on hunters and gatherers, respectively, are likely responsible for many of these differences.[11]

Female superiority at a given task is generally not something that people feel required to explain, justify, or remedy. I am unaware, for example, of any initiatives to decrease the "verbal fluency gap" between girls and boys. However, for those tasks at which males excel – such as mathematical reasoning – once again comes the insistent search for a social cause and demands for intervention. Someone must be to blame for the "mathematical reasoning gap," although not for the "verbal fluency gap." Thus, many have attributed higher male scores on tests of mathematical aptitude to different expectations that parents and teachers have for the two sexes. Moreover, the argument continues, girls downplay their mathematical skills in order to appear feminine. While widely accepted, these arguments are largely lacking in support.[12] First, they do not explain why girls do *better* than boys in calculation, since, for most people, mathematics *is* calculation. Second, if these arguments were valid, one would expect the greatest sex differences to be on tests with very visible results or where evaluation is particularly subjective. That is, when protected by anonymity, girls would do relatively better than they do when everyone can see how well they perform and where the person evaluating them knows their sex. However, the reality is just the opposite. Girls get *better* grades than boys in school, even in math classes. The female disadvantage shows not in classroom *achievement* but on tests of mathematical *aptitude*, and as classes require increasing amounts of aptitude, girls increasingly decline to take the classes.

Males and females also differ in their sexual attitudes and behaviors.[13] Common stereotypes of men's being more interested

---

11 See, e.g., Irwin Silverman & Marion Eals, Sex Differences in Spatial Abilities: Evolutionary Theory and Data, in The Adapted Mind: Evolutionary Psychology and the Generation of Culture 533 (Jerome H. Barkow, Leda Cosmides & John Tooby, eds.) (1992).

12 See Kimura, supra note 10.

13 See generally David M. Buss, The Evolution of Desire (1994).

in casual sexual relationships and more willing to use coercion to achieve them have a basis in fact. Men often see sexual opportunity where women see sexual threat. The sexual conflict that occurs when men and women work side-by-side in the workplace is often a predictable, though regrettable, consequence of a conflict between male and female sexual psychologies, and it is that conflict – rather than the commonly blamed "ideology of patriarchy" – that manifests itself as sexual harassment.

All of these sex differences – the temperamental differences that lead men disproportionately to seek high status, the cognitive differences that lead to male dominance of certain professions that impose high spatial and mathematical demands, and the differences in sexual strategies that lead to rape and sexual harassment – have important legal and policy ramifications. If the biological account is correct, then commonly urged policy responses are likely to be ineffective. If one assumes, for example, that it is employer discrimination that is largely responsible for keeping women out of the executive suites, then the appropriate course would be to strengthen the discrimination laws or their enforcement. Unless the concept of "illegal discrimination" is extended to include all "underrepresentation" of women, however, that course is unlikely to be terribly successful in achieving the desired parity. Similarly, enhancing female self-esteem in mathematics is unlikely to substantially increase female representation in mathematical fields.

An understanding of biological origins of many sex differences can be important in at least two ways. First, if intervention is felt desirable, understanding the origins of the forces that one is seeking to overcome is highly desirable. Second, an understanding of the origins *may* actually affect the judgment of whether intervention is desirable in the first place. Consider, for example, the relatively low representation of women at the highest corporate levels. Some people may object to the lack of proportional representation at all levels of the corporation and in all jobs as a matter of principle. For such people, the origins of the differences may be relevant to the strategy to be chosen to achieve proportional representation but not to the initial decision whether something ought to be done at all.

However, many people despair over the lack of women in certain positions not because they believe that justice demands 50/50 representation as a matter of principle, but because they assume that the lack of proportional representation is due to discrimination. Thus, they view women's career choices not as manifestations of their own preferences and abilities but rather as "choices" forced upon them by employers and society, neither of which will allow them to follow the dictates of their own preferences.

Many people are uncomfortable with biological explanations of social phenomena, believing such explanations to imply either the inevitability or the virtue of the status quo. To provide such explanations is, some say, to commit the "naturalistic fallacy," that is, reasoning from what *is* to what *ought* to be. But science can explain only the "is" and not the "ought." The discovery that all manner of social ills, from rape to child abuse, derive in part from biological predispositions does not justify those behaviors. Nor does it imply that efforts to reduce the prevalence of such behaviors are necessarily doomed, for a central finding of evolutionary psychology is the flexibility (albeit along predictable lines) of human behavioral responses.

Some believe that we should not base law and policy on one or another specific view of human nature, but even a moment's reflection reveals that sentiment to be misguided. What, after all, is law but an attempt to shape human behavior? And what could be more essential to that enterprise than an understanding of the nature of the beast we are trying to control? One would think a zookeeper guilty of malpractice if he sought to treat all animals the same rather than understanding the "psychology" of each separate species, and one should have no different a view of someone who seeks to influence human behavior while remaining completely unconcerned with human motivations.

Laws often rest on an implicit view of human nature, and they should. Programs designed to create incentives for some favored behavior are based on a belief that the incentive will increase the likelihood of that behavior. In behaviorist terms, the programs are based on a belief that a particular stimulus acting on a human organism will result in a predictable behavioral response. Such a prediction is impossible without at least an implicit theory of the mind.

Much current policy relating to sexual equality is already based upon a specific, though often unarticulated, theory of human nature – the traditional social-science assumption that humans, unlike all other mammals, possess a sexually monomorphic mind. For the most part, the law has implicitly adopted the SSSM, often to the detriment of sound social policy. For example, use of statistical evidence in discrimination cases rests on the explicit assumption that in the absence of discrimination there would be equality in outcomes.[14]   That assumption, in turn, implicitly rests on an assumption that male and female preferences and capacities are identical. With respect to some preferences and capacities, that is a correct assumption, but it is not always so. The apparently increasing hostility to sex classifications demonstrated by the Supreme Court in its ruling that the Virginia Military Institute could not exclude females may reflect a deepening conviction on its part that sex is a largely arbitrary criterion that is irrelevant to public policy.[15] The alternative offered here is that the male and female mind differ (on average) in important ways that are relevant to real-world outcomes. In short, the question for policy makers is not *whether* they should base policy on a particular view of human nature, but rather it is a question of *which* view of human nature they should embrace.

We should not, however, expect too much from science. A robust consensus on the nature of man and woman does not foreordain consensus on policy responses. Pre-existing values are important and are not derivable from scientific fact. Thus, liberals,

---

14   See Kingsley R. Browne, Statistical Proof of Discrimination: Beyond "Damned Lies," 68 Wash. L. Rev. 477 (1993).

15   See United States v. Virginia, 518 U.S. 515 (1996).

conservatives, radicals, and libertarians will probably derive liberal, conservative, radical, and libertarian conclusions from the same science.

The forces that must be countered by those seeking to use biological learning to inform policy making should not be underestimated, for they push from many directions. Those (especially on the left) who adhere to the prevailing social-determinist view of human behavior predictably reject any substantial biological contribution to behavior. Similarly, those (especially on the right) who reject the entire theory of evolution do not find much explanatory value in Darwinian perspectives on the human condition, although they might find some Darwinian insights congenial on a political level. But most disconcerting is the tack taken by some who actually employ Darwinian principles in their own work, but who also have adopted the political tactics of those who attempt to exclude the findings of behavioral biology from academic discourse. Let me provide a couple of examples that involve my own work.

Much of the prior discussion in this essay about the "glass ceiling" and the "gender gap" in compensation draws from a lengthy piece on the subject that appeared in the *Arizona Law Review.*[16] In that piece, I drew on literature from biology, psychology, and anthropology, as well as law. In a nutshell, my thesis was that, although discrimination against women exists, the current fashion of automatically attributing sex disparities in pay or position to sex discrimination ignores the fact that men and women are biologically predisposed to make, on average, different choices, because of their average differences in temperament, and that those choices can have tangible consequences. I emphasized that nothing that I said justified treating men and women differently in the workplace or suggested that there was not substantial overlap in the distribution of temperament between men and women.

---

16 Sex and Temperament, supra note?.

Reflexive accusations of biological determinism are, of course, to be expected, and there is no way to insulate oneself from such attacks other than to abandon the biological inquiry altogether. And, of course, legitimate criticism is always appropriate. No extensive work can be perfect, and fair criticism can substantially aid in the search for truth. Unfortunately, other criticisms were more discouraging, including some from people who purport to believe that insights from behavioral biology can be useful to policy makers. For example, in an article urging the integration of law and biology, Oliver Goodenough referred to my work as follows:

> Some contemporary scholars seem prone to dwell on the differences [between the sexes], in the process giving ammunition to those who would perpetuate per se barriers to women's entry into areas of society from which they have been barred in the past.[17]

A parsing of Goodenough's criticism illustrates the psychic costs that will continue to be paid by those seeking to unite law and biology, at least if the research is perceived to have certain kinds of political implications. This is not to suggest that such research should be immune from criticism but rather that the criticism should adhere to scholarly methodology.

Goodenough dismisses my 135-page article in a single sentence on two seemingly separate grounds, neither of which rests on any assertion of error on my part. First, Goodenough complains that I am "prone to dwell" on the differences between the sexes. Second, he contends that my work "giv[es] ammunition" to people whose political views he finds uncongenial. Neither of these criticisms is, I submit, an appropriate one.

---

17   Oliver R. Goodenough, Biology, Behavior, and Criminal Law: Seeking a Responsible Approach to an Inevitable Interchange, 22 Vt. L. Rev. 263, 287 (1997). Immediately following the citation to my article, the reader is helpfully directed to "a cogent caution on contemporary abuse." Id. n.86.

Being "prone to dwell" on something is, of course, a bad thing, a pejorative phrase that connotes attention to a matter that is excessive according to some standard. We would not, after all, suggest that the career of a cancer researcher who devoted his life to curing cancer indicated that he was "prone to dwell" on the causes and cures of cancer, and we would not condemn Albert Einstein for being "prone to dwell" on the nature of the universe. So, what is the standard by which my attention to sex differences reflects "dwelling" rather than a "scholarly focus?" Goodenough provides none, and none is readily apparent. Although my article was long, it was minuscule in comparison with the body of literature on sex differences that it was attempting to synthesize. If his point was that devoting 135 pages to the effect of biology on modern workplace outcomes was excessive because the effects of biology are trivial, if not nonexistent, then it should be my conclusions, rather than my propensity to "dwell," that should have been challenged.

The second criticism was that my research "giv[es] ammunition" to those who would like to exclude women from the workplace. Significantly, Goodenough does not identify who those people are, and I am unaware of anyone having relied upon my work in this way. But apparently the fact that someone someday might do so is sufficient to impugn the effort. Explicit statements that my argument would *not* justify discrimination against women, but rather that it merely explains that disparities will exist even in the absence of discrimination, are apparently insufficient to relieve me of the burden of that criticism.

One can, and in many cases should, take steps to avoid inadvertent good-faith misunderstandings of one's work. Indeed, that is simply good communication. However, there is little, if anything, one can do to avoid the deliberate misrepresentation of one's work to suit someone else's agenda. When that kind of misrepresentation occurs, the criticism appropriately lies with the person who is misrepresenting the work, rather than the one whose work is misrepresented.

Another recent example of the kind of criticism that one risks by writing about biological matters came in an article discussing the application of biological theories to female violence.[18] The author, Cheryl Hanna, described the "explicitly sexist and racist" views of 19th Century criminologist Caesar Lombroso, who believed, she says, that women "were not just biologically different, but inferior." Hanna tells us that "Lombroso's work has been rightfully [sic] discredited as sexist and racist as well as methodologically unsound, although sadly still survives [sic] in much of contemporary discourse." First among the contemporary discourse cited is my glass-ceiling article, which is cited for the proposition that "biological differences between men and women explain gender discrimination in the workplace." That is not an accurate characterization of my article, which suggested not that biological sex differences explain discrimination, but that because of biological sex differences some average sex differences in workplace outcomes will exist even without discrimination. These are, of course, dramatically different points.

More significant for current purposes, however, is the characterization of my work as representing a survival of the "sexist and racist" science of the 19th Century. No error in my work is cited, nor is any particular point in my article even identified as being sexist. It is apparently deemed sufficient simply to invoke the term "sexist," because in politically charged areas name calling has seemingly come to be an acceptable form of scholarly criticism. Like Goodenough's criticism this is not an argument that is susceptible of refutation.

These criticisms are particularly dismaying coming from scholars who attempt to incorporate biological learning into their scholarship. Unfortunately, there seems to be a felt need to identify some "bad" biology person in order to create an appearance of moral authority to speak on behalf of "good" biology. Thus, at conferences on law and biology one often hears the equivalent of

---

18   Cheryl Hanna, Ganging up on Girls: Young Women And Their Emerging Violence, 41 Ariz. L. Rev. 93 (1999) (footnotes omitted).

"sociobiology bad/evolutionary psychology good." However, biology will never be incorporated into mainstream public policy discussions as long as its proponents appear to believe that they have so little positive to offer that they must enhance the appearance of the good by constructing straw men whom they claim to be bad. If proponents of biology resort to the same kind of arguments as their opponents –pejorative labeling, questioning of motives, and ruling certain areas of inquiry presumptively out of bounds – the opponents will win.

Knowledge is power, and like other forms of power it can be misused. But we do not decline to gather epidemiological or environmental data, for example, because it might be used (or misused) by partisans involved in tort or environmental litigation. Rather, we attack the science when it is bad, and we attack reliance on the science when that reliance is unfounded. We should do no differently when it comes to biology and behavior. If we cannot adhere to rigorous standards of scholarly inquiry, we can hardly expect our opponents to do so.

Mongolia: Avoiding Tragedy in the World's Largest Commons

Robert D. Cooter[*]

Abstract
In Mongolia, 300,000 nomadic people herd 25 million animals over an unfenced area twice the size of France. Current economic theories assert that efficiency requires privatizing land until the savings from reduced congestion equal the costs of exclusion. However, the fundamental tradeoff in Mongolia is different. In Mongolia, privatization solves the problem of congestion at the cost of aggravating the problem of spreading risk. Assigning exclusive use-rights over particular pastures to families solves the problem of congestion among herds, and increases the transaction costs of moving the herds across climatic zones in response to inclement weather. Thus, efficiency requires privatizing land until the savings from reduced congestion equals the increase in the transaction cost

* Professor of Law, University of California at Berkeley School of Law

of insuring against climatic risk. Customary law responds to this tradeoff with a different legal regime for different seasons of the year. Families enjoy relatively open access to summer pasture. In contrast, customary law assigns families exclusive use-rights to winter pasture. These facts about Mongolia generalize: Open-access resources are susceptible to inefficient congestion because users receive the average product, not the marginal product. Privatizing eliminates averaging, which also concentrates risk.

Mongolia: Avoiding Tragedy in the World's Largest Commons[2]

In Mongolia 300,000 nomadic people herd 25 million cattle, sheep, goats, yaks, horses, and camels over an unfenced area twice the size of France.[3] The steppe, mountain, and desert pastures of Mongolia are the world's largest "commons."[4] Although low rainfall makes the land vulnerable to degradation from over-grazing, it

---

2 Chris Clague, Robin Mearns, Peter Murrell, and Tom Ginsburg read and corrected the first draft of this manuscript. The basic argument was clarified by suggestions from Peter Murrell. IRIS (Institutional Reform and the Informal Sector) and USAID organized and financed my travel to Mongolia and my participation in a colloquium on law and economics. Special thanks are due to Cindy Clement, Jim Anderson, and participants in the colloquium, especially Tumur Sorogjoogiln (Dr. in Law and Member of Parliament) and B. Ochbadrakh (Deputy Chairman, State Commission for Privatization). Participants in the colloquiums included B. Sarantuya (judge), R. Jaianchoijil (judge), B. Ochbadrah (Privatization Commission), D. Byasgalan (National Development Board), Altantsetseg (Chamber of Commerce), Batjargal (Law and Arbitration Bureau), L. Boldhuu (Ministry of Justice), J. Delgertsetseg (Member of Parliament), B. Dolgor (Parliament office), D. Dugerjav (Law Drafting Department, Ministry of Justice), Erdenechimeg (Consultant to Parliament), D. Minjuur (legal consultant) Davaasurengjin Naranchimeg (Law School, Mongolia National State University), Soyol-Erdene (lecturer, Economic College, S. Tumur (Member of Parliament), and Turbaya (Law Drafting Department, Ministry of Justice).

3 The population of Mongolia at the end of 1992 was 2,215,000, of whom 330,100 are herders and their families. Almost all herders are nomadic, although some have established permanent living sites near towns or paved roads. 1992 Statistical Yearbook as reported in the Consultancy Centre (1994), pages 1 and 2. For details on Mongolia's 25 million livestock, see Economist Intelligence Unit, table on page 44.

4 "Four broad ecological-territorial zones can be distinguished in Mongolia on the basis of prevailing ecological conditions, geographical boundaries and herding methods. These are: the Altai mountain zone, the Hangai-Hentii mountain zone, the steppe zone and the Bogi-steppe zone." Bazargur, D., C. Shilrevadja, & B. Chinbat, page 2. The zones are explained at length in Figure 1 on page 10 and related discussion.

remains largely undamaged after more than a millennium of use.[5] How have Mongolians avoided the tragedy of the commons? Published research and personal observations suggest an explanation based on property rights as developed through customary law.[6]

"Open-access" refers to a property regime in which a broad group of people can freely graze their animals on pastures, whereas

---

5   Here is a typical opinion: ". . . although there is probably no overgrazing problem, there are local problems, especially where customary tenure arrangements have been undermined." Institute of Development Studies at University of Sussex, U.K. and associated Mongolian institutions (1993), page ii.

   A less typical view alleges significant degradation of the land during collectivisation, which continues under new circumstances: "The thirty years under collectivisation (1959-1989) constituted a period in which questions of territorial organisation and land management were ignored or avoided.   As a result, a substantial proportion of natural pasture has become degraded and traditional techniques have been forgotten . . .   We consider that collectivisation marked the starting point for costly errors in relation to land tenure and pastoral techniques . . . In recent years, some herders have begun to move unsystematically and gain uncontrolled access to grazing of neighboring brigades and districts.   In order to guard against this, other herders have adopted the defensive and historically unprecedented strategy of spending all four seasons at their winter and spring places.   If they perceive that their important winter and spring pastures are likely to be grazed out by others during other seasons, the customary users of these areas may choose to remain in those pasture areas themselves to prevent such encroachment. The overall consequence however is that substantial areas of pastures have become damaged through overuse." Bazargur, D., C. Shilrevadja, & B. Chinbat, page 1 and page 6.

6   The Institute of Development Studies at University of Sussex, U.K. and associated Mongolian institutions, have recently conducted field research on livestock and land in Mongolia under the title Policy Alternatives for Livestock Development in Mongolia (PALD).   A series of useful reports have been published.   I visited Mongolia in June of 1994 to participate in a colloquium on business law sponsored by IRIS (Institutional Reform and the Informal Sector) and USAID.   I taught the economic analysis of contracts to Mongolian judges and drafters of their civil code and land law.   These teaching session gave me the opportunity to discuss the ideas presented in this note.   I also spent two days in the countryside with a translator and a member of Parliament who is especially interested in land.

   "Mongolian herding communities are generally organised around the management of viable grazing territories, and have effective customary rules and procedures to manage the resources of these territories.   The period of collectivisation to some extent weakened these customary tenure systems, but they are re-emerging rapidly under economic reform.   They have important weaknesses however, and cannot cope on their own with the rapid and far-reaching changes triggered by privatisation and the move to a market economy . . .   Given ecological and other constraints, private freehold tenure of grazing land by individual households is not a viable general solution.   Different mixes of public and private freehold and leasehold, at individual and group level, offer the best solutions, and provide the flexibility needed to adapt the tenure system to varying local conditions .. ." from summary in Institute of Development Studies at University of Sussex, U.K. and associated Mongolian institutions (1993).

   ". . .improving the living standards of herders and at the same time enabling them to remain as "valley keepers", or careful custodians of their local environment, will not be achieved by focusing exclusively on households as atomistic units with private herds.   In fact herding households were never so individualistic as this even prior to the 1921 Revolution.   They formed collective units of ownerhip within which they were able to decide some of their own socio-economic problems . .   Research has usually shown that policy measures not in accordance with our livestock farming traditions are inappropriate." Bazargur, Shilrevadja, & Chinbat, page 1.

"private ownership" refers to a property regime in which an individual or a small group of people has exclusive rights to graze their animals on particular pastures. In this context, "privatization" means converting the legal regime from open-access to private ownership. Current theories of land privatization derive from Demsetz's classic paper, as elegantly developed by subsequent scholars such as Ellickson, Eggertsson, Field, and Ostrom.[7] Unfortunately, these theories do not fit the facts of Mongolia. In the first section of this paper, I briefly describe the tragedy of the commons, recapitulate Demsetz's theory of privatization, explain why it does not fit the facts of Mongolia, and propose an alternative. I also suggest why this alternative generalizes beyond Mongolian pasture. In subsequent sections of the paper I relate my theory to the past and future of Mongolia.

Theory

A pasture is congested if an additional animal grazing on it reduces the food available to other animals. As congestion increases, a pasture may be "overused" in two senses of the word. First, the actual number of pastured animals may exceed the number that maximizes the joint profits of their owners. When a pasture is over-used in this sense, a smaller number of better nourished animals would increase profits to their owners. Second, the actual number of animals may exceed the carrying-capacity of the land. When a pasture is over-used in this sense, the land degrades.

Placing an additional animal on a congested pasture deprives other animals of grass and increases the pressure on the land. If the affected animals and land belong to him, the owner will consider these costs when deciding whether to add an additional animal. Private ownership of animals and land internalizes congestion costs

---

7 In an elegant article, Ellickson (1993) traces the historical evolution of property rights, drawing upon the theme that private property rights are created when the "dead weight loss" from group rights exceeds the "transaction costs" of private property. Also see Field (1989), Ostrom (1990), Eggertsson (1990 and 1992), and Ellickson (1991). An economic account of property rights in the West from Roman times is found in Bouckaert.

and avoids over-use. In contrast, if the affected animals and land belong to someone else, the owner may ignore the effects on other animals and the land when deciding whether to add an additional animal. Open-access to land externalizes congestion costs and causes over-use. This tragic outcome, however, presupposes political paralysis that obstructs collective action. In close-knit communities, people typically avoid the tragedy by changing the law.[8] The change in law may involve privatizing the land.

Demsetz predicted *when* privatization would occur. As explained, privatization reduces congestion costs. Privatization also creates costs of excluding non-owners, such as registering property rights, demarcating boundaries, monitoring trespassers, and prosecuting violators. Demsetz considered the trade-off between the costs of congestion and the costs of exclusion as central to privatization. In so far as he is right, efficiency requires privatizing land until the savings from reduced congestion equal the costs of exclusion. Demsetz predicted that privatization would occur at the efficient point in history. As time passes, population growth and capital accumulation increase congestion, whereas the costs of exclusion remain constant or diminish. Demsetz predicted that privatization would occur at the tipping point when congestion costs surpass exclusion costs.

This theory of land privatization overlooks the most fundamental tradeoff in Mongolia.[9] Inclement weather persistently endangers Mongolian herds. Mongolians respond to inclement weather by shifting herds across micro-climates. Shifting herds requires negotiating with impacted families. Negotiations are perfunctory under an open-access rule, because no one can exclude others from the land. In contrast, negotiations are extensive under a private property rule, because permission to trespass must be

---

8 This point was made by McCloskey concerning open fields in England and by Cooter concerning tribal land in Papua New Guinea.

9 The classical tradeoff between the costs of congestion and exclusion has some application to Mongolia. One paper discusses the fact that some families now find that they must stay all year at winter pastures to guard against others grazing them. See Bazargur, D., Shilrevadja, C., & Chinbat, B. (1993), page 6. This is a cost of exclusion. In addition, the costliness of fencing materials prior to the mass production of barb wire raised the cost of boundary maintenance in many areas of Mongolia. Surveying and registering privatized land is discussed in Whytock (1992), page 62. Finally, the classical analysis may apply to congested pasture around wells and transportation links.

Robert D. Cooter

obtained from numerous individuals or small groups. Negotiations
are the transaction costs of insuring against climatic risk. Thus a
change from open-access to private property increases the
transaction costs of insuring against climatic risk.[10]

In choosing between open-access and private ownership of land
in Mongolia, the decisive tradeoff concerns the cost of congestion
and the cost of insurance against climatic risk. Private ownership
lowers the cost of congestion and raises the transaction cost of
insuring against climatic risk. Conversely, open-access raises the
cost of congestion and lowers the transaction cost of insuring
against climatic risk. Thus private property is more efficient when
congestion is high and climatic risk is low, whereas open-access is
more efficient when the opposite is true.[11] These facts are
summarized by the northeast and southwest cells in Figure 1.

Figure 1 encompasses two more possibilities. When climatic
risk and congestion are both low, efficiency requires open-access,
as indicated by the southeast cell in Figure 1. When climatic risk
and congestion are both high, their relative values must be
compared to determine the more efficient property regime. This
fact is indicated by "?" in the northwest cell in Figure 1. In general,
the efficient use of Mongolia's pasture requires privatizing use-rights
until the gain from reduced congestion equals the loss from more
costly insurance against climatic risk.

Figure 1: Efficient Property Rule

Climatic Risk

Congestion		High	Low
	High	?	Private
	Low	open-acccess	open-acccess

---

10 Mearns (1993b) stresses the central role played by unpredictable, inclement weather in the formation
of property rights. He tests and largely confirms the following hypothesis:
The hypothesis outlined earlier, based on the economic dependability of resources model, was that
territorial behaviour among pastoralists in the more equilibrial grazing ecosystems of Mongolia,
characterised by relatively high forage density and predictability, would correspond to a geographically
stable territorial system . . ., while in less equilibrial ecosystems, characterised by relatively low resource
density and predictability, would be territorially unstable and feature increased mobility and dispersion
. . ." page 97.

11 similar argument is developed in Mearns (1993b).

The tradeoff between congestion and climatic risk changes with the seasons in Mongolia. I will contrast winter and summer. Winter forage comes primarily from pastures where wind thins the snow cover and animals can dig for dry grass. High quality winter pasture is scarce relative to the number of animals. Most unintended deaths of animals occur during the harsh winter months. In winter the animals may freeze from extreme cold or starve when impenetrable ice covers the grass. Winter weather makes moving the herds difficult, so they typically remain at the same pasture for the duration of the winter season. Survival of the herds during the harsh winter requires reserving lands for winter pasture and constraining the number of animals.

The animals must accumulate fat in the summer in order to survive the winter. To accumulate fat, the animals need green grasses. In summer, more precipitation and sunshine cause more grass to grow. The distribution of summer grasses depends upon local variations in rainfall. Late in the summer, Mongolians move the herds quickly from one pasture to another in order to add weight for the approaching winter.[12] Animals who remain in a region afflicted by summer drought may be too thin to survive the winter.

I summarize the difference between winter and summer in terms of congestion and climatic risk. Congestion and climatic risk are both relatively high in the winter. Furthermore, animals cannot be moved in winter to reduce climatic risk. High congestion and low mobility make private property the more efficient regime. In contrast, congestion and climatic risk are both relatively low in the summer. Furthermore, animals can be moved to reduce climatic risk. Low congestion and high mobility make open-access the more efficient regime.

Mongolian customary law responds to these facts about efficiency by imposing a different property regimes for different seasons. Customary law allocates exclusive use-rights over specific

---

12 quick movement of animals in late summer is called the "otor."

winter pastures to specific families.[13] The winter pastures of a family cannot be grazed by another family's herds at any time during the year.[14] Thus Mongolian customary law protects winter pasture from over-use by recognizing exclusive use-rights for families. In contrast, specific families have relatively weak claims in customary law to specific summer pastures. In summer the property rule resembles open-access.[15] Mongolians insure against climatic risk in the summer at relatively low transaction cost by open access to uncongested pastures.[16] As explained, herds move many times in the late summer to take advantage of local variations in rainfall.

I must add another detail to my sketch of private winter pastures. As explained, herds typically remain at a family's winter pasture for the duration of the winter season. In an unusual winter, however, the families in a region may find that their own winter pastures cannot sustain their herds. To escape unpredictable cold or precipitation, the endangered families may attempt to move to a different micro-climate. Families apparently have the customary right to relocate an endangered herd elsewhere. Sometimes families relocate endangered herds to areas reserved by local government for emergencies. Other times the endangered families relocate their herds on the winter pastures reserved for other families, and the two groups must share. Thus the exclusive right to use winter pasture is not absolute. The reciprocal duty to share with endangered families limits a family's customary right to exclude others from its winter pastures. Enforcing this duty requires negotiations with impacted families and state officials, as I discuss later.

---

13 The most distinguished scholar of Mongolian land arrangements describes the facts as follows: "Customary law in Mongolia does recognize individual rights in winter pasture sites, although not in all parts of the country, and not as permanent, inalienable rights." Mearns (1993a), page 59.

14 Families typically begin moving towards their winter pasture in October and arrive in November, remaining until all animals have given birth in March or April. The general pattern of cyclical movement through the seasons has been mapped for various localities. For example, see Institute of Development Studies at University of Sussex, U.K. and associated Mongolian institutions (1991), pages 27-33.

15 A Mongolian saying: "If I put my hut down, the place is mine today and tomorrow it is someone else's."

16 This point is explained at the level of general theory by Nugent and Sanchez (1993) at page 89, who write "the extremely high local variability of rainfall in ASARs implies that the risk to the individual herdsman can be reduced substantially by gaining access to the largest possible grazing area."

Researchers on Mongolia believe that its common pastures have suffered little degradation.[17]   Mongolians avoid the tragedy of the commons by privatizing the congested resource, by which I mean winter pasture.   Some degradation has occurred in Mongolia on pasture near wells and transportation links, where congested resources are not privatized.   A similar solution was found by Eggertsson in the open pastures of the mountains of Iceland.[18]

The facts about Mongolia have wider application. Open-access resources are susceptible to inefficient congestion because users receive the average product, not the marginal product. Privatization causes each of them to receive the marginal product, but the elimination or averaging also concentrates risk.   To illustrate, consider fishing along an open access river. Fishermen will relocate to the spots where the fishing is best, thus tending to equalize the catch. However, the best spots will suffer congestion. Technically, people will decide to fish by equating their opportunity cost to the average value of the catch per fisherman, which exceeds the marginal product (some fishermen catch fish that others would have caught). In response to congestion, assume that families privatize the shore of the river by assigning exclusive fishing rights to particular parts of it. Privatizing the shore reduces congestion at the best fishing spots. However, the dispersion in the catch increases among fishermen, because they cannot move along the bank to the spots where fishing is best.

---

17 Soil erosion seems slight, except where motor vehicles churn the roadless steppe into dust. The more subtle form of degradation concerns a deterioration in the type of plants. One study suggests that collectivization resulted in signification degradation of this kind through subsidies for winter fodder. See Mearns (1993a), pages 21-25. Also see Bazargur, Shiirevadja, and Chinbat, page 1. Other studies find little evidence of such degradation. See Institute of Development Studies at University of Sussex, U.K. and associated Mongolian institutions (1993), page ii.

18 Eggertsson (1991) found that families are allowed to put animals on the open summer pastures in the mountains in proportion to the size of their lowland fields, where fodder is cut to feed the animals in the winter. The total number of animals allowed on the summer pastures are determined by their carrying capacity. In Mongolia, no one limits the total number of animals on the common summer pastures. Rather, nature provides the limit by severely constraining winter food for the animals.

Brief History

Having sketched my basic claim, I now offer some details. Understanding Mongolian customary law involves understanding the role allowed for it by the state. The centralized state is apparently as old as Mongolia. According to a Chinese historian,[19] precursors of the Mongolians called the "Xiongnu," whose armies breached China's Great Wall around 200 BC and reached the Yellow River, organized themselves according to the "system of 10." This system placed a leader over each group of 10 soldiers, with leaders aggregated into successive groups of 10, until the pyramid of authority reached the head of state. This system was adopted by Ghengis Khan, whose empire stretched from the Caspian Sea to Beijing at his death in 1227. After his death, his heirs divided the empire and it declined, until the Manchu emperor of China ended Mongolia's independence by conquest in 1644. The Manchus divided the country into districts with a governor over each one and continued the system of centralized, unitary administration.

Manchu rule disintegrated in the early 20th century. During the ensuing instability, Russian soldiers and Mongolian nationalists defeated the Chinese in 1921.[20] With backing from the Soviet Union, Mongolia created the world's second communist state in 1924.[21] Under the leadership of a native Stalin, Mongolia subsequently attacked its feudal heritage with ruthless vigor. The economy mirrored Russia, with centralized planning, priority for heavy industry, and collectivized agriculture.

Having led Mongolia into communism, Russia led Mongolia out of it. Perestroika after 1984 was succeeded by democracy and economic liberalization in Mongolia after 1989. Unlike Russia, however, Mongolia's communist party continues in power, having

---

19 Ssu-Ma Chien, pages 163-164.
20 The general reference is Bawden. Also see Petrov. He discusses attack of a White Russian Army on the Chinese in Mongolia on pages 215-216. Subsequently the Red Army and its Mongolian sympathizer destroyed the White Army and its Mongolian sympathizers in Mongolia. Note also that a combined force of Mongolians and the Russian Red Army defeated the Japanese in 1939 (Bawden, page 329), and subsequently the Russians prevented annexation by the People's Republic of China. "Inner Mongolia," which is a province of China, has suffered a fate similar to Tibet. The Chinese government in Taiwan still asserts that Mongolia is a province of China.
21 Bawden, chapter 6, pages 238-289.

won wide majorities in free elections in 1990 and 1992. Mongolian's national income declined even more precipitously than other post-communist countries after 1989,[22] primarily because Mongolia was even more dependent than other countries on Russian subsidies and trade.[23]   Mongolia's economic future probably lies in providing over-populated Asia with access to an unspoiled natural world, but Mongolians have little understanding as yet of a service economy.[24]

Mongolia is currently divided into 22 large units (21 "aimags" and the capital city), which are subdivided into 325 small units ("sums"), which are subdivided into 1,581 of the smallest units ("bags").[25]   The aimag and sum governors in the communist era enjoyed broad powers to allocate resources and resolve disputes in the countryside.[26] They have been centrally appointed in the past, although now local legislatures influence the process and their authority seems ambiguous.[27]

Some historians say that there was no private ownership of land in Mongolia from 1206 to 1992.[28] The central government certainly claimed formal ownership of land in Mongolia since the Manchu conquest in 1644.[29]   Individuals could own use-rights under the Manchus, but the power of local administrators over land was secured by state ownership.   Since the Mongolian state already claimed ownership of all rural land, "collectivization" of agriculture did not mean that the state appropriated rural land.   Rather,

---

22. The estimated fall in national income exceeded 40% in 4 years. The year-by-year estimates are as follows: 1990-2.5%, 1991-16.2%, 1992-7.6%, 1993-15.0%. See Economist Intelligence Unit. Also see Hahm (1993).

23. Soviet financial assistance, which ended in 1991, had averaged 30% of GDP. See Hahm, page 1. "In the first months of the 1990's, Mongolia was still under the hegemony of the Soviet Union, receiving aid equal to 25% of GDP and conducting 95% of its trade within the CMEA." Korsun and Murrell (1994a), page 3.

24. To illustrate, Mongolia has no minister of tourism and reports no statistics on income from tourism. See Economist Intelligence Unit.

25. These facts were true as of May 1994. See Consultancy Centre, IAMD, page 1.

26. Although Mongolia has courts at the sum level, the relative role of courts and administrators in resolving local disputes is unclear. See Supreme Court of Mongolia.

27. Peter Murrell thinks that these local officials are caught between their dependence upon the center and the growing independence of the herders. (Private communication from Murrell to Cooter.)

28. Whytock (1992), page 10.

29. "Land . . . became the property of the Emperor after the Manchu dynasty was established. Land use was then allocated "administratively," for pasture, agriculture, mineral deposits, military frontier guards, horse relay stations, and lamaist monasteries. When the Manchu dynasty was deposed in Mongolia, the Bogdo-Khan became the supreme owner of the land. Intermediate officials—khoshun governors, "feudal lords"—exercised their right of land use within designated boundaries under both periods." Shirendyb (1976), page 524, cited Whytock (1992), page 12.

"collectivization" meant that the state appropriated animals and reorganized herding. Private herds were appropriated in the 1950s and their former owners were forced into collectives.[30] The collectives hired the former owners as employee-members to continue tending the animals. The employee-members of the collectives received productivity bonuses and were allowed to keep a small number of their own animals, just as the Russian collectives allowed small family plots for agriculture.[31]

Mongolian families traditionally kept mixed herds of horses, goats, sheep, cows, yaks, and camels. Mixing animals reduces risk and draws upon complementary abilities in different species.[32] The collectives originally attempted to group all the animals of a particular type together in order to achieve economies of scale and lower the cost of veterinarian services and other applications of scientific knowledge. The policy of homogenous grouping failed and was reversed.

The collectives formally dissolved after 1990 and the herds were distributed to private families.[33] Some collectives were reconstituted as cooperatives and continue many of their former practices. In other cases, families abandoned such organizations and went their own way. Today families typically own many of the animals that they tend, although families also participate in sharing arrangements or tend other people's animals for pay.[34] Current

---

30 Everyone in the rural population became members of state farms ("negdel") in the 1950s. See Institute of Development Studies at University of Sussex, U.K. and associated Mongolian institutions (1991), page 4. The steps in creating and dismantling Mongolia's collectives are described in Mearns (1993a), pages 10-12.

31 The number of privately owned animals increased substantially after 1989. By 1990, about 1/2 of pastoral family income came from privately owned animals. Institute of Development Studies at University of Sussex, U.K. and associated Mongolian institutions (1991), circa page 9.

32 For example, sheep and horses eat different grasses, goats lead sheep to forage, and some animals keep others warm during the winter.

33 According to Hahm (1993), page 1, Mongolia began dismantling its centrally planned economy in the first quarter of 1990 and restrictions on private ownership of herds were eliminated in 1991. However, Peter Murrell, who was in Mongolia at the time, states that he did not observe these events beginning until January of 1991. (Private communication from Murrell to Cooter.) In any case, rural families were eager to acquire ownership of herds, although the method of distributing the animals caused disagreements. Animals were typically distributed on a per capita basis to members of rural organizations or residents of rural districts. Problems arose when people left towns to return to the countryside in order to claim a share in the distribution of the herds. See, for example, Institute of Development Studies at University of Sussex, U.K. and associated Mongolian institutions (1991), page 17. A discussion of privatization by vouchers and outmigration from cities is in Institute of Development Studies at University of Sussex, U.K. and associated Mongolian institutions (1991), page 9.

34. Mongolian families typically group together to cooperate and share tasks during part of the year. For a more complete account, see note 50.

organizational and institutional arrangements are tentative, fluid, and complicated. Privatization and the freeing of agricultural prices after 1990 caused a sharp improvement in the terms of trade between the country and the city. The relative improvement in rural incomes provoked an urban backlash and the restoration of some restrictions on agricultural markets.[35]

Mongolia's constitution now recognizes ownership of land by the state and natural persons of Mongolian citizenship, but not by private institutions or foreigners.[36] The current Mongolian constitution, however, forbids private ownership of "pastures," and the government classifies 77% of the land as pastures.[37] Current plans to extend private ownership of land in Mongolia do not include pastures.[38] A vigorous political debate concerns privatizing some resources that pastoralists use other than pastures. Nomadic families typically live in circular tents called "gers," which move several times in the summer. Families traditionally construct permanent ger-sites on their winter pasture, including stables and corrals. In recent years, permanent ger-sites have developed on the edge of towns, near transportation links, or close to rural employers. Current discussions envision extending private ownership to permanent ger-sites.[39] Otherwise, current discussions of private ownership of land concern towns and non-agricultural users.

State and Custom

I have explained that the state owned all of Mongolia's land during most of its history, and the state still owns all pastures.

---

35. State orders for basic agricultural products were implemented by the Mongolian Agricultural Commodities Exchange and the Central Procurement Cooperatives Union. Dismantling quotas and freeing prices have caused an increase in rural incomes and raised the price of meat in urban areas. The authorities reintroduced "mandatory" state orders for meat in Government Order no. 53 in March of 1993. The Order specifies direct state procurement for four slaughterhouses instead of through market channels. See Hahm (1993), pages 23-25.

36. Whytock, page 54. Even foreigners can own use-rights to Mongolian land under the current constitution. Whytock (1992), page 49.

37. Article 6, clause 3. See Whytock (1992), page 6.

38. Report on draft Land Law and amendments to Civil Code is discussed in Institute of Development Studies at University of Sussex, U.K. and associated Mongolian institutions (1993). However, these plans are evolving and changing rapidly in response to various political pressures.

39. The governing party is discussing a proposal to give .5 hectares to each settled family around the ger site.

However, families owned use-rights by customary law, especially use-rights to winter pasture, which I identified as the legal mechanism to avoid congestion. Some scholars believe these rights have existed continuously since the Mongolian empire's creation in the 13th century.[40] In any case, nomadic families had use-rights over pasture that the state owned after the Manchu conquest in 1644, and use rights were inherited or sometimes traded.[41] Disputes about use-rights were ultimately resolved by the governor in the region. Resolving such disputes according to custom served the interest of the governors by promoting smooth administration.

What happened to customary law during collectivization? Some researchers believe that the most important features of customary law persisted through collectivization.[42] For example, a collective typically divided and dispersed its herds for winter, "employing" its member-families to keep its animals on their winter pastures. Thus the collectives often, but not always, respected the exclusive use-rights of families to winter pasture.[43] Custom survived, not because of its favored legal status, but because it served everyone's interests.[44]

Privatization of cooperatives and state farms proceeded after 1990 by distributing assets (especially livestock) and restructuring organizations or dissolving them.[45] The weakening of the collectives strengthened customary law by removing ideological and

---

40 Land tenure allegedly conforms to the following pattern since the founding of an independent Mongolian empire in 1206: "Private households exercised customary use rights over specific areas, defined in relation to the ecological resource base, and they customarily owned areas of pasture used during the winter and spring. In addition they had customary rights to areas for common, rotational grazing during the summer. Some of these traditional, customary rights continue to exist. For example, it has not been forgotten that unwritten, customary laws demanded high penalties for unauthorized access to someone else's pasture." Bazargur, D., Shilrevadja, C., & Chinbat, B. (1993), page 5.

41 Whytock (1992), pages 11-12.

42 Whytock (1992), pages 13-14.

43 "It is common knowledge which winter/spring pasture sites are customarily owned by whom, and priority is always given to the holder of these customary rights. Under collectivisation, this was formalized by the administrative allocation of shelters, although this did not necessarily respect customary tenure rights. . . ." Mearns (1993a), page 21.

44 Mongolia's civil code, derived from Russia, does not discuss customary ownership or its legal status. This fact remains true in the draft of a proposed new civil code that I saw in Mongolia.

45 Korsun and Murrell (1994b), pages 14-17.

institutional impediments to it. Customary law guarantees reasonably secure use-rights.[46] Today, violation of property rights by private persons are compensable by civil judgments in courts or punishable by fines imposed by administrators.[47] Unfortunately, the constitution provides weak protection against violation of property rights by the state, including regulations and takings.[48] Owners of property in Mongolia enjoy much less security from state interference than in Western countries. Weaknesses in the bundle of ownership rights continue to undermine incentives to improve real property.[49]

I have explained that customary law insures against climatic risk through reciprocal duties to share. As collectives declined, small groups of families have joined together to cooperate along traditional lines.[50] However, insuring against climatic risk can involve moving herds across climatic zones. Such movements cross administrative boundaries and affect many resident families. For example, the administrators must decide whether to reserve certain pastures for emergency use, when to move herds on to reserve pastures, and whether to permit herds from other districts to cross into its district or pasture in it. Local administrators either take the lead in these movements or facilitate the decisions of endangered families. Local administrators routinely performed this task under the old system of centralized control. To illustrate, in winter of 1986-87, snow covered the whole of Dornogobi aimag too deeply

---

46 I probed this fact repeatedly in seminars with district court judges.

47 Whytock (1992), 44-45.

48 Whytock (1992), pages 32-37.

49 Whytock (1992), page 50.

50 The smallest unit of cooperation, called the "khot ail," consists of 3-5 families, with customary use of specific areas, customary ownership of winter and spring pastures, private ownership of herds, cooperative herding on a daily basis, and nomadic moves made in response to ecological conditions. See Table 1 page 4 and discussion of it. The khot ail are joined into larger units of cooperation around springs, and still larger units of cooperation in ecological areas. These traditional groups apparently strengthened as collectives dissolved. Bazargur, D., Shilrevadja, C., & Chinbat, B. (1993), pages 4-5. A fact about Mongolia that strikes a legal anthropologist is the absence of clans or tribes. The Manchus sought to destroy such affiliations by suppressing family names and recognizing only first names and patronymics. However, Mearns believes that the decline in solidarity around the kinship group dates from at least the 13th century. Mearns (1993a), page 8. For a discussion of the historical evolution of social units in Mongolia, see Mearns (1993a), page 5. Careful field work by Mearns found that the khot ail varies in size from 2 to 10 families. See Mearns (1993a), pages 44-45.

for animals to dig for food, so the central authorities instructed the neighboring aimag to deliver tons of fodder to Dornogobi without charge.[51]   With the decline of government authority, sharing arrangements must be made privately. Insurance against climatic risk is one example of services diminished or lost to nomadic pastoralists by privatization.[52]   This fact may have contributed to some opposition to abolition of state farms.[53]

Predictions

Privatizing herds and strengthening traditional use-rights of families should have two economic effects.[54]   First, more security of families over their winter pasture enables more animals to survive the winter in the long run (but not necessarily in the short run).[55] The survival of more animals in the winter increases the pressure on common summer pastures.[56]

Second, privatization creates obstacles to the movement of herds endangered by inclement weather.   As explained, the movement of endangered herds requires cooperation among

---

51 Institute of Development Studies at University of Sussex, U.K. and associated Mongolian institutions (1991), page 43. Apparently fodder was often dropped from helicopters to remote areas in winter under the old system of centralized controls.

52 Consistent with this account of insurance is the fact that the economically viable units are larger in the drier, riskier Gobi area than in wetter north, and privatization of collectives proceeded more slowly in the south. See Mearns (1993a), page 3 and page 12.

53 Under communism, rural people received health, education, and veterinarian services from the sum administration, often through collective enterprises. Interview data reports an attachment of rural people to collective organizations and the lamenting of their demise, although there is no lamenting of the privatization of herds. See Policy Alternatives for Livestock Development in Mongolia (Working Paper No. 2, August 1991) especially page 14. In general, social services have declined sharply in Mongolia. For example, educational expenditures declined absolutely and relative to the government budget since 1989. See Consultancy Centre, IAMD, especially pages 8-10.

54 The re-emergence of local institutions increases the security of traditional use-rights. However, general legal uncertainty undermines settled expectations. I presume that the first effect, which strengthens customary rights, will prove stronger than the second. For a discussion, see Mearns (1993a), page 26.

55 If exclusive rights to winter pasture broke down, open-access would result in an short run increase in the number of animals on winter pasture. However, short-run over-use of winter pastures would result in a long run decline in the number of animals surviving the winter.

56 Proposals are being discussed in Ulaanbaatar to give families ownership over the permanent structures erected on winter pasture and the land under them, and to formalize exclusive use-rights to winter pasture.

families. The scope of cooperation may involve many families if inclement weather affects a whole region of the country. The involvement of many families requires collective choice about which herds to relocate, and when and where to relocate them. Collective choice involves an active role for officials, not just bilateral negotiations among families.[57] Privatization undermines the political mechanisms for collective choice and reduces official discretion.[58] In other words, privatization increases the transaction costs of insurance against climatic risk, and less insurance against climatic risk results in more winter deaths of animals.

I have predicted that privatizing winter pastures reduces winter-kill caused by congestion and increases winter-kill caused by climatic risk. The former effect should prove stronger than the latter effect in the long run (although not necessarily in the short run[59]), and the aggregate number of animals should rise, especially when two additional factors are considered. Prices for animal products will rise as the government lifts controls and restrictions,[60] which will prompt families to obtain more fodder to feed animals in the

---

57 Formal rules of land tenure restrict herders to pastures in their own sum, but "trades" and reciprocal agreements often occur. See Institute of Development Studies at University of Sussex (1991), page 33.

58 Note, however, that much of Mongolia's rapid privatization has simply transferred power to insiders already controlling the organization being privatized. The structural changes are less than the word "privatization" connotes. See Korsun and Murrell (1994b).

59 If economic disruptions continue to cause a decline in production of fodder on farms, the number of livestock may decline. See discussion in footnote 61.

60 The government eliminated price controls on meat and subsequently re-imposed them. The government does not currently attempt to control the price of such animal products as milk and wool, although it recently forbade the export of raw cashmere. See Institute of Development Studies at University of Sussex, U.K., and Institute of Agricultural Economics, National Agricultural University, Mongolia (1994). The government apparently follows a meandering course towards free markets in agricultural products.

61 Note that Mearns (1993a), pages 21-25, found that an increase in subsidized winter fodder by collectives caused the degrading of 5% of pasture in Erdene sum. However, the prospects are bleak for applying mechanization to increase fodder production in the short run, because agriculture is currently declining relative to pastoralism. See Whytock, (1992), page 52. Furthermore, the break in trade with Russia has caused petroleum prices to rise sharply, which reduces the use of agricultural machines. See Institute of Development Studies at University of Sussex, U.K., and Institute of Agricultural Economics, National Agricultural University, Mongolia (1994), page 7. However, the end of Mongolia's isolation will bring access to superior technology, which may eventually decrease relative prices of fodder. Note that higher petroleum prices have reduced the use of jeeps in hunting wolves, and herders are now complaining about sharp increases in loss of livestock to wolves. See Institute of Development Studies at University of Sussex, U.K. and associated Mongolian institutions (1991), page 31.

winter.[61]   Furthermore, the number of nomadic pastoralists is increasing due to population growth and the return of urban families to the countryside.[62]

If the pressure to over-graze summer pastures increase in the future as I predict, Mongolians will need mechanisms other than winter-kill to avoid over-use of summer pastures. The obvious legal device is to create exclusive use-rights to summer pastures. The creation of exclusive use-rights to summer pastures involves a trade-off between congestion and insurance. As noted, privatization lowers congestion and increases the cost of insurance. To achieve an optimum, privatization should proceed until the saving in congestion costs equal the increase in the transaction cost of insuring against climatic risk. Consequently, I predict the gradual evolution of exclusive use-rights in places where summer pastures become over-crowded,[63] combined with attempts to find new ways to protect against inclement weather.[64]

---

62 Population has moved from town to country at least since 1991, partly as a response to urban unemployment and partly as a response to the revival of barter trade caused by run-away inflation. Whytock, (1992), page 8. Also see Institute of Development Studies at University of Sussex, U.K., and Institute of Agricultural Economics, National Agricultural University, Mongolia (1994), page 6.

63 Livestock "offtake" (animals sold and slaughtered for meat consumption) increased from 1988 until 1991, began declining in 1991 and has apparently continued to decline. This is presumably explained by the initial liberalization of meat prices, followed by the subsequent imposition of price controls, as Mongolia returned to its traditional policy of providing artificially cheap meat to the towns. Liberalization of livestock products other than meat (wool, cashmere, skins, hides) has also been partially repealed. Thus the year-to-year variations in livestock "off-take" depends upon transitory policies which, I believe, market forces will presumably undermine. See Institute of Development Studies at University of Sussex, U.K., and Institute of Agricultural Economics, National Agricultural University, Mongolia (1994), table on page 2, and page 7.

64 On way for an individual family to lower climactic risk is to obtain more winter fodder for the animals. Another way is to negotiate an arrangement for mutual aid with people in another climactic zone.

Conclusion

Privatizing pasture land in Mongolia aggravates climatic risk by increasing the transaction costs of moving herds from one micro-climate to another. These facts point to a fundamental tradeoff when privatizing a public-access resource. Open-access resources are susceptible to inefficient congestion because users receive the average product, not the marginal product. This fact distorts incentives and leads to inefficient congestion. However, averaging also spreads risk. Conversely, privatization concentrates risk. This phenomenon should occur generally, although seeing it is easiest in a harsh environment like Mongolia's.

Mongolian customary law has evolved efficient solutions to the problems of a pastoral economy in a harsh environment. Mongolian customary law has evolved for more than a millennium in response to the conditions of a pastoral economy. Customs provides the key to vexing questions that Mongolia now faces concerning rural economic development.[65] Development should proceed by strengthening customary law, not undermining it.[66] The reasons why the state should not allot land to families in violation of customary law are the same as the reasons against forced collectivization: Force disrupts a delicate balance between congestion and climatic risk.[67] Legal reforms need to be integrated with customary law in this country, so advice on reform should be based on extensive knowledge of the country and intensive interaction with reformers in the country.

---

65 Institute of Development Studies at University of Sussex, U.K. and associated Mongolian institutions (1993). The summary recommends private individual freehold for winter-spring shelters with restrictions (transferable within families but not saleable), and to recommend for "public individual leasehold" of land around winter shelters, and "public group leasehold" for summer and winter pastures. "Public v. private" means "state v. private" title. "Individual v. group" means right held by "named individual v. family or other cooperative group." "Freehold v. leasehold" means lease or ownership. In other words, if we imagine a dimension of property rights from relatively private and exclusive to relatively public and open, then Mongolian pastoral property could be ordered on this dimension as follows: winter structures < winter pasture < summer pasture. The report recommends the legal development of these three kinds of property into private ownership, private lease, and public lease, respectively.

66 Whytock (1992), page 22, warns against "any legal change that does not fully consider contextual factors .....". Mearns (1993a, pages 61-62) proposes to reconcile the flexibility and certainty through a system of "rolling leases" for rural land.

67 Means holds that individual tenure of pasture land is "rarely appropriate." See Mearns, (1993a), page 57.

References

Bawden, C.R. The Modern History of Mongolia (Praeger, New York and Washington, 1968).

Bazargur, D., C. Shilrevadja, and B. Chinbat. "Territorial Organisation of Mongolian Pastoral Livestock Husbandry in the Transition to a Market Economy "(Policy Alternatives for Livestock Development in Mongolia (PALD), Research Report No.1, no date).

B. Bouckaert. "What Is Property?," 13 Harvard J. Law & Public Policy 775-816 (1990).

Butler, W. E. The Mongolian Legal System: Contemporary Legislation and Documentation (1982).

"Civil Code of the Mongolian People's Republic". Xerox, English translation supplied by IRIS.

Consultancy Centre, IAMD, "Report of the Fact-Finding Study on Pre-School Strengthening in Mongolia" (Xerox, Ulaanbaatar, Mongolia, 1 June 1994), sponsored by National Center for Children and the Save the Children Fund.

Cooter, Robert D. "Inventing Market Property: The Land Courts of Papua New Guinea," 25 Law and Society Review 759-801 (1991).

Demsetz, Harold. "Toward a Theory of Property Rights," 57 American Economic Review 347 (1967).

Economist Intelligence Unit. Country Report: Mongolia (1st Quarter 1994; Economist Intelligence Unit, 15 Regent Street, London, UK).

Eggertsson, T. (1990). Economic Behavior and Institutions (Cambridge University Press).

Eggertsson, T. (1992), "Analyzing Institutional Successes and Failures: A Millennium of Common Mountain Pastures in Iceland," 12 International Review of Law and Economics 423-437 (1992).

Ellickson, R. (1991). Order Without Law (Harvard University Press).

Ellickson, R. (1993). "Property in Land," 102 Yale Law Journal 1315.

Field, Barry C. "The Evolution of Property Rights," 42 Kyklos 319 (1989).

Ginsburg, Tom. "The Transformation of Legal Institutions in Mongolia, 1990-1993, 30 Issues & Studies: A Journal of Chinese and International Affairs 77-113 (1994).

Hahm, H. "The Development of the Private Sector in a Small Economy in Transition: The Case of Mongolia" (World Bank Discussion Papers, East Asia & Pacific Region Series, China and Mongolia Department No. 223, apparent date 1993).

Humphrey. "Pastoral Nomadism in Mongolia: The Role of Herdsmen's Cooperatives in the National Economy," 9 Development and Change 133 (1978).

Institute of Development Studies at University of Sussex, U.K. and associated Mongolian institutions (1991). Policy Alternatives for Livestock Development in Mongolia (PALD) (Working Paper No. 2)". "Transformation of a Pastoral Economy: A Local View from Arhangai and Dornogobi Provinces" (August 1991).

Institute of Development Studies at University of Sussex, U.K. and associated Mongolian institutions (1993). Policy Alternatives for Livestock Development in Mongolia (PALD) (Policy Options Report No. 1). "Options for the Reform of Grazing Land Tenure in Mongolia."

Institute of Development Studies at University of Sussex, U.K., and Institute of Agricultural Economics, National Agricultural University, Mongolia (1994). Policy Alternatives for Livestock Development in Mongolia (PALD) Policy Option Paper No. 2)". "Options for the Reform of Livestock Marketing" (3rd draft version, April 1994).

Korsun, G., and P. Murrell (1994a). "Ownership and Governance on the Morning After: The Initial Results of Privatization in Mongolia" (Center for Institutional Reform and the Informal Sector, University of Maryland at College

Park, Working Paper No. 95, 1994).

Korsun ,G., and P. Murrell (1994b). "The Politics and Economics of Mongolia's Privatization Program: A Brief History" (Center for Institutional Reform and the Informal Sector, University of Maryland at College Park, Working Paper No. 103, 1994).

McCloskey, "D.N. The Persistence of English Common Fields" and "The Economics of Enclosure," European Peasants and Their Markets (1975; W.N. Parker and E.L. Jones, eds.), pages 73 and 123, respectively.

Mearns, Robin (1993a). "Pastoral Institutions, Land Tenure and Land Policy Reform in Post-Socialist Mongolia," (Policy Alternatives for Livestock Development in Mongolia (PALD), Research Report No. 3, February 1993).

Mearns, Robin (1993b). "Territoriality and Land Tenure Among Mongolian Pastoralists: Variation, Continuity and Change," 33 Nomadic Peoples 73-103 (1993).

Murrell, P., K. T. Dunn and G. Korsun. "The Culture of Policy Making in the Transition from Socialism: Price Policy in Mongolia" (Center for Institutional Reform and the Informal Sector, University of Maryland at College Park, 1992, Working Paper No. 32).

"The MPR Law on Economic Entities," (Xerox, Translation Copyright IRIS, University of Maryland, Translation from Mongolian, Third Version).

Nugent, Jeffrey B., Nicolas Sanchez, "Tribes, Chiefs, and Transhumance: A Comparative Institutional Analysis," Economic Development and Cultural Change 87-113 (1993).

Ostrom, E. Governing the Commons: Evolution of Institutions for Collective Action (Cambridge UP, 1990).

Petrov, Victor P. Mongolia: A Profile (Praeger, New York, 1970).

Policy Alternatives for Livestock Development in Mongolia (PALD), "Transformation of a Pastoral Economy: A Local View from Arhangai and Dornogobi Provinces" (Working Paper No. 2, August 1991).

Potkanski, T., & Szynkiewicz, S. "The Social Context of Liberalisation of the Mongolian Pastoral Economy: (Policy Alternatives for Livestock Development in Mongolia (PALD): A Research and Training Project No. 4, 1993).

Rubin, P. H. "Growing a Legal System, With Special Reference to the Post-Communist Economies," (Center for Institutional Reform and the Informal Sector, Working Paper No. 63, June, 1993).

Shirendyb. "Some Aspects of the History of Land Rights in Mongolia," 3 J. of the Ango-Mongolian Society no. 1, 25-43 (1976).

Ssu-Ma Chien, Records of the Grand Historian of China, (translated from the Shih chi of Ssu-Ma Ch'ien, Volume II: The Age of Emperor Wu 140 to circa 100b.c. (translated by Burton Watson, Columbia University Press, New York and London, 1968).

1992 Statistical Yearbook (1993).

Supreme Court of Mongolia. "Mongolian State Law of Courts" (English translation, Xerox, 3/3/93 No. 34 (534).

"Tax Law of the MPR" (Unofficial translation, Xerox, undated, supplied by IRIS).

Whytock , Christopher A. " Mongolia in Transition: The New Legal Framework for Land Rights and Land Protection" (Center for Institutional Reform and the Informal Sector, Country Report No. 7, May 16, 1992).

Evolutionary Models in Law:
Pros and Cons

E. Donald Elliott[*]

Dr. Margaret Gruter is living testimony to the existence of altruism (although not perhaps in the precise biological sense of self-sacrifice to promote the reproductive success of genetically-related kin). For over two decades, she has given generously of her time, her wisdom and her personal fortune to advance the progress of knowledge in law by incorporating insights from the biological sciences, particularly ethology and evolutionary theory. Rare in the post-Renaissance world, Margaret is that thoroughly admirable creature — a patron of scholars, as well as a scholar herself. As I

[*] Professor (Adjunct) of Law, Yale Law School and Georgetown University Law Center. Partner, Paul, Hastings, Janofsky & Walker, Washington, DC. Formerly, Julien and Virginia Cornell Professor of Environmental Law and Litigation, Yale Law School. B.A. (1970) and J.D. (1974), Yale University.

An earlier version of this paper was presented at the first conference of the Society for Evolutionary Analysis in Law, at Pace University Law School, October 16-17, 1998 and at the Georgetown University Law Center-Olin Foundation Conference on Evolution and Legal Theory, April 16, 1999.

wrote in the introduction to one of her books, <u>Law and the Mind</u>, she has truly begun the field of law and evolutionary biology,[2] not only through her own seminal scholarship,[3] but also through the Gruter Institute, which has stimulated the work of others. It is a great honor to contribute to this volume honoring her.

In what follows, I reflect on one particular type of use of evolutionary theory in law. In recent years, increasing numbers of legal scholars have turned to evolutionary biology for insights into the nature of law. As I noted in a 1997 review article, one of several different ways that legal scholars have sought to draw on evolutionary biology to improve our understanding of law is as a metaphor or model to describe the processes of legal change.[4] There is a long tradition in law of attempting to understand processes of legal change by analogy to biological evolution.[5] The modern renaissance of interest in evolutionary models in law traces primarily to the work of Paul Rubin, and also George Priest and Robert Clark.[6]

This paper attempts to assess the pros and cons of using biological evolution as an analogy to explain processes of legal change, a view that elsewhere I have called the "bio-mimetic" thesis,

---

2 See E. Donald Elliott, Introduction to MARGARET GRUTER, LAW AND THE MIND: BIOLOGICAL ORIGINS OF HUMAN BEHAVIOR (Sage, 1991).

3 Margaret Gruter, Law in Sociobiological Perspective, 5 FLORIDA ST. L. REV. 181 (1977).

4 See E. Donald Elliott, Law and Biology: The New Synthesis?, 41 ST. LOUIS U.L.REV. 595, (1997) (describing "models of legal system dynamics" as one of three ways that evolutionary biology has been used in law).

5 E. Donald Elliott, The Evolutionary Tradition in Jurisprudence, 85 COLUM. L. REV. 38 (1985). See also E. Donald Elliott, Holmes and Evolution: Legal Process as Artificial Intelligence, 13 J. LEGAL STUD. 113 (1984).

6 See Paul Rubin, Why Is the Common Law Efficient?, 6 J. LEGAL STUD. 51 (1977); George Priest, The Common Law Process and the Selection of Efficient Rules, 6 J. LEGAL STUD. 65 (1977). Robert Clark, The Interdisciplinary Study of Legal Evolution, 90 YALE L.J. 1238 (1981); Robert Clark, The Morphogenesis of Subchapter C: An Essay in Statutory Evolution and Reform, 87 YALE L. J. 90 (1977). For critical discussions of the concept, see also Goodman, An Economic Theory of the Evolution of the Common Law, 7 J. LEGAL STUD. 393 (1978); Cooter, Kornhauser & Lane, Liability Rules, Limited Information and the Role of Precedent, 10 BELL J. ECON. 366 (1979); Landes & Posner, Adjudication as a Private Good, 8 J. LEGAL STUD. 235 (1979); Cooter & Kornhauser, Can Litigation Improve the Law Without the Help of Judges?, 9 J. LEGAL STUD. 139 (1980); Terrebonne, A Strictly Evolutionary Model of Common Law, 10 J. LEGAL STUD. 397 (1981); Note, The Inefficient Common Law, 92 YALE L.J. 862 (1983). Elliott, supra note 5.

that the dynamics of change in law imitate evolutionary change in biology.[7]

The conclusion reached is a mixed one. The analogy between law and biological evolution is helpful to some degree in focusing attention on the relationship between the structural features of legal systems through an accessible and broadly understandable analogy to relative familiar concepts of biological evolution. On the other hand, the analogy between law and biological evolution can be taken too far. A dogmatic claim that the processes of evolutionary change in law and biology are *identical* (or "isomorphic") rather than merely *similar* is probably misleading and unhelpful, and actually obscures important features of the dynamic of legal change.[8]   Indeed, it is often the *differences* between biological evolution and legal evolution that are the most enlightening,[9] but most scholars are so taken by the analogy to biological evolution that they overlook a careful account of the differences as well as the similarities between evolution in biology and evolution in law.

In addition, the analogy to biological evolution comes with a fair amount of unwanted intellectual baggage, largely as a result of the unfortunate history of Social Darwinism, and to a lesser degree, the speculative nature of Sociobiology.

Finally, the very familiarity of Darwinian evolutionary theory is both its great advantage and also a great shortcoming. Although most non-specialists *think* that they understand biological evolution, often their actual understanding is actually limited to a few shorthand phrases such as "survival of the fittest" that they remember from high school biology. Lawyers and legal scholars (not renowned for their intellectual modesty) need to be cautioned that their understanding of the subtleties of modern evolutionary theory based on high school biology is probably about comparable to biologists understanding of modern jurisprudential theory based

---

7 See Elliott, supra note 4.
8 M.B.W. Sinclair, Evolution in Law: Second Thoughts, 71 U. DET. MERCY L. REV. 31 (1993).
9 See Elliott, supra note 4, 41 ST. LOUIS L.REV. at 601, n.33 (responding to Sinclair, supra note 8, by pointing out that the "similarities and *differences*" between law and biological evolution make the comparison useful (original emphasis)).

on their recollection of high school civics. As in any serious interdisciplinary work, a serious investment in learning another discipline (or better yet, recruiting a co-author!) is generally required. However, law professors may be less likely to make the necessary investment when a well-known theory such as evolution is involved than if the analogy were to a more patently abstruse subject such as "chaos theory" or "complex adaptive systems."

Overall, the bio-mimetic view that evolution in legal systems mimics evolutionary change in biology is dangerous medicine — it can be helpful if used carefully with proper professional supervision, but it comes with some dangerous side-effects that we must watch.

In what follows, the pros and cons of using an analogy of evolution in biology to understand law are explored.

Pro #1-Focus on System Dynamics.

Unlike most other models of legal decisions, evolutionary models focus attention on "system dynamics" -- the immanent logic and relationships of overall decision systems -- rather than on the motivations of judges and individual aspects of legal doctrines. Because legal systems are comprised of individual actors who are (at least to some extent) making policy decisions as an act of will, most other accounts of lawmaking, particularly judicial lawmaking, tend to focus their attention on individual decisions by individual decisionmakers.

Evolutionary models, by contrast, focus attention at a different level of organization. From the standpoint of evolutionary models, individual decisions are of little significance -- just as whether a particular animal survives and reproduces is in itself of little moment to the species. Whether individual actions will be the "noise" of random variation or the beginnings of a significant trend is seen as a function of the logic of the overall system in which the individual decision is embedded, and more specifically, the relationship between the system and its environment (i.e. the larger political and cultural system within which it is embedded).

By focusing attention on a quite different level of legal organization, one which has not previously been as thoroughly explored as many others, evolutionary models hold the promise of bringing into focus significant patterns that have previously escaped attention. In short, they contemplate the ecology of the forest, not the trees, and different patterns can be apprehended at that level of organization.

Pro #2-A Shared Grid.

Until the rise of "law and economics," most legal scholars were sole practitioners. We made pins one at a time in the way described by Adam Smith before the rise of interchangeable parts and assembly lines. Each legal scholar was involved in the business of inventing her own "innovative reconceptualizations" of law.[10]   A few particularly influential legal scholars developed a small following of disciples and former students who might perpetuate their conceptual framework, and perhaps even extend it slightly, but by and large each legal article was like a painting -- a unique and individual work of art that could perhaps be grouped into a "school" of influences, but which stood fundamentally as an isolated work. Whatever value this may have had as art, or as a means of self-development and an aid to teaching, it was not a science. If each law professor invents his or her own private language for thinking about law, there can be no cumulative effect to legal scholarship. Traditional law professors are like Sisyphus, rolling the same stone up the same hill over and over, only to see it fall back and begin again, as insights are apprehended, described, lost, and re-discovered in different words.

By adapting a shared conceptual framework from another discipline, law and economics opened up the possibility of scientific progress in understanding law. As one legal scholar built on and extended (or falsified) the insights of her predecessors, it was possible for legal scholarship to develop cumulative insights in

---

10 See Bruce Ackerman on the nature of legal scholarship, The Marketplace of Ideas, 90 YALE LAW JOURNAL 1131 (1981).

which one work built on and extended what was known previously. This cumulative progress of research was made possible in part by the existence of the shared conceptual framework provided by economics (and also by propositions that were specified with sufficient definiteness to be debatable, if not always empirically falsifiable). When Richard Posner announced his famous thesis that the common law was "efficient," we more or less knew what he meant in a way that was somewhat more specific than when Myres McDougal contended that international law was shaped by a "world community."

When most legal scholars cite prior work in their fields, most of what they cite consists of competing paradigms, alternative conceptual frameworks for explaining the phenomena at issue. When scholars in the law and economics tradition cite prior work, they cite work which attempts to use a more or less shared framework which has been elaborated and worked out in another discipline.

The existence of a shared framework is potentially helpful as a fixed grid -- a measuring stick of sorts -- against which legal phenomena can be measured, and measured in manageably commensurate terms by multiple observers. (Of course, like all grids or models, law and economics brings some relationships into sharp focus at the price of suppressing others.)

Evolutionary models of law also offer legal scholars a shared vantage point on legal phenomena. The shared grid provided by evolutionary biology is at least comparable, and perhaps more refined and specific, than that provided by economics. For example, when Mark Roe writes about "path dependance,"[11] it is possible for others to know what he is talking about. Of course, not everyone shares this lingo, but at least those "in the know," who

---

11 Mark J. Roe, Chaos and Evolution in Law and Economics, 109 HARV. L. REV. 641 (1996). Another example is provided by the Spring 1999 newsletter of the Gruter Institute, which has served as a clearinghouse and forum for scholars interested in evolutionary biology. It uses terms such as "epigenesis" and "reciprocity" as words of art that have relatively precise meanings drawn from evolutionary theory but adapted to describe cognate phenomena in law.

have invested in learning some basic evolutionary biology, can share a grid drawn from evolutionary biology for talking about law. Working with a shared grid is fundamentally different from the situation that would exist if each scholar had made up her own terms for describing the phenomena she observed. For example, it is possible to argue that Elliott has misapplied the concept of "founder effects" in a way that it is not possible to argue that Ackerman has misapplied the concept of "constitutional moments" (but only that perhaps he is internally inconsistent). This shared framework drawn from evolutionary biology opens up the possibility of cumulative development in scholarship in this tradition, like that which has occurred in law and economics, but in few other areas of legal scholarship, as one generation of scholars stands on the shoulders of the previous.

Pro #3-The "Pluto Effect."

The advantages described above would inhere in any relatively specific shared grid that could manage to get itself broadly accepted among legal scholars. There is, however, a more powerful (and debatable) claim that is made by proponents of evolutionary biology. At base this claim is that evolutionary biology is more than a metaphor that is arbitrarily overlaid on legal phenomena. Rather, evolutionary models claim to have power because they describe what is really going on. The claim here is that the dynamics of legal systems and the dynamics of biological systems both obey common rules, or at least that biological evolution and legal evolution are both special cases of a more general phenomenon. This more general theory of how open systems adapt as a result of selection by the environment might be called the field of "complex adaptive systems," or "evolutionary models" more generally. Biological evolution by natural selection with genetic inheritance and mutation might be regarded as a special case of the more general phenomenon by which open systems adapt in the direction of greater fit with their environment. If this is true, then evolutionary models of law are not an arbitrary grid or metaphor superimposed on legal change, but in fact describe the underlying processes or mechanisms of change — in other words the underlying process by which legal change occurs.

As the recent history of natural science illustrates, there are strong predictive advantages in deducing the underlying mechanisms, rather than merely imposing an arbitrary metaphor or grid. Elsewhere I have called this the "Pluto Effect,"[12] evoking the fact that scientists were able to predict the existence of the planet Pluto from its effect on the orbits of other planets before they were able to see or otherwise detect its existence. In other words, they knew that Pluto *had* to exist based on other effects. This heuristic advantage in making predictions occurs if, but only if, a description is not merely arbitrary metaphor but something more. A metaphor is different from a valid theory in that the metaphor may be fashioned to account for all the known data, but precisely because the comparison is arbitrary and fashioned to account for only the known data, the metaphor will not necessarily have predictive power. When humans believed that the planets were the chariots of the gods, they could not have predicted the existence and location of Pluto.

Similarly, if the "selective relitigation" effect or other evolutionary mechanisms really do account for a significant portion of the variance in legal change, we ought to be able to use the theory to make testable predictions of corollary phenomena — to find Pluto where it is predicted to be, so to speak.

Pro #4-A Richer (But Still Manageable) Theory of Human Motivations.

At base, all theories about law are theories about human behavior, and thus every jurisprudential theory builds at least implicitly on a theory of behavior. The model of human behavior posited by classical law and economics is quite parsimonious, purporting to capture a great deal of the variance in human affairs

---

12 Elliott, supra note 4, 41 ST. LOUIS L.REV. at 604-606.

with a theory of human motivations so simple that it has been criticized by some as mere "nominalism."[13]

Evolutionary biology also provides an alternative theory of human behavior and motivations.[14] The evolutionary theory of human behavior is a candidate to develop a corollary theory of jurisprudence, just as Bentham's theory of human behavior has ultimately spawned law and economics. Some of the most promising current work in law and evolutionary biology is by young scholars such as Owen Jones and Kingsley Browne, who analyze conventional legal problems that have proven intractable to other models of human behavior but can be understood productively from the perspective of an evolutionary understanding of human nature.[15]

Many of the early converts in the modern renaissance in interest in evolutionary theories of jurisprudence were drawn to it precisely because the underlying theory of human behavior and motivations posited by economics seemed to them too incomplete and constraining.[16] It should be noted, however, that the theories of human motivations posited by economics and evolutionary biology are at least first cousins, and overlap and make similar predictions in many areas. Evolutionary biology shares with economics the perception that humans may be motivated at least in part by a desire

---

13 Arthur Leff, Economic Analysis of Law: Some Realism About Nominalism, 60 VIRGINIA L. REV. 451 (1974).
14 There is large and growing literature on the nature of human nature from the perspective of evolutionary biology. See, e.g. MICHAEL MCGUIRE & ALFONSO TRIOSI, DARWINIAN PSYCHIATRY (Oxford, 1998); ROBIN WRIGHT, THE MORAL ANIMAL: EVOLUTIONARY PSYCHOLOGY AND EVERYDAY LIFE (Pantheon, 1994); MATT RIDLEY, THE RED QUEEN: SEX AND THE EVOLUTION OF HUMAN NATURE (MacMillan, 1993); TIMOTHY H. GOLDSMITH, THE BIOLOGICAL ROOTS OF HUMAN NATURE: FORGING LINKS BETWEEN EVOLUTION AND BEHAVIOR (Oxford Univ. Press, 1991). See also FRANS DE WAAL, GOOD NATURED: THE ORIGINS OF RIGHT AND WRONG IN HUMANS AND OTHER ANIMALS (Harvard, 1996); ROBERT D. ALEXANDER, THE BIOLOGY OF MORAL SYSTEMS (1987).
15 Owen D. Jones, Evolutionary Analysis in Law: An Introduction and Application to Child Abuse, 75 NORTH CAROLINA LAW REVIEW 1117 (1997); Kingsley R. Browne, Sex and Temperament in Modern Societies: A Darwinian View of the Glass Ceiling and the Gender Gap, 37 ARIZ. L. REV. 971 (1995).
16 See William Rodgers, Bringing People Back: Toward a Comprehensive Theory of Taking in Natural Resources Law, 10 ECOLOGY L. Q. 205 (1982).

to accumulate material wealth. However, for evolutionary biology, wealth maximization is not an end in itself but rather a secondary or instrumental goal that aids in reproductive success.

Evolutionary biology posits a more complex set of motivations than economics. Notably, modern evolutionary biology has developed a sophisticated theory of "altruism," behaviors in which animals appear to sacrifice narrow self-interest for the good of the group. This theory of altruism may help to account for the fact that many of the legal scholars interested in evolutionary biology are also interested in environmental law, a field difficult to explain in terms of self-interest, narrowly defined. Because evolutionary biology is more complex than economics, Ockham's Razor suggests that legal scholars would be well-advised to turn to evolutionary biology if, but only if, an area of legal behavior is not well-explained by simpler models of behavior.

On the other hand, the theory of human behavior posited by evolutionary biology, while more complex than economics, is nonetheless sufficiently simple and manageable that it can usefully be deployed to explain legal phenomena. This literature is particularly helpful in explaining the emergence and function of norms and other cultural phenomena including law as mechanisms to preserve cooperative group or community dynamics. Perhaps the most significant development (at least for lawyers) in recent years is a robust theory of the evolution of cooperation — and its limits.

Con #1-Familiarity Breeds Contempt.

Few theories in intellectual history have been as influential in wide-ranging areas as Charles Darwin's theory of the evolution of species by natural selection. Ironically, its success is also its greatest enemy. The intellectual influences of evolutionary theory are all around us, and most people have some familiarity with the theory.

On one hand, this familiarity is an advantage for legal scholars using evolutionary metaphors because it is possible to speak about complex system phenomena in language that most people can understand, at least to some degree. On the other hand, much of what many non-specialists "know" or think they know about evolutionary theory is either outright wrong, or over-simplified at best. Thus, the legal scholar using evolutionary metaphors may have to start out by correcting unstated, popular misconceptions about evolutionary theory before being able to use these metaphors successfully.

Con #2-Guilt by Association.

Evolution by environmental selection is such a powerful and simple idea that its proponents have sought to analyze many social and cultural phenomena in evolutionary metaphors, sometimes with unfortunate results. In a sense, evolution has been over-sold. Two movements in American intellectual history that illustrate this tendency are Social Darwinism and Sociobiology.

Social Darwinism was a movement in the early 20th century that sought to explain many social and political phenomena in terms of analogies to evolutionary theory in biology. Often associated with the social theories of Herbert Spencer, Social Darwinists became associated with non-interventionist government policies, in part because evolution had already produced "the best of all possible worlds" (in the words of Voltaire's Dr. Pangloss). Profoundly statist and conservative in its implications, Social Darwinism was interpreted (at least by its opponents) as a profound rationalization of the status quo, as for example by suggesting that the poor were poor because they were less "fit." Few lawyers have not heard Justice Holmes' famous line in the <u>Lochner</u> case rejecting Social Darwinism as a Constitutional theory: "The Constitution does not enact Mr. Herbert Spencer's <u>Social Statics</u>," although most of us are no longer familiar with the social theories at issue.

Sociobiology is a modern second-cousin of Social Darwinism. Reaching its heyday in the late 1970's and early 1980's, Sociobiology proposed speculative explanations for a wide range of social and cultural practices in terms of evolutionary theory.[17] And like Social

---

17 See, e.g. E. O. WILSON, SOCIOBIOLOGY: THE NEW SYNTHESIS (Harvard, 1975).

Darwinism before it, Sociobiology also produced a strong intellectual counter-reaction, particularly from feminists and other progressive forces who, rightly or wrongly, were suspicious that Sociobiology was also inherently statist. They feared that Sociobiology would also necessarily provide rationalizations in terms of evolutionary theory for whatever exists (such as the subordination of women and minority groups). Many scientists objected to Sociobiology on different grounds: that it was profoundly non-empirical and merely speculative in its methods.

As a result of the past excesses of Social Darwinism and Sociobiology in applying evolutionary theory, it is hard to think of an intellectual move that provokes more suspicion in some circles than to analyze social and political phenomena by analogy to biological evolution. To be blunt, evolutionary models are "politically incorrect."

While this intellectual history has little to do with the use of evolutionary models of legal change in the sense at issue in this paper, the fact remains that evolutionary models come with a lot of baggage, and that those of us who choose to use them in our work will have to spend a lot of time and energy dealing with hostility and misunderstanding that are directed at other past (mis)uses of evolutionary models to describe social phenomena.

Con #3-Where's the Beef?

It has been roughly 20 years since the modern renaissance in the use of evolutionary models of law began. In that time, it is difficult to think of any major insights of great interest to lawyers and legal scholars that have emerged from the application of evolutionary models to the law (except of course for the original thesis about the selection of inefficient rules for selective re-litigation). While it is true that not many legal scholars have been plowing this particular vineyard, but rather using biology in other ways to understand law, nonetheless it is worth asking if evolutionary models of legal change are so promising, why have they produced so little of value to date?[18]

My own answer to the question of why evolutionary models of law have produced so little is twofold. First, evolutionary models tend to speak to legal phenomena at a high level of generality, primarily at the level of overall system dynamics. Law at the wholesale level is rarely the concern of most lawyers, who are more concerned about the details of how this or that Constitutional law case will be or was decided by the Supreme Court. From the standpoint of evolutionary theory, these small movements in the law, which are of the greatest interest to lawyers (and clients!), are grandly dismissed as semi-random variations around a larger trend. In short, evolutionary theory generally speaks only to the very largest trends, the global movements in law, not to the details of doctrinal change. Legal change at this level is rarely of great concern to most lawyers and legal scholars except for the few who are drawn to the most abstract and general of studies. Evolutionary models of law may provide a very useful jurisprudential undergirding for the budding legal scholar in her thinking about how the law works and may help lead her to think about interesting and important legal problems, as it has many great legal scholars in the past. However, it is rare that the topic of the typical law review article will benefit much from the explicit invocation of evolutionary models of legal system dynamics.

The second reason why evolutionary models of law have produced so little to date is less fundamental. To date, most legal scholars have focused exclusively on the *similarities* between legal

---

18 Much the same critical assessment could be made of previous waves on enthusiasm for evolutionary models in law. Elsewhere I have catalogued the fact that many of America's most famous legal scholars such as Holmes, Wigmore, Corbin and Pound all were serious devotees of evolutionary models of law. See Elliott, supra note 5. However, even among these giants of the past, it is hard to think of any great insight into the nature of law that is specifically attributable to their evolutionary jurisprudence. This may be because the best of their work is about law, rather than about the evolutionary metaphors that undergird their understanding of the processes of legal change. Contemporary legal scholars might do well to follow their example and keep the primary emphasis on law, rather than on their scholarly apparatus, whether evolutionary or drawn from some other discipline.

system dynamics and evolution in biology. This is perhaps understandable in that the analogy between biological evolution and legal process is so aesthetically striking that it is natural enough to become fascinated with it. The correspondence between biological evolution and legal process is at best a rough one, however. Among other things, even common law lawmaking systems differ among themselves structurally in significant ways (for example, in the degree to which they respect stare decisis). For this reason alone, it seems highly unlikely that they would *all* correspond precisely to biological evolution. As one moves past gross similarities to increase the resolution and make more refined comparisons, it becomes increasingly apparent that there are also important *differences* between the processes of legal evolution and biological evolution. To take but one famous example (borrowed from Lamark): genes are not consciously seeking to find adaptive solutions; judges, on the other hand, may at least sometimes plan solutions that increase the fit between the legal system and its larger cultural and political environment. It is an interesting and important question to what degree law responds to planned, foresightful changes, and to what extent law is shaped by the invisible hand of selection by the environment. The point for the moment, however, is merely that law and biology differ in that law is clearly the joint product of these two forces, one of which (willed, self-conscious change) does not have a good analogy in the biological version of evolution.

Acknowledging differences is not a refutation of the usefulness of evolutionary analogies, but rather a caution that scholars should exploit rather than suppress or elide the differences between the process of biological evolution and legal evolution. The mechanisms of biological evolution are now relatively well-worked out at a theoretical level. As a result, deviations in structure from the biological paradigm should have predictable consequences. By using biological evolution as a starting point, or base case, and paying close attention to the differences, as well as the similarities, between the processes of evolution in biology and in law, legal scholars ought to be able to develop interesting and testable predictions about how changes in the structure of law-making institutions should affect their outputs.

Investing in A Balanced Portfolio.

In the final analysis, young legal scholars are like investors -- they invest in learning other disciplines in the hopes of an eventual payoff in terms of the insights about law to be gained in their scholarship.

Law and economics is like a blue chip stock -- its record is well established, but it is also already broadly owned by many other investors, so the likely returns may be less than for some riskier investments. Evolutionary theory is more like an Internet growth stock; its returns to the individual who chooses to invest in it may be higher, but it is more speculative and hasn't yet established its worth in the marketplace.

A balanced portfolio will contain some of each.

Law-Related Education,
Moral Development,
and the Sense of Justice[*]

Wolfgang Fikentscher[**]

Introduction

Can moral development in general, and the sense of justice in particular, be learned during a human lifetime? Answering, as a hypothesis, the question in the positive raises at least three theoretical issues:

(1) Are moral development and the sense of justice learnable <u>in toto</u>, or only in part so that there have to be certain predispositions for this learning. What might these predispositions be?; (2) does this learning take place all through a human being's lifetime, "non-phase oriented," or are there certain phases or periods of intensified receptivity ("windows"), in childhood, adolescence or later, during

---

[*] Enlarged text of a lecture, given on March 27, 1998, at the Conference: "Windows for Justice: Does learning affect the behavior of children and adolescents?   An interdisciplinary and international inquiry into how learning about law and literacy affects the moral development, civic capacity and sense of justice of children and adolescents." Sponsored by Gruter Institute for Law and Behavioral Research, Portola Valley, CA, and Georgetown University Law Center, Washington, D.C

[**] Professor of Law, University of Munich, Law School, Munich, Germany.

which morals, law and justice are taken up in the human repertoire, and, if so, does this phase-centered learning occur typically, preferably, or in the extreme exclusively?; (3) what does "learning" mean in this context: is it an active or a passive behavior, a conscious or sub-conscious focusing on morals, law and justice, or mere imitation?

These theoretical issues cannot be adequately discussed in the context of this paper. I will concentrate on three less profound, preparatory topics. They are all, more or less, of preliminary character, not of the fundamental nature which would of neccessity be touched upon when one would try to stake out the total terrain indicated by the conference tide.

Our present conference is designed to serve as a stock-taking of what can be understood by the windows for justice in moral development, what approaches have been made in pertinent studies–especially work on "street law"–thus far, and into which directions further studies should go.[1] Therefore, it seems to me advisable to confine myself to the following subjects of inquiry:

1. Starting from practice: what is the meaning of "street law" when taught to children and adolescents, apparently as one of the most successful attempts so far at fostering the understanding of law and justice (A.)?

2. How closely related to teaching "street law" in the United States are similar attempts to stimulate the understanding of law and justice, practiced in Germany where I collected some material concerning the subject (B.)?

3. What can be said about the "windows," the sensitive phases, in children and adolescents with regard to their age? For example: do certain "windows" concern a basic understanding of human rights, national and international? Are there typical age groups which should be studied separately, and how are these age groups to be defined in time periods and designations (C.)?

---

1 The older expression for law-related education at high schools is "street law." The present article uses both terms interchangeably.

4. Are there age-group independent issues of learning the sense of justice (D.)?

A. Meanings of street law

The term street law seems to be in use for at least five different topics of study or activities (I.-V.). Furthermore it is closely related to other areas of studies or activities in the social sciences (VI.).

I. Street law as the law of children's rights

It appears that among the original meanings of street law there was the idea of teaching children and adolescents how to know and use their rights as citizens when addressed by police or other law enforcement agents. It may be that the discussion of issues of street law in many places, such as some law schools, never got much beyond this meaning.

Even in the context of this rather narrow meaning, three fields should be distinguished:

1. Children's and adolescents' rights against police and other law enforcement agencies.
2. Children's and adolescents' rights against teachers, school personnel, school boards, etc.
3. Children's and adolescents' rights against their parents, foster parents and other educators.

II. Street law as an embodiment of legal rules concerning the social status of children

Street law used in a wider sense seems to consist of at least three categories. Here I am relying on material received from the street law project of Georgetown University Law Center.

1. Legal education at high schools, for example, taught by law students who would receive credit for teaching as part of their law school's curriculum. The materials contain the following fields of such education, taught in classes or seminars:

(1)   The structure of the legal system of the United States

(2)   Basic constitutional law, with particular weight on the constitutional rights of the individual

(3)   Procedural rights in criminal and juvenile law

(4)   The basic rules of evidence

(5)   Rights within the family

(6)   Rights of consumers

(7)   Housing rights

(8)   Other individual rights (e.g. social security)

(9)   The fundamentals and the operation of legal trials

(10) Legal terminology

(11) Legal forms and how to use them

(12) Responding to police and other law enforcement agents

(13) Avoiding potential legal problems by the inspection of merchandise, etc

(14) Writing letters with legal contents or of legal importance:

2. First Amendment cases concerning free speech of students (a field of particular importance, according to the materials).

3. Teaching techniques of street law: case studies, mock trials, video clips etc.

III. Children's and adolescents' sense of justice

The sense of justice is a field of study in legal theory, in particular legal ethology.[2]   Obviously, children and adolescents develop their own sense of justice. However, this area of street law in a wider sense appears to have been assigned minor importance compared to the more technical questions mentioned under I. and

---

2 The Gruter Institute for Law and Behavioral Research, under its President Dr. Margaret Gruter, J.S.M., the Institute's founder, has early entered into seminal research on the sense of justice in ethological perspective: M. Gruter and M. Rehbinder, Editors, Der Beitrag der Biologie zu Fragen von Recht und Ethik, in Schriftenreihe zur Rechtssoziologie und Rechtstatsachenforschung, Band 54 (1983); M. Gruter, Editor, Behavior, Evolution and the Sense of Justice, American Behavioral Scientist (Vol. 34, Jan/Feb. 1991) Sage Publications, Newbury Park, CA; and M. Gruter, R.D. Masters, Editors, The Sense of Justice: An Inquiry into the Biological Foundations of Law, Newbury Park CA, 1992: Sage.

II. The fields mentioned in the available materials include:
1. Legal policies, rationales and values contained in statutes and case law.
2. The teaching of competing values, and the understanding that a case can be argued from two sides.
3. Legal values such as fairness, due process, and justice.
4. Balancing the rights of individuals and interests of society.

Specific high school education in the doctrines and theories concerning the sense of justice could not be found in the available materials.

IV. Street law as "the law of the street"

In the sources, now and then street law is used in the sense of the law of the street. However, this occurs only if street law in urban settings is discussed. In this context, street law takes the meaning of the self-styled or inherited rules that govern teen gangs. They contain rules of gang discipline that are applied in a mafia manner whenever insiders or outsiders of the gang do not behave in the expected way.

As a minimum, four legal issues are raised by street law in this "law of the street" sense:
1. In anthropology, the rules that govern gangs, illegal conspiracies, pirate ships etc. pose the problem whether they can be called "law." Of course, this depends on the definition of law, and in particular, whether justice, the sense of justice, an idea of justice, the aim of justice, etc. has to be included in this definition as a conceptual requisite. The authorities differ, and this is not the place to go into details.[3] There may be mentioned in passing the famous debate between H.L.A. Hart and Lord Devlin, and the discussions about the positism of legal realism in the thirties and forties.[4]

---

3 See, e.g., Pospisil, Leopold, Ethnology of Law, 3rd ed., Menlo Park 1985: Cummings, 1-10.
4 Hart, H.L.A., The Concept of Law, Oxford 1991: Clarendon; Devlin, Patrick, Law and Morals, Birmingham 1961; Martin, Michael, Legal Realism: American and Scandinavia, New York 1997; P. Lang; Fikentscher, W. Methoden des Rechts: vol. 2, Anglo-amerikanischer Rechtskreis, Tubingen 1975: Mohr.

2. Again, viewed anthropologically, this type of street law has to be discussed under the heading of "unofficial law," and this may only be mentioned here, too. "Unofficial law" is a subject of legal anthropology of considerable importance and actuality.[5]

3. Under state and federal law, and related policy-making, the illegality of gangs, conspiracies, etc. are of concern, as well as issues of juvenile criminology, and prevention of crime. The context with the "sense of justice" consists in the belief of many of the members of youth gangs that peer pressure and like-mindedness are setting the rules of desired behavior. Is this part of what may be called the "sense of justice?"

4. In terms of legal philosophy, the "law of the street" as the "law" of violent gangs evokes recollections of an ongoing debate that has been phrased by St. Augustine in the following words: Romota iustitia quid sunt regna nisi maga latrocinia? (but for justice, what else are kingdoms than great robber caves?). It will be noticed that the curricula of German street law teaching devote more attention to the legal philosophical background of everyday law (see Part 2, infra.).

V. Street law as general legal education for non-lawyers

A rather different approach to "street law"' is being taken in the "Course in Practical Law" published by Arbetman, McMahon and O'Brien.[6] According to its materials, the Georgetown Street Law Clinic also seems to favor this meaning of the term "street law."

Here, street law appears as a general basic legal education for non-lawyers. In German, this would be called "Allgemeine Rechtskunde" (general knowledge of the law). This type of street law is the widest in scope. It covers nearly all fields of law and

---

5. Rouland, Norbert, Legal Anthroprology. Stanford 1994: Stanford U. Press (orig. Paris 1988; transl. from French by Ph.G. Planet).

6. Arbetman, Lee, Edward McMahon and Edward L. O'Brien, Street Law: A Course in Practical Law, 5th ed. Minneapolis/St. Paul 1994: West Publ. Co.

presents them in a way which is accessible to anyone who did not receive a formal legal education, but is interested in the working of the law and its various fields. This approach is not limited to urban settings, nor to adolescent citizens. It amounts to a general civic education. The Georgetown Street Law Clinic successfully provides for such education.

Interest in the sense of justice as demonstrated in the ethology of law ("Law and Behavior"), legal philosophy, and anthropology of law does not frequently show up in this general teaching of the basics of the law. It is difficult enough to cover nearly all the subcategories of law in a manner which is to be understandable for everyone. Hence, it cannot surprise that the contents pages and the index of this course does not mention the keywords "justice," let alone "sense of justice." The sense for law and justice, e.g., for due process, is being taught by discussing cases in "clinical manner," for example in moot courts.

> "Street law" as a general legal education for non-lawyers, especially at high schools, has a high impact on civic education, and may influence legal understanding in general on the national and international level.

VI. Other areas neighboring street law (esp. literacy programs)

There should be mentioned some other fields of interest attached to "Street Law," according to the materials, such as literacy programs, prison programs, etc. In particular, the literacy clinic seems to have interesting connections with what is called street law.

VII. Evaluation

Street law in the senses III. and IV., supra (the children's sense of justice, and street law as the law of the street) come closest to what in former years has been discussed on conferences and in publications sponsored by the Gruter Institute for Law and Behavioral Research.[7] Meaning No. I. (childrens' responses to

---

7. See note 2, supra.

policemen, etc.) and No. II. (the body of the law concerning the status of children) fall outside of this scope, at least in parts. Meaning No. V. (general legal and civic education) seems to be of general importance for national and international education in a democracy.

Some of these activities particularly those mentioned under III. and IV., may require the collaboration of legal philosophers,[8] sociologists,[9] comparatists,[10] psychologists, criminologists, and experts in the clinical training by law schools.[11] In view of the many different meanings the term "street law" has come to represent in recent years, it might be advisable to prefer the term "law-related education" for future use.

B. Education in law and justice at German schools
I. Jurisdiction for education

In Germany, law and administration of educational and school matters is under the jurisdiction of the states (Laender). The federal government has only general directive powers. Thus, education in understanding the law is a matter for the states.

II. The four types of German schools

Typically, the school system in the German states consists of four categories:

-elementary school (Grundschule, ages 6 to 10, and Hauptschule, ages 11 to 16)

-intermediate school (Realschule) (ages 10 to 16) which includes learning foreign languages; may be continued in Fachschule (16-19)

-high school (Gymnasium) (ages 10 to 19) leading to a final exam (Abitur) that qualifies to enter university

---

8. Cf., Atiyah, P.S., and Robert Sommers, Form and Substance in Anglo-American Law, Oxford 1987: Clarendon.
9. Cf., Friedman, Lawrence and Harry Scheiber, Legal Culture and the Legal Profession, Westview 1995.
10. Cf., Damaska. Mirjan, The Faces of Justice and State Authority, New Haven 1986: Yale University Press.
11. See note 6, supra, for examples.

-vocational school (Berufsschule) (ages 16 to 19) (for those who have completed elementary school or Realschule at 16).

III. Street law activities in German schools[12]

All four types of school in obviously all German states offer some education in the meaning of law and justice, the working of the rule of law in the courts, and the functions of the legal profession:

1.   At elementary schools (Grundschule and Hauptschule), basics of law are taught in combination with the neighboring fields of social sciences such as economy, sociology, labor relations, and educational theory.

2.   At intermediate schools (Realschule) the educational law provides for an option:

   a) As a rule, law is taught together with economics. The course is called "Economics and Law" (Wirtschafts-und Rechtslehre). Teachers have a degree in economics.

   b) If there are enough students and financial means, the students of the age groups 10 and 11 (ages 16 and 17) receive a qualified education in law (Rechtskunde) taught by a professional legal practitioner, for a period of 15 double hours in each of the two years.

3.   At the high school level, again there is an option for the students:

   a) As a rule, law is offered in a course called "Economics and law" (Wirtschafts-und Rechtslehre), and additionally in the course on "Sociology" (Sozialkunde). The teachers have a degree in economics, or in sociology. The teacher's exam in economics comprises macro-and microeconomics and private law.

---

12. My information is gained from four experts in German legal education in the school system. For the teaching practice in my home state, Bavaria, I contacted Ministerialrat Steiner and his aid, Mr. Mutter, both from the Bavarian State Ministry of Education. Mr. Steiner referred me to Dr. Heckl, who specializes in the teaching of law at high schools within the framework of a government financed scientific research project. Also, there exists a Federal Association of Teachers of Law at High Schools. I had an exchange with Mr. Limbeck, Bochum, Northrhine-Westphalia, the secretary of this Association. All were helpful and responsive. The text above presents some results of this fact-finding work.

b) If there are enough students and financial means available, the same opportunity for a law course by a legal professional is offered as at the Realschule (see before). This amounts to twice the amount of 15 double hours for students of the age groups 16 and 17.

Students interested in legal education are permitted to include law into their final high school examination (Abitur) among those fields of Abitur which are optional. The <u>Abitur</u> consists of mandatory and optional fields. I studied examples of examination questions. For me, the questions asked look quite advanced: they are simple on the surface, but would cause difficulties even for law students in their first and second years.

The <u>Abitur</u> enables those who passed it to enter university without more, in particular without a college or university entrance test or exam. Germany does not have college. Students enter university at age 19. It is planned to lower that age to 18 to enhance international compatibility. Thus, the study of law begins at that age, and there is no college in between. Since studying at a university is free for every <u>Abiturient</u> (Abitur-holder) and no tuition has to be paid, there are no essential social barriers for those who want to enter university.

All high school law courses, as well as the exams offered after these courses, attribute ample consideration to underlying issues of <u>justice and the sense for justice</u>. For example, the students are asked to comment upon the "Nuremberg Laws" of 1935 which legalized and required the discrimination of the Jewish minority during the Hitler dictatorship.

Curricula for teaching law and issues of justice at Bavarian high schools are regularly overhauled and adapted to changing needs. The last curriculum for the teaching of economics and law at Bavarian high schools I found was an ordinance of Jan. 28, 1992.[13]

Legal education on high school level seems to be similar or at least comparable in all sixteen German states. There exists a

---

13. Official Gazette of the Bavarian Ministry of Education, Cultus, Sciences, and Art, Part I 1992, 425 ff, Special Publication No. 9.

Federal Association of Teachers of Law at High Schools, represented by Mr. Limbeck, Bochum.[14]

4. At all vocational schools, legal education corresponding to street law is covered in the class on sociology (Sozialkunde). Moreover, at some vocational schools which prepare their students for legally relevant professions such as merchant, manager, or business consultant, law is given a broader spectrum. Sociology teachers and teachers in professional legal areas are equipped to teach their fields through a corresponding teachers' education: they possess the diploma in merchant's activities, economy, or law proper.

5. In sum, there seems to be an elaborate system of teaching law and the sense for justice in German schools. Also, apparently there are enough teachers available to cover the diversified teaching requirements. However, I could not find practical activities such as clinics, workshops or the like through which the students may get involved themselves in the implementation of law in situations of real life. This does not mean that these practical involvements do not exist, but the initiative seems to be left to the teachers. To my knowledge, there is no official Bavarian program of practical studies in applying to real situations what has been studied in class. This contrasts to the moot trials held as part of clinical street law programs in the U.S.

IV. Literature

Literature on the teaching of street law in German schools is voluminous. Only some more or less typical quotes can be made here. Albert Molzahn, in "Rechtskunde" <u>Zeitschrift fuer den Unterricht an allgemeinbildenden und berufsbildenden Schulen</u>, No. 1, June 1985, pp. 5 ff., at 6, makes the point that law should be taught at high schools <u>as a cultural value</u>. In this context, he mentions the following aspects:

---

14. Mr. Limbeck offered his support for the Windows for Justice Project of the Gruter Institute. He himself is familiar with the high school system in Wisconsin.

-the human image of the autonomous person surrounded by legal and moral norms,

-the idea of law as an instrument of peace and security,

-the rule of law and social responsibility, and

-justice, not as a political ideal but rather as a personal virtue.

The same author, in "Rechtskunde," No. 2, Jan. 1986, pp. 4 ff., accentuates <u>behavioral aspects</u> of the law. He mentions a theory of human acting and tries to define <u>behavior relevant to law</u>.

Much attention is given to the role of <u>reality</u> in dealing with practical situations of legal relevance, in contrast to theoretical knowledge (at 5).

In "Rechtskunde," No. 6, Jan. 1988, the same author discusses the importance of <u>legal philosophy</u> for teaching law at high schools. Referring to <u>Rawls</u>, the necessity of protecting possession is accentuated (at 8). Teaching the law at high schools should not so much lead to simply knowing the law (this is the task of the law schools) but rather make use of the educative effect of law for high school students (at 9).

In "Rechtskunde," No. 10, Jan. 1990, the same author mentions the most serious deficiencies in understanding the law among lay persons, and consequently the need to overcome these deficiencies:

-not being able to distinguish between criminal and civil law

-not knowing that most contracts are binding even without formalities

-not being able to read a contract with the necessary understanding of what is meant

-neglecting bargaining chances in negotiating a contract

-not being aware of one's own right and duties

-underestimating criminal punishment

-not being able to distinguish between criminal and misdemeanor charges

-not being able to identify illegal administrative acts

-neglecting one's rights as a party to a procedure

-to misunderstand or underrate the role of law in society and state

The results of such omissions are said to be the non-realization of one's rights, running avoidable risks, and misunderstanding the legal aspects of one's social and political environment.

Authors most quoted in the discussion of the necessity of teaching law and justice at high schools include, besides John Rawls: H.L.A. Haft, Talcott Parsons, Jurgen Habermas, Edmund Husserl, A. Schuetz, Lawrence Kohlberg, Gustav Radbruch, Norbert Hoerster, Ludwig Wittgenstein, George Mead, and O. Hoeffe.

V. Practical examples

As an example from the teaching materials, I take the following case from an article by Volkard Trust, on euthanasia, in "Rechtskunde," No. 6, Jan. 1988, pp. 11 ff., at. 16:

"Bernd, 19 years old, is seriously handicapped since a tragic swimming accident two years ago. He is immobilized from the cervical spine down. Formerly, he was a top sportsman. Now he cannot move from his bed and is totally dependent on the care by his parents. He cannot even move his arms and must be fed.

For some time he has lost any interest in staying alive. Depression has developed, and repeatedly he asks to be relieved from his painful suffering by a lethal injection. Please discuss whether Bernd's express wish should be granted." (transl. W.F.)

Other cases and problems which could be found in German materials concern reckless bicycling; demonstrations becoming violent; violations of sports rules; omitted assistance (unterlassene Hilfeleistung). However, I did not find a hazing case, probably because these initation practices of fraternities and sororities are not known or kept secret.

C. The sensitive phases (windows) for learning the law and a sense of justice
I. Comparison with linguistics

Linguists tell us that there are phases of sensitivity for learning to speak languages without accent. Once these "windows for language-learning" are passed, a language can no longer be learned with such a result that the listener cannot guess the provenance of the speaker by the accent she has. General experience teaches that the older a person is, generally the harder it is to learn a foreign language at all. Details cannot be offered here.

Generalizing from this linguistic observation it may be stated that abilities to learn are influenced by age. The rule seems to be that a young person is more able to learn than an older one. A German proverb goes: <u>Was Hänschen nicht lernt, lernt Hans nimmermehr</u> (What Johnny didn't learn, John will learn no more).

II. Sensitive phases ("windows") for law and justice

If law is something that can be learned, and if the sense for justice is something than can be learned by, or along with, learning the law, there should be sensitive phases ("windows") for learning the sense for law and justice. It cannot be denied that an older person can study law and learn legal prescripts. What is meant here is the internalization of the feeling for the just.

What may those windows be, expressed in age groups of children and adolescents? Before empirical data are available which are one major target of any future project, only speculation can help. The following are speculations, based on unrepresentive observations of children and adolescents, common-sensical experiences of a family father, not more. Here, a project on the study of the learnability of the sense for justice will have to produce empirical and replicable proof.

It seems that a human being in the course of her maturing development between birth and, let us say, the age of 18 or 19, undergoes successive stages of receptivity with regard to things to be learnt, to be discovered, and to experienced. It may be wrong to generalize as to these successive stages. Some people may undergo a quicker development that others. With some, the receptive phases may follow a different order than with others. Some will demonstrate a continual process of mental and corporeal maturing. For some there may be longer or shorter periods of stagnation. Some will tend to mature and then enter a stage of relative "perfection," that is, give the impression that they have reached the status of being "grown-up." Others will show a tendency of steady development of their mental and bodily status in a positive, acceptable manner. Again others are those of whom one might say that "they will never be grown-up" people, etc.

However, one truth seems to be evident, that a newly born baby, both in natural and normative respect, behaves differently from a 25-year old person, and that this difference is due to what technically may be called ontogenetic evolution. Given that evolution, its path and stages can be subjected to investigation. On this basis, incomplete as it may be for lack of empirical proof, three stages of personal development are distinguishable:

1. There is what may be called the infant phase, encompassing about the first three or four years of a human life (0 to 3 or 4). This phase is characterized by an almost complete dependence of the child on the mother, and to a possibly lesser degree on the father or other persons of reference (Bezugsperson). This rather complete dependence must be mirrored in the understanding by the child of what is right and wrong. Since the infant has not yet developed rules of right and wrong for herself, she relies on the judgment of others, mainly the mother, and this gives rise for a keen understanding of regularity and rule-following. Hence, infants see the main reason for injustice in deviations from a rule. The contents of this rule is not equally important. The rule as such is what counts.

2. Secondly, there follows a period during which the contents of rules becomes more interesting. But since the child knows that contents must be learned, she will be interested in substantive contents of legal rules. Knowledge is accquired, along with what is right and wrong. This phase may be roughly dated from age 5 to 11, and it might be identified as the phase of discovery. The child and respectively the adolescent sets out to discover the world in its good and bad qualities. The mind turns to the contents of things, however in a receptive, still mostly uncritical way, not in that radically inquisitive, disbelieving manner that is typical for the next period, puberty.

During the first part of this period of discovery, interest in justice may be formal, and stimulated by the desire to avoid conflicts (see III. B.2)a), infra). Hence, the phase of discovery may have to be divided into two sub-phases: a content-related discovery for reasons of conflict-avoidance, and a content-related discovery out of genuine interest in learning.

Furthermore, it occurs during this total phase of (5 to 11 years of age) that a child or adolescent—as a result of this discovery—may have to learn that there is no perfect justice in this world.

3. Thirdly, puberty, marks a major step in the development of a girl or boy. Parents talk of the "difficult age" of the adolescent. The phase of puberty is characterized by the inclinination of the adolescent to new orientations. These orientations are not only rule-fixed (as has been described for the infant period), and no longer predominantly receptive (as in the discovery period), but critical and challenging. The period of puberty (including pre- and post-puberty) may roughly be assumed for the years between the 12th and 18th year of age.

4. Let us assume that after puberty, a human is grown up. On the whole, civic life and looking around for a partner to live with starts at about 20.

5. This amounts to four phases, three of which are being focussed here as the stages or "windows" during which a member of the human society learns and internalizes, each one in his or her own way, the difference of right and wrong. However, dividing the receptivity for the sense of justice into phases and age groups does not exclude the possibility of phase-independent developments in learning and internalizing the sense of justice. This eventuality will be considered in Part D, infra.

Having given names to these three stages (the infant, the discovery, and the puberty stage), and having assigned to them, if arbitrarily, a period of years of a human life span, a more detailed description of each of these three periods or stages or "windows" is in order.

III. Characterization of the sensitive phases
1.c.a. In general

With regard to the sense of justice, learned by learning the law and its corollaries, the three periods of infancy, discovery, and puberty can be described as follows:

1. The infant phase constructs an interdependent system of trust and obedience, above all in the relationship to the mother. The child acts, and refrains from acting, without considering whether the mother is right. From that comes a feeling of being able to rely on someone and, of necessity, also a liking for regularity. The parents say: "Remember that. Stop doing that,"— references to rules. This "infant phase of trust and obedience" contributes to a sense of justice, above all to an inclination for equal treatment, equal rights and equal justice. Authorities speak of regular functioning (Regelwerken). Emotions making orientation easier to develop. Empathy for unequal treatment ought to be called for.

2. The second, the acquisitive and discovery phase, is suitable for the acquisition of basic knowledge and feeling for that which may be called basic criminal law. One can, probably, bring in the Ten Commandments here as well. Children between the ages of five and ten are receptive to that which, in general, is held by grown-ups to be right and wrong. That's exactly why they can understand a Turkish child's being made to wear a head scarf. Here begins comparative law. In the second "discovery" phase it is a matter of substantial basic learning, of basic contents, not merely of equal rights. Group play, numbering off, and story-telling count. One sees that parents make mistakes too, a great shock for many children. It is this discovery phase which

seem to be particularly relevant to "learning" human rights, most of all today: international human rights.

3. The phase of puberty, or new orientation, brings on something totally new: a sense for the actually suitable. Suum cuique is being asked for and understood. Distributive justice is beginning to claim the interest of the adolescent: now one criticizes a football team's having won a game in spite of having played badly. Interests in sports grow, along with growing sense for fair play, and also for accepting having lost the game. Now, one accepts umpires, referees, judges, and is already capable of making decisions and value judgments of one's own. In the discovery phase, the sports teacher is accepted as the umpire; in puberty, sports teacher and umpire assume different roles. Someone who in spite of doing poorly in school has still been promoted, tells himself and others that he's been lucky. Self-doubt and world-weariness grow. Idols are sought: many things begin to totter. The youth sects see their chance. A new form of orientation offered is quickly grasped at. One goes into new value relationships; they may be of a doubtful kind, to which one the more firmly adheres.

4. Sometime every person ought to be "grown up" and see oneself and others in tenable perspective. Commutative justice, substantive contents of law and morals, and—consequently—distributive justice have been learned.

Thus, according to the above, the sensitive phases are geared to equal treatment in the phase of trust and obedience, to basic elements of right and wrong during the phase of acquisition and discovery, and to that which is actually suitable during the phase of puberty and new orientation.

1.c. A corrobaration from negotiation theory[15]

15. Murnigham J. Keith and Madan M. Pillutian, Asymmetric Moral Imperatives in Ultimatum Bargaining, in: Kramer, Roderick M. and David M. Messick, Editors, Negotiation as a Social Process, Thousand Oaks 1995: Sage Publications, pp. 240-267. See also Lawrence Kohlberg's six stages of moral development, Lawrence Kohlberg. The Meaning and Measurement of Moral Development. Clark University. Heinz Werner Institute, 1981 (concerned with morals, not with law). William Damon, The Moral Development of Children, Scientific American, August 1999 , 73-78.

Negotiation theory studies children's and adolescent's fairness-oriented behavior. The results demonstrate a similar division of age groups. To the three main periods, 0-4, 5-11, and 12-19, negotiation theory adds a sub-group of the 5 to 7-year old.

1. Young children, in negotiating, "tenaciously" defend their positions, insisting on possession and equal treatment.

2. a) At age 5 to 7, this striving for positions and equal treatment becomes rationalized by a growing interest in conflict-avoidance and peace-keeping.

   b) Children more than 7 years old increasingly become "equity-oriented" and are willing to listen to arguments of moral and legal substance.

3. At the age described above as the phase of puberty, elements of competition and rivalry are being added to equality (1) and equity (2 a and b).

Thus, we find the same phases. Moreover, based on the foundation of this description of age-patterned behavior in negotiations, there seems to be a general trend from egalitarian equality to measured equity, and from there to rivalry. From economic anthropology, the three elements of allocation –reciprocity, equitable distribution, and competitive rivalry–are well known. Piagetism would parallel a child's and cultural developments. In-depth study of these parallel phenomena is in order; its preliminary results cannot be presented here.

D. Non-phase-oriented research

Age-group independent issues would call for non-phase oriented research.

Going beyond the four periods of age with their specific problems regarding the sense of justice, there may indeed be a "general part" of issues applicable to all four groups. Hagen Hof (personal communication) indeed suggested, in this context, as age-group independent "learning tools" for the sense of justice:

-change of perspectives as a methodological approach;

-confrontation with the enlargement of scope, or with contrasts, as a means of forming a growing sense of justice;

-letting things appear more relative and thus less important; and
-teaching comparisons.

There may be added, in taking up some other suggestions by H.
Hof, the demonstration of key values such as personal respect, trust
and reliance, freedom from foreign influence ("freedom from") and
to take initiatives ("freedom to"), and the insistence on personal,
value-oriented and traditional ties, etc.[16]
    And there are ethological generalities, too. Phase-independent
factors influencing the sense of justice may be non-kin reciprocity,
understanding of being ostracized, peace-keeping activities, and
social exchange.
    All these non-age-group related aspects of the learning and
internalization of the sense of justice need to be studied along with
the age-group oriented.

E. A Summary:
The idea of a project "Windows for Justice"

A project dealing with sensitive phases for learning the sense of
justice based on age-group phased and non-phased phenomena
should contribute to a detailed study of the issues raised in sections
A. through D. of this paper, and on this basis may concentrate on
the three questions mentioned in the introduction to this paper.
Again, they concern:

(1) the learnability of law and of the sense for justice in the
    ontogenetic evolution of the human being, and her ensuing
    understanding of the law and laws underlying aim, justice;

(2) the expressions this learning finds in human behavior, for
    example in respecting international human rights, in
    particular with regard to the sensitive phases ("windows")
    for the development of the sense for justice, but also for
    phase-independent phenomena of the learning process;

(3) the nature of this learning process as such, against the
    background of possible genetic predispositons, and the

---

16. Cf., Hof, Hagen, Rechtsethologie, Heidelberg 1996: R.v. Decker's Verlag, 186 ff.

results of epigenetic transmission theory building up on these predispositions.

Regulating Sexual Behavior:
Richard Posner's *Sex and Reason**

Robert H. Frank**

Margaret Gruter is an important intellectual entrepreneur. Over the years, she and her colleagues in the Gruter Institute have brought scholars from diverse backgrounds together in ways that have forever changed their thinking. The following paper was spawned by such a meeting in March of 1993, when Margaret invited me and several others to discuss Richard Posner's *Sex and Reason.*

We are in Richard Posner's debt for his intelligent, informed effort to bring reason to bear on how sexual behavior ought to be regulated. He has provided persuasive evidence that sexual behavior is responsive to costs and benefits. But even if it were highly unresponsive, weighing the costs and benefits, including unintended side effects, of our attempts to regulate it would nonetheless be valuable. This cost-benefit analysis, which the

* A shorter version of this essay originally appeared in *Economics and Philosophy.*
** Goldwin Smith Professor of Economics, Ethics, and Public Policy, Cornell University.

courts have always been reluctant to undertake, is well launched with *Sex and Reason.*

Posner wants us first to strip away our moral prejudices and view sexual desire as an ordinary human appetite—on a par, say, with our appetite for food. Next, he asks us to view the behaviors by which people try to satisfy their sexual appetites as having been chosen by weighing the relevant costs and benefits. Posner correctly anticipates that many critics will take this approach to imply that sexual passions play no role. But he emphatically resists this inference:

> By deeming sexual behavior rational, I do not commit myself to denying the importance of emotion and of prerational preference, or to exaggerating the degree of conscious calculation. From the genes and perhaps from early childhood development as well, we obtain our basic sexual drive and preferences. But how we translate these into actual behavior depends on social factors--including opportunities, resources, and constraints. Sex is a means to human ends, and the efficient fitting of means to ends, whether done consciously or unconsciously, is the economist's notion of rationality. (p. 436.)

This response is fair enough, as far as it goes. Most people clearly do have goals and, if not always, then at least much of the time they do the best they can to achieve them.

Yet there remains something troubling about Judge Posner's portrayal of sex as rational choice. Unlike many of his critics, however, I will argue that the problem lies not with the rational choice model per se, but with the specific narrow version of it that Posner and most contemporary neoclassical economists employ. This version of the model assumes both an implausibly narrow set of human objectives and a curiously naive view of the manner in which people actually pursue them. Not surprisingly, the welfare implications of the analysis are highly sensitive to the assumptions we make in each of these areas. I will attempt to show that more plausible assumptions yield conclusions more in keeping with our intuitions and with existing theories and evidence on human behavior.

Yet despite my objections, I hope it will be clear that I am proposing a "friendly amendment" to Posner's theory. For it is my firm view that the rational choice framework, suitably broadened, can teach us as much about sexual behavior as it has about behavior in other domains.

I. The Impulse-Control Problem

A troubling feature of the narrow rational choice perspective is that it appears to rule about the possibility that people might regret having chosen behaviors whose consequences were perfectly predictable at the outset. Yet such expressions of regret are common. Many people wake up wishing they had drunk less the night before, but few wake up wishing they had drunk more.

It is likewise a puzzle within the narrow rational choice framework that people often incur great expense and inconvenience to prevent behaviors they would otherwise freely choose. For example, the model has difficulty explaining why some people pay thousands of dollars to attend weight-loss camps that will feed them only 1500 calories per day.

Welfare analysis based on the rational choice model assigns considerable weight, as it should, to people's own judgments about what makes them better off. In this framework, it is not clear how one could ever conclude that a risk freely chosen by a well-informed person was a wrong choice. By itself, the fact that the choice led to a bad outcome is clearly not decisive. If someone is unlucky enough to be killed crossing the street, for example, we would not conclude that his decision to cross the street was necessarily a bad one.

Posner's version of the rational choice model suggests that criticizing someone's decision to have an unprotected sexual encounter that resulted in AIDS would be similarly problematic. If the person knew the risks and yet freely chose to ignore them, this model makes it hard to say more than that he was just unlucky.

Compelling evidence from psychology, however, suggests why expressions of regret may often be genuine, why people might impose constraints on their own behavior, and why risks freely chosen by a well-informed person may not be optimal from his own point of view. This evidence concerns behavior in the realm of intertemporal choice.

The rational choice model says that people will discount future costs and benefits exponentially at their respective rates of time preference. With exponential discounting, the choice between two alternatives will be the same no matter when the choice is made. Consider, for example, the pair of choices A and B:

> A: $100 tomorrow vs. $110 a week from tomorrow.
> B: $100 after 52 weeks vs. $110 after 53 weeks.

If future receipts are discounted exponentially, people will always make the same choice under alternative A as they do under alternative B. Since the larger payoff comes a week later in each case, the ordering of the present values of the two alternatives must be the same in A as in B, irrespective of the rate at which people discount. When people confront such choices in practice, however, there is a pronounced tendency to choose differently under the two scenarios: most pick the $100 option in A, whereas most choose the $110 option in B.

Richard Herrnstein, George Ainslie, George Loewenstein and others who have studied intertemporal choices experimentally have amassed substantial evidence that individuals tend to discount future costs and benefits not exponentially, as assumed by the rational choice model, but hyperbolically.[1] Under hyperbolic

---

1 Two of the most important earlier papers on this issue are Chung and Herrnstein, 1967; and Ainslie, 1975. The most detailed and current summary of the relevant evidence appears in Ainslie, 1992. See also Elster, 1979; Schelling, 1980; Thaler and Shefrin, 1981; and Winston, 1980. For a series of papers that discusses economic applications of the hyperbolic discounting model, see Elster and Loewenstein, 1992.

discounting, the psychological impact of a cost or benefit falls much more sharply with delay than it does under exponential discounting. One consequence is that preference reversals of the kind just observed are all but inevitable under hyperbolic discounting. The classic reversal involves choosing the larger, later reward when both alternatives occur with substantial delay, then switching to the smaller, earlier reward when its delay falls below some threshold. Thus, from the pair of alternatives labeled B above, in which both rewards come only after a relatively long delay, most subjects chose the larger, later reward; whereas from the pair labeled A, most chose the earlier, smaller reward.

So, why would people pay thousands of dollars to attend a weight-loss camp that will feed them only 1500 calories per day? If they tend to discount future costs and benefits hyperbolically, the answer is clear: they really *want* to eat less, but they know that without imposing constraints on themselves they will lack the willpower to do so.

The tendency to discount future costs and benefits hyperbolically gives rise to a variety of familiar impulse-control problems and, in turn, to a variety of strategies for solving them. Anticipating their temptation to overeat, people often try to limit the quantities of sweets, salted nuts, and other delicacies they keep on hand. Anticipating their temptation to spend cash in their checking accounts, people enroll in payroll-deduction savings plans. Foreseeing the difficulty of putting down a good mystery novel in midstream, many people know better than to start one on the evening before an important meeting. Reformed smokers seek the company of nonsmokers when they first try to kick the habit, and are more likely than others to favor laws that limit smoking in public places. The recovering alcoholic avoids cocktail lounges.

Effective as these bootstrap self-control techniques may often be, they are far from perfect. Many people continue to express regret about having overeaten; having drunk and smoked too much; having saved too little; having stayed up too late; having watched too much television; and so on. The exponential discounting model urges us to dismiss these expressions as sour grapes. But from the perspective of the hyperbolic discounting model, these same expressions are coherent. In each case, the actor chose an inferior option when a better one was available, and later feels genuinely sorry about it.

Impulse-control problems appear to lie at the root of some of the most destructive forms of human behavior, both to self and to others. Wilson and Herrnstein, for example, suggest that impulse-control problems are an important cause of criminality, and there is evidence of a similar relationship involving compulsive gambling.[2]

Statutory law itself implicitly recognizes the force of impulse-control problems in some contexts. For instance, the law of homicide is relatively lenient in the case of a husband who has murdered his wife's lover upon encountering them in bed. Most countries impose at least some restrictions on gambling. Entrapment law implicitly acknowledges the injustice of tempting a normally law-abiding citizen to break the law, and in many jurisdictions it is illegal to leave one's keys in a parked car.

Impulse-control problems arise with particular force—and often with severe consequences—in the domain of sexual behavior. Someone who eats too much stands to gain a few pounds, but sexual indiscretions have become a life-and-death matter. Most people know by now that "safe sex" is the most sensible option for sexually active single persons. Yet many ignore this knowledge in the moment of decision. People who confront life-threatening and relationship-threatening impulse-control problems have an interest in the regulation of sexual behavior—their own as well as others'—that is fundamentally different from the one suggested by the dispassionate focus of the rational choice model.

In an analysis so thoroughly committed to the rational choice model in its narrow form, there is no room even to acknowledge impulse-control problems in mature adults. The single, fleeting

---

2 Wilson and Herrnstein, 1985; see also Mischel, 1961.

reference to impulsivity in Posner's 442-page book comes in reference to teenagers, and even here he adds a parenthetical remark that downplays its significance:

> Teenagers are on average more impulsive, hence on average less responsive to incentives, than adults are (although Chapter 10 presented evidence of rational behavior by teenagers toward abortion). (p. 331).

Posner's framework cannot accommodate the notion that people might improve their lives by deliberately restricting their own options. He states, for instance, that "rarely is a person made better off by having an option removed." (p. 253).

Trying to analyze sexual behavior with a model that denies the existence of impulse-control problems is like trying to build a barn without a hammer. Many of the laws and social norms that define acceptable behavior simply cannot be understood without reference to the fact that people confront powerful temptations to engage in sexual activity that is contrary to their long-run interests.

Consider, for example, the laws and norms regarding adultery. Spouses may strongly wish to remain in their marriages and realize that their prospects for doing so will be higher if they remain sexually faithful. And yet they may also recognize the potential lure of extramarital romance. Anticipating this conflict, most wedding ceremonies attempt to strengthen the partners' resolve by having them make public vows of fidelity. And in most societies, these vows are backed up by legal and social sanctions against adultery.

Posner appears puzzled by such practices, which he regards as having arisen from arbitrary religious beliefs:

> ...our sexual attitudes and the customs and laws that grow out of them and perhaps reinforce or even alter them by some feedback process, are the product of moral attitudes rooted in religious beliefs rather than in the sort of functional considerations examined in the preceding chapter. (p. 236.)

But why not use the same functionalist perspective to examine the content of morality? Elsewhere I have argued that moral sentiments appear to help solve a variety of impulse-control problems.[3] Consider, for example, the iterated prisoner's dilemma. As Rapoport, Axelrod, and others have shown, the tit-for-tat strategy fares well against alternative strategies in the repeated prisoner's dilemma.[4] Self-interested persons thus have good reasons to play tit-for-tat, yet to do so they must first solve an impulse-control problem. Playing tit-for-tat means cooperating on the first interaction, which in turn implies a lower payoff on that move than could have been had by defecting. The reward for playing tit-for-tat lies in the prospect of a string of mutually beneficial interactions in the future. The rational choice model with exponential discounting says that if the present value of the current plus future benefits is larger by cooperating now, the actor will cooperate. But if people discount hyperbolically, this does not follow. Because the gain from defecting comes now, whereas its cost comes in the future, the hyperbolic discounter confronts an impulse-control problem.

The moral sentiment of sympathy, which figured so prominently in Adam Smith's early writings, helps to solve this problem. Someone who feels sympathy for the interests of his trading partner faces an additional cost of defecting, one that occurs at the same time as the gain from defecting. Because of this cost, the person who sympathizes with his trading partners is less likely to defect, and is thus more likely to reap the long-run gains of cooperation.

Similar issues arise when we compare the behavior of a hyperbolic discounter who regards thrift as a moral virtue with that of someone who regards saving as morally neutral. The first person will be better able to resist the temptation to consume most of his current income. And at some point in the not too distant future, even the spendthrift is likely to view his own plan as inferior. Suppose, for example, that the two start with the same income and

---

3 See Frank, 1988, chapter 4.
4 See Rapoport and Chammah, 1965; and Axelrod, 1984.

that the first saves 20 percent, the second only 5 percent. If the rate of return is ten percent, only eleven years will elapse before the high saver's consumption overtakes the low saver's. After 20 years, the high saver's consumption is 16 percent greater; after thirty years, 35 percent greater.

The rational choice model with exponential discounting suggests that the difference between these two life histories is merely a reflection of differing preferences, and hence not a proper subject for welfare comparisons. Once we acknowledge hyperbolic discounting, however, we are more inclined to take the low saver's expressions of regret at face value, and to trust our intuition that the thrifty person really has done better.

Posner's ideal world is one in which people regard sex as a matter of moral indifference. In such a world, everyone, married or single, would essentially be a sexual free agent. No doubt such a world would be an improvement in some ways over one saddled with outmoded and often capricious rules of sexual morality. Yet surely not all moral rules regarding sex are maladaptive. Although some of the costs of behavior in the sexual domain may have vanished with the discovery of antibiotics and the pill, many others remain. The lure of sexual attraction is powerful and immediate, whereas the costs of many sexual behaviors come only after substantial delay. The evidence regarding hyperbolic discounting suggests that impulse-control problems will continue to confront people in the sexual domain. Moral sentiments have helped solve such problems in the past, and can continue to do so in the future. Before we embrace Posner's call for a morally neutral attitude toward sex, we should inquire what alternative mechanisms might take the place of moral sentiments.

Posner attempts to persuade us that people are rational in the sexual domain by citing evidence that partial derivatives in behavioral equations have the signs predicted by the rational choice model. He notes, for instance, that unprotected sex among homosexual males has gone down in the face of the risk of AIDS.

Yet surely this does not imply that the unprotected sex that does still occur must be rational.

Posner employs similar evidence in an attempt to show that rape is primarily a substitute for consensual sex rather than misogyny:

> Contrary to a view held by many feminists, rape appears to be primarily a substitute for consensual sexual intercourse rather than a manifestation of male hostility toward women or a method of establishing or maintaining male domination. Donald Symons, for example, points to anthropological evidence that the incidence of rape rises with bride price; thus the more expensive it is to obtain marital sex, the more likely men are to resort to force. (p. 384.)

But here, too, the fact that the derivative has the expected sign tells us little. To be rational in the pursuit of an activity means to pursue that activity until its marginal cost is equal to its marginal benefit. The observation that costs and benefits have *some* influence on behavior does not by itself imply that people are rational. Indeed, as Gary Becker has pointed out, income effects alone give us downward sloping demand curves, independent of whether people are rational.

II. Positional Externalities

My second line of criticism rests more squarely in the domain of neoclassical economics. In the neoclassical tradition, Posner correctly recognizes externalities as an important and often legitimate source of demand for regulation. But there is an important class of externalities that he and many other writers in this tradition ignore. This class I call "positional externalities." It includes behaviors that alter important social frames of reference, which in turn affect individual valuations. One example is the well-documented effect of economic growth to raise the absolute level of income considered necessary for the achievement of an acceptable standard of living.[5] Elsewhere I have argued that positional externalities are the most plausible explanation for a variety of restrictions on the freedom to contract in the labor market.[6]

To illustrate, consider workplace safety regulations. Traditional neoclassical economic theory holds that competition will produce the optimal amount of workplace safety. Workers survey their options and choose the job with the wage-safety combination that best satisfies their preferences. This argument suggests that mandating higher safety levels will reduce welfare.

Marxists and other critics of the market system have long countered that labor markets are not effectively competitive, and that safety regulation is needed to prevent employers from exploiting workers. The puzzle for both camps is to explain why safety regulations are most binding in those labor markets that on traditional measures are the most highly competitive. Once we acknowledge that people care not only about absolute wealth but about relative wealth as well, a ready explanation is at hand.

For example, consider a representative "community" composed of two such individuals, A and B, each of whom faces a choice between working in a safe job at a salary of $400/mo or an "unsafe" job at a salary of $500/mo. The safe job pays less only because of the costs of maintaining higher safety. The lone adverse consequence of working in the unsafe job is a modest reduction in life expectancy. A and B choose independently and each picks the job that promises to deliver the highest utility. The satisfaction each gets from a particular job depends on three factors: 1) absolute income; 2) relative income; and 3) job safety. A's utility function has the form $U = X + R + S$, where

> X = A's monthly income in dollars;
> R = A's satisfaction from relative position
> > = 200 if A's income exceeds B's,
> > 0 if the two have equal incomes, and
> > -200 if A's income is less than B's;

---

5 See, for example, Runciman, 1966; Easterlin, 1973; Hirsch, 1976; and Sen, 1983.
6 See Frank 1985a; 1985b, chapters 7 and 8.

and

S = 200 if A has a safe job, 0 if an unsafe job.

B's utility function is symmetrically defined.

Given these opportunities and preferences, the utilities of the four possible combinations of choices are as summarized in Table 1.

		B's Choice	
		Safe job @ $400/mo	Unsafe job @ $500/mo
A's Choice	Safe job @ $400/mo	U = 600 each (Second best for each)	U = 700 for B, 400 for A (Best for B, Worst for A)
	Unsafe job @ $500/mo	U = 400 for B, 700 for A (Best for A, Worst for B)	U = 500 each (Third best for each)

Table 1. Job Safety Choices When Relative Income Matters.

The utility functions used to generate Table 1 tell us that having the safer job is worth $200/mo to each worker. And since the cost of providing the extra safety is only $100/mo, it might seem that the safer job would be the obvious best choice for each. Yet the payoffs in Table 1 confront A and B with a prisoner's dilemma, so there is no reason to feel confident that a socially optimal combination of choices will emerge. On the contrary, the choice of the unsafe job is a dominant strategy for both players, even though each does worse under that combination of choices than if each were to have chosen the safe job. Under these circumstances, there is little mystery about why A and B might favor regulations that mandate greater levels of workplace safety.

Analogous reasoning suggests the possible attraction of a variety of similar regulations on individual choices about the sale of babies and sex. From an individual seller's perspective, the income gained from participating in such transactions is advantageous for two reasons: first, because of the utility of the additional consumption it will support; and second, because it will improve their position in purely relative terms. From the collective vantage point, the second payoff is spurious, since any one person's advance in relative terms necessarily entails a relative decline for others.

Of course, merely to observe that positional concerns render the sale of sex and babies misleadingly attractive to individuals is not to say that these activities should be proscribed completely. On the contrary, the relative position argument says individual incentives are misleadingly high for virtually *everything* we might sell for money—not just safety, babies and sex, but also our leisure time, future job security, and a host of other environmental amenities. The problem is not that we exchange these items for money, but that we sell them too cheaply. In the case of workplace safety, the solution is not to ban risk, but to make it less attractive to individuals. Analogously, the best response in the sexual domain may not be to ban prostitution or the sale of babies, but rather to make these activities less attractive to potential sellers.

The logic of positional externalities also suggests a clear rationale for laws favoring monogamy over polygyny. In polygynous species in the animal kingdom—which is to say most species—dominant males enjoy enormous reproductive payoffs. In one colony of seals, for example, 4 percent of the adult males sired almost 90 percent of all offspring.[7] Not surprisingly, payoffs of this magnitude stimulate intensive competition among males for access to fertile females. This competition manifests itself variously in the form of physical combat and elaborate forms of displays and courtship rituals. And although this competition does often lead to genetic innovations that serve the interests of the species as a whole, for the most part it is profoundly wasteful.

---

7 Dawkins, 1976.

Peacocks as a group, for example, would be better off if each individual's tailfeathers were to shrink by a significant proportion. But these feathers are an important form of courtship display, and the gain to any individual bird from having shorter tailfeathers would be more than offset by the reproductive penalty.

In polygynous human societies, males who rank high in the wealth distribution tend to have disproportionately many wives. Here, too, the struggle for position is often costly. Laws favoring monogamy might thus be viewed as an arms-control agreement of sorts. By preventing the concentration of reproductive success in the hands of a small minority of men, they reduce the incentive to engage in costliest aspects of the struggle to move forward in the relative wealth distribution.

In Posner's narrow version of the rational choice model (which is also the one used by most economists writing today), people care about absolute wealth but not about relative wealth. In this model, the individual pursuit of maximum utility leads to an efficient allocation of resources (abstracting from such difficulties as impulse-control problems, among others). Thus it is natural for Posner to say, in reference to a woman's right to hire another woman to bear a child for her, "I do not see how regulation of that right could be inimical to women's interests as a whole." (p. 424)

There is abundant evidence, however, that concerns about relative wealth loom also large for most people. Under this broader, and more realistic, view of preferences, there is no longer any presumption that individual decisions yield socially optimal allocations. Because one person's forward movement in any wealth hierarchy entails backward moves for others, income-generating activities are misleadingly attractive to individuals. The logic of the broader model thus suggests the possible attraction of policies that make the pursuit of additional wealth less attractive. Taxes on income, workplace safety regulation, and a variety of restrictions on commercial sexual activity fall into this category.

I offer one final speculation about how positional externalities might give rise to demands for regulation of the public display of sexual imagery. Almost all societies have at least some such regulations, which range from legal limitations on hardcore pornography to informal standards governing the use of nudity in magazine advertisements. I suggest that the demand for these restrictions may stem in part from the well-documented finding in experimental psychology that perception and evaluation are strongly dependent on the observer's frame of reference.[8] The ability of the frame of reference to affect perception is called the adaptation effect.

The power of sexual imagery to arouse depends at least in part on its power to surprise or even shock the viewer. But just as the adaptation effect tells us that we cannot predict whether a given light source will seem bright or dim unless we first know the ambient light level, neither can we predict whether a given sexual image will shock the observer unless we have detailed information about the kind of sexual imagery the observer has become accustomed to.

In the 1950s, laws and social norms in the U.S. prevented major national magazines from accepting ads that used nude photographs to draw readers' attention. Advertisers have powerful incentives to chip away at the margins of these norms, and the cumulative result of their efforts has been a continuing shift in the standards that define acceptable imagery. First we saw the nude silhouette; then increasingly well-lighted and detailed nude photographs; and more recently, photographs of what appear to be group sex acts. Each innovation achieved just the desired effect—namely, to draw the reader's instant and rapt attention. Inevitably, however, competing advertisers have followed suit and the effect has been merely to shift the frame of reference for what is considered attention-grabbing. Photographs that once would have shocked readers now often draw little more than a bored glance.

Whether this is a good thing or a bad thing naturally depends on one's view about the public display of sexual imagery. Perhaps the earlier, stricter norms were ill-advised in the first place, the

---

8 See, for instance, Helson, 1964; and Scitovsky, 1976.

legacy of a more prudish and repressive era. And yet even those who take this view are likely also to believe that there are *some* kinds of photographic material that ought not to be used in advertisements in national magazines. There is, in any event, a divergence between the individual and collective payoffs from an escalation in the explicitness of sexual imagery. And once we recognize this divergence, we see the possible attraction of at least some restrictions on the display of sexual imagery.

Concluding Remarks

The rational choice model, even in its most narrow form, has provided countless insights into human behavior. Yet many important behaviors are destined to remain mysterious to scholars armed with only the narrow model. In this essay, I have suggested that two simple modifications to the model can shed light on many common forms of sexual regulation. One modification is that people tend to discount future costs and benefits not exponentially but hyperbolically. The special feature of hyperbolic discounting is that it gives rise to impulse-control problems. People often realize that their true interests are best served by one choice and yet feel irresistibly drawn to another. Anticipating this difficulty, they employ a variety of strategies for steering clear of choices they will later regret. Many laws and institutions—marriage vows, divorce laws, and monogamy, for instance—may be understood as strategies of this sort.

My second modification is to suggest that people care not only about absolute wealth but about relative wealth as well. This modification implies that a seller faces two rewards whenever she sells something in the marketplace—namely, an increase in her absolute wealth and an increase in her relative wealth. The second of these incentives in illusory from the collective vantage point, and this may help explain why we often limit various types of market exchange—among them the sale of labor, safety, babies, and sex. By contrast, the narrow version of the rational choice model implies that such regulations always reduce welfare.

Neither of the modifications I propose is controversial. There is strong evidence that people often discount hyperbolically, and overwhelming evidence that people care about relative wealth. These modifications sharply alter many of the most important implications of the narrow model. In particular, they suggest why intervention may sometimes be more attractive than doing nothing.

Of course, showing that individual choice does not produce the best outcome is not the same as showing that a given regulation will improve matters. Collective intervention is also an imperfect enterprise, and we are all acquainted with cases in which the even the most clearly motivated regulations have made matters worse. Posner is right that before we debate the practical consequences of a given regulation, it is useful to examine whether there was a sound theoretical case for that regulation in the first place. His narrow version of the rational choice model is unfortunately not always a suitable mechanism for trying to answer that question. The alternative version of the model I have sketched provides theoretical support for many of the regulations Posner discusses. It is time for the public policy debate to focus on the practical question of how well these regulations actually work.

References

Ainslie, George. "Specious Reward: A Behavioral Theory of Impulsiveness and Impulse Control," *Psychological Bulletin, 82,* July, 1975: 463-96.

_____. *Picoeconomics: The Strategic Interaction of Successive Motivational States within the Person,* New York: Cambridge University Press, 1992.

Chung, Shin-Ho and Richard Herrnstein. "Choice and Delay of Reinforcement," *Journal of the Experimental Analysis of Behavior, 10,* 1967: 67-74.

Dawkins, Richard. *The Selfish Gene,* NY: Oxford University Press, 1976.

Duesenberry, James. *Income, Saving, and the Theory of Consumer Behavior,* Cambridge, Mass.: Harvard University Press, 1949.

Easterlin, Richard. "Does Economic Growth Improve the Human Lot? Some Empirical Evidence," In *Nations and Households in Economic Growth: Essays in Honor of Moses Abramovitz,* Paul David and Melvin Reder, eds., Palo Alto, CA: Stanford University Press, 1973.

Elster, Jon. *Ulysses and the Sirens,* Cambridge: Cambridge University Press, 1979.

Elster, Jon and George Loewenstein, eds., *Choice Over Time,* New York: Russell Sage, 1993.

Frank, Robert H. "The Demand for Unobservable and Other Nonpositional Goods," *American Economic Review, 75,* March, 1985a: 101-116.

_____. *Choosing the Right Pond: Human Behavior and the Quest for Status,* NY: Oxford University Press, 1985b.

_____. *Passions Within Reason: The Strategic Role of the Emotions,* NY: W. W. Norton, 1988.

Helson, Harry, *Adaptation-Level Theory,* New York: Harper and Row, 1964.

Hirsch, Fred. *Social Limits to Growth,* Cambridge, MA: Harvard University Press, 1976.

Mischel, W. "Preference for Delayed Reinforcement and Social Responsibility, *Journal of Abnormal and Social Psychology, 62,* 1961: 1-7.

Runciman, W. G. *Relative Deprivation and Social Justice,* New York: Penguin, 1966.

Schelling, Thomas. "The Intimate Contest for Self-Command," *The Public Interest,* Summer, 1980: 94-118.

Scitovsky, Tibor, *The Joyless Economy,* NY: Oxford University Press, 1976.

Sen, Amartya. "Poor, Relatively Speaking," *Oxford Economic Papers,* 1983: 153-67.

Thaler, R. and H. Shefrin. "An Economic Theory of Self-Control," *Journal of Political Economy,* 89, 1981: 392-405.

Wilson, James Q. and Richard Herrnstein. *Crime and Human Nature,* New York: Simon & Schuster, 1985.

Winston, Gordon. "Addiction and Backsliding: A Theory of Compulsive Consumption," *Journal of Economic Behavior and Organization, 1,* 1980: 295-394.

The Biological Basis of
The Undue Influence Doctrine[*]

Lawrence A. Frolik[**]

The law review article that this piece is based upon is an example of what Margaret Gruter and the Gruter Institute have achieved: attempts by law professors to synthesize law and biology and to draw upon the insights of evolutionary psychology to illuminate law and legal doctrine. Simply put, without Margaret's efforts to educate law professors about the wisdom of biology, this article and the insights that it contains would never have occurred.

I. Introduction

Our common law heritage reflects society's fundamental values. It is the repository of our aspirations and values, and as those basic values change or are reinterpreted, so must the common law. Laws that remain constant over time demonstrate that they are well aligned with deeper societal values, else they would have been long since modified. When the law is constant, we can assume that indicates a very substantial agreement as to the underlying values. Since the law is agreeable to most, change is unnecessary.

[*] This is an adaption of an article originally published in 57 University of Pittsburgh Law Review 641 (1996)

[**] Professor of Law, University of Pittsburgh School of Law, Pittsburgh, PA.

The common law of probate, of intestate succession, although not static, has been relatively calm. In particular, the common law doctrine of undue influence, now over 200 years old, has remained remarkably fixed. As such, it represents a congruence of law and deeply held social values. If so, just what are those values that the doctrine of undue influence supports?

The attraction and the stability of the undue influence doctrine are attributable to its grounding in basic, instinctual human attitudes towards one's offspring. Simply put, it is human nature for decedents to promote the interests of their descendants even if others, such as friends, other relatives, or faithful employees, seem more deserving based upon their behavior.

The doctrine finds support in the deeply-held cultural belief that favors the passing of wealth along lineal lines of descent. That belief, in turn, arises out of our common genetic heritage. We are the result of generations of genetic imprinting that created reproductive instincts and a predisposition to assist the survival of our descendants. In short, we favor our offspring because our ancestors favored us. As a result we share an unconscious impulse to promote our genetic survival by assisting our genetic descendants. One way we collectively express that instinct is by the use of the doctrine of undue influence.

II. The Doctrine of Undue Influence

The doctrine of undue influence permits an otherwise valid will or testamentary gift to be overturned on the basis that the testamentary bequest represented not the will of the testator, but that of the influencer.[1] As a result, the testator[2] was the victim of undue influence. Originating in the 1780s, the specific elements of the doctrine have been in place for almost 200 years without substantial change.

Apparently, the earliest case that relied on the undue influence doctrine was reported in 1787. In the English case, *Mountain v.*

---

1 The term "influencer" will be used to denote the individual, individuals, or institution who wrongly influenced the testator for his, her, their, or its gain.
2 The term "testator" will be used as a gender neutral term.

Bennet,[3] the plaintiffs challenged a will in which the testator, Bennet, left substantial real estate holdings to his wife, whom he had secretly married only a few months before executing the will. Bennet's heirs claimed that the wife had overcome Bennet's free will to have herself named the beneficiary of the will. As proof, they submitted correspondence by her to a man named Parry, to whom she bragged about the amount of control that she had over Bennet. She later married Parry. The plaintiffs prevailed after the jury was instructed by the judge to reject the will if "the dominion or influence" of another prevented the exercise of independent discretion by the testator.[4]

The next significant case, *Kinleside v. Harrison,*[5] involved a conspiracy to commit undue influence by the testator's vicar, his housekeeper, and a family friend. Though the challenge to the will failed, the case did establish the "confidential relationship"[6] doctrine, which holds that the existence of a confidential relationship in itself is probative of possible undue influence. In America, the undue influence doctrine can be traced back to 1839 in the New York case of *Gardner v. Gardner,*[7] in which a court found no undue influence by a second wife over the objections of children from the first marriage.

During the nineteenth century the doctrine of undue influence was gradually developed in a number of cases. Over time it came to have a fairly standard definition, expressed as: "Something must operate upon the mind of a person allegedly unduly influenced which has a controlling effect sufficient to destroy the person's free agency and to render the instrument not properly an expression of the person's wishes, but rather the expression of the wishes of

---

3   29 Eng. Rep. 1200 (1787) (Eng.).

4   Id. at 1211.

5   161 Eng. Rep. 1196 (1818) (Eng.).

6   Confidential relationship is defined as the relation which exists between client and attorney, principal and agent, principal and surety, landlord and tenant, parent and child, guardian and ward, ancestor and heir, husband and wife, and executors or administrators and creditors. Robins v. Hope, 57 Cal. 493 (1881). In these cases the law, in order to prevent undue advantage from the unlimited confidence or sense of duty which the relation creates, requires the utmost degree of good faith in all transactions between the parties. Ballentine's Law Dictionary 244 (3d ed. 1969).

7   22 Wend. 526 (N.Y. 1839).

another or others."[8]   Undue influence is the destruction of the free agency of the testator, and the substitution of the will of another.

The elements of the doctrine of undue influence took a few years to evolve, with earliest cases often mixing together undue influence, duress and lack of capacity. By the twentieth century, however, the modern version of undue influence had been worked out so that today almost all jurisdictions recognize five elements or variants on them as being the necessary components of a cause of action. They are:

1. the testator was susceptible to the influence of others;
2. the testator and the alleged influencer had a confidential relationship;
3. the influencer used that relationship to secure a change in the testator's distribution of property under the will;
4. there was in fact a change of the distribution plan because of the influencer's actions; and
5. the change was unconscionable or at least did not express the true desires of the testator.

The traditional elements of the undue influence doctrine, when listed and examined in the context of the case law, seem to make sense. They do, that is, if you accept the notion that there is anything like undue influence. Think about it for just a moment, and ask yourself how is it that one person can unduly influence another, absent the use of duress, misinformation, or fraud? Just what is the difference between legally permitted influence and "undue influence?"

For example, suppose I befriend my childless, widowed, elderly uncle who lives in a nursing home. Over time I become his close advisor and confidant. At age 80, he announces that he intends to write a new will. He has no lawyer, no accountant; only me, to advise him. To help my uncle draft a new will, I call up my college roommate, Eric, now a lawyer, who comes to the nursing home. I introduce him to my uncle and leave the room. The next day Eric returns while I am visiting my uncle. We discuss the will and note

---

8   Hardee v. Hardee, 309 S.E.2d 243, 245 (N.C. 1983).

that it leaves everything to me. My uncle signs the will without witnesses (this is Pennsylvania and none are needed) and asks me to pay Eric, promising to repay me (prior to his moving to the nursing home I often paid for things that he needed and he usually repaid me). I pay Eric.[9] My uncle dies two days later without repaying me.

Now, is this undue influence at the expense of my cousins, or has my uncle merely favored the nephew who was the most kind and helpful to him? All of my actions towards my uncle could be interpreted as having been part of scheme to ease my way into his life and capture his estate. Conversely, I could be seen as the "very model"[10] of a helpful nephew, a most deserving beneficiary of my uncle's gratitude. How to choose between these two interpretations?

Since the actions are the same, the preferred explanation depends on my *motives* for my behavior. If I acted kindly towards my uncle with no thought of reward, I should not be found guilty of undue influence.

The world of motives, however, does not divide so easily into those with pure motives and those of base ones. Most of us operate under a number of motives, some saintlike, others less praiseworthy. A potential beneficiary who acts kindly towards an older person may do so for any number of reasons ranging from altruism to obligation, from the enjoyment of the act of kindness to an intense hope for a bequest. Those who are kind to the old may not themselves understand their conflicting motives.

The use of the doctrine of undue influence to overturn gifts by testators who had the capacity to make a valid will rests on assumptions about human nature and particularly about older persons that are very problematical. The doctrine of undue influence assumes that someone can substitute his or her will for that of another.

---

9   Even though I pay the lawyer, his client is my uncle. Model Rules of Professional Conduct Rule 1.7 cmt. (1992).

10 "The very model of a major general." Gilbert & Sullivan, Pirates of Penzance (RCA Records 1966).

What is the assumption about human psychology that supports the concept of undue influence? In particular, since almost all unduly influenced testators are older, what does the doctrine suggest about the rights of older persons to leave their property as they see fit? Without belaboring the point, little in modern psychology supports the doctrine of undue influence. Certainly, individuals can become caught up in cults, but in those cases there is a real issue of the competency of the cult victim. But in most undue influence cases, the victim is not placed under the psychological pressure, duress, fear of rejection, and religious dogma duress that we associate with cults. Certainly, the testator has a close (confidential) relationship with the alleged undue influencer, but that is true for the vast number of gifts made by will. To whom else should decedents leave their wealth? The answer, of those who sue to overturn a will on the basis of undue influence, is, naturally, to those who have sued to overturn the will.

Under probate law, however, the interests and wants of those who petition to void a will count for nothing. Rather, for hundreds of years testators have been free, with the exception of the rights of spouses, to leave their property as they wish. Freedom of testamentary disposition has been described as "one of the basic tenets of our social structure."[11] The doctrine of undue influence, by permitting courts to void testamentary gifts by testators, undercuts this basic principle.

The success and longevity of the doctrine of undue influence suggests that courts (and society) believe that older persons are susceptible to the schemes of others in a way that is not true of younger people (almost no cases of undue influence involve younger persons), and so execute wills that represent the wishes of an influencer. But this reasoning makes little sense if we accept that the testator had the capacity to write a valid will, since the very definition of capacity is that the testator "knew" what he or she was doing. Can a testator really be said to have capacity and yet write

---

11 Joseph W. deFuria, Jr., Testamentary Gifts Resulting from Meretricious Relationships: Undue Influence or Natural Beneficence?, 64 Notre Dame L. Rev. 200, 200 (1989).

a will as if he or she was in the thrall of another? Surely, if a testator is unwittingly carrying out the wishes of another, it is bizarre to say that the testator has the legal capacity to write a will. If the will emanated from the influencer and not the testator because the latter lacked the requisite capacity, the will should be voided because of a finding of a lack of capacity. Indeed, almost all undue influence cases cite a finding of diminished capacity along with the finding of undue influence.

A finding of a lack of testamentary capacity is not required as the basis for invalidating the will, however, if the elements of undue influence are present. The two ways of voiding a will, testamentary incapacity and undue influence, interact as if on an imaginary seesaw. In concert they operate to overturn otherwise valid wills; as the extent of incapacity rises, the degree of undue influence declines, and conversely, as incapacity declines, the greater must be the proof of undue influence. As stated by one court, "[t]he facts constituting the undue influence are required to be far stronger in the case of a testator whose mind is strong and alert than in the case of one whose mind is defective or impaired by disease or advancing age."[12] Testamentary incapacity and undue influence operate as the proverbial one-two punch to bring down suspect wills.

Courts are reluctant to rely solely on a finding of incapacity for fear that to do so would gradually raise the standard of the degree of testamentary capacity needed to execute a valid will. Were that to happen, many older persons of marginal capacity would be barred from writing a will or revising a preexisting will, thereby causing more estates to pass by intestacy or preventing some individuals from changing their testamentary bequests. Either of these outcomes would conflict with the societal goals of avoidance of intestacy and protection of the rights of individuals to leave their estates to whomsoever they please. Therefore, selective reliance upon the undue influence doctrine (rather then finding a lack of testamentary capacity) helps preserve the low level of capacity that is needed to write a valid will. In instances where there is not even

---

12 Dunklin v. Black, 275 S.W.2d 447, 449 (Ark. 1955).

a hint of undue influence, the doctrine permits testators with very low levels of capacity, too low even for them to manage their own property during life, nevertheless to direct its passage at their deaths.

The support that the doctrine of undue influence provides for the low testamentary capacity standard comes at a cost, however, by permitting a will to be invalidated because of judicial disapproval of the testamentary plan of distribution.[13] A finding of undue influence requires convincing a court that the testator left an unnatural gift to someone with whom the testator had a close (confidential) relationship. This has the practical effect of placing almost any unusual gift at risk since few testators leave a substantial gift to a mere acquaintance or a stranger. The willingness of courts to overturn these unnatural or unusual bequests seems itself unnatural, but closer examination of the categories of cases in which undue influence is found discloses deeply held societal attitudes about the proper disposition of assets that explain the judicial willingness to overturn wills on the basis of the substantive testamentary plan of distribution.

The answer lies in our biological heritage. We are predisposed to leaving a legacy to our children by our own genetic and cultural legacies, which impel us towards leaving our children as well equipped as possible for reproductive success.[14] Genetically, we are designed to want to assist our children to be reproductively successful; culturally, that translates into socializing them, educating them, and bestowing material well-being upon them. As individuals we feel the pull towards creating an estate and leaving it to our descendants. Consequently as a culture we embrace and endorse the right of wealth accumulation and the freedom of testation. Leaving one's wealth to one's descendants is a firmly established cultural norm. The desire for dynastic support is so strong that

---

13 Of course, in some cases the finding of undue influence will be made by a jury. If the case is appealed, however, the ultimate decision will be made by the appellate court judges.

14 Martin Smith et al., Inheritance of Wealth As Human Kin Investment, 8 Ethology & Sociobiology 171 (1987).

society, in deference of other values, has found it necessary to enact the Rule Against Perpetuities to limit accumulation of wealth across time. Conversely, more radical attempts to bar inheritance find almost no support.

Cultures can and have expressed the desire to aid descendants in different ways. Primogeniture, for instance, comes to mind as one alternative that expresses the desire to assist progeny in a distinct manner.[15] Other cultures have adopted alternative methods. For the last few hundred years, however, our culture and social norms have favored equal division among the children (assuming there is no surviving spouse). Indeed, when the testamentary pattern of a will violates that norm, eyebrows are lifted and questions are asked. While an unequal treatment of children might not be considered wrong, still it at least invites an explanation and creates the presumption that the disadvantaged children did something to incur the displeasure of the testator. As a culture or society, we share the unarticulated belief that testators without spouses can be expected to leave their wealth to their lineal descendants and to do so in roughly equal proportions.[16] When a will transgresses the norm, everyone, judges and juries included, is likely to look for a reason. It is not sufficient to state the obvious–that a testator may do what he or she feels best. If the unusual property division is challenged by a lawsuit, the burden of going forward (merely the legal term for the question, "So why did you do that?") often shifts, if only in a practical sense, to those who would defend the acts of the testator. It is human nature, in a word, that is the basis for the doctrine of undue influence, for it is that concept that permits both the law (society) to overturn bequests that are found to be "unconscionable."

Courts are thus drawn to the doctrine of undue influence by the common sense notion that something is amiss when testators violate

---

15 Primogeniture has been explained in Darwinian terms as the means by which a wealthy father, by leaving everything to one son, gives him the economic status and means to become a successful adulterer and beget many bastard children. A wealthy daughter gains no such advantage. Matt Ridley, The Red Queen 239 (1994).

16 John H. Beckstrom, Sociobiology and Intestate Wealth Transfers, 76 Nw. U. L. Rev. 216 (1981).

the norm and favor outsiders over their descendants, or even if they unduly favor one child over the others. If courts were bound to the basic binary capacity test–did or did not the testator have the requisite capacity–they would have no way of intervening even if they disliked the testamentary plan of distribution. To overtly declare that bequests could be overturned merely because courts thought them to be unwise, however, would be indefensible judicial intervention. The doctrine of undue influence circumvents that dilemma by inventing a new category: the testator whose will expresses the intent of another. Never mind that the doctrine has no objective limit in its applicability, since almost any bequest can be seen as reflecting the notion that it was somehow the result of the acts of the beneficiary. To prove undue influence, there is no need to show that the influencer actually requested that the gift be made, much less actually prove that the influencer forced his or her will upon the testator. A mere showing of the opportunity to do so (a confidential relationship) is usually enough for a finding of undue influence.

The willingness of courts to apply the undue influence doctrine, however, is likely to be severely tested in the years to come. With the projected increase in the number of older Americans, the number of undue influence claims is likely to grow exponentially. The growth in numbers of older testators will increase the potential numbers of undue influence challenges, since successful undue influence claims are almost always associated with older testators. Other factors will also contribute to a sharp rise in undue influence claims. First, the value of assets held by older testators is growing rapidly. As the stakes increase, so will the number of challenges to wills by older testators. Second, the fastest growing age cohort is the group over age 85. A substantial number of these individuals will experience a loss of mental capacity and therefore be more susceptible, or will be thought of as being more susceptible, to undue influence. These very old testators are also more likely to outlive friends, close relatives, and even children and thus to take up with individuals who might have designs on their assets. Third, the conditions which bring forth will contests are increasing at a more rapid rate than the growth in the number of older persons.

Claims of undue influence are most likely to occur when the testator makes a substantial testamentary gift to someone other than his or her closest relative. (This assumes that there is no surviving spouse of long duration; surviving spouses of a recent marriage, however, are often accused of undue influence by children of previous marriages. Disproportionate gifts to relatives can also trigger undue influence claims.[17]) In a traditional nuclear family, i.e. a surviving parent who was married only once and had "x" number of surviving children, the conditions that support undue influence may exist, but the doctrine is more likely to be successfully invoked under broken or blended family situations. For example, a divorced or widowed testator may be lonely and more likely to take up with a friend or lover and leave him a substantial bequest. The testator's children may resent the perceived interloper taking away "their" inheritance. Similarly, a divorced testator may remarry and have children from the first marriage, stepchildren from the second marriage, and children from the second marriage. The possibility is ripe for perceived "unfairness" in the distribution scheme when so many have a legitimate claim for a bequest.

Another factor also that will contribute to an increase in claims of undue influence is the likelihood of some elderly upon retirement to move, often far away from family and longtime friends. Alone in a new environment they acquire new friends, new professional advisors, and new religious advisors; any one of whom can be accused of being an undue influencer. In addition there are an increasing number of frail older persons who receive home health care and so are exposed to caretakers who have an extraordinary opportunity to forge a close relationship.[18]

---

17 E.g., Murray v. Laird, 446 So. 2d 575 (Miss. 1984); Troyer v. Plackett, 617 P.2d 305 (Or. 1980); Rosenberg's Estate v. Strure, 246 P.2d 858 (Or. 1952).
18 Charles Longino, From Sunbelts to Sunspots, Am. Demographics, Nov. 1994.

With the probable increase in the number of claims of undue influence, it will be interesting to observe the law's reaction. If, as this article has postulated, the attraction of the doctrine is our culturally shared belief in the obligation of a testator to leave assets to lineal descendants, the doctrine may find less support as more complex family arrangements fail to produce a "natural" scheme of testamentary distribution.

Is it time to step away from the doctrine of undue influence? Possibly, but that is not a viable option. It is too deeply ingrained in case law and too closely aligned with public prejudices to be swept aside. The more attainable goal is the diminution of successful will challenges based upon undue influence. Courts need to become more skeptical as to the ease with which older persons can be influenced when making out their wills. Certainly, the standard for challenging a will in which an attorney excessively participates in the drafting for his or her own benefit should be maintained (although as pointed out, this could better be handled as a transgression of professional responsibility). Other claims of influence, however, should be resisted absent a clear showing of severely reduced mental capacity on the part of the testator.

Absent such a sea change in societal attitudes towards the elderly and testation, however, the doctrine of undue influence will continue to be applied. The only hope is to limit its use by understanding the motives and fears that give it continued vitality.

The genetic drive to favor one's lineal descendants is a very real drive, but it is not an instinct, such as the beating of a heart, that we cannot overcome or temper. Indeed, an awareness of its influence on our behavior and attitudes is the first step in controlling it. Though we need not succumb to it, neither do we need to reject it in toto. It is enough that we are aware of its existence and bend to its will only to the degree that reason dictates. Just as levees can contain, but not control, a powerful river, so should the doctrine of undue influence be kept under a watchful judicial eye else it wash away the best-laid testator plans.

The Nature of Business:
Bringing the Insights of Biologically Informed Behavioral Science to Business and the Law

Oliver R. Goodenough*

Introduction

Law is an applied behavioral science. Not only is law's essential purpose regulating human behavior, but the legal system and its workings are themselves human behavior. Anyone seeking to understand the law must start with a theory—express or implicit—of why people act the way they do. This simple understanding is one of the intellectual gifts I have received from Dr. Margaret Gruter over the last decade. In her extraordinary and productive career she has also tirelessly reminded the legal academy of the importance of the mind as the initiator of behavior and of the influence of

* Professor of Law, Vermont Law School, South Royalton, VT.

evolutionary biology in giving content to the mind's work. By her writings,[1] her organizational talents, her force of personality and her perseverance, she has brought the insights of biologically informed behavioral science to a place of prominence in legal scholarship. Her creation, The Gruter Institute for Law and Behavioral Research, has become the world's leading intellectual organization devoted to these questions, sponsoring research, writing, conferences and training around the globe.[2]

The founding of the Society for Evolutionary Analysis in Law ("SEAL") in 1998 provides clear and convincing evidence that Dr. Gruter's work has born human fruit. And as she enters her 9th decade she is still catalyzing new interdisciplinary approaches, forging new connections, and ferreting out new sources of support. Too often celebratory volumes such as this must dwell on past achievements. Not so with Dr. Gruter.

As a Gruter Institute Research Fellow, over the past decade I have benefitted in many ways from the opportunities that Dr. Gruter creates. In the upcoming year I will be director of a new project:

---

1   As author, editor and contributor, Dr. Gruter has participated in more than 14 publications on these issues since 1976. These publications include: Gruter, M., Die Bedeutung der Verhaltensforschung für die Rechtswissenschaft, Schriftenreihe zur Rechtssoziologie und Rechtstatsachenforschung, Band 36, Berlin: Duncker & Humblot.,1976; Gruter, M., Law in Sociobiological Perspective, Florida State University Law Review, Vol. 5, p.181-218,1977; Gruter, M., The origins of legal behavior, Journal of Biological Structure, 2:43-51, 1979; Gruter, M., Soziobiologische Grundlagen der Effektivität des Rechts, Rechtstheorie, Zeitschrift für Logik, Methodenlehre, Kybernetik und Soziologie des Rechts, 11 Band, Heft 1, Berlin: Duncker & Humblot, 1980, p. 96-109; Gruter, M. and Bohannan, P. (eds.), Law, Biology and Culture: The Evolution of Law. San Francisco: Ross-Erikson, 1983; Gruter M. and Rehbinder, M., Der Beitrag der Biologie zu Fragen von Recht und Ethik, Gruter, M. and Rehbinder, M. (eds.), Schriftenreihe zur Rechtssoziologie und Rechtstatsachenforschung, Band 54. Berlin: Duncker & Humblot, 1983; Gruter, M. and Masters, R.D. (eds.), Ostracism: A Social and Biological Phenomenon. Elsevier: New York; Gruter, M. and Rehbinder, M. (eds.), Ablehnung—Meidung—Ausschluss. In: Schriftenreihe zur Rechtssoziologie und Rechtstatsachenforschung, Band 60, Berlin: Duncker & Humblot, 1986; Gruter, M. (ed.), Behavior, Evolution and the Sense of Justice, American Behavioral Scientist, Volume 34. Newbury Park, California: Sage.1991; Gruter, M., Law and the Mind: Biological Origins of Human Behavior. Newbury Park, California: Sage, 1991; Gruter, M. and Bohannan, P. (eds.), Law, Biology and Culture, (2d Ed.) McGraw-Hill Primis 1992; Gruter, M., Rechtsverhalten - Biologische Grundlagen mit Beispielen aus dem Familien-und Umweltrecht. Verlag Dr. Otto Schmidt. Köln, Germany, 1993.

2   Information on the programs and achievements of the Gruter Institute is available on its web site, at www.gruterinstitute.org.

the Gruter Institute Business Initiative. In the past, the Gruter Institute has brought together interdisciplinary teams from such areas as medicine, biology, ethology, neuroscience, anthropology, political science, economics and law. Recurring centers of attention have been law and governmental policy. Within the law, crime, family issues, environmental problems, reproductive rights, and intellectual property have been frequent themes.[3] Less attention has been given to date to the impact that this work can have on economic activity, in particular business. The Initiative will seek to redress this. Much of the law involves the structuring and regulation of business and finance. As adults, working, shopping and other economic activities consume the majority of our waking hours. The discipline of economics is the one area of behavioral study with pervasive influence over the law. As a country "the business of America is business." Given the importance of business in law and society and the rapid advance of biologically informed behavioral science, there has been surprisingly little work bringing the two together.

The purpose of this paper is to lay out the intellectual starting points for the Gruter Institute's goal of helping to integrate the study of biology, business and law. In the process it may remind us of the ongoing need for Dr. Gruter's work both in and beyond her chosen discipline of the law.

The Insights of Biology

In this volume it is hardly necessary to belabor the contributions that evolutionary biology and its related fields have made to our understanding of how living things—including humans—operate. While there is some rear-guard skirmishing,[4] the notion of that human behavior is purely a social construct is simply untenable. Indeed, with a few exceptions, even the "biophobes" in the behavioral sciences would not take so extreme a position. After

---

3 A comprehensive bibliography of Gruter Institute-sponsored works also appears at www.gruterinstitute.org.

4 See, e.g., Gould, Stephen J., The Mismeasure of Man (2d ed.), New York: W.W. Norton & Co., 1996.

decades of vilification, there is an emerging consensus that humans are a composite of biology and culture, of genes and experience, of nature and nurture.[5] As E.O. Wilson put it in his recent book, CONSILIENCE:

> A century of misunderstanding, the drawn-out Verdun and Somme of Western intellectual history, has run its exhausting course, and the culture wars are an old game turned stale. It is time to call a truce and forge an alliance. Within the broad middle ground between the strong versions of the Standard Social Science Model and genetic determinism, the social sciences are intrinsically compatible with the natural sciences.[6]

We may legitimately argue about the makeup of the bio-social mix, but denial of its existence is right up there with the flat earth as a scientific proposition.

In some ways, public understanding is out ahead of the academy on this issue. It is worth remarking on the degree to which the realization that biology influences people's behavior has penetrated the popular conciousness. As the ECONOMIST editorialized in an August 1997 special issue with Darwin on the cover:

---

5 See, e.g., Blakemore, Susan J., The Meme Machine, New York: Oxford University Press, 1999; Boyd, R. and Richerson, P. Culture and the Evolutionary Process, Chicago: University of Chicago Press, 1985; Cavalli-Sforza, L.L. and Feldman, M. Cultural Transmission and Evolution: A Quantitative Approach, Princeton, N.J.: Princeton University Press, 1981; Flinn, M.R. Culture and the Evolution of Social Learning, Evolution and Human Behavior, Vol. 18, p.23-67, 1997; Goldsmith, Timothy H., The Biological Roots of Human Behavior: Forging Links Between Evolution and Behavior, New York: Oxford University Press, 1991; Goodenough, Oliver R., Mind viruses: culture, evolution and the puzzle of altruism, Social Science Information, Vol. 34, p. 287-320, 1994; Goodenough, O.R. and Dawkins, R. The St. Jude mind virus. Nature, Vol. 37, p. 6492, 1994; Lumsden, C.J. and Wilson, E.O. Genes, Mind and Culture, Cambridge: Harvard University Press, 1981; and Wright, Robert, The Moral Animal: The New Science of Evolutionary Psychology, New York: Pantheon Books, 1994.
6 Wilson, Edward O., Consilience, The Unity of Knowledge, New York: Knopf, 1998.

Recent science shows that, even more than you might suppose, people are animals. Evolutionary imperatives have left their signature on the human mind in ways that are both obvious and subtle, much as they have left their mark on the behavior of other creatures. Like other animals, humans are driven to eat, survive and reproduce—and as science reveals ever more about the complexities of these drives and the behavior that express them in the animal world, it sheds ever more light on human nature.

This realization is also reaching the world of business. After all, business, like the law, is human behavior, although of somewhat different kind. And if the insights of evolutionary biology and its related fields into people are becoming generally accepted, it is time for a systematic and directed program that will bring those insights to bear on business. In short, it is time for what Margaret Gruter, as a kind of living emblem of E.O. Wilson's process of "consilience," does so well. This is the impetus behind the Gruter Institute Business Initiative.

We believe that many areas of business can be illuminated by an understanding of biology, evolution, neuroscience and the law. Management issues of leadership, motivation, interpersonal dynamics, corporate culture and gender relations all implicate biological factors and the legal framework which regulates our conduct. Sales and marketing efforts succeed by mobilizing human desires and compulsions. Work as diverse as Gordon Getty's *Total Return Economics*[7] and Jack Hersleifer's classic *Economics from a Biological Viewpoint*[8] suggest that the winds of economics and finance follow evolutionary patterns. Even the business cycle may have parallels in the mathematics of population growth and crash.

---

7 Getty, Gordon P., Total Return Economics, 1999. Copy on file with the Author.
8 Hirshleifer, Jack, Economics from a Biological Viewpoint, Journal of Law and Economics, Vol. 20, p. 1-52, 1977.

The Nature of Business: A Broad Field of Enquiry

Of course, a combination with so much potential has occurred to others, and the inquiry into the nature of business is already underway. Business scholarship is starting to recognize that there are significant insights into behavior just waiting to be applied.[9] Nigel Nicholson, Professor and Dean of Research at the London Business School, wrote a ground-breaking 1998 article in THE HARVARD BUSINESS REVIEW entitled *How Hardwired Is Human Behavior?* Nicholson reviews a number of the tenants of evolutionary psychology and suggests that managers of businesses should start taking them into account:

> What are executives to make of the evolutionary psychologist's view of the world? One alternative is to disagree, on the grounds that it is nurture, not nature, that makes us who we are. Another route is to consider the implications of evolutionary psychology as you consider managerial problems. Or on the far end of the continuum, you can use that perspective as you design your company.[10]

Coming at the problem from the other side, scientists such as E.O. Wilson, Frans de Waal and Helen Fisher are increasingly speaking to business audiences about their work. As an example of the two worlds coming together, the June 1999 Forbes CEO Conference was entitled "Corporate Darwinism."[11] Against this background of existing activity, the Gruter Institute Business

---

9 A small sampling of these efforts includes: Chattoe, Edmund, The Use of Evolutionary Algorithms in Economics: Metaphors or Models for Social Interaction?, Many- Agent Simulation and Artificial Life, E. Hildband and J. Stender, Eds., Amsterdam: ISO Press, 1994; Livia Markoczy and Jeff Goldberg, Management Organization and Human Nature, Managerial and Decision Economics, Vol. 19, p.387-409 (1998); Nigel Nicholson, Seven Deadly Syndromes of Management and Organization, The View from Evolutionary Psychology, Managerial and Decision Economics, Vol. 19, p. 411-426 (1998).

10 Nicholson, Nigel, How Hardwired is Human Behavior? Harvard Business Review, July-August 1998, 134-147, Reprint 98406, at 146-147.

11 Information on this conference, whose speakers are scheduled to include E.O. Wilson, Frans deWaal, Stuart Kaufman, Benoit Mandelbrot and Daniel Goleman, has appeared at www.forbes.com/conf/CEO99/index.htm.

Initiative hopes to accelerate the process, combining people and ideas to bring the interaction of business, biology and law to rapid and rigorous fruition.

The Gruter Institute Business Initiative intends to keep law as an important ingredient in the interaction. Business and law are deeply intertwined, whether it be in workplace rules, corporate structures, or the regulation of financial markets. The knowledge gained in the process will often be only half digested if it is not taken into account by the legal system as well as by management, labor, finance and the other players in the business world.

Fields for Investigation

As a starting point, the Initiative will divide the areas in which biologically informed thinking can illuminate business issues into four broad, and sometimes overlapping, fields of study. The first field involves <u>workplace behavior</u>. Wherever humans go, whether to work or play, at home or at the office, they bring with them the needs and drives that make them humans. At a deeply important level, human behavior is not fully "rational." Our actions are the result of a combination of cognitive agents and deeply rooted motivations. On the job, in addition to the the supposedly economic agenda of the business itself, there are issues of hierarchy, status and aggression, group cohesion, conflict resolution, gender relations, and risk assessment in which our human nature makes itself all too clearly evident.[12] Only by confronting this mix can we make intelligent choices—and intelligent laws—about life in the workplace. Furthermore, these dynamics play out in the cubicles and the boardrooms. Nobody is "above" these considerations. A knowledge of "Boardroom Primatology" should be invaluable in understanding many problems of mergers and acquisitions.

The second field involves <u>marketing, sales, and negotiation</u>, focusing on the arts of communication and persuasion. In order to sell something, or to negotiate successfully, it is necessary to

---

12 See, e.g., Nicholson, supra note 10, and generally Goleman, Daniel, Working with Emotional Intelligence, New York: Bantam Books, 1998.

influence the behavior of people outside the organization, to convince them to take actions which will be to your benefit. Negotiation tactics and the non-verbal cues which underlie so many of them deeply reflect human nature.[13]   Among good marketers there is a widely-shared working understanding of the influence of biologically-fixed desires on getting attention and making a sale. The power of a bikini-clad Swedish Women's Beach Volleyball Team to sell beer is not rooted in the more rational areas of the masculine mind. Cornell professor Robert Frank has argued that the status games behind many aspects of consumerism are deeply rooted in our evolved psychology.[14]

Web sites and other computer products need to be not only user-friendly, but also, at a deeply effective level, user-attractive. The line between computer video games and day-trading web sites is shrinking. Consumer protection laws should take into account how human brains perceive and process product-related information.   Here the insights of such disciplines as cognitive neuroscience and evolutionary psychology will not so much open people's eyes as they will refine, strengthen and direct the existing vision.

The third field is <u>organizational behavior</u>, viewed broadly to include both the human interactions that create organizations and the dynamics of organizations themselves. There is an academic history of viewing organizations through an evolutionary lens. For instance, the field of "Community Ecology" uses biologically influenced tools drawn in part from population ecology to explain the competitive life-cycles of organizations.[15]   Researchers in

---

13 See, e.g., Drolet, Aimee L. and Morris, Morris, Michael W., Rapport in Conflict Resolution: Accounting for how Nonverbal Exchange Fosters Coordination on Mutually Beneficial Settlements to Mixed Motive Conflicts, Stanford Graduate School of Business Faculty Research Paper, Number 1477, 1998, available at www-gsb.stanford.edu/research/paper/abstract/rpindex.htm.

14 E.g. Frank, Robert H., Luxury Fever: Why Money fails to Satisfy in an Era of Excess, New York; Free Press, 1999. See also Miller, Geoffrey F., Waste: A sexual critique of consumerism, 1998, essay on file with the author.

15 See, e.g., Astley, W.G., The Two Ecologies: Population and Community Perspectives on Organizational Evolution, Administrative Science Quarterly, Vol. 30, p. 224-241, 1985; Dollinger, M. The Evolution of Collective Strategies in Fragmented Industries, Academy of Management Review, Vol. 15, No. 2, 1990; Hannan, M. & Freeman, J., The Ecology of Organizational Mortality: National Labor Unions 1836-1985; American Journal of Sociology, Vol. 94, p. 25-52, 1988; Hawley, A., Human Ecology: A Theory of Community Structure, New York: Ronald Press, 1950; Tushman, M., Newman, W., and Romanelli, E., Managing the Unsteady Pace of Organizational Evolution, California Management Review, Vol. 29, No. 1, p. 1-16, 1986; Tushman, M. & Romanelli, E. Organization Evolution: A Metamorphosis Model of Convergence and Reorientation, in Cummings, L.L. & Staw, B. Research in Organizational Be

cultural evolution are turning their attention to organizational sub-sets in society as well.[16] As work goes forward in this field, other useful disciplines will include ecology, population dynamics, information theory, and other biologically grounded approaches to interacting groups. Additional issues to be attacked include mergers and acquisitions, corporate cultures, learning organizations, accounting and business evaluation, strategies for growth, and organizational self-reinvention.

The final field in this classification involves the more general questions of <u>economics and econometrics</u>. Economic activity is human biology at work. Making this connection explicit will enrich the theory and practice of the study of economics. Game theory has provided one productive avenue for communication between evolutionary and economic research. This shared approach, however, is grounded in the rational actor model which has been at the core of traditional economic thinking. The success of this model as the basis for economic theories results from its accuracy in emulating *one* of the ways the human brain works. Its failures result from the same factor. There are a number of other ways that the brain works, as some economic scholarship is starting to realize. One promising set of developments has taken the label "behavioral economics," and has started to examine more nuanced models of human cognition, including evolutionary psychology.[17] On a somewhat different line of approach, biologically informed analysis can help solve such formal problems in the behavior of markets.[18]

---

16 Current work in progress by David Sloan Wilson and by Robert Boyd and Peter Richerson focus on these issues. See, e.g., work presented at "The Biology of Belief and Trust: Has Natural Selection Shaped a Capacity of Subjective Commitment?" at the ISR Evolution and Human Adaptation Program, University of Michigan, April 9-10, 1999.

17 See, e.g., Ulan, Thomas S., The Growing Pains of Behavioral Law and Economics, Vanderbilt Law Review, Vol. 51, p. 1747-1763, 1998, and see also the other articles in that useful symposium issue.

18 See, e.g., Bikhchandani, Sushil, Hirshleifer, David, and Welch, Ivo, Learning from the Behavior of Others: Conformity, Fads, and Informational Cascades, Journal of Evolutionary Perspectives, 12:3:151-170, Summer 1998.

Method of Approach

How does one stimulate an intellectual initiative as broad and as deep as the application of evolutionary thinking to the world of business? Perhaps fools rush in where angels fear to tread, but the history of the Gruter Institute demonstrates that planning and persistence can move academic mountains. In its strategy for carrying out this program, the Institute will pursue three staged, if overlapping, objectives. The first stage will identify issues and resources; the second will bring the resources to bear on the issues to develop useful applications; the third will bring these applications to the business and academic communities. The Initiative will also target revenue sources, both from grants and from information consumers, to help support its activities. Except where specifically commissioned work is being carried out, the intellectual content will be subject to an open, academic model of general dissemination, subject to the normal author's rights in a particular expression of the ideas developed.

The first steps have been taken. As of the Spring of 1999 there has already been a very productive gathering of scholars at Berkeley to launch the first stage. Participants from institutions as varied as Stanford Business School, Boalt Hall School of Law and the Department of Biology at the University of California at Davis made significant progress in narrowing the issues of workplace behavior and in sketching in the outlines of other applications. Additional sessions are planned for the upcoming months.

In pursuing these stages, those working on the project will (i) identify existing scholars, scholarship and programs which bring biological, neurological and evolutionary knowledge to bear on business and the laws governing business; (ii) work with these scholars to identify an intellectual framework for applying these disciplines to business; (iii) identify and make contact with scholars, programs, and business people with an eye to recruiting teachers, customers and funders; (iv) work to identify and pursue new funding sources interested in supporting work in this field; (v) plan conferences, training seminars, publications, and other programs which are to be the near-term fruit of this process; and (vi) develop strategies and opportunities for the Institute and its community to provide consulting services to businesses on these matters. The list is not surprising. As with most strategies the trick is more in the execution than in the conception.

Conclusions?—No, Beginnings

This essay is not really susceptible to a conclusion; rather, it marks a beginning, yet another beginning on an ambitious intellectual project under the leadership of Margaret Gruter. The ground looks fertile. Dr. Gruter knows how to make new fields bloom. I look forward to helping in the garden.

Der evolutionären Entwicklung von Werten auf der Spur
Ein Werkstattbericht

Herbert Helmrich[*]

Gliederung

I.   Margaret Gruters weiterführender Ansatz

II.   Der Tier-Mensch-Vergleich

III. Motivierte Verhaltenssysteme und der Rechtsgüter- bzw. Rechtswerteschutz insbesondere im Strafrecht

IV.   Die funktionale Ordnung motivierter Verhaltenssysteme und ihr rechtlicher Schutz

1.   Funktionsbereich der Selbsterhaltung

2.   Funktionsbereich der Fortpflanzung

3.   Funktionsbereich der Koordination

V.   Motivierte Verhaltenssysteme und Rechtsgüterschutz – eine zufällige Korrelation oder ein evolutionärer kausaler Prozeß?

---

[*]   Member, Legislature, State of Mecklenberg - Vorpommern, Schwerin, Germany.

I. Margaret Gruters weiterführender Ansatz

Margaret Gruter kann auf eine mehr als 25jährige Befassung mit den Beziehungen, die zwischen Biologie und Recht bestehen, zurückblicken.[1] Es ist ihr Ziel „die Kluft zwischen Biologie und Recht zu überbrücken"[2]. Bei ihren interdisziplinären Bemühungen stieß sie immer wieder auf die „intellektuelle Isolation", die, wie sie schreibt, „als unvermeidliches Nebenprodukt entsteht, wenn verschiedene akademische und professionelle Disziplinen ihre Interessen- und Fachgebiete definieren"[3].

Sie hält die Überbrückung der Kluft zwischen Biologie und Recht für erforderlich, um durch eine bessere - biologische - Kenntnis des Menschen und seiner Sozialstrukturen zu geeigneteren Gesetzen, besserer Gesetzesauslegung und -anwendung zu kommen. Sie schreibt: „Um effektiv bleiben zu können, darf das Gesetz aber sich nicht zu weit vom Verhalten entfernen. Regeln, deren Zweck sich gegen starke biologische Prädispositionen richten - solche Regeln werden oft aus ideologischen oder religiösen Gründen eingeführt -, sind entweder kurzlebig, werden mißachtet oder beides."[4]

An drei von ihr behandelten Beispielen, nämlich der Verhaltensbegünstigung, der Familienstruktur (Einehe) und dem Umweltrecht sei der weiterführende Ansatz von Margaret Gruter kurz erläutert.

Das Verhalten nahe Verwandte zu begünstigen ist nach einer weitverbreiteten Auffassung, die auch Gruter und der Verfasser teilen, als evolutionsstabile Strategie durch Sippen- bzw. Verwandtenselektion (kin selektion) selektiert worden.[5] Gruter legt dann dar, daß das Recht eine derartige Verhaltenstendenz auf

---

1 GRUTER, Margaret: Die Bedeutung der Verhaltensforschung für die Rechtswissenschaft, Schriftenreihe zur Rechtssoziologie und Rechtstatsachenforschung, Bd. 36, Berlin 1976; GRUTER, Margaret und REHBINDER, Manfred, Hrsg., Ablehnung – Meidung – Ausschluß, Schriftenreihe zur Rechtssoziologie und Rechtstatsachenforschung, Bd. 60, Berlin 1986.
2 GRUTER, Margaret: Rechtsverhalten, Köln 1993, S. 3.
3 GRUTER, a. a. O., S. 23.
4 GRUTER, a. a. O., S. 18.
5 WICKLER, Wolfgang: Funktionen des Verhaltens, in: Psychobiologie, hrsg. von Klaus Immelmann u. a., Weinheim/München 1988, S. 92 ff.

unterschiedliche Weise berücksichtigt[6]; so etwa im Erbfolgerecht: nahe Verwandte erhalten mehr als entferntere; im Erbschaftssteuerrecht: der Steuersatz steigt mit der „Entfernung"[7]; bei Unterhaltspflichten: sie sind nahen Verwandten am ehesten zuzumuten[8]; im Strafprozeß brauchen nahe Verwandte nicht gegeneinander auszusagen[9]. Dies gilt auch im deutschen Recht.

Zur Frage, ob wir als Menschen zur Einehe biologisch prädisponiert sind, stößt sie auf widersprüchliches Material. Hier widersteht sie dem Versuch, die auseinanderstrebenden Fakten in einer eigenen Ideologie zu verzerren und läßt die Frage offen. Ehe nicht weitere Daten vorliegen muß von einer kulturell tradierten Verhaltensweise ausgegangen werden, der keine biologische Prädisposition zugrunde liegt.

Zum Umweltrecht konstatiert sie, daß wir eine Spezies sind, die in ihrer phylogenetischen Geschichte die Umwelt aus Eigeninteresse ausgebeutet hat und die in erster Linie auf der Grundlage kurzfristiger Zielsetzungen handelt. Deshalb schlägt Gruter vor, um die „erforderlichen Veränderungen erreichen zu können muß bei der Erziehung angesetzt werden"[10].

Daraus ergibt sich als weiterführender Ansatz, daß wir nur bei gut biologisch abgesicherten Prädispositionen den weiteren Schritt gehen können, um zu prüfen, ob sich diese im Recht niedergeschlagen haben oder dort niederschlagen sollten. Eine ideologische Verzerrung der Fakten müssen wir vermeiden und stets damit rechnen, daß die Probleme auch erst, wie die Umweltprobleme in geschichtlicher Zeit, als zivilisatorische oder kulturelle Probleme aufgetaucht sein können.

Diesen Grundsätzen ist der Verfasser gefolgt. Er verdankt Margaret Gruter und dem Gruterinstitut vielfältige Anregung und Unterstützung. Dies war wichtig, denn der Verfasser ist auch immer

---

6 GRUTER, a. a. O., S. 50 ff.
7 A. a. O., S. 52.
8 A. a. O., S. 54.
9 A. a. O., S. 74, Anm. 11.
10 A. a. O., S. 185.

wieder auf die „intellektuelle Isolation" gestoßen, die Margaret Gruter beschreibt.[11]

Im folgenden wird der Verfasser einige Ergebnisse seiner eigenen Untersuchungen und Überlegungen in Form eines vorläufigen Werkstattberichts darstellen. Das heißt einerseits, daß hier einige Kenntnisse der evolutionstheoretischen Annahmen nicht diskutiert werden können, sondern vorausgesetzt werden müssen und daß zum anderen Sachverhalte nur verkürzt wiedergegeben und nur in wenigen Punkten mit den nötigen Literaturangaben versehen werden können. Es kann deshalb hier nur um eine plausible Darstellung der Ergebnisse gehen, deren Ableitungen weitgehend nur angedeutet werden können. Hier und da werden die abschließenden Ergebnisse auch noch offengelassen.

Zunächst sei mit einigen Anmerkungen begonnen wie der Verfasser mit dem Tier-Mensch-Vergleich umgeht und kurz geschildert, was er unter motivierten Verhaltenssystemen, die prädisposinierte menschliche Verhaltensweisen mit hervorbringen, versteht (II.). Sodann wird er darlegen, welchen Zusammenhang er zwischen motivierten Verhaltenssystemen und insbesondere Vorschriften des Strafrechts sieht (III.). Daran schließt sich die Darstellung verschiedener motivierter Verhaltenssysteme und deren Zusammenhang mit dem Recht, speziell mit dem Rechtsgüterschutz, an (IV.). Zum Schluß wird kurz erörtert, ob dieser Zusammenhang nur eine zufällige Korrelation ist, oder ob zwischen den Verhaltenssystemen und dem Rechtswerteschutz ein evolutionärer kausaler Zusammenhang besteht (V.).

Die letzte Erörterung läuft darauf hinaus, ob der Mensch der Aufgabe bzw. Funktion der Verhaltenssysteme Wertcharakter beimißt und ihnen in Sollensvorschriften Anerkennung zollt und sie zu schützen sucht. Damit müßte auch das Verhältnis von Sein und Sollen, zumindest partiell, neu definiert werden. Damit würden Natur- und Geisteswissenschaften näher aneinander rücken.

---

11 Siehe Anm. 1

II. Der Tier-Mensch-Vergleich

Zunächst geht der Verfasser davon aus, daß das Recht in erster Linie der Verhaltensregelung dient. Deshalb muß das Verhalten und die Verhaltensregelung beim Tier-Mensch-Vergleich im Vordergrund stehen. Hierfür können wir uns auf die Entdeckung und den Nachweis von Konrad Lorenz[12] stützen, daß es außer den morphologischen Merkmalen auch Verhaltensweisen gibt, die sich bei einer Tierart von Generation zu Generation stereotyp vererben. Es sind reflex- oder programmgesteuerte Verhaltensweisen, die er Erbkoordinationen nannte. Hierfür ist die Homologiemethode zunächst für den Merkmalsvergleich bei verschiedenen Tierarten, dann aber auch für den Tier-Mensch-Vergleich, entwickelt worden. Diese Methode befaßte sich fast ausschließlich mit dem Vergleich des beobachtbaren Verhaltens und kam deshalb kaum über den Vergleich von Erbkoordinationen hinaus. Sie hatte deshalb ihre größten Erfolge in der Erforschung von Mimik, Gestik und in der Babyforschung.[13] Sonstige soziale Verhaltensweisen, wie z. B. der Aufbau von Hierarchien, konnten mit dieser Methode im Tier-Mensch-Vergleich kaum untersucht werden. Dennoch werden allgemein tiefe gemeinsame phylogenetische Wurzeln des Hierarchieaufbaus bei den Tieren und beim Menschen angenommen.[14]

Diesem Dilemma – keine Vergleichbarkeit des Verhaltens, aber dennoch tiefe phylogenetische Wurzeln – versucht der Verfasser dennoch, durch die Entwicklung eines Konzepts biologisch-funktionaler und motivierter Verhaltenssysteme, zu begegnen. Dies erscheint möglich, weil wir heute über die neuronale Verankerung von Motivationen im Gehirn und besonders in den Arealen des Limbischen Systems wesentliche, bessere und präzisere Kenntnisse haben als zu der Zeit, als die bisherige Homologiemethode entwickelt und anfänglich mit ihr erfolgreich gearbeitet wurde.

---

12 LORENZ, Konrad: Vergleichende Bewegungsstudien an Anatiden in: Über tierisches und menschliches Verhalten, 11. Aufl., München 1974, S. 13-113.

13 HASSENSTEIN, Bernhard: Verhaltensbiologie des Kindes, 4. Aufl., München/Zürich 1987, bes. S. 66 ff.

14 VOGEL, Christian, ECKENSBERGER, Lutz: Arten und Kulturen – Der vergleichende Ansatz, in: Psychobiologie, S. 563 – 608, 584.

Biologisch-funktionale und motivierte Verhaltenssysteme erfassen über die äußerlich in Erscheinung tretende und beobachtbare Verhaltensweise hinaus die Motivation, die die Verhaltensweise mit hervorbringt sowie die Funktion der Verhaltensweise.

Biologisch-funktional heißt dabei, diese Verhaltenssysteme müssen im evolutionstheoretischen Sinne als verbesserte Anpassung bzw. Fitneß der Selbsterhaltung sowie der Fortpflanzung dienlich sein. Das Konzept motivierter Verhaltenssysteme, das der Verfasser entwickelt, ist nichts wesentlich Neues. Damit sollen lediglich Ergebnisse der Motivationsforschung und der Verhaltensforschung zusammengeführt und gemeinsam genutzt werden. Das Konzept der Verhaltenssysteme ist vorwiegend von Bowbly[15] in Abwandlung der früheren Instinktkonzepte entwickelt worden. Es fußt auf der Evolutionstheorie und bietet deshalb für den Tier-Mensch-Vergleich gute Voraussetzungen. Dieses Konzept stellt zwar das Verhalten als Forschungsgegenstand in den Vordergrund, untersucht aber auch die dazugehörigen Motivationen. Die Motivationsforschung beschäftigt sich vorwiegend mit dem Menschen und ist überwiegend in der Psychologie angesiedelt. Nicht alle Psychologen nutzen die Möglichkeit Motivationen aus der Phylogenese herzuleiten. Alle Motivationsforschung befaßt sich aber gleichzeitig mit den aus den Motivationen ableitbaren Handlungen. Der „Motivationsbegriff als Bezeichnung der motivationalen Disposition im menschlichen und tierlichen Verhalten"[16] dürfte sich aber weitgehend durchgesetzt haben.

Als besonders einfaches und gut untersuchtes Beispiel mag hier, für ein biologisch-funktionales und motiviertes Verhaltenssystem, die Nahrungsbeschaffung und ihr Verzehr dienen. An vergleichbaren Verhaltenssequenzen sind bei Schimpansen und dem Menschen nur noch das zum-Mund-führen, das Kauen und das Schlucken der Nahrung geblieben – wahrscheinlich drei durch Lernen nur geringfügig modifizierte Erbkoordinationen. Die

---

15 BOWBLY, John: Bindung, München 1975, S. 73 ff. sowie derselbe: Trennung, München 1976, S. 107 ff.
16 SCHNEIDER, Klaus, SCHMALT, Heinz-Dieter: Motivation, 2. Aufl., Stuttgart/Berlin/Köln 1994, S. 15.

Nahrungsbeschaffung ist nur noch über die Motivation und die Funktion vergleichbar. Der Schimpanse sucht und pflückt am Boden und auf Bäumen Obst und Blätter. Der Mensch kann dies zur Not auch noch, aber in der Regel geht er in der arbeitsteiligen Geldverkehrswirtschaft einkaufen und arbeitet vorher, um Geld zu verdienen. Seine Arbeit - wie auch immer sie geartet sein mag – erfüllt neben allen sonstigen Funktionen als Teilfunktion in der Regel auch die der Nahrungsbeschaffung. So kann sie teilweise als Funktionsäquivalent des Beerenpflückens beim Schimpansen angesehen werden. Der Weg dieser weiten Auseinanderentwicklung führte über Jäger- und Sammlergesellschaften, wo schon das Anlegen von Vorräten hinzukam. Dann folgte die Viehhaltung und der Ackerbau. Die Natural- und Tauschwirtschaft wurde ergänzt und später verdrängt durch die Geldverkehrswirtschaft. Die Agrargesellschaften waren die Vorstufe zu unserem heutigen Leben in der Industriegesellschaft, die sich derzeit wiederum rasant verändert. Deshalb können wir nicht immer nach vergleichbaren Verhaltensweisen suchen, sondern nur nach ihren Funktionsäquivalenten.

Die biologische Funktion der Nahrungsbeschaffung und ihres Verzehrs besteht im Ausgleich des ständigen Kalorienverbrauchs und der Zuführung sonstiger Nahrungsbestandteile, die Schimpansen und Menschen in fast gleicher Weise zur Lebenserhaltung und Fortpflanzungsfähigkeit benötigen.

Die Motivation für diese Verhaltensweisen ist der Hunger. Zwar wissen wir nicht ob und wie Tiere Hunger fühlen oder wahrnehmen, aber wir kennen weitgehend die neuronalen und physiologischen Mechanismen, die die beobachtbare zunehmende und abnehmende Nahrungsaufnahmebereitschaft steuern und die bei uns der Hunger begleitet. Diese inzwischen erforschten Mechanismen sind denen beim Menschen sehr ähnlich. Das gleiche gilt für die Verdauung, also die Nahrungsumwandlung, die die biologisch-funktionale Kalorienzufuhr bewirkt. Diese Herleitung läßt den Schluß zu, daß wir es beim Hunger mit einer phylogenetisch entstandenen Motivation zu tun haben. Dabei ist, wie bei den Verhaltensweisen, zu berücksichtigen, daß es für den Menschen auch andere Motivationen gibt, um zu essen. Das ändert aber nichts daran, daß auch die ursprüngliche biologische Grundfunktion, wegen der das System in der Phylogenese selektiert worden ist, nach wie vor besteht und existenznotwendig bleibt.

Nach diesen hier nur sehr grob umschriebenen Kriterien wird im folgenden das Vorliegen biologisch-funktionaler Verhaltenssysteme geprüft, also:

- Vergleich der Verhaltensweisen,
- Vergleich der biologischen Funktion,
- Vergleich der Motivation,
- Vergleich physiologischer und neuronaler Mechanismen,
- zusätzlich Kulturenvergleich zur Feststellung von Universalität des Verhaltens.

Je nach Forschungs- und Erkenntnisstand werden bei den zu untersuchenden motivierten Verhaltenssystemen kaum je für alle Kriterien ausreichende Daten vorliegen. Dann geht es um eine Abwägung, ob das Vorliegen eines solchen System angenommen werden kann. Außerdem sei kurz angemerkt, daß die verschiedenen motivierten Verhaltenssysteme unterschiedlich organisiert sind.[17] Anders als Hunger und Durst wird z. B. das Sexualverhalten vorwiegend hormonell gesteuert und bedarf eines Partners. Bei der Inzestvermeidung knüpft die Evolution an die mit der Blutsverwandtschaft im Tierreich regelmäßige Nähe und Vertrautheit an, nicht jedoch an die Blutsverwandtschaft selbst. Auch deshalb wechselt die Bedeutung der oben angegebenen Kriterien von System zu System.

Um Mißverständnisse zu vermeiden soll hier noch einmal die Sonderentwicklung des Menschen hervorgehoben werden. Er kann praktisch jede Motivation und alle damit verbundenen Verhaltensweisen unterdrücken. Er besitzt hierfür eine prinzipielle Entscheidungsfreiheit. Er ist in diesem Sinne nicht zwingend biologisch determiniert. Motivierte Verhaltenssysteme sind meist bei

---

17 EIBL-EIBESFELDT, Irenäus: Die Biologie des menschlichen Verhaltens, 3. Aufl., München/Zürich 1995, S. 105 f.

den Primaten, aber sicher beim Menschen nur Verhaltensanlagen, die der Entfaltung der Entwicklung, eventuell auch der Einübung bedürfen. Das Paarungsverhalten und die dazugehörige Motivation stellen ein weiteres motiviertes Verhaltenssystem dar. Es hat immer wieder Menschen gegeben denen es gelungen ist - etwa Mönchen in Klöstern - diese Motivation niederzuhalten und die Verhaltensweisen nicht auszuüben. Der Mensch kann sich sogar verhungern lassen, z. B. wenn ein Hungerstreik bis zur letzten Konsequenz durchgehalten wird. Seine Flexibilität und seine willensmäßig gesteuerte Freiheit gegenüber motivierten Verhaltenssystemen befähigen ihn dazu.

III. Motivierte Verhaltenssysteme und der Rechtsgüter- bzw. Rechtswerteschutz insbesondere im Strafrecht

Um unter IV. die einzelnen Verhaltenssysteme, und jeweils damit im Zusammenhang die Berührungspunkte, mit dem Recht zu erörtern sei vorab generell der Gedanke der Korrelation von biologisch-funktionalen und motivierten Verhaltenssystemen und Rechtsgütern besonders im Strafrecht erläutert.

Der Verfasser hatte sich schon einige Zeit mit dem Verhältnis von Biologie und Recht beschäftigt. Ihm war die Vorstellung von Instinkten und später Verhaltenssystemen in biologischen Funktionskreisen vertraut. Und dann stieß er mehr zufällig auf die Tatsache, daß der besondere Teil des Deutschen Strafgesetzbuches nach Funktionsbereichen wie Straftaten gegen Ehe und Familie, Straftaten gegen die Organisationsstruktur des Staates (Straftaten gegen Verfassungsorgane sowie bei Wahlen und Abstimmungen), Straftaten gegen das Eigentum usw. aufgebaut ist. Bei näherem Zusehen ergab sich, daß Ordnung und Aufbau des besonderen Teils des Strafgesetzbuches (StGB) nach den jeweils verletzten Rechtsgütern richtet. Diese Ordnung richtet sich also nach den Angriffsobjekten, die die Straftäter schädigen. Die Beschreibungen der Angriffsobjekte wiesen eine Ähnlichkeit mit den Beschreibungen der erörterten Verhaltenssysteme auf. Die Angriffsobjekte werden als Rechtsgüter bezeichnet und schon ihre allgemeine Definition weist auf Ähnlichkeiten hin. So heißt es etwa in einem gängigen Kommentar: Rechtsgüter seien „die von ihrer konkreten Erscheinungsform in bestimmten Gütern, Zuständen, Lebensbeziehungen usw. abstrahierten ‚Rechtswerte', welche die ‚Bauelemente der Sozialordnung' bilden".[18] Und es heißt dort weiter, daß es auf die ihnen „innewohnenden Wirkungsmöglichkeiten" ankomme, und ihre Bestimmung als werthafte soziale Funktionseinheiten wird besonders hervorgehoben.[19]

Diese „Bauelemente der Sozialordnung" sollen durch das Strafrecht geschützt werden, indem die Angriffe auf sie unter Strafe gestellt werden. Sie sind zum großen Teil auch im Grundgesetz (GG) als Grundrechte geschützt. Der Verfasser geht jedoch vom Strafrechtsschutz aus, weil dort die Rechtsgüter bzw. Rechtswerte und die Art ihrer Störung konkreter gefaßt sind.

Zur Konkretisierung an einem Beispiel bleiben wir bei dem oben behandelten Nahrungsaufnahmesystem und erörtern die dazu passenden Rechtsvorschriften. Im Strafrecht lautet die Vorschrift:

§ 170 b StGB – Verletzung der Unterhaltspflicht

Wer sich einer gesetzlichen Unterhaltspflicht entzieht, so daß der Lebensbedarf des Unterhaltsberechtigten gefährdet ist oder ohne die Hilfe anderer gefährdet wäre, wird mit Freiheitsstrafe bis zu drei Jahren oder mit Geldstrafe bestraft.

Unterhalt und Lebensbedarf weisen schon auf Nahrung hin. Geschützt werden soll der Unterhaltsberechtigte vor der Gefährdung seines Lebensbedarfs.[20] Was genau zum Lebensbedarf zählt ergibt sich aus dem Bürgerlichen Gesetzbuch, besonders aus seinen § 1610. Gemeint sind danach in erster Linie Nahrung, Bekleidung und Unterkunft. Diese drei Begriffe stehen für den gesamten Funktionskreis der homöostatischen Verhaltenssysteme. Sie haben die Funktion, die organismische Struktur des einzelnen Individuums, auch bei wechselnden Umweltverhältnissen, im

---

18 LENCKNER in Schönke/Schröder, Vorbem. §§ 13 ff., Rdn. 9.
19 LENCKNER, a. a. O., m. w. Nachw.; zum Rechtsgutbegriff umfassend AMELUNG, Knut: Rechtsgüterschutz und Schutz der Gesellschaft, Frankfurt 1972.
20 LENCKNER, a. a. O., § 170 b, Rdn. 1.

Gleichgewicht zu halten. Neben der festen Nahrung ist es die flüssige Nahrung. Als Motivation ist es neben dem Hunger der Durst. Für dessen phylogenetische Ableitung gilt vergleichbares wie oben für den Hunger ausgeführt. Außerdem zählt dazu das System des Wärmeausgleichs. Schimpansen und Menschen müssen in ihrem Körper etwa die gleiche Temperatur erhalten. Bei geringen Abweichungen kann der Körper hierfür selbst sorgen. Der Mensch benötigt darüber hinaus in den meisten Gegenden der Welt Bekleidung und bei Witterungsunbilden eine Unterkunft. Als viertes der homöostatischen Verhaltenssysteme gehört der Schlaf dazu. Auch dazu gehört als Schlafplatz eine Unterkunft. Mit der Sicherstellung des Lebensbedarfs durch den Unterhaltsanspruch im Zivilrecht und durch die oben zitierte Strafvorschrift soll also erreicht werden, daß die homöostatischen Verhaltenssysteme, die sämtlichst nicht erlernt sind, sondern phylogenetische Wurzeln haben, zum Zuge kommen können. Wir schauen also bei dieser Untersuchung nicht auf den Straftäter und seine Tat, sondern auf das Opfer und darauf, welche Rechtsgüter und Handlungs- bzw. Entfaltungsmöglichkeiten beim Opfer zerstört oder geschädigt werden und deshalb geschützt werden sollen.

Ein Gedanke aus der Evolutionstheorie, der dieser Korrelation von Verhaltenssystemen und Schutzgütern eine gewisse Plausibilität verschafft, sei noch angefügt. Die erörterten homöostatischen Verhaltenssysteme sind als überlebenswichtige Systeme schon im Tierreich in der Evolution selektiert worden. Sie sind auch beim Menschen noch mit gleicher Funktion vorhanden und für sein Überleben wirksam und erforderlich. Aus dieser Sicht liegt es nahe, daß die Rechtsordnung als Verhaltensregelung ihr Wirksamwerden durch Gewährung eines Unterhaltsanspruches schützt und zusätzlich ihre Störung durch das Vorenthalten des Unterhalts, die Verletzung der Unterhaltspflicht, bestraft. Hierauf wird zum Schluß zurückzukommen sein.

IV. Die funktionale Ordnung motivierter Verhaltenssysteme und ihr rechtlicher Schutz

Die Bemühungen, die menschliche Natur zu analysieren, seine Bedürfnisse, Triebe, Motivationen und Emotionen zu katalogisieren und zu ordnen, hat eine lange Tradition. Einen guten Überblick gibt Ernst-Joachim Lampe.[21]

Üblicherweise werden die Hauptfunktionsbereiche der Selbsterhaltung und der Fortpflanzung, früher auch Arterhaltung genannt, unterschieden. Daneben wird noch ein dritter Funktionskomplex genannt, der als „soziales Verhalten"[22] oder „Einordnung in einen größeren Verband"[23] bezeichnet wird. Bischof schreibt diesem Verhaltensbereich die Aufgabe zu, „eine Gruppe selbständiger Individuen zu koordinieren".[24] Der Verfasser wird ihn im folgenden als den Funktionsbereich der Koordination bezeichnen.

Einzelheiten über diese drei Funktionsbereiche sowie die Einzelfunktionen und die dazugehörigen Verhaltensweisen ergeben sich aus den folgenden drei Grafiken. Bei dieser Zusammenstellung der Funktionsbereiche hat sich der Verfasser eng an die Darlegungen von Norbert Bischof zu einer Taxonomie der Motive angeschlossen.[25]

1.Funktionsbereich der Selbsterhaltung

a) Homöostatische Verhaltenssysteme – Nahrungsaufnahme in fester und flüssiger Form, Wärmeausgleich und Schlaf

Diese Verhaltenssysteme sind oben bereits als Beispielsfall erörtert worden. Darauf kann verwiesen werden. Sämtliche aufgeführten Kriterien liegen bei allen vier Verhaltenssystemen eindeutig vor. Der rechtliche Schutz dieser Verhaltenssysteme,

21 LAMPE, Ernst-Joachim: Rechtsanthropologie, Berlin 1970, S. 201-264.
22 IMMELMANN, Klaus/SCHERER, Klaus R./VOGEL, Christian: Was ist Verhalten?, in: Psychobiologie, S. 11 f.
23 SCHNEIDER, Klaus/SCHERER, Klaus R.: Motivation und Emotion, in: Psychobiologie, S. 257 ff.
24 BISCHOF, Norbert: Das Rätsel Ödipus, München/Zürich 1985, S. 295.
25 BISCHOF, Norbert, a. a. O., S. 330 ff. u. 291 ff.

zusammengefaßt durch das Rechtsgut, Unterhalt zur Deckung des Lebensbedarfs, liegt ebenfalls eindeutig vor. Es sei nur noch darauf hingewiesen, daß völlig unabhängig voneinander einerseits die Biologen diese vier Verhaltenssysteme in einem Oberbegriff als homöostatische Verhaltenssysteme zusammenfassen und die Juristen völlig unabhängig davon, ebenfalls unter ihren Oberbegriffen Unterhalt und Lebensbedarf (§ 170 b StGB, § 1610 BGB), die gleichen Funktionseinheiten (Essen, Trinken, Regulierung der Körpertemperatur, Schlafen) zusammenfassen.

b) Das Verhaltenssystem der Immunreaktionen und das System des Hygieneverhaltens

Diese beiden Systeme haben für unseren Zusammenhang keine besondere Bedeutung. Sie werden aber aufgeführt, weil sie besonders von Bischof benannt werden. Die geringe Bedeutung des Immunsystems für unseren Zusammenhang ergibt sich aus der Tatsache, daß das Immunsystem in erster Linie inner- und mikroorganismisch arbeitet[26] und die Verhaltensweisen sich erst im Krankheitsfalle zeigen. Das es ein solches System gibt ist überhaupt erst in den letzten 20 Jahren, im Zusammenhang mit den AIDS-Erkrankungen, ins allgemeine Bewußtsein gedrungen. Das Strafgesetzbuch schützt Angriffe auf das Immunsystem durch die Vorschriften gegen Körperverletzung und Totschlag (§§ 223, 212 f. StGB).[27] Die verletzten Rechtsgüter sind Leben und Gesundheit.

Das System des Hygieneverhaltens ist ein sehr unmittelbar persönliches Verhalten, zu dem Kratzen, Jucken und Fellpflege und beim Menschen besonders das Waschen zu zählen ist. Diese Verhaltensweisen funktionieren auch beim Menschen noch selbsttätig und bedürfen kaum des strafrechtlichen Schutzes. Erst in der Massengesellschaft gibt es inzwischen hygienische

---

26 BISCHOF, Norbert, a. a. O., S. 332; eine ausführliche Darstellung findet sich bei WEISS, C. und JELKMANN, W.: Funktionen des Blutes, in: Physiologie des Menschen, hrsg. von Schmidt/Thews, 25. Aufl., Berlin u. a. 1993, S. 423 ff und 447 ff, 453 ff; vgl. auch BIRBAUMER, Niels/SCHMIDT, Robert F.: Biologische Psychologie, Berlin/Heidelberg 1990, S. 44 u. 45.

27 ESER in Schönke/Schröder: Kommentar zum Strafgesetzbuch, 24. Aufl., München 1991, § 223 Rdn. 6a und § 212 Rdn. 3 jeweils mit umfangreichen Nachw.

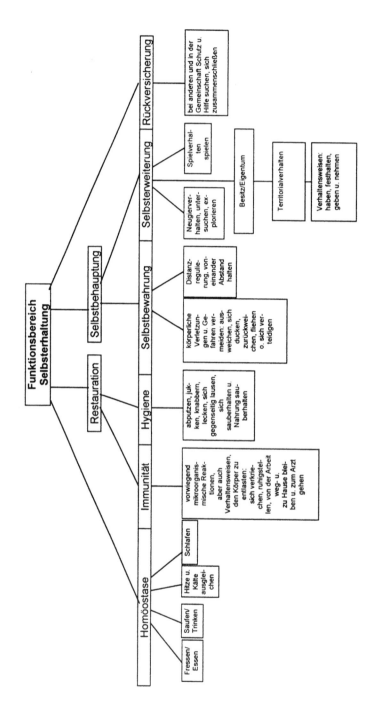

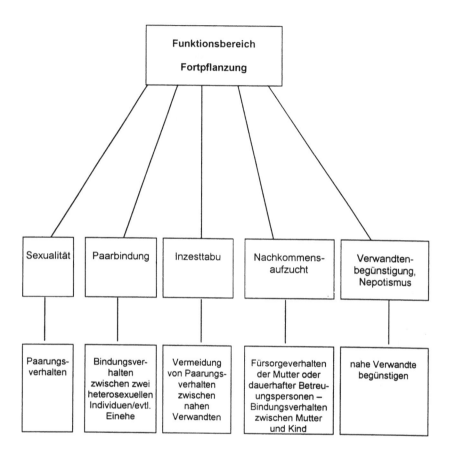

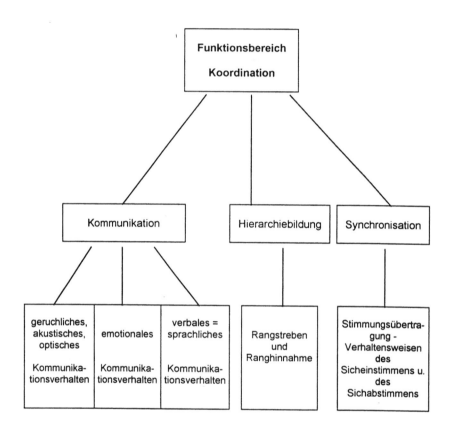

Schutzvorschriften für öffentliche Toiletten, Badeanstalten und in der Nahrungsaufbereitung und –versorgung, die hier nur am Rande erwähnt werden müssen.

c) Verhaltenssysteme der Verletzungs- und Gefahrvermeidung

Hier werden zwei Verhaltenssysteme gemeinsam behandelt, weil aus ihnen gleichartiges Verhalten resultiert und weil sie vielfach durch Lernprozesse gekoppelt sind.

Das System der Verletzungsvermeidung wird durch das Gefühl des Schmerzes begleitet und das Gefahrvermeidungssystem durch das Gefühl der Furcht.[28] Das aus beiden Systemen resultierende Verhalten kann insgesamt als Vermeidungsverhalten gekennzeichnet werden. Konkret besteht es darin, sich vor Angegriffen oder widrigen Umweltumständen zu ducken, ihnen auszuweichen, eventuell auch durch Verstecken, zu fliehen ggf. aber sich auch zu verteidigen oder zum Gegenangriff überzugehen. Der Schmerz ist physiologisch und psychisch eines der am besten untersuchten Systeme.[29] Das Verhalten, die Neurophysiologie und damit seine phylogenetische Kontinuität und die entsprechende Vermeidungsmotivation sind eindeutig belegt. Hinzuzufügen ist noch, daß in dieses System neben den genannten Verhaltensweisen auch noch die Schutzreflexe einzubeziehen sind, mit denen auch der Mensch - etwa beim Zurückziehen der Hand von einer heißen Herdplatte - ohne Nachdenken reflexartig reagieren kann.

Das System der Furcht ist etwas schwerer zu erfassen, aber seine neurophysiologische Verankerung kann ebenfalls als belegt gelten. Die Motivation ist bei Tier und Mensch eindeutig. Neben dem oben genannten Vermeidungsverhalten finden wir als Ausdrucksverhalten auch das ängstliche oder das angstverzerrte Gesicht sowie das Zittern und auch die Furcht- oder Angststarre.

Wichtig ist hervorzuheben, daß wir sowohl beim Kind als auch noch beim Erwachsenen angeborene Auslöser nachweisen können,

---

28 Auf die Unterscheidung von Furcht und Angst kann hier aus Platzgründen nicht eingegangen werden.

29 Umfangreiche Nachw. findet sich in ECCLES, Die Psyche des Menschen, Ernst Reinhardt Verlag, München/Basel 1985, S. 113, 114; BIRBAUMER/SCHMIDT, a. a. O.,S. 349 f.

wie großer Lärm beim Kind auch das Klippenerlebnis und die Fremdheit von Situationen und Personen. Beim Erwachsenen unterscheiden wir natürliche Schlüsselreize und deren Derivate von kulturellen durch Beobachtung erlernte Schlüsselreize und schließlich Schlüsselreize, die mehr oder weniger verstandesmäßig benutzt werden, um Gefahren einzuschätzen und zu vermeiden. Die Furcht ist ein Vermeidungssystem, das dem Schmerz- und Verletzungssystem praktisch vorgelagert ist. Die Funktion leuchtet dahingehend ein, daß ein großer Überlebens- und Fortpflanzungserfolg anzunehmen ist, wenn Verletzungen nicht erst eintreten müssen, sondern wenn typische Gefahrensituationen das Vermeidungsverhalten schon vorher auslösen. Daran knüpft auch die Koppelung beider Systeme an. Verletzungssituationen werden durch Konditionierung oder beim Menschen auch durch verstandesmäßige Einsicht an das Furchtsystem gekoppelt, so daß schon durch das Auftreten der Furcht beim Erkennen der herannahenden Situation das Vermeidungsverhalten ausgelöst werden kann. Diese Antizipation möglicher Schädigungen und die darauf folgende Vermeidungsreaktion ist mit Sicherheit in der Evolution von großem Vorteil gewesen. Beide Systeme können also als eindeutig belegt angesehen werden.

Die geschützten Rechtsgüter sind Körper und Gesundheit sowie das Leben. Der Schutz findet sich in den § 211 ff. und 223 ff. StGB. Hinsichtlich des rechtlichen Schutzes ist auch noch hervorzuheben, daß wir im Recht auch das Verteidigungsverhalten abgebildet finden, das aus diesen Systemen anstelle von Flucht auftreten kann. § 32 StGB regelt die Notwehr, wodurch das Verletzen anderer in Notwehrsituationen straffrei gestellt wird.

d) Verhaltenssystem der Distanzregulierung

Die Arbeiten über dieses Verhaltenssystem sind in der Werkstatt des Verfassers über eine beginnende Literatursammlung und erste Überlegungen noch nicht hinausgekommen. Es handelt sich zunächst um die jedem bekannte Tatsache, daß wir beim Fahrstuhlfahren Fremde nicht aus nächster Nähe voll anblicken, sondern den Blick nach unten senken, daß wir ferner in einer Schlange, in der wir anstehen, wenn es der Platz einigermaßen erlaubt, eine gewissen Distanz zu den vor uns und zu den hinter uns Stehenden einhalten. Hierüber gibt es von Desmond Morris gute Bilddokumentationen. Dieses Verhaltenssystem ist im täglichen Umgang von einiger Bedeutung. Seine phylogenetischen Wurzeln dürften unbestritten sein.[30] In der veränderten Umwelt des Menschen hat sich hieraus entwickelt, was wir den Intimbereich und die Privatsphäre nennen, in die wir nur besonders vertraute Personen eindringen lassen.

Der Schutz dieser Privatsphäre schlägt sich im Recht nieder als Schutz vor der Ausspähung des gesprochenen Wortes (§ 201 StGB), als Schutz vor der Verletzung des Brief- und Postgeheimnisses (§ 202 StGB), neuerdings als Schutz vor dem Ausspähen von Daten auf Computern (§ 202 a StGB) und schließlich überhaupt als Schutz vor Verletzung von Privatgeheimnissen (§ 203 StGB). Hinzugezählt werden kann auch das Recht am eigenen Bild. Diese Störungen der Privatsphäre muten sämtlichst sehr modern an. Sie sind aber nur die zivilisatorisch technisch ausgeformten Angriffsarten, die in früheren Gesellschaften die sogenannten Späher oder Spitzel mit dem eigenen Ohr und den eigenen Augen ausübten. Im Grundgesetz ist die Privatsphäre in dieser Ausprägung durch das Grundrecht auf Einhaltung des Brief-, Post- und Fernmeldegeheimnisses, gemäß Artikel 10 GG, geschützt.

e) Verhaltenssystem der Neugier/Exploration

Das Explorationsverhalten ist bei Tieren, Kindern und erwachsenen Menschen durch Beobachtung gut dokumentiert.[31] Die phylogenetische Kontinuität zwischen Tieren und Menschen im Hinblick auf dieses Verhaltenssystem wird allgemein bejaht. Es wird alles untersucht was als neuartig oder zu dem bisherigen als diskrepant erkannt wird. Bischof bezeichnet die einschlägigen Reizeigenschaften, die das Explorationsverhalten auf den Plan treten

---

30 EIBL-EIBESFELDT, a. a. O., S. 475 ff.
31 MORRIS, Desmond: Der nackte Affe, München 1968, S. 117 ff.; EIBL-EIBESFELDT, a. a. O., S. 788 ff.

lassen als Komplexität, Erwartungswidrigkeit, Wechsel, Mehrdeutigkeit, Inkongruenz, Unbestimmtheit und Fremdartigkeit.[32] Er schreibt: „Je informationsreicher ein Reiz ist desto schwerer fällt die Entscheidung wie er zu beantworten sei. ‚Ihn zu verarbeiten' heißt also, angemessene Reaktionen im verfügbaren Verhaltensrepertoire herauszusuchen oder neu zu entwickeln. Genau darum scheint es zu gehen, wenn ein Tier oder ein Mensch ‚exploriert'."[33] Neurophysiologische Untersuchungen sind dem Verfasser kaum bekannt. Untersuchungen zum Aufmerksamkeitsverhalten und zum Orientierungsverhalten befassen sich auch mit der Gehirntätigkeit bei Erwartungswidrigkeit (mismatch).[34] Damit können wir auf der Basis von Hirnstromexperimenten schon erste Aussagen über das zum Neugierverhalten gehörende Orientierungsverhalten machen. Die Funktion des Explorationsverhaltens dürfte eindeutig sein. Wer mehr kennt, wer mehr weiß, wer sich seine Umgebung bekannter und damit vertrauter gemacht hat, hat größere Möglichkeiten sich in schwierigen Situationen zu behaupten, was einer besseren Angepaßtheit bzw. einer besseren Fitneß entspricht.

Einen spezifischen strafrechtlichen Schutz im Strafgesetzbuch gibt es – soweit dem Verfasser bekannt – in den freiheitlichen westlichen Gesellschaften nicht. In den Diktaturen gibt es ihn auch nicht, aber er wäre dringend nötig. Formuliert wird der Schutz des Neugierverhaltens als Freiheit der Forschung, die eine späte kulturelle Ausformung des Neugierverhaltens ist. Außerdem gehört hierher, die Freiheit sich aus allen öffentlich zugänglichen Quellen informieren zu dürfen, also die Informationsfreiheit, die ihrerseits eng gekoppelt ist mit der Pressefreiheit. Es sind besonders wichtige Freiheitswerte, die in Artikel 5 GG ihren verfassungsrechtlichen Schutz gefunden haben.

f) Verhaltenssystem des Besitzes/Eigentums

Die Bezeichnung als Verhaltenssystem des Besitzes/Eigentums

---

32 BISCHOF, Norbert, a. a. O., S. 240.
33 BISCHOF, Norbert, a. a. O.

benennt, worum es beim Menschen im Endergebnis geht. Diese menschlichen abstrakten Oberbegriffe verdecken jedoch, daß es sich in Wahrheit um zwei Verhaltenssysteme handelt denen unterschiedliche Motivationen zugrunde liegen. Der Verfasser vertritt die Auffassung, daß unterschieden werden müssen einmal das Verhaltenssystem des Territorialverhaltens (unbewegliche Habe: Territorium, Areal, Grundstück, evtl. Haus) und zum anderen das Verhaltenssystem des Habens, Nehmens und Gebens (bewegliche Habe: Werkzeuge, Instrumente, Bekleidung, Auto usw.). Juristisch kann man sowohl an beweglicher wie auch an unbeweglicher Habe Besitz und Eigentum erwerben. Beide Begriffe werden vielfach auch in der Umgangssprache benutzt. Biologen und Soziologen unterscheiden deshalb auch meist nicht zwischen diesen beiden Besitz- und Eigentumsarten. Der Verfasser unterscheidet beide Arten, weil sie aus unterscheidbaren Motivationen resultieren.

aa) Verhaltenssystem des Territorialverhaltens

Das Suchen, Erobern und Behaupten eines Territoriums ist im Tierreich weitverbreitet. Das Verteidigen eines Territoriums resultiert, nach weitverbreiteter Auffassung, aus der räumlichen Bindung an den vertrauten Lebensbereich. Wir finden die Territorialbindung und –verteidigung auch bei Schimpansengruppen und in Steinzeitpopulationen sowie in Stadtstaaten und in sonst staatlich verfaßten menschlichen Gesellschaften.[35] Die phylogenetische Kontinuität dieser Motivationen sieht der Verfasser als eindeutig an.

Der rechtliche Schutz findet sich in den Vorschriften über den Landesverrat und die Gefährdung der äußeren Sicherheit (§§ 93 bis 101 a StGB) und in den Vorschriften über Straftaten gegen die Landesverteidigung (§§ 109 – 109 k StGB). Als Schutzobjekt wird einerseits die äußere Machtstellung der Bundesrepublik Deutschland angegeben, die gefährdet werden kann durch Landesverrat, Hochverrat und durch die Gefährdung der inneren

---

34 BIRBAUMER/SCHMIDT, a. a. O., S. 484 ff.; zu ereigniskorrelierten Gehirnpotentialen eben
   da, S. 501 ff.
35 EIBL-EIBESFELDT, a. a. O., S. 455 ff.

Stabilität[36], und andererseits der Schutz der Landesverteidigung, was natürlich auf das Territorium der Bundesrepublik Deutschland zielt. Die einzelnen Vorschriften zielen auf das Intakthalten der Kampfkraft der Bundeswehr.

bb) Verhaltenssystem des Habens, Gebens und Nehmens

Dieses Verhaltenssystem basiert nur auf sehr einfachen angeborenen Verhaltensweisen. Mit dem Haben ist zunächst tatsächlich nur das gemeint, was man unmittelbar in der Hand hat. Nicht menschliche Primaten kennen an beweglichen Gegenständen keinen Dauerbesitz. Säuglinge und Kleinstkinder, außer einem Tuch, einem Stofftier oder einem Schnuller, wonach sie immer wieder verlangen, ebenfalls nicht. Für die Entwicklung von Dauerbesitz muß sich bei Kindern erst im Bewußtsein ein weiterer Zeithorizont aufspannen. Erst mit einem aufgespannten Zeitbewußtsein konnte das „Besitzverhältnis" an beweglichen Gegenständen auf Dauerbesitz umgestellt werden. Ob sich mit der Entwicklung des Zeitbewußtseins in den letzten 5 – 8 Millionen Jahren, nach der Trennung der Hominiden von den nicht menschlichen Primaten, eine phylogenetische Prädisposition für Dauerbesitz entwickelt hat, muß zur Zeit offen gelassen werden. Sie könnte sich am beginnenden Werkzeugbesitz und in der langen Zeit der Sammler- und Jägergesellschaften am Anlegen von Vorräten entwickelt haben.

Die Anlage zum kurzfristigen Besitz ist an Primaten und Kleinkindern im Kulturenvergleich gut belegt. Sie ist aus dem Blickwinkel von zwei Akteuren zu betrachten, aus der Sicht des Habenden und aus der Sicht desjenigen, der es wegnehmen oder abbekommen möchte. Auf der Seite des Habenden haben wir die Verhaltensweisen des Festhaltens und des Abwehrens. Auf der Seite des anderen haben wir neben dem Versuch des Wegnehmens auch die Verhaltensweise - wie Eibl-Eibesfeldt sagt - „der Akzeptanz, der

---

36 STREE in Schönke/Schröder, vor §§ 93 ff., Rdn. 1 u. 2.

Besitznorm" sowie des Bittens und des Bettelns.[37] Von Schimpansen wissen wir, daß auch Stärkere und Ranghöhere Schwächere und Rangniedere anbetteln, insbesondere um Futter, obwohl sie es auch an sich reißen könnten. Bei Kindern im Kulturenvergleich hat Eibl-Eibesfeldt, die entsprechenden Verhaltensweisen auf beiden Seiten der Akteure eindrucksvoll filmisch dokumentiert.

Sollte sich beim Menschen mit der Aufspannung des Zeitbewußtseins keine Prädisposition auf Dauerbesitz entwickelt haben, dürfte der Dauerbesitz auf dem Instrumentalcharakter der beweglichen Gegenstände beruhen. Mit der Erweiterung des Zeithorizonts erweitern sich auch die Zwecke, die man mit den Gegenständen verfolgen kann. Schimpansen können Futterbrocken fressen, sie können mit Steinen Nüsse knacken und damit werfen, mit Grashalmen können sie in Termitenhaufen nach Termiten stochern, mit Ästen können sie bei Imponierveranstaltungen ihre Kraft darstellen usw. usw. Der Mensch konnte und kann mit seinem Zeitbewußtsein und in der von ihm selbst geschaffenen Umgebung mit beweglichen Gegenständen immer mehr Zwecke verfolgen, so daß die alte Besitzmotivation durch typisch menschliche Motivationen erweitert werden konnte. Auf die alte Besitzmotivation, die phylogenetischen Ursprungs ist, werden bewußte Zweckmotivationen als rationale Beweggründe aufgepfropft. Hierauf konnte zunächst der Tauschhandel und später die Geldverkehrswirtschaft aufbauen.

Deshalb werden in unserem Recht Besitz und Eigentum als Funktionseinheiten geschützt. An erster Stelle steht die Sachbeschädigung (§ 303 StGB). Rechtsgut ist das Eigentum. Zweck ist es, daß nicht nur der Substanz–, sondern auch der Gebrauchswert einer Sache geschützt wird. Ebenfalls wird das Eigentum durch die Verbote des Diebstahls (§§ 242 ff. StGB), der Unterschlagung (§§ 246 ff. StGB) und der Hehlerei (§§ 257 ff. StGB) geschützt. Im übrigen werden Besitz und Eigentum umfangreich im

---

37 EIBL-EIBESFELDT, a. a. O., S. 483 f.

Bürgerlichen Gesetzbuch besonders (§§ 558 ff. BGB, Besitz und §§ 903 f., 958 ff. BGB, Eigentum) geschützt. Ferner genießt das Eigentum, gemäß Artikel 14, auch verfassungsrechtlichen Schutz.

Auf die Frage eines gesonderten Verhaltenssystems des Gebens, Abgebens und Schenkens kann hier aus Platzgründen nicht eingegangen werden. Hier müßten Probleme der Reziprozität von Verhalten etc. behandelt werden. Diese schlagen sich in zivilrechtlichen Rechtsprinzipien nieder, was nicht in diesem Kurzbericht behandelt werden kann. Am Rande sei nur erwähnt, daß nach deutschem Recht der Schenker die geschenkte Sache zurückverlangen kann, wenn der Beschenkte sich groben Undanks schuldig macht (§§ 530 ff. BGB). Wenn bei vielen Menschen das Beschenktwerden ein Gefühl der Verpflichtung auslöst, dann muß man, zumindest im Zusammenhang mit der genannten Vorschrift, gründlich prüfen, ob es hier eine phylogenetische Wurzel gibt.

g) Verhaltenssystem des Spielens

Das Spielverhalten ist ebenfalls durch wissenschaftlich-experimentelles Beobachten gut dokumentiert.[38] Evolutions-theoretisch war die Entstehung des Spielverhaltens ein großer Schritt, weil es dadurch möglich wurde, die vorher nur für den Ernstfall an Instinkte gebundene und überwiegend determinierte Verhaltensweisen unabhängig vom Ernstfall, also spielerisch, zu üben und zu trainieren. Für jeden leicht beobachtbar ist es wie Hunde und Katzen das Jagen und Fangen, auch das Kämpfen spielerisch üben und es so für den Ernstfall verfügbar machen und verfügbar halten. Eine große Rolle hat das Spielverhalten auch in Koppelung mit dem Explorationsverhalten im sozialen Leben. Hier kann schon spielerisch erforscht werden, welches Sozialverhalten noch zulässig ist und welches nicht mehr. Dieses Austasten im Sozialverhalten ist bei Kindern sehr gut beobachtbar.

Die phylogenetische Kontinuität zwischen Tier und Mensch wird allgemein bejaht. Als Nachweis hierfür gilt auch das

---

38 HASSENSTEIN, Bernhard, a. a. O., S. 330 ff.; GRAMMER, Karl: Biologische Grundlagen des Sozialverhaltens, Darmstadt 1995, S. 164 ff.; EIBL-EIBESFELDT, a. a. O.,S. 788 ff.

Spielgesicht des Schimpansen, dem zwingend als mimisches Verhalten ein neuronales Programm zugrunde liegen muß. Sonstige neurophysiologischen Untersuchungen sind dem Verfasser nicht bekannt.

Störungen des Spielverhaltens haben bisher wohl nirgends strafrechtliche Relevanz erlangt. Das deutsche Strafrecht regelt allerdings das Spiel in seiner Ausformung als Glücksspiel und Lotterie. Sie bedürfen der staatlichen Genehmigung und diese Vorschriften gelten heute allgemein der „Absicherung eines ordnungsgemäßen Spielbetriebs".[39] Vor der letzten wesentlichen Änderung 1974 waren die Vorschriften dahingehend ausgestaltet, daß „die Mitspieler vor Vermögensgefährdung durch Ausbeutung ihrer Spielleidenschaft" geschützt werden sollten. Diesem Schutzzweck dienen die neueren Vorschriften nicht mehr in der bisherigen Deutlichkeit, obwohl sie diesen Schutzzweck auch noch verfolgen.

h) Verhaltenssystem der Rückversicherung

Das Verhaltenssystem der Rückversicherung ist an jungen Rhesus-Affen und an Menschenkindern, hinsichtlich ihrer Rückversicherung bei der Mutter als sichere Basis, gut untersucht.[40] Für das Verhalten Erwachsener untereinander besteht dieses System mit leicht abgewandelter Thematik fort. Hier wird Schutz und Halt, also Rückversicherung, bei anderen vertrauten Gruppenmitgliedern und letztlich in der schützenden Gruppe überhaupt, gesucht.[41] Die überlebens- und fortpflanzungsdienliche Funktion ist offensichtlich.

Dieses System wird verfassungsrechtlich durch die Garantie der Versammlungs- und Vereinigungsfreiheit in den Artikeln 8 und 9 GG geschützt.

---

39 STREE/ESER in Schönke/Schröder, § 284, Rdn. 1.
40 BOWLBY, John: Bindung, S. 211 f.
41 BISCHOF, Norbert, a. a. O., S. 334 ff., 162 ff.; vgl. dazu auch die Untersuchungen an niederländischen Einzelhändlern von Mulder und Stemerding mitgeteilt in: ZIMMER, Dieter E.: Die Vernunft der Gefühle, München 1981, S. 199 f.

i) Der Freiheitsdrang

Im vorstehenden Verhaltenssystem wurden die geschützten Rechtsgüter als Versammlungs- und Vereinigungsfreiheit bezeichnet. Das Grundgesetz kennt weitere Freiheitsrechte, nämlich die Glaubens-, Gewissens- und Bekenntnisfreiheit (Art. 4 GG) und das Recht der freien Meinungsäußerung (Art. 5 GG). Schon die Bezeichnungen dieser Freiheitsrechte weisen darauf hin, daß es sich um typische Ausprägungen menschlicher Freiheitsvorstellungen handelt. So wie diese Begriffe ist auch der Freiheitsbegriff selbst geistesgeschichtlich, auf der Basis der philosophischen und religionsphilosophischen Bemühungen in den letzten 3000 Jahren, entstanden. Er ist einer unser höchsten Wertbegriffe. Im Zusammenhang mit ihm sprechen wir auch vom Freiheitsdrang. Für diesen Gesamtbegriff menschlichen Geistes gibt es kein korrelierendes motiviertes Verhaltenssystem. Konrad Lorenz sagte schon von den Instinkten, daß es keinen allgemeinen Überlebensinstinkt gibt. So sind auch die motivierten Verhaltenssysteme nur „in der kleinen Münze" der Motive, wie Hunger und der Verhaltensweise Essen, wie Durst und Trinken, wie Neugier und Explorieren usw., bei den Tieren und als Anlagen bei den Menschen in ihrer phylogenetischen Ausstattung repräsentiert. Erst ihr Zum-Zuge-Kommen und Zusammenspiel insgesamt ermöglichen das Überleben und die Fortpflanzung. Deshalb können sich auch Biologen nicht mit dem allgemeinen Freiheitsbegriff und einem korrespondierenden Freiheitsdrang beschäftigen.

Eine einzige Ausnahme würde der Verfasser machen wollen, für eine Anlage sich körperlich frei bewegen zu können und sich auch räumlich fortbewegen zu können. Biologen sprechen davon, daß Tiere und Menschen, und bei Kindern besonders deutlich ablesbar, einen Bewegungsdrang besitzen. Dieser korreliert sicher mit den verschieden ausgestalteten Verboten im Strafrecht, die sich dagegen richten, daß gegen andere Menschen Gewalt angewandt wird. Dies wurde schon oben bei dem Verbot der Vergewaltigung erwähnt und gilt etwa auch teilweise für die Nötigung (§ 240 StGB), den Raub (§ 249 StGB) und die Erpressung (§ 253 StGB), zu deren geschützten Rechtsgütern jeweils auch die Freiheit zählt. An vorderster Stelle sind hier die Freiheitsberaubung (§ 239 StGB) sowie der

Erpresserische Menschenraub (§ 239 a StGB) und die Geiselnahme (§ 239 b StGB) zu nenennen. Dort ist jeweils neben dem allgemeinen Freiheitsbegriff als Rechtsgut auch die Fortbewegungsfreiheit genannt. Hierbei muß jedoch stets berücksichtigt werden, daß mit dem Freiheitsbegriff, nach menschlichem Werteverständnis, wesentlich mehr gemeint ist, als von der biologischen Motivation sich körperlich frei und auch fortbewegen zu können abgedeckt wird.

2. Funktionsbereich der Fortpflanzung

Wegen der allgemeinen Bekanntheit dieses Funktionsbereiches und der vielfältig bekannten Forschung hierzu, begnügt sich der Verfasser in diesem Kurzbericht mit Stichworten. Nur zur Paarbindung und zum Inzesttabu werden kurze Ausführungen gemacht.

a) Verhaltenssystem der Sexualität

Die phylogenetische Kontinuität und die Funktion des Paarungsverhaltens liegen auf der Hand. Die Freiheit des Paarungsverhalten unter Menschen war stets durch Vergewaltigungsverbote in unterschiedlicher kultureller Ausformung geschützt (§§ 177 ff. StGB). Das Schutzgut wird heute als sexuelle Selbstbestimmung bezeichnet, was besonders auf die damit verbundene Freiheitsbeschränkung hinweist. Es hat auch immer kulturelle Beschränkungen gegeben, wie heute noch in verschiedenen Kulturen. In Deutschland ist die Strafbarkeit des außerehelichen Beischlafs erst vor 30 Jahren aufgehoben worden.

b) Verhaltenssystem der Paarbindung

Hier wird insbesondere immer wieder die Frage, ob der Mensch eine genetische Prädisposition zur Einehe besitzt erörtert. Die vielfältigen Untersuchungen hierzu geben keine eindeutigen Daten her, mit denen sich eine derartige Prädisposition begründen ließe.[42]

---

42 SCHMIDT, Frank-Hermann: Verhaltensforschung und Recht, Schriften zur Rechtstheorie, Heft 98, Berlin 1982, S. 69 ff., zusammenfassend S. 88.

Zu dieser Einschätzung der Untersuchungslage kommt auch Margaret Gruter. Wir finden gerade bei den uns am nächsten stehenden Primaten eher eine Anlage zur Promiskuität. Die Entwicklung einer derartigen Anlage in den letzten 5 – 8 Millionen Jahren, nach dem sich der Hominidenstamm von den nicht menschlichen Primaten getrennt hat, kann nicht ausgeschlossen werden.

Die sehr weit verbreitete Einehe dürfte auf anderen Bindungsmechanismen beruhen, die sehr stark kulturell geprägt sein müssen. Der rechtliche Schutz der Einehe muß deshalb, solange nicht andere Daten vorliegen, als weitestgehend kulturbedingt angesehen werden.

Der Verfasser geht deshalb nicht davon aus, daß es sich bei der ehelichen Paarbindung um ein phylogenetisch prädisponiertes Bindungsverhalten handelt. Deshalb gibt es hier zwischen dem rechtlichen Schutz der Einehe keine Korrelation zu einem prädisponierten Bindungsverhalten. Der Schutz von Ehe und Familie hat verfassungsrechtlichen Rang und ist im Art. 6 GG geregelt. Dabei kann hervorgehoben werden, daß es bei dem Schutz der Familie auch um den Schutz des biologisch motivierten Mutter-Kind-Bandes geht. Die Mutter-Kind-Dyade ist biologisch prädispodiniert.

c) Verhaltenssystem des Inzeststabu´s

Die phylogenetische Anlage zur Vermeidung des Paarungsverhalten zwischen nahen Verwandten dürfte zwischenzeitlich ausreichend geklärt sein.[43] Eine der wichtigsten Untersuchungen dazu, dürften die Untersuchung an Kibbuz-Kindern in Israel sein. Die Kinder aus einem Kibbuz wachsen dort von Kleinstkindalter an gemeinsam auf. Es wurde festgestellt, daß alle gemeinsam aufgewachsenen Kinder später nur über Kibbuzgrenzen hinaus und nicht untereinander heiraten. Aus dieser und anderen Untersuchungen ergibt sich die Erklärung, daß sich die enge körperliche und psychische Vertrautheit von Kindern, die wie

---

43 Vgl. zu den Untersuchungen zum Inzesttabu: BISCHOF, Norbert, a. a. O., S. 369 – 387, bes. 384 ff. (Kibbuz-Kinder).

Geschwister aufwachsen, kaum mit dem psychischen Geschehen des Flirtens und der sexuellen Annäherung vertragen. „Normalerweise" zeigen Geschwister kein sexuelles Interesse aneinander. Für einen derartigen Mechanismus gibt es auch bei Primaten Anhaltspunkte. Diese Auffassung und Erklärung dürfte sich zwischenzeitlich durchgesetzt haben, der Verfasser folgt ihr.

Die biologische Funktion besteht darin, daß zumindest dauerhafte Fortpflanzung unter nahen Verwandten zu erblichen Schäden und damit Leistungsminderungen bei der Nachkommenschaft führt und derartige Individuen ihrerseits nur einen geringeren Fortpflanzungserfolg haben.

Der Beischlaf zwischen nahen Verwandten ist gemäß § 173 StGB verboten. Als Rechtsgut gilt „die Freihaltung der engsten Familie von sexuellen Beziehungen; daneben werden als Strafgrund auch Gefahren für die psychische Entwicklung des Partners (minderjährige Tochter, Geschwisterinzest)"[44] und die Gefahr eugenischer und genetischer Schäden genannt. Die Gefahr eugenischer und genetischer Schäden ist unter Juristen umstritten.[45] Der Verfasser steht auf der Seite derer, die derartige Schäden für ausreichend nachgewiesen halten.

d) Verhaltenssystem der Nachkommensaufzucht

Über das Mutter-Kind-Band ist in den letzten 40 Jahren soviel geforscht worden, daß hier wohl die Feststellung ausreicht, daß hier eine Prädisposition vorliegt. Die Funktion für die Weitergabe der eigenen Gene ist offensichtlich. Auch hier kommt es nicht zwingend auf die Blutsverwandtschaft an. Es kommt hier in erster Linie auf die dauerhafte Bindung an eine fürsorgliche Betreuungsperson an. Es geht um gute physische und psychische Voraussetzungen für eine gesunde Entwicklung des Säuglings, des Kindes und des heranwachsenden Menschen. Dieses Ziel wird durch eine große Anzahl von Jugendschutzvorschriften rechtlich verfolgt. Die Hauptvorschrift im Strafgesetzbuch, die diesem Ziel dient, findet

---

44 LENCKNER in Schönke/Schröder, § 173, Rdn. 1.
45 Nachw. hierzu bei LENCKNER, a. a. O.

sich im § 170 d, die die Verletzung der Fürsorge- und
Erziehungspflicht unter Strafe stellt. Das geschützte Rechtsgut ist die
„gesunde körperliche und psychische Entwicklung von
Jugendlichen unter 16 Jahren".[46]

e) Verhaltenssystem der Verwandtenbegünstigung

Hierbei dürfte es sich um eine auf der Basis von kin selektion
entstandene evolutionsstabile Strategie handeln.[47] Dies ist auch, wie
oben schon mitgeteilt, von Margaret Gruter richtig beurteilt worden.
Die diversen Schutzvorschriften für dieses evolutionsstabile
Verhalten, mit denen das Recht hierauf zumindest weitgehend
Rücksicht nimmt, sind oben ebenfalls bereits mitgeteilt worden.

3. Funktionsbereich der Koordination

a)Kommunikationssysteme

Die Kommunikation hat die Funktion einander Signale geben zu
können, und die komplexere Kommunikation sich über Situationen
und das Verhältnis zueinander zu verständigen. Das hat Regelungs-
und Koordinationscharakter. Ohne die verschiedenen Formen der
Kommunikation (chemische, akustische, optische, haptische,
geruchliche) hier zu behandeln, soll hier nur festgestellt werden,
daß wir mehr emotionale und mehr rationale (symbolisch abstrakt
durch Sprache und Schrift) unterscheiden können. Die emotionale
Kommunikation hat sich schon nonverbal bei den Tieren entwickelt
– bei den höheren nicht menschlichen Primaten wohl auch schon
mit symbolischen Anteilen. Beim Menschen ist die emotionale
Kommunikation nach wie vor vorhanden (Mimik, Gestik,
Stimmlage, Weinen usw.). Sie wird jedoch von der Wort- und
Schriftsprache überlagert und zum Teil zurückgedrängt.

---

46 LENCKNER, a. a. O., § 170 d, Rdn. 1 m. w. Nachw.
47 Vgl. BISCHOF, Norbert, a. a. O., S. 186 ff. mit dem Verw. auf die Arbeit von William D.
   Hamilton, The Genetical Theory of Social Behavior in Journal of Theoretical Biology, 1964

Verhaltenssystem korrekter Informationsvermittlung

Hier kann nur für unseren Zusammenhang ein Punkt angesprochen werden. Es sind dies in der Kommunikation die Erscheinungen, die als List, Täuschung und Lüge bezeichnet werden. Es handelt sich um unzutreffende oder zurückgehaltene Informationen. Gibt es in den Kommunikationssystemen eine Tendenz, die auf die Abgabe zutreffender Informationen gerichtet ist? Kurz gefragt: Hat der Satz „Du sollst nicht lügen!" eine phylogenetische Wurzel? Mit diesem heiklen Problem hat sich kaum jemand befaßt. Von Biologen kennt der Verfasser zu diesem Thema nur Stellungnahmen von Wickler[48] und de Waal[49]. Beide bejahen eine biologische Basis. Der Verfasser vertritt auch diese Auffassung. Die an sich nötige umfassende Diskussion kann hier nicht ausgebreitet werden, deshalb müssen Stichworte genügen. Auch Tiere, insbesondere Schimpansen, können täuschen. List und Täuschung sind sicher gegenüber Raubfeinden und gegenüber Beutetieren eine fitneßfördernde Strategie. Ist dieses Phänomen erst einmal in der Welt, so ist es auch unter Freunden zur Erlangung eigener Vorteile nicht mehr zu vermeiden.

Insbesondere de Waal bringt, wie der Verfasser meint, richtigerweise hiermit das Rotwerden und das Verlegenwerden in Zusammenhang, das wir alle kennen und das auftritt, wenn ein Mensch beim Täuschen oder Lügen ertappt wird. Sicher ist das deutlich sichtbare Rotwerden nicht erlernt, sondern angeboren.

De Waal bringt diesen Komplex im Anschluß an Richard Alexander mit dem Vertrauen in Verbindung, außerdem mit dem guten persönlichen Ruf eines Menschen sowie mit der Regeleinhaltung. Er ist der Auffassung, daß ein Selektionsprozeß dahin gewirkt haben könnte, daß ein Individuum in der Kooperation mit anderen dadurch Vorteile hatte, daß es zuverlässig war. Das könnte erklären, daß es im Falle von Täuschen und Lügen, also von Unzuverlässigkeit, beim Ertapptwerden der

---

48 WICKLER, Wolfgang: Die Biologie der zehn Gebote, München 1975.
49 de WAAL, Frans: Der gute Affe, München/Wien 1997, S. 144 – 147.

„Unzuverlässigkeitsbeweis" nach außen durch Rotwerden sichtbar wurde. De Waal bringt auch im Anschluß von Steven Pinker weitere evolutionstheoretische Argumente.[50]

Der Verfasser wird hierfür noch eine ergänzende Ableitung vorlegen, die davon ausgeht, daß Regeleinhaltung in ständig zusammenlebenden Gruppen notwendig war und ist. Das vertraute Zusammenleben und die Kooperation unter Mitgliedern einer Gruppe ist ein anderer Sachverhalt als die Situation gegenüber Raubfeinden und Beutetieren. Letzteren gegenüber sind List und Täuschung stets von Vorteil und der Erfolg wird mit Triumph gefeiert. Ihnen gegenüber bzw. in derartigen Situationen gibt es kein Rotwerden. Etwas anderes ist Täuschung, Lügen und Verrat in der eigenen Gruppe.

Das regelhafte Verhalten bei Wirbellosen erfolgt zunächst durch determinierte Verhaltensweisen, also durch Erbkoordinationen, die durch bestimmte Auslöser auf den Plan gerufen werden. Werden im Tierreich in den Verhaltensweisen erste Freiheitsgrade und eine zunehmende Lernfähigkeit erreicht, wird das flexiblere Verhalten durch Konditionierung wieder festgestellt. So wird wieder Regeleinhaltung garantiert. Die Regel lautet immer: „In gleicher Situation, gleiches Verhalten." Durch das Leben in Gruppen und die Ausbildung von Hierarchien und die weitere Ausbildung von Synchronisationsverhalten[51] entsteht bereits im Tierreich der Vorläufer unseres Sollens, d. h. die Vorform unseres Verhaltens nach Sollensregeln. Die dominanten Tiere setzen den subdominanten Tieren gegenüber durch, wie sich diese verhalten sollen. Die Synchronisationsmechanismen führen zu Gruppendruck, der die einzelnen Gruppenmitglieder zu gesolltem Verhalten anhält.[52] Ein Verstoß gegen die „Sollensregel", das Alpha-Tier zu grüßen oder ihm den Vortritt zu lassen, löst in der Regel unmittelbar Sanktionen

---

50 de WAAL, a. a. O., S. 147, besonders Anm. 18.
51 Zur Hierarchiebildung und zur Synchronisation vgl. die Ausführungen zu den beiden nächsten Verhaltenssystemen.
52 Zur Übertragung auf dem Menschen vgl. die Experimente von MILGRAM, S.: Das Milgram-Experiment, Zur Gehörsamsbereitschaft gegenüber Autorität, Reinbek 1974; und zum Gruppendruck und zur Isolationsangst vgl. das Experiment von Salomon E. Asch mitgeteilt in: LINSENMAIR, Eduard K./MIKULA, Gerold: Soziale Einflüsse, in Psychobiologie, S. 471 ff.

(Strafe) aus. Verstöße gegen das Sollen des Gruppendrucks führt ebenfalls zu Unbill und Nachteilen. Von Tieren wissen wir, daß sie bei unbeabsichtigten Regelverstößen noch vor einer Reaktion ihres Interaktionspartners erschrecken können.[53] Das bedeutet, daß sie in der Lage sind ihr Verhalten insoweit zu „überwachen". Das „Überwachen und Erschrecken" weisen auf einen Mechanismus hin, der im Tier selbst bei der Regeleinhaltung mithilft. Die Bildung eines solchen Mechanismus ist sehr wahrscheinlich. In der Evolution werden oft Mechanismen selektiert, die antizipatorisch arbeiten. Das Erschrecken, das den wahrgenommenen und nicht gewollten Regelverstoß begleitet oder das bereits das Verhalten eines beginnenden Regelverstoßes abstoppt, antizipiert die auf den Regelverstoß folgende Sanktion oder Unbill. Gruppendruck und dominante Tiere könnten den Selektionsdruck erzeugt haben, der ein derartiges Frühwarnsystem vor Regelverstößen im Tier selbst selektiert hat. Selbst dem Menschen ist noch bei Regelverstößen nicht ganz wohl zumute. Es liegt nahe anzunehmen, daß sich die hier auswirkenden Mechanismen die biologische Basis dessen sind, was wir entsprechend menschlich überhöht und in Fortentwicklung auf dem Sonderweg des Menschen heute das Gewissen nennen. Die Basis des Gewissens und das Gewissen selbst würden sich damit als ein im Menschen selbst liegendes Frühwarnsystem vor Regelverstößen darstellen. Daß der Mensch außerdem sein Gewissen befragt, wenn er nicht weiß wie er künftig handeln soll, weil für sein Problem keine Regel besteht, ist eine Weiterentwicklung.

Zurück zum Erschrecken vor dem unbewußten Regelverstoß. Jede bewußte Täuschung unter vertrauten Gruppenmitgliedern ist ein Regelverstoß.[54] Hier kann sich, wenn diese Anlage entfaltet und entwickelt ist, das schlechte Gewissen melden. Das bewußte

---

53 HENDRICHS, Hubert: Lebensprozesse und wissenschaftliches Denken, Freiburg/München 1988, S. 132, 196.
54 Die Ableitung hierfür kann hier aus Platzgründen nicht dargelegt werden.

Täuschen und das damit verbundene Verheimlichen können das
Gewissen überspielen. Erst beim Ertapptwerden tritt das Rotwerden
auf den Plan. Das Rotwerden wird von einer erheblichen Erregung,
die vom Überwinden des Gewissens und dem Ertapptwerden
ausgelöst wird, begleitet. Als Verhaltensweise beim Menschen
können wir das Kopf- und Körperabwenden und das Kopfsenken
beobachten. Ferner bezeichnen wir diese Regungen auch als
Verlegenheit, die sich bis zur Scham steigern kann. Das Rotwerden
und die damit wohl verbundenen Gesten der Verlegenheit und der
Scham scheinen dem Verfasser deshalb eher als
Beschwichtigungssignale. Dabei muß man sich vor Augen halten,
daß dieses Repertoire in vorsprachlicher Zeit entstanden sein muß,
also zu einer Zeit als die Individuen auf emotionale Kommunikation
viel stärker angewiesen waren und sich alles in unmittelbaren face-
to-face-Interaktionen abspielte. Deshalb ist auch Täuschen hier der
angemessenere Begriff und nicht Lügen. Hinzukommt, daß die
emotionale Kommunikation viel schneller arbeitet als die verbale
Kommunikation. Das Rotwerden, als Erregungssignal und die
Gesten, würden dann bedeuten: „Ja, ja, ich weiß, das war oder ist
falsch." Das Rotwerden gehörte also zu einem
Beschwichtigungsgebaren, nach einer versuchten oder erfolgten
Täuschung dem Interaktionspartner gegenüber, wiederum um
Sanktionen und Unbill zu vermeiden. Damit könnten Funktion und
Funktionsweise sowie der Selektionsdruck für eine biologische
Anlage des Gewissens und des Rotwerdens, nach Ansicht des
Verfassers, plausibel erklärt werden. Auf diesen Ausführungen
ließen sich auch Überprüfungsexperimente an Tieren und
Menschen entwerfen.

Als Beispiele von Tieren sei einerseits der Hund genannt, der
erschrickt, wenn er im Spiel versehentlich zu fest zubeißt. Dies gilt
auch beim Spiel mit seinem „Herrchen".[55] Der verlegene Hund, der
einen Regelverstoß begangen hat, kneift, als Beschwichtigungsgeste
und als Andeutung von submissiven Verhalten, den Schwanz
zwischen die Hinterbeine.

---

55 KONRAD, Lorenz berichtet von einer solchen Situation, nach der sein Hund längere Zeit
   untröstlich war.

Die höheren Säugetiere, die in Gruppen leben und über das genannte Repertoire verfügen, finden wir bevorzugt als Dressurtiere im Zirkus. Wenn sie und ihre menschlichen Dompteure diese Fähigkeiten nicht gemeinsam besäßen, würden die Dressurakte nicht gelingen. Sie hätten ohne ein angeborenes Verständnis für Regeleinhaltung und Sollen, für Lohn und Strafe und für das Mißlingen und Gelingen von Dressurakten keine gemeinsame Kommunikationsbasis.

Zur Frage, ob es für den Satz: „Du sollst nicht lügen!" eine biologische Prädisposition gibt, mußte selbst in diesem Werkstattbericht länger ausgeholt werden. Entsprechende noch detailliertere Ausführungen und Belege dafür, wird der Verfasser demnächst vorlegen. Nach den obigen Ausführungen können wir festhalten, daß es in der Evolution in erster Linie um Täuschung ging. Lügen ist ein Begriff, der in unserem Sinne erst nach dem Spracherwerb entstand und seine heutige Bedeutung erhielt. Als Ergebnis läßt sich sagen, daß es gegen Täuschung und Lügen unter vertrauten Personen wohl einen Hemmechanismus gibt. Der Mensch in seiner Freiheit hat dies als Anlage phylogenetisch erworben. Er kann diese Anlage zurückdrängen und nicht nutzen. Er kann als Gegenstück dazu sich das Pokerface anerziehen, das nicht errötet. Und dennoch muß darauf hingewiesen werden, daß selbst unter Ganoven und Verbrechern oft strenge Regeln herrschen, deren Einhaltung das genannte Repertoire wieder sicherstellen hilft. Dabei sei am Rande bemerkt, welchem Wertesystem und welchem Regelsystem (ob christlich, schiitisch, demokratisch oder diktatorisch) der einzelne Mensch auch immer angehört, der oben erörterte Gewissensmechanismus funktioniert weitgehend unabhängig vom Inhalt der Regeln. Er ist ein Frühwarnsystem gegen Regelverstöße, gegen die in einer Gesellschaft internalisierten und herrschenden Regeln. Der Satz: „Du sollst nicht lügen!" hat also als biologische Basis nicht ein motiviertes Verhaltenssystem, das nach einem Verhalten in eine bestimmte Richtung strebt, wie etwa der Hunger. Wir können aber eine Hemmung gegen das Täuschen und Lügen ausmachen.

Dementsprechend sind auch die Rechtsvorschriften, die sich mit Lügen und Täuschen befassen, besonders ausgebildet. Als erstes muß noch einmal darauf hingewiesen werden, daß das geschilderte Repertoire von Regeleinhaltung, Sollen und Hemmung gegenüber Täuschen und Lügen in die Funktionskreise Kommunikation und Koordination gehören. Wir finden ein Verbot des Täuschens bzw. Lügens nur dort, wo es in erster Linie auf die Wahrheit ankommt und wo die Straftatbestände als „eigenhändige und abstrakte Gefährdungsdelikte" ausgestaltet sind, nämlich bei den Aussagedelikten, also in erster Linie beim Meineid (§§ 153 ff. StGB). Als Rechtsgut gilt nach herrschender Meinung in erster Linie die Rechtspflege als staatliche Funktion. Die Gerichte sind in unserer Ordnung herausragende Institutionen der Koordination menschlichen Verhaltens. Der Richter kann nur gerechte Urteile sprechen, wenn er die Wahrheit erfährt. Die Rechtspflege als staatliche Funktion wird noch genauer bezeichnet als „das öffentliche Interesse an einer wahrheitsgemäßen Tatsachenfeststellung in gewissen gerichtlichen und sonstigen Verfahren."[56] In den übrigen Rechtsvorschriften, die sich mit Lügen und Täuschen befassen, geht es stets in erster Linie um andere Rechtsgüter, wie beim Betrug (§§ 263 ff. StGB) und zum Teil beim Untreuetatbestand (§ 266 StGB – Treuebruchstatbestand) sowie bei den Fälschungsdelikten (§§ 146 – 152 a StGB – Geld- und Wertzeichenfälschung; §§ 267 – 282 StGB – Urkundenfälschung). Diskriminiert durch die Strafvorschrift wird jeweils in erster Linie die Störung des Geldverkehrs und des Verkehrs mit schriftlichen Urkunden oder des Vermögens, gleichzeitig aber auch immer die Angriffsart gegen diese Rechtsgüter, durch Täuschen und Lügen. Außerdem ist aus den Beleidigungsvorschriften die Verleumdung (§ 187 StGB) hierher zu zählen.

b) Verhaltenssystem des Rangstrebens und der Ranghinnahme (Hierarchiebildung)

Die Hierarchiebildung finden wir im Tierreich und in den

---

56 LENCKNER in Schönke/Schröder vor §§ 153 ff, Rdn. 2.

menschlichen Gesellschaften. Tiefe phylogenetische Wurzeln der Hierarchiebildungen in menschlichen Gesellschaften werden zwar angenommen, aber der Verhaltensvergleich zwischen Tier und Mensch in Hierarchien erwies sich bisher als kaum durchführbar. Der Verfasser glaubt den Vergleich mit Hilfe des Konstrukts der motivierten Verhaltenssysteme eher lösen zu können, als dies bisher möglich war. Als erstes gehört dazu aber auch eine genaue Vorstellung von den Verhaltensweisen, die – hier als Beispiel – in Schimpansengruppen[57] zu beobachten sind. Jane Goodall[58] und Frans de Waal[59] schildern mehrstufige Hierarchien mit einer Spitze (Alpha-Tier), mit einem Mittelbau und einem unteren Hierarchierand. Ein Tier im Mittelbau zeigt Verhaltensweisen in zwei Richtungen. Es hat sich seinen Rang erobert und muß ihn erhalten. Es zeigt Dominanzverhalten gegenüber niederrangigen Tieren. Es ist aber dem Alpha-Tier – eventuell noch einem Zwischenrang – gegenüber subdominant und zeigt diesem gegenüber Respekt durch entsprechendes Grußverhalten und durch Demutsgebärden, kurz, es zeigt submissives Verhalten. In jedem Tier ist also beides angelegt. Das Alpha-Tier befand sich vorher auch im Mittelbau. Deshalb müssen für das Verhaltenssystem beide Fähigkeiten gesehen werden: die Fähigkeit einen Rang anzustreben und zu behaupten, und gleichzeitig die Fähigkeit sich mit einem subdominanten Rang, wenn auch vielleicht nur auf Zeit, abzufinden. Das dies bei Tieren nicht generell vorausgesetzt werden kann wissen wir aus der Forschung an Tieren, die nicht in derartigen Hierarchien leben.[60] Wenn z. B. ein Tupaja-Männchen in einem Kampf einem anderen unterlegen ist, besitzt es nicht die Fähigkeit seine Furchterregung in der Nähe des Siegers wieder herunterzuregeln. In einem Käfig mit dem Sieger wird es an

---

57 Männchen und Weibchen haben dort eigene unterschiedliche Hierarchien, untereinander sind Weibchen erwachsenen Männchen gegenüber regelmäßig subdominant. In der menschlichen Gesellschaft haben sich diese Unterschiede weitgehend abgeschliffen. Deshalb wird hier darauf nicht gesondert eingegangen.

58 GOODALL, Jane: Wilde Schimpansen, Reinbek bei Hamburg 1991.

59 de WAAL, Frans: Wilde Diplomaten, München 1991; derselbe: Der gute Affe, München 1997.

60 Z. B. Forschungen an Tupajas vgl. BISCHOF, Norbert, a. a. O., S. 325 ff.

Furchterregung, physiologisch an Nierenversagen, eingehen. In der Freiheit würde es fliehen und nicht zurückkehren. Bei Schimpansen gibt es nach Auseinandersetzungen, oft sehr schnell, die Versöhnung, die insbesondere durch gegenseitiges Berühren und Groomen angezeigt wird. Die Rangentscheidung ist aber gefallen und bleibt – auf Zeit – auch festgestellt. Damit ist deren Verhalten auf Sicht - etwa der Vorrang beim Fressen, beim Behaupten bestimmter Plätze und eventuell auch beim Kopulieren mit bestimmten Weibchen - geregelt und damit koordiniert. Jedes Mal kräftezehrender Streit und/oder Kampf werden vermieden. Das Verhalten einen Rang zu behaupten oder nach einem höheren Rang zu streben, ist ähnlich. Es besteht vornehmlich in Imponier- und Drohgebärden, eventuell auch in Tätlichkeiten und im Kampf. Nach unten dient es besonders der nachhaltigen Einschüchterung und nach oben der Herausforderung. Dabei sind die anwesenden Gruppenmitglieder nicht ohne Bedeutung. Sie können beschwichtigend wirken, was besonders von hochrangigen Weibchen berichtet wird. Sie können aber auch für eine Seite unterstützend „wirken" und/oder auch tatsächliche Unterstützung leisten. De Waal schildert eindeutige Koalitionsbildungen.

In Kenntnis der Gefahren des Anthropomorphismus[61] seien die Facetten dieses Verhaltens noch etwas eingehender geschildert, und weil es sich um einen Kurzbericht handelt sei ohne weitere Erklärungen der Bogen zu menschlichen Verhalten geschlagen.

Der Imponierende wird von den anderen beobachtet, angesehen und macht dadurch auf sich aufmerksam. Er agiert sich in eine Mittelpunktrolle. Dieses Agieren wird beim Menschen auch mit einem Streben assoziiert, das als Geltungsdrang bezeichnet wird. Dabei wird der schon erreichte Status herausgestellt; man erheischt Ansehen und Achtung. Hieraus leitet sich eine Forschungsstrategie ab, um aus einer Primatengruppe das Alpha-Tier herauszufinden. Dabei wird notiert, welches Tier am häufigsten

---

61 Hier folgt der Verfasser der Auffassung de Waals, das wir auch bei der Beschreibung tierlichen Verhaltens nicht ganz auf die an menschlichen Erscheinungen entwickelte Sprache und entsprechend auf den Menschen bezogene Begriffe verzichten können.; siehe ausführliche dazu de WAAL: Der gute Affe, München/Wien 1997, S. 81 – 86.

angesehen wird, auch auf welches am häufigsten geachtet wird. Dieses Tier hat, menschlich ausgedrückt, das höchste „Ansehen" und genießt die höchste „Achtung".

Weiter ist das Rangstreben verbunden mit einer Wettbewerbssituation. Der Akteur hat Konkurrenten, oder wenn er das Alpha-Tier herausfordert tritt er in eine Auseinandersetzung mit diesem ein. Hierbei muß er Anstrengung und auch Kraft darstellen und beides notfalls auch aufwenden. Er muß eine hohe „Leistung" erbringen. Verständlicher werden die Verhaltensweisen, wenn wir ihnen Motivationen zuordnen können. Dem Verhalten des Rangstrebens und des Rangerhalts ist insgesamt die Machtmotivation zuzuordnen. Dem Rangverlust oder einem fehlgeschlagenen Rangstreben korrespondiert das submissive Verhalten. Beides hat physiologisch eine hormonale Entsprechung. „Bei Rhesus-Affen fand man, daß der Plasmatestosteronspiegel mit dem Wechsel der Rangstellung schwankt.[62] Er steigt, wenn eine dominante Position erreicht oder erfolgreich verteidigt wird und fällt bei Rangverlust. Beim Menschen, in seiner selbst geschaffenen Umwelt, haben sich die einzelnen Bestandteile des Rangstrebe- und Rangerhaltungsverhaltens ausdifferenziert und in der Komplexgesellschaft teilweise verselbständigt. So finden wir das Wettbewerbsverhalten gesondert im sportlichen Wettbewerb und im wirtschaftlichen Wettbewerb. Beide fordern Anstrengungen und schlagen sich in Leistungen wieder. Hier sind die Wettbewerbsmotivationen, die Motivation die Konkurrenz zu überflügeln und die Leistungsmotivation zuzuordnen. Dies gilt auch auf geistigem Gebiet im Lern- und Forschungswettbewerb und deren Leistungen.

Daß der Gedanke der Ausdifferenzierung wohl richtig ist, zeigen Plasmatestosteronmessungen bei Tennis- und Schachspielern und bei Medizinstudenten vor und nach der Promotion. Beim Match-Sieger und nach gut gelungener Doktorprüfung steigt der Plasmatestosteronspiegel. Beim Verlierer bleibt er gleich ebenso

---

62 EIBL-EIBESFELDT: a. a. O., S. 431.

beim Prüfling, der mit seiner Leistung nicht zufrieden ist. Diese beim
Menschen gesondert benannten Motivationen dürften dem alten
Motivationssystem der Machtmotivation entstammen.

Auf der Basis der Machtmotivation und des Rangstrebens und
der Fähigkeit einen niederen Rang hinzunehmen bzw. zu
akzeptieren, entstehen die Rangverhältnisse und damit die
Hierarchien.

Bei den menschlichen Hierarchien unterscheidet der Verfasser
hier der Einfachheit halber Hierarchien ersten und zweiten Grades.
Zu Hierarchien ersten Grades zählt er einfache Behörden,
Unternehmen und alle Zusammenschlüsse natürlicher Personen, in
denen es über- und untergeordnete Positionen gibt. Hierarchien
zweiten Grades entstehen, wo Hierarchien als Institutionen oder
auch demokratisch verfaßte Institutionen in Hierarchien einander in
Über- und Unterordnung zugeordnet werden. Derartige Hierarchien
entstehen als Hierarchien zweiter Ordnung, wo die Koordination
von Millionen Menschen geleistet werden muß. Deshalb bezieht
sich der rechtliche Schutz derartiger Hierarchien im Strafgesetzbuch
sowohl auf die Institutionen als auch auf die darin agierenden
Menschen und zwar in erster Linie auf die Spitzen dieser
Hierarchien.

Für uns von Interesse sind hier die Straftaten gegen die innere
Sicherheit (gegen die Verfassungsorgane §§ 105 – 106 a StGB). Nach
§ 105 StGB wird bestraft, wer mit Gewalt oder durch Drohung die
Parlamente des Bundes oder eines Bundeslandes oder einen ihrer
Ausschüsse, die Regierung oder eines der Verfassungsgerichte
nötigt. Nach § 106 StGB werden die Mitglieder dieser Organe gegen
Gewalt und gegen Drohung mit einem empfindlichen Übel
geschützt, also die Abgeordneten und die Regierungsmitglieder je
einzeln. An erster Stelle ist als schützenswerte Person der
Bundespräsident genannt. Der Bundespräsident ist darüber hinaus
auch noch nach § 90 StGB gegen Verunglimpfung geschützt.
Desgleichen sind nach § 90 a StGB auch der Staat und seine

Symbole gegen Verunglimpfung geschützt sowie nach § 90 b StGB auch die Verfassungsorgane. Die oben kurz geschilderte Hierarchie in Schimpansengesellschaften galt für eine Größenordnung von 30 – 60 Individuen. Unsere Staatsorganisation umfaßt 80 Millionen Menschen. Für diese Art, in der Menschen sich in Staaten organisieren, kann man sicher die Auffassung vertreten, dies sei nicht vergleichbar. Fragt man jedoch nach dem Prinzip, nach dem beide sehr unterschiedlichen Formen von Gesellschaften aufgebaut sind und wie die Individuen koordiniert werden, muß man in beiden Fällen wohl akzeptieren, daß ein Koordinationsmechanismus die Hierarchiebildung ist und daß diese die Aufbaustruktur abgibt. Nachdem der nächste Koordinationsmechanismus, die Synchronisation, behandelt worden ist kommt der Verfasser auf das Problem der Vergleichbarkeit noch einmal zurück.

c) Verhaltenssystem der Synchronisation

Dieses System ist darauf gerichtet, daß Verhalten mehrerer Individuen gleichgerichtet zu synchronisieren. Der wohl älteste Mechanismus dazu ist die Stimmungsübertragung bzw. das gegenseitige Einstimmen auf eine gleichartige Motivationslage.[63] Nach Auffassung der Biologen hat diese Funktion etwa das Wolfsheulen. Ein Beispiel dafür ist auch die Art wie Vögel oder ein Vogelschwarm in Abflugstimmung geraten. Das Gähnen bei Primaten wird hierher gezählt, um gemeinsam zur Ruhe zu kommen. Das Gähnen wirkt auch beim Menschen noch ansteckend. Ebenfalls steckt das gemeinsame Hetzen gegen einen Feind die Gruppenmitglieder untereinander an. Am meisten bekannt ist sicher auch die gemeinsame Flucht einer Gruppe von Tieren. Das Fluchtverhalten steckt an ohne Rücksicht darauf, ob das zuerst fliehende Tier wirklich eine echte Gefahr erkannt hat. Kummer berichtet von einem Prozeß der Richtungsbestimmung für Kolonnenmärsche bei Primaten in Äthiopien, was schon mehr sein

---

63 BISCHOF, Norbert, a. a. O., S. 295 f., 297 f.

dürfte als reine Stimmungsübertragung.[64] Da auch bei uns die emotionale Kommunikation noch eine große Rolle spielt, sind auch beim Menschen Fälle der Stimmungsübertragung vielfältig. Hierher gehören das gemeinsame Singen, das Schunkeln, rhythmische Bewegungen, auch das Klatschen sowie das schon erwähnte Gähnen, das Marschieren und Singen, das Angriffsgebrüll wie das Hetzen bei Tieren, gemeinsam Beten, Kulttänze und gemeinsam in Panik geraten. Selbst das Fernsehen kann einen derartigen Prozeß vermitteln wie viele Menschen 1989 mit Tränen der Freude und der Rührung zu Hause an sich selbst erlebt haben.

Diese überwiegend emotional getönte Synchronisation vollzieht sich beim Menschen auch rational durch Worte. Wir können gemeinsam ergriffen sein von Worten. Wir können uns aber auch durch Worte zu gemeinsamen Handeln untereinander abstimmen. Diese Prozesse sind für Steinzeitpopulationen beschrieben worden, wo diese Funktion zum Teil durch Kulthandlungen erfüllt wird, aber auch das Abhalten von Palavern, wo so lange aufeinander eingeredet wird bis sich eine einheitliche oder doch von einer sehr breiten Mehrheit getragene Meinung herausbildet etwa über die Frage bei Nomaden, ob sie weiterziehen wollen oder nicht. Kummer beschreibt diesen Prozeß der Gleichrichtung von Auffassungen an einem Beispiel, indem vor der Entscheidung ein ständiges Hin- und Herlaufen von Zelt zu Zelt zu beobachten war bis eine Einigkeit im Clan hergestellt worden ist.

An die emotional getönten Synchronisationsprozesse schließen sich in der Evolution mit dem Spracherwerb durch den Menschen mehr rational bestimmte Synchronisationsprozesse durch Wort und Sprache an, wobei das auch emotionale Beeinflussen oder gar Mitgerissenwerden nie ganz unwirksam geworden ist. Mit der Fähigkeit, in der vom Menschen selbst geschaffenen Umwelt, größere und große Menschengruppen in Stadtstaaten und Staaten zu organisieren und zu versorgen entstand auf der geschilderten Grundlage das demokratische Abstimmen. Zumindest in der

---

64 KUMMER, Hans: Weiße Affen am Roten Meer, München 1992, S. 334.

deutschen Sprache hat sich dafür noch nicht einmal ein neues Wort herausgebildet. Abstimmungen gab es bei den Griechen und den Römern. Aus dem Mittelalter kennen wir Kaiser-, Königs- und Herzogswahlen. Die Wahlkämpfe des 20. Jahrhunderts mit der abschließenden Stimmabgabe sind funktionsäquivalente Verhaltensweisen zum Palaver und zu Abstimmungsprozessen in Steinzeitpopulationen, angepaßt an die Organisationsmöglichkeit für große Menschenmassen. Diese Stichworte müssen hier genügen. Auch wenn man auf den ersten Blick über diesen Zusammenhang erstaunt sein mag ist der Verfasser überzeugt davon, daß dem Sichabstimmen zu gleichgerichtetem Tun eine phylogenetische Anlage zugrunde liegt mit der Funktion in Gruppen lebende Individuen zu koordinieren.

Dieser so entstandene Abstimmungsprozeß wird im Strafgesetzbuch umfassend in den §§ 107 – 108 d umfassend geschützt gegen Wahlfälschung, gegen Fälschung von Wahlunterlagen, gegen die Verletzung des Wahlgeheimnisses, gegen Wählernötigung und schließlich gegen Wählerbestechung. Letztere war schon im alten Rom strafbar.

Zu b) und c) erst, wenn man das Zusammenspiel beider phylogenetisch entstandenen Koordinationsmechanismen überblickt, ergibt sich wie funktional sinnvoll wir sie heute noch nutzen. Wir setzen das Synchronisationsprinzip ein, um uns auf die hierarchischen Spitzen auf Zeit zu einigen. Da wir alle in uns angelegten Verhaltenssysteme zurückdrängen oder durch Ausbildung und Training fördern können, hat es in der Geschichte immer Gesellschaften gegeben, die mal mehr nach dem hierarchischen System und mal mehr nach dem demokratischen Synchronisationsprinzip organisiert waren. Nach den dem Verfasser bekannten Beispielen sind wohl stets beide Mechanismen bei der Koordination des Menschen wirksam gewesen. Welche Organisationsstrukturen Menschen für am richtigsten hielten, ist immer durch vielfältigste Ideologien mal so und mal so begründet worden.

Zu c) ist noch nachzutragen, daß die aus der Machtmotivation ausdifferenzierte Wettbewerbsmotivation durch gesonderte Gesetze und im sogenannten Nebenstrafrecht für den wirtschaftlichen Wettbewerb geregelt und geschützt ist. Schon der Name dieser Gesetze zeigt die Schutzrichtung an. Es sind das Gesetz gegen Wettbewerbsbeschränkungen (Kartellgesetz) und das Gesetz gegen den unlauteren Wettbewerb. Durch beide Gesetze soll sichergestellt werden, daß das Wettbewerbsverhalten zum Zuge kommen kann und nicht durch Beschränkung wie Kartellabsprachen und unlautere, d. h. unfaire, Wettbewerbshandlungen behindert oder gar verhindert wird.

V. Motivierte Verhaltenssysteme und Rechtsgüterschutz – eine zufällige Korrelation oder ein evolutionärer kausaler Prozeß?

Zunächst sei hervorgehoben, daß der besondere Teil des Strafgesetzbuches die Straftatbestände in 29 Abschnitten regelt. Keine Straftaten wurden erwähnt aus dem Abschnitt 11, der sich mit Religion und Weltanschauung beschäftigt, aus dem Abschnitt 24 - Konkursstraftaten, aus dem Abschnitt 27 - gemeingefährliche Straftaten, aus dem Abschnitt 28 - Umweltstraftaten und aus dem Abschnitt 29 - Straftaten im Amte. Damit konnte hinsichtlich der übrigen Abschnitte, überwiegend für die Grundtatbestände und die darin geschützten Rechtsgüter, eine Korrelation mit phylogenetisch entstandenen Verhaltensanlagen festgestellt werden. Der Verfasser hält diese Korrelation nicht für zufällig. In den Grafiken zu den drei Funktionsbereichen Selbsterhaltung, Fortpflanzung und Kommunikation sind motivierte Verhaltenssysteme aufgeführt worden, die das Überleben und die Fortpflanzung von in Gruppen lebenden Tieren ermöglichen. Sie sind für diese Funktionen in der Phylogenese selektiert worden. Sie decken auch heute noch wichtige Funktionen in der menschlichen, staatlich verfaßten Gesellschaft ab. Die Menschen haben im Laufe ihrer Geschichte erkannt, wo Ausfälle von motivierten Verhaltenssystemen zu Störungen in der Gesellschaft führten und sie haben diesen Funktionseinheiten Wertcharakter beigemessen und sie als Rechtsgüter, insbesondere durch Verbotsvorschriften gegenüber dem Störer (dem Straftäter), unter Schutz gestellt. Dabei handelt es sich zum Teil um höchste Werte, die ihr teilweise verfassungsrechtlicher Schutz zeigt. Sind die motivierten Verhaltenssysteme in einfacheren Gesellschaften und Umwelten die Bausteine dieser Gesellschaften, so werden in der oben zitierten Definition unsere Rechtsgüter zurecht als Bauelemente unserer Sozialordnung bezeichnet.[65] Entsprechende Verbote finden wir bereits teilweise in den ältesten uns überkommenen Gesetzestexten.[66] Der Verfasser hält dies für die Entwicklung der menschlichen Gesellschaften für einen zwingenden evolutionären Prozeß. Die wichtigen funktionalen, motivierten Verhaltenssysteme sind mit der Sonderentwicklung des Menschen und seinen Kommunikationsmöglichkeiten als Werte „zur Sprache gekommen". Die Trennung von Wert und Wirklichkeit und von Sein und Sollen, wie sie insbesondere von den Neukantianern in aller Schärfe vertreten worden ist[67], dürfte in dieser Form nicht mehr zu halten sein. Um dies noch deutlicher zu machen muß allerdings nicht nur die Ableitung der Werte, sondern auch die Ableitung wie es evolutionär zu Sollensregeln gekommen ist, noch vorgelegt werden. Dies wird im Zusammenhang mit den Wertüberlegungen, die hier in einem Werkstattbericht kurz vorgestellt wurden, geschehen.

Die Rechtswissenschaft, als Geisteswissenschaft, steht den Naturwissenschaften näher als sie selbst wahrhaben möchte. Vielleicht ist sie ja zum Teil Naturrechtswissenschaft.

---

65 Vgl. Anm. 18
66 Vgl. dazu OEHLER, Dietrich: Wurzel, Wandel und Wert der strafrechtlichen Legalordnung, Walter de Gruyter & Co. Verlag, 1950.
67 Vgl. statt aller RADBRUCH, Gustav: Vorschule der Rechtsphilosophie, 2. Aufl., Göttingen 1959, S. 19.

LITERATURVERZEICHNIS

AMELUNG, Knut — Rechtsgüterschutz und Schutz der Gesellschaft, Frankfurt 1972

BIRBAUMER, Niels/ — Biologische Psychologie, Berlin/Heidelberg

SCHMIDT, Robert F. — 1990 zitierweise: BIRBAUMER/SCHMIDT

BISCHOF, Norbert — Das Rätsel Ödipus, München/Zürich 1985

BOWLBY, John
- Bindung, München 1975
- Trennung, München 1976

DE WAAL, Frans
- Wilde Diplomaten, München/Wien 1991
- Der gute Affe, München/Wien 1997

ECCLES, John C. — Die Psyche des Menschen, München/Basel 1985

EIBL-EIBESFELDT, Irenäus — Die Biologie des menschlichen Verhaltens,3.Aufl., München/Zürich 1995

GOODALL, Jane — Wilde Schimpansen, Reinbek bei Hamburg 1991

GRAMMER, Karl — Biologische Grundlagen des Sozialverhaltens, Darmstadt 1995

GRUTER, Margaret
- Die Bedeutung der Verhaltensforschung für die

Rechtswissenschaft, Schriftenreihe zur Rechtssoziologie und Rechtstatsachenforschung, Bd. 36, Berlin 1976;
- Rechtsverhalten, Köln 1993

GRUTER, Margaret
REHBINDER, Manfred
Ablehnung – Meidung – Ausschluß, Schriftenreihe zur Rechtssoziologie und Rechtstatsachenforschung, Bd. 60, Berlin 1986

HASSENSTEIN, Bernhard
Verhaltensbiologie des Kindes, 4. Aufl., München/Zürich 1987

HENDRICHS, Hubert
Lebensprozesse und wissenschaftliches Denken, Freiburg/München 1988

IMMELMANN, Klaus,
SCHERER, Klaus R.,
VOGEL, Christian,
SCHMOOK, Peter
Herausgeber
Psychobiologie, Weinheim/München 1988 zitierweise: IMMELMANN u. a., Hrsg. Psychobiologie

KUMMER, Hans
Weiße Affen am Roten Meer, München/Zürich1992

LAMPE, Ernst-Joachim
Rechtsanthropologie, Berlin 1970

LINSENMAIR, Eduard K./
MIKULA, Gerold, Hrsg
Soziale Einflüsse in: Immelmann u. a., Psychobiologie, Weinheim/München 1988, S. 455 – 486

LORENZ, Konrad
Vergleichende Bewegungsstudien an Anatiden (1941), in: Über tierisches und menschliches Verhalten, Bd. II, 11. Aufl., München 1974

MILGRAM, Stanley   Das Milgram-Experiment, Reinbek bei
                          Hamburg 1982

MORRIS, Desmond   Der nackte Affe, München 1968
OEHLER, Dietrich   Wurzel, Wandel und Wert der
                          strafrechtlichen Legalordnung, Walter de
                          Gruyter & Co. Verlag, 1950

RADBRUCH, Gustav   Vorschule der Rechtsphilosophie, 2.
                          Aufl., Göttingen 1959

SCHMIDT, Frank-Hermann   Verhaltensforschung und Recht,
                          Schriften zur Rechtstheorie, Heft 98,
                          Berlin 1982

SCHNEIDER, Klaus/   Motivation, 2. Aufl., Stuttgart/Berlin/Köln
SCHMALT, Heinz-Dieter   1994

SCHNEIDER Klaus/   Motivation und Emotion, in: Immelmann
SCHERER, Klaus R.   u. a., Hrsg. Psychobiologie,
                          Weinheim/München 1988, S. 257 – 288

SCHÖNKE/SCHRÖDER   Kommentar zum Strafgesetzbuch, 24.
                          Aufl., München 1991 zitierweise:
                          Kommentator in Schönke/Schröder, §§

VOGEL, Christian   Arten und Kulturen – Der vergleichende
ECKENSBERGER, Lutz   Ansatz in: Immelmann u. a., Hrsg.,
                          Psychobiologie, Weinheim/München
                          1988, S. 563 - 608

WEISS, C. und   Funktionen des Blutes, in: Physiologie
JELKMANN, W.   des Menschen, hrsg. von Schmidt, Robert
                          F./Thews, Gerhard, 25. Aufl.,
                          Berlin/Heidelberg 1993

WICKLER, Wolfgang — - Funktionen des Verhaltens, in: Immelmann u. a., Hrsg. Psychobiologie, Weinheim/München 1988, S. 76 – 100
- Die Biologie der zehn Gebote, München 1962

ZIMMER, Dieter E. — Die Vernunft der Gefühle, München 1981

Rules of Respect

Hagen Hof*

1. Introduction

Law demands respect. Whether its origins are the legislature or a judge, law demands being obeyed by its addressees. But respect in this general sense is not subject to the following thoughts. "Rules of respect" are norms in the most simple case, which intend that one person pays respect to another one. Not respect for law in general, but *respect for another person* is our subject.

At this point allow me to render respect to *Margaret Gruter.* She has been the first to concentrate scientific efforts on law and behavioral research. For more than twenty years[1] she has been trying to find ways to this unexplored land, and whoever has tried to go on there could use her landmarks for his orientation.[2] She has organized and sponsored many initiatives for conferences and projects, which have brought together legal scholars and behavioral scientists. The network of scholars that she has created from the

---

* Dr. iur. Ahornweg 5, Barsinghausen, Germany.
1 A first step in this direction was her German book "Die Bedeutung der Verhaltensforschung für die Rechtswissenschaft" (1976).
2 Cf. to the list of her publications in this volume.

243

United States to Germany and back has become more and more elaborate. All these various initiatives demand our respect. The best way to pay it may be to go ahead in the direction she has marked: going on in research on the interrelations between law and behavior. I will try to show that rules of respect may be a new way into this field.

2. Definition and Examples

Within the wide range of the regulation of human behavior by law, by politics, by religion, by ethics and education, the rules of respect are to be found everywhere.[3]   Above all the various differences in their expression in these fields, we will find *three major types* of these rules. At first there are norms, which aim to keep somebody's distance from another person.[4] Second, there are rules to take into account the interests of another person.[5]   Third, there are rules which aim to protect somebody against invasive behavior by another.[6]   Thus the rules of respect include three different kinds of norms by means of their common functions between the partners in behavior.

Some of the most important examples for rules of respect are the *Human Rights*, which aim to preserve life, freedom, security, and property of the individual.[7] They typically have in common the main criteria of rules of respect: they are oriented to a central value

---

3   Cf. Hof (1996) p. 186-200.

4   In German "Abstand halten." For example the request "Please don't disturb" at the door of the hotel room, or "No admittance" to a special room.

5   In German "Rücksichtnahme." For example to keep midday rest in a flat.

6   In German "Schutzgewähr." For example rules for industrial safety or to obviate child labour.

7   Cf. to amendment IV to the Constitution of the United States: "The right of the people to be secure in their persons, houses, papers and effects, against unreasonable searches and seizures, shall be not violated . . . ."
    Later on the resolution of the United Nations 217 A (III), 10th December 1948, especially Art. 3, 17, and the European Convention on Human Rights of 20th March 1952 Art. 2 (right to live), 5 (rights of freedom and security) with the additional protocol of 13th December 1957 (private property).
    Further the Canadian Bill of Rights (10th August 1960, Part 1, Chapter 1 Nos. 1, 3, 6, 7): "(Right to life) Every human being has a right to life, and to personal security, inviolability and freedom . . . (Fundamental freedoms) Every person is the possessor of the fundamental freedoms including freedom of conscience, freedom of religion, freedom of opinion, freedom of expression, freedom of peaceful assembly and freedom of association . . . (Peaceful enjoyment of property) Every person has a right to the peaceful enjoyment and free disposition of his property, except to the extent provided by law . . . (Home inviolable) A person's home is inviolable."
    Last not least the Canada Act of 1982 especially no. 7 (Life, liberty and security of person). For the development of the theorie of international human rights cf. Bosselmann p. 235-250.

like life, freedom, security or property of the individual. To preserve it, they order especially the state and its administration to keep "hands off" or not interfere with this value.[8] This implies that the state and its administration have to take into account these values in their decisions. If somebody attacks one of these values, the state, its administration and its judges as well have to protect it. In short, human rights are prototypes of rules of respect.

This can be confirmed by some other examples: The protection of individual life, of individual freedom and of private property can be regarded as special expressions of respect for *human dignity.*[9] This topic underlines more than any other the respect which has to be paid to the individual. In the German Grundgesetz human dignity is on top of its order of values.[10] The state, its administration, its legislation, and its judges are equally obliged to render respect to human dignity and to protect it.[11]

Another example is the First Amendment to the Constitution of the United States of America:

> "Congress shall make no law respecting an establishment of religion, or prohibiting the free exercise thereof; or abridging the freedom of speech, or of the press, or the right of the people peaceably to assemble, and to petition the Government for a redress of grievances."

At the one hand this amendment demands for taking into consideration the religion and the political rights, while it simultaneously aims to protect them. This shows the close

---

8 For example "shall not be violated," "is inviolable," cf. footnote 7.
9 Cf. for Germany Maunz/Dürig Art. 1 Abs. 1 Rdn. 6-15.
   Moreover the preamble of the Constitution of Canada: "Whereas every human being possesses intrinsic rights and freedom designed to ensure his protection and development; Whereas all human beings are equal in worth and dignity, and are entitled to equal protection by the law;
   Whereas respect for the dignity of the human being and recognition of his rights and freedoms constitute the foundation of justice and peace . . . ."
10 Art. 1 Abs. 1 Grundgesetz: "Die Würde des Menschen ist unantastbar. Sie zu achten und zu schützen ist Verpflichtung aller staatlichen Gewalt."
11 Art. 1 Abs. 3 Grundgesetz.

connection between these two types of the rules of respect. Moreover this amendment *protects not only individuals, but even groups and institutions,* as we find this in the human rights catalogues of the above mentioned constitutions, too.[12]

3. Respect for Nature

Up to now we have dealt with norms that render respect to other persons, to groups or institutions, in short rules of respect for the social sphere of human life. But we must not forget that our life is influenced not only by other men and women, but that it is determined by climate and the weather, by the landscape,[13] by plants and animals; in short by our environment, as it is created by nature.[14] There are serious experts who show that respect can be paid and must be paid to nature, especially to animals and plants, but even to the landscape.[15] I will try to refer some of their thoughts as far as they are important for our subject, before I shall explain my own position, which has grown in connex and in contrast to their thoughts.

Taylor pleads expressis verbis for "respect for nature."[16] He understands humans as members of the earth's community of life[17] and denies a general human superiority in relation to animals and plants.[18] They have in this view an inherent worth,[19] which grows out of their autonomous existence. Taylor concentrates his thought

---

12 For Germany cf. Art. 4, 5, 8, 9 and 19 Abs. 3 Grundgesetz.

13 The landscape has special influence on the individual, which finds its expression not only in his dialect, but also in the quality of his or her everyday life and its organization, which may be determined by the facilities or hindrances of traffic, of weather and climate, of the available food, air and water. So we can say, that the landscape is the spatial basis of human life. Nevertheless Taylor (1986, p. 18) is right with his statement, that inanimate objects (like landscapes) are not moral subjects.

14 To special aspects of an ethic of the bioculture cf. Taylor (1986) p. 53-58.

15 To the structural symmetry between human and environmental ethics cf. Taylor (1986) p. 41-47.

16 Cf. Taylor (1986), (1997).

17 Cf. Taylor (1986) p. 44, 101-116, (1997) p. 83, 94-97, for the "deep ecology" Dewall p. 23.

18 Cf. Taylor (1986) p. 45, 46, 129-156, (1997) p. 101-114.

19 Cf. Taylor (1986) p. 13, 46, to his distinction between "intrinsic values," "inherent values" and "inherent worth" there p. 73-80, (1997) p. 83-84.

on animals and plants, they are "teleological centers of life,"[20] because these "living things" have a good of their own as we find it similar in humans.[21] It is this inherent worth, which has to be estimated by humans, to whom they have to pay respect.[22] This respect for nature is more than a special behavior against animals and plants. It is an attitude,[23] which results from a biocentric view of nature.[24] This view comprises the insight, that nature and its phenomena like animals and plants have a worth of their own, which demands respect.[25]

Here the thoughts of Taylor seem to go around in a circle. In contrast to the traditional anthropocentric view,[26] which focuses on humans and their interests in the biosphere, he prefers a multicentric approach, which accepts animals and plants as entities of their own with an inherent worth. Thus "respect for nature" is

---

20 Taylor (1986) p. 119-129, 149, 157, (1997) p. 99-101. This view is not possible with regard to inanimate objects (p. 123, 124).

21 Cf. Taylor p. 64-71, (1997) p. 80-82.

22 Cf. Taylor (1986) p. 71: "To have the attitude of respect for nature is to regard the wild plants and animals of the Earth's natural ecosystems as possessing inherent worth."

23 Cf. Taylor (1986) p. 80-98, (1997) p. 85-93.

24 Cf. Taylor (1986) p. 44, 59-98. This view leads in two directions: On the one hand to a multicentric understanding of life, which accepts animals and plants as partners within the earth's community of life. On the other hand, Taylor assumes that humans are an integral part of the system of nature (1986, p. 117).

25 Necessarily incompatible with this is the exploitative attitude, which thinks of nature as nothing more than a vast repository of resources to be developed, needed, and consumed by humans for human ends (Taylor (1986) p. 95).

26 For a list of anthropocentric arguments cf. Taylor (1986) p. 11: "Future generations have as much right to live a physically secure and healthy life as those of the present generation. Each of us is therefore under obligation not to allow the natural environment to deteriorate to such an extent that the survival and well-being of later human inhabitants of the Earth are jeopardized. We also have a duty to conserve natural resources so that future generations will be able to enjoy their fair share of benefits derived from those resources. Even our present responsibility to protect endangered species of wildlife is linked to human values. Thus it is sometimes argued that a varied gene pool of plant and animal species is needed for developing new ways to protect humans from diseases, to get rid of harmful bacteria, to learn how to control certain insects and other "pests," and to produce new sources of food through genetic engineering. We also have a duty, the argument continues, to preserve the beauty of wild nature so that those of future generations can have as much opportunity to experience and appreciate it as we do. It would be unfair of us to destroy the world's natural wonders and leave only ugly trash heaps for others to contemplate. Thus a whole system of standards and rules governing our present conduct in relation to the Earth's natural environment can be grounded on human needs and interests alone."

not only the result of his thoughts, but even hidden in their basis and beginning.[27] This is no fault of his theory, it is a consequence of his multicentric approach, which poses a real alternative to the anthropocentric views.

Stone goes further; he also regards nature and its phenomena as entities with an inherent worth, and postulates legal rights[28] of animals and plants and even of landscapes, of nature in general. In this way he tries to make up a certain equilibrium of legal weapons between man and nature, which forces to take care of nature's phenomena and its rights in political, economic and legal decisions.[29]

On first view this seems to be acceptable. We even know rights of institutions, that means of artificial persons, which exist only because and so far as they are accepted by law.[30] But there is an important difference between animals, plants, landscapes and nature on the one hand and these institutions on the other hand: Behind these institutions and within them there are humans. These institutions are nothing but instruments[31] that provide additional possibilities to act for humans, which they would not have as only natural persons. Thus the rights of the institutions derive from the rights of humans. In contrast to that, animals, plants, landscapes and nature need no humans to exist. To realize the rights Stone assigns to them, however, they would need human agents.

The approaches both of Taylor and Stone create numerous difficulties. Because all the systems of human law we find in the different countries all over the world are typically anthropocentric, they regulate the behavior of humans and human interests in nature.

---

27 So even Taylor himself (1986, p. 119): "The biocentric outlook includes a certain way of conceiving of each entity that has a life of its own."

28 Taylor does not deny that animals and plants can have legal rights. He even shows that, for example, the Endangered Species Act of 1973 (USA) gives legal protection to certain species-populations of animals and plants. "On the basis of that law certain species-populations acquire the legal right to exist." (p. 223) Without such norms there are no legal rights of animals and plants (p. 224), but they have moral rights (p. 251-255).

29 Cf. Stone (1974), critical to this Birnbacher (1995) p. 65-73. Stone himself mitigates his ideas in (1995) p. 84-87, 98-101: He now pleads for the construction of a new ethic.

30 Cf. Birnbacher (1995) p. 69.

31 Similar Attfield p. 124.

To give these systems a biocentric view, to create rights of animals and plants, seems to be impossible. It would require a fundamental new orientation of the whole system of law. There is no hope to find the political majorities that would be necessary for that. Therefore it seems to be more promising, with *Bosselmann*[32] to search for possibilities, to interpret the existing law appropriate to ecological requirements, as far as it lege artis is possible. As rules of respect are to be found in German law, in the law of the United States, and in international law as well, I will try to show that they can be used as starting-points for an ecological orientation of the existing law.

4. Another approach

At first I want to sum up some facts, which make up the basis of the following thoughts:

> All phenomena of nature and all human beings as well are products of evolution.[33] So they have a common origin and in a certain sense they are relatives to each other. This view is oriented to the facts of evolution and therefore it is independent from any religious, philosophical or political system. Evolution might be the work of God as a creator,[34] it might be only a result of natural mechanisms, or it might be an embodiment of some higher principles of creation. Which of these explanations may be favoured is unimportant for the result, each of them

---

32 Cf. Bosselmann p. 47-79, 109-126, 330-332.

33 Cf. Taylor (1986) p. 111: ". . . our common origin with other living things . . . it was the same order of evolutionary processes, governed by the same laws of natural selection and genetic transmission, that gave rise to our existence and to the existence of every other species . . ."

34 Even if one would deny evolution, he must accept that all "living things" are combinations of the same chemicals, and that there are a lot of parallels in their behavior, which indicate that humans, animals and even plants are in some traits relatives to each other.

leads to the insight, that all existing phenomena are products of evolution.

As autonomous products of evolution, animals and plants and all human beings as well have an inherent worth, as Taylor has shown.[35] This worth is independent of an evaluation by humans or anyone else. It is a result of their existence and finds a special expression in the mechanisms and the modes of behavior, which aim to maintain their existence.

Like all other living beings, humans value the facts of their environment, whether they are conductive or obstructive[36] to human interests.[37] In consequence, humans value the inherent worths of all other creatures and phenomena of nature, too. And as a consequence of this evaluation, human behavior depends on the tribute he or she pays to them. What tribute someone pays to phenomena of nature depends on his attitude to them. This attitude will be formed and directed by his interests. If these are merely egotistical, there will be respect neither for other persons nor for the phenomena of nature. Conversely, he may pay respect to some persons or to his own dog or cat. But he also may pay respect to all living creatures, as do Buddhists.

Thus the value of a phenomenon of nature depends on several determinations:

-On the egotistic motivations of those who are valuing something.

-On the inherent worth of the object, which is valued.

-On the acceptance of this inherent worth by the valuing person.

-This acceptance may be influenced by social values or norms[38]

---

35 Taylor (1986) p. 73-80 distincts the "intrinsic values" or "inherent values," which are placed on an object by man and therefore "must be relativized to this view," from the "inherent worth" of an entity, which is a result of its existence. Similar to this Regan's understanding of "inherent values" (1983) and Rescher's thoughts on "intrinsic values" (p. 180, 184, 186).

36 Cf. Randall p. 203, 204.

37 Perhaps this is one of the most important, but often neglected criteria for the distinction between the different forms of life on earth and inanimate things.

38 These are not only the result of an addition of the values of the individuals (so Randall p. 204), but they are an expression of the convictions of an important part of the specific society.

like rules of respect, which demand to keep "hands off" of something, or to take into account the interests of this object, or aim to protect it. These values or norms can help the individual with his orientation and valuing, either in a positive sense of identification with these social values or norms, or in a negative sense of non-identification with them.

In our everyday life we often pay respect to animals, especially when they seem to be dangerous.[39] We also pay respect to plants, which are very beautiful, rare, or when they are able to defend themselves, like stinging nettles or roses. Moreover there are examples for paying respect to a beautiful landscape. And we feel ourselves motivated to protect it against plans to destroy it for commercial purposes. All these examples show, that in our everyday life we keep "hands off" not only from other humans, but also from animals, plants and landscapes as the most important phenomena of nature. So rules of respect are an important element of our common behavior, and in this quality they perhaps can be used as starting-points of an ecological orientation of our behavior and the different modes of its regulation, for example by law, bypolitics, by education or by ethics.

Rules of respect aim to confine egotism, to support individual motivations, to take into consideration the interests of others, by keeping distance from them, or protecting them. They can be expressed in rights of others, or in duties of the individual to keep distance from another one, to protect him, or to take his interests into account. Human rights contain a combination af both: the rights of the individual are complemented by the duty, especially of the state, to respect them.[40]

---

39 Within this acceptance, which is typical for rules of respect, we can differ between harmless individuals or species like the hare, an elephant as an example for an endangered species, and the bacteria, which cause a deadly illness like smallpox. They need not all to be paid the same respect. But with regard to their existence, they can claim respect, as far as they are not dangerous for humans. Cf. also Taylor (1986) p. 264-269 (principle of self-defense).

40 For ethical duties cf. Taylor (1986) p. 171-191.

In the case of the phenomena of nature this construction is not available, as there are almost no rights of animals, plants or landscapes accepted by law. But there are many legal norms, which aim to protect animals, plants and landscapes or other phenomena of nature. These rules are norms of respect. They contain the duties to keep "hands off" these phenomena, to take them and their further existence in consideration, and to protect them. In these qualities rules of respect can even be extended to other phenomena, which up to now are not yet protected.

A duty of humans to do this results from the ethical responsibility of man for nature. This responsibility derives from the position of a trustee, which humans have in relation to animals and plants and other phenomena of nature with regard to several aspects:

-the common origin of animals, plants and humans,

-the interests of future generations,

-the interests of humans to get food and medicine from
      previously unknown other species, and

-the responsibility, which grows with the possibilities of
      man to destroy nature.

In consequence, rules of respect can be used as an instrument equally in favor of other persons and of the phenomena of nature. They can be regarded as a switch-box of human behavior in both directions.

5. The system of key values

Because rules of respect are to be found in law and ethics, as well as in politics and education,[41] they should be regarded as key values[42] of human society which are important for the orientation of the individual as well as the state and community.

An analysis of German law has shown that besides the rules of respect, other key values are: confidence, freedom, bonding, the individual assignment of behavior, of objects and areas, security,

---

41 Cf. Hof (1996) p. 186-200.
42 Cf. Hof (1996) p. 184-186.

competition, equal treatment and justice.[43] This enumeration is not complete, other key values may be added. All of them make up a system of the key values, in which these cling together, but also correct and confine each other.[44] In this system the rules of respect are in a dominant position: On the one hand they enclose others, which have a spatial dimension like freedom and the individual assignment of objects and areas.[45] On the other hand they overlap security as a key value as far as they aim to protect somebody or something.[46] Furthermore they are a constitutive element of justice, which includes respect of the partner and the acknowledgement of his justified interests.[47]

Moreover this system of key values is a part of a greater system of regulation of human behavior, which includes special concepts of regulation like law, politics, ethics and education.[48] This greater system itself is different from the all embracing system of behavior, which includes the drives and hindrances, and all other elements of innate and learned behavior and of their determination by the genes, by cultural influences, by the individual itself and by the relevant situation. Via the phenomena of keeping distance from another individual[49] there are connections to the rules of respect, which are expressed in law and politics, in ethics and education as well.

6. A Bridge to Foreign Cultures

It may be one of the tasks of further research to analyse the systems of key values of different countries. We surely will find that there are many differences in the weight of the various key values

---

43 Cf. Hof (1996) p. 186-360.
44 Cf. Hof (1996) p. 361-366.
45 Cf. Hof (1996) p. 361-363.
46 Cf. Hof (1996) p. 362.
47 Cf. Hof (1996) p. 345, 363.
48 Cf. Hof (1996) p. 361-382.
49 From the results of psychological and ethological research the individual is surrounded by an individual space, which makes possible to keep in distance to others. It is structured in several zones: The intimate distance (0-40 cm), the personal distance (0,40-1,20 m), the social distance (1,20-4 m), and the public distance (4-8 m). For details cf. Eibl-Eibesfeldt (1995) p. 478-480, Hof (1996) p. 190.

in accordance to the historical development of the system of values of the particular society. The insight in these differences may help us to understand the characteristics of other societies. For example, it is to be expected that key values like respect for others, freedom or security find special expressions respectively in German, in the United States, in Japan, Russia, and Iran. Up to now we know that there are some differences in the laws and in the value systems of these countries, but we lack a systematic approach.

The key values, and among them especially the respect for others and the respect for nature, could be used for this research. Moreover, the rules of respect can be used in everyday life as an instrument of better understanding other individuals and peoples. In spite of the delimitation they cause or perhaps because of this delimitation, the rules of respect can be used as bridges to that which seems strange to us in the behavior of other individuals and people. This results out of the acceptance of the partner in behavior, which is characteristic of rules of respect. This acceptance enables us to bridge the differences that up to now have been pointed out in relation of humans to the phenomena of nature.

References

Attfield, R.: Biozentrismus, moralischer Status und moralische Signifikanz. In: Birnbacher (1997) p. 117-133.

Birnbacher, D.: Juridische Rechte für Naturwesen. Eine philosophische Kritik. In: Nida-Rümelin/v. d. Pfordten (1995), p. 63-80.

Birnbacher, D. (1997, Edtr.): Ökophilosophie. Stuttgart.

Bosselmann, K.: Ökologische Grundrechte. Zum Verhältnis zwischen individueller Freiheit und Natur. Baden-Baden 1998. Especially V. International Human Rights and the Environment, p. 234-332.

Dewall, B.: Die tiefenökologische Bewegung. In: Birnbacher (1997) p. 17-59.

Ehrenfeld, D.: Das Naturschutzdilemma. In: Birnbacher (1997) p. 135-177.

Eibl-Eibesfeldt, I. (1995): Die Biologie des menschlichen Verhaltens. 3rd Edn. München.

Gruter, M. (1976): Die Bedeutung der Verhaltensforschung für die Rechtswissenschaft. Berlin.

Hof, H. (1996): Rechtsethologie. Recht im Kontext von Verhalten und außerrechtlicher Verhaltensregelung. Heidelberg.

Maunz, Th./Dürig, G.: Grundgesetz. München.

Nida-Rümelin, J./v.d.Pfordten, D. (1995, Edts.): Ökologische Ethik und Rechtstheorie. Berlin.

Randall, A.: Was sagen die Wirtschaftswissenschaftler über den Wert der biologischen Vielfalt? In: Birnbacher (1997) p. 202-215.

Regan, T. (1983): The Case for Animal Rights. Los Angeles.

Rescher, N.: Wozu gefährdete Arten retten? In: Birnbacher (1997) p. 178-201.

Schweitzer, A.: Kultur und Ethik. München. Edn. 1990.

Stone, C. (1974): Should Trees Have Standing? Toward Legal Rights for Natural Objects. Los Altos.

Stone, C.: Eine ökologische Ethik für das einundzwanzigste Jahrhundert. In: Nida-Rümelin/v.d.Pfordten p. 81-102.

Taylor, P.W. (1986): Respect for Nature. A Theorie of Environmental Ethics. Princeton, New Jersey.

Taylor, P.W.: Die Ethik der Achtung für die Natur. In: Birnbacher (1997) p. 77-116.

Zimmermann, B. (1992): Kanadische Verfassungsinstitutionen im Wandel: Unitarisierung durch Grundrechtsschutz. Berlin.

Legal Procedure
as a Place of Aggression

Raimund Jakob*

I. Procedure as a Fight

According to legal theoreticians, it is the aim of every juridical procedure to restore peace. Peace is disturbed where in human relations conflict or aggression takes its place. It is almost normal that conflict and aggression appear together. One aim of judicial procedure is—under the aspect of the psychology of law—to master aggression and conflict. This should happen by means of a formalization of the underlying conflict and its resolution by an independent authority. In this context jurists tend to overlook that a procedure can not only be a place of execution and a scene of aggressions, but that it itself contains aggressive features. Not the least destructive features can be found in procedure itself (cf.

* Dr. Raimund Jacob, Lecturer of Law, University of Salzburg, Institut fuer Grundlagenwissenschaften, Salzburg, Austria.

Gruen, 1993, passim). As far as penal procedure is concerned the so-called public opinion leaves no doubt about society's desire for revenge. The examples shown in this contribution are taken from legal practice in German-speaking countries.

The classical judicial civil procedure is called in German "Rechtsstreit"—"Streit" meaning fight or struggle. Aggression is the impetus for an attack, for a belligerent behavior. Civil procedure thus is necessarily connected with aggression, normally with immediate personal aggressions of the parties to the conflict. In this context we have to keep in mind that it is not necessarily the wish of the parties to the conflict to restore peace. Usually for the lawyer the legal procedure has the character of work. Aggressions can result when the client entrusts a lawyer with representation in a certain procedure, who is well known as being aggressive ("hired gun"). This is true for institutions and individuals as well.

Apart from this, civil law also has a non-contentious procedure, which in Austria is called "ausserstreitiges Verfahren." This expression, however, is misleading; it should only express that here we are confronted with an atypical judicial procedure. Typically, a judge has to decide a fight. Let us only think of the Last Judgement, where the powers of good fight the powers of darkness. Naturally the good has to win. The mentioned atypical procedures are often apt to work off personal aggressions. Wherever law enforcement takes place, aggression is involved. This happens in case of the determination of support for a divorced partner or the realization of children's right of access after a divorce. Also, administrative procedures can be the place of aggressions—not only when taking place before an administrative court, but even before that. Thus, for instance in a building case, the consensus between "good" neighbors has to be found.

That the judicial procedure can in many ways be a place of aggression becomes especially clear in criminal procedure. In the material scope the punishment is an instrumentalized aggression to serve the accomplishment of a certain aim of punishment. Or in the meta-scope, where the procedure takes place and the detention before the trial as an instrumentalized aggression is imposed in view of the ascertainment of the truth. In cases of extremely abominable offences even personal aggressions of the legal personnel appear. A fact becomes visible: namely that on the part of the legal staff, aggressive measures and ways of behavior are applied in recognition of their legal authority, or even without it. This may happen consciously as well as unconsciously. Also in civil procedure one's own concerns may play a role, as for instance in a case of divorce.

In practice it is certainly difficult to draw a border between instrumentalized and personal aggression. Often personal aggression in legal matters is actually only pretended instrumentalized aggression. Think of the case of a prisoner in chains. Also the lawyer who enjoys the fight and needs it, finds a forum for the realization of this need in the court (cf. Redmount, 1973, p. 80ss.).

II. As to the Linguistic and Notional Problems

First of all it should be noted that the professional jargon of jurists in procedural matters is similar to the language used in warlike conflicts. This begins when speaking of the procedural "opponent" responding to the "hostile party" and ends with the "lost" procedure and the "disputed" (combated "bekaempft") decision. Legal life and war interface each other when speaking of aggression in international law where weapons are directed intentionally against targets on foreign territory. We shall meet with these kinds of analogies more often.

It is the time now to explain which notion of aggression is used here. I do not intend to contribute to the controversial discussion for the reasons for aggression. It seems that for the present article the question whether endogenous or exogenous reasons are to be hold responsible for it are of secondary importance (psycho-analysis and ethology normally prefer endogenous reasons). Mainly because here it is not the question "why," but the question "how" aggressions take place and how they can possibly be avoided and coped with. The position I take here is orientated on the statements of psycho-analytical theory (cf. Laplanche & Pontalis, 1975, p. 40ss.). But this shall not exclude that an "instinctively" aggressive lawyer additionally is supported in his future aggressive behavior in legal matters by the successes he has gained because of his past aggressive performance.

III. Role and Aggression

In the 1960s, clients expected their lawyers to leave the court with a scowl, and walk in different directions after a civil suit or after a procedure on an insult of honor. They would have even expected them almost to insult each other verbally and to threaten each other with a disciplinary pursuit in front of their professional board. With the granting of the mandate to their lawyer, the clients had somehow bought the "theater at the court." The performance there had to have an aggressive tendency and it had to be a hero-play (cf. Rasehorn, 1980, p. 328ss.).

Should one party to the conflict find the lawyers of both parties eating their dinner together in a good mood, this behavior was regarded as suspicious, if not as a betrayal. The argument that two fellow students had met again privately would in this context not be accepted as plausible. At this time the parties to the conflict had expected their representatives to fully identify themselves with the represented interests. The lawyer had to demonstrate publicly that he were an enemy both of the opponent and also of his representative.

Why is it that today clients do not expect this behavior of their lawyers? Different explanations are possible. One reason may be found in the context of television. It seems that the different Anglo-American proceedings which are shown in many television series to the European audience have influenced their ideas about and their expectations of the legal procedure. Another explanation may be found in the flood of rules in the last decades and in the intricacy of legal life. Intricacy means uncertainty and thus uncertainty in regard of the outcome of the procedure. This uncertainty can be minimized if the representative undertakes some of those contacts which oneself does not exercise any more with the opponent. This fact has something to do with socialization. It seems that we also find here parallel orders of events that occur in military conflicts ("limited conflict" or "surgical intervention").

In penal procedure the public prosecutor describes the person's offence who disregarded the law and so represents the society's desire for revenge and retribution. The individual's gratification of drives may not go unpunished if all other members of society have to live without this gratification (Freud, XXII, p. 195ss.; cf. Gruter, 1976, p. 79s.). The judge now has to decide about the presence and the gravity of a norm violation. The more he unconsciously recognizes himself in the offence in question, the more he feels that which he rebukes and hates in himself, the more severe the verdict. In order to avert this unconscious inner conflict, an expert will be asked for an opinion based on rationally clear reasons. It is the task of this expert to help the judge to avoid injustice. But in fact, he will be used as a helpmate to condemn those features most despised by the judge and so support the judicial verdict (cf. Freud, XII, p. 48s.).

Those procedures play a special role where women are the victims of a crime such as rape, sexual abuse and the like. One can notice here that female judges and public prosecutors tend to identify themselves with their male colleagues more than with other women (cf. Jakob, 1997, p.328). Also, here the identification with the men is made easier by the fact that in reaching the verdict the judge's own inclinations towards norm violations are averted. It may be that this situation will change if there is a sufficient representation of women within the legal staff in combination with the passage of enough time to get used to this fact. Male judges often feel that women as the victims of a crime are responsible themselves for the terrible events. This might be due to the fact that the women's sense of self-worth is still guided by male patterns. This leads to self-sacrifice, self-contempt and the preparedness for a sacrifice. At the same time the man's belief in his superiority is strengthened, and his contempt of the female is furthered.

IV. Argumentation and Aggression

For the actualization of aggressive tendencies, generally all ways of behavior are apt. Any behavior can be aggressive, be it a negative (omission), a positive (activity), a symbolic (irony) or an effectively performed one. As it gives a bad impression to show aggression openly, ironic and cynical forms of expression are apt for legal argumentation. Covert aggression is a speciality of legal argumentation. Correspondence preceding a hearing might often be quite aggressive. It is intended to threaten the opponent and to make him give in. In legal procedure we are confronted with different possibilities to exert aggressions. In order to illustrate this, civil procedure is used as an example. One possibility is to try to use the law of civil procedure, pleadings and the like, to harm the other party. This might happen because of the aggression or it might aim at making the opponent seem to the court unworthy. This happens by describing certain events or personal ways of behavior such as drinking, lying and such.

Other possibilities to actualize aggressive tendencies are offered by the language as a means of legal argumentation. We have to distinguish here whether the argumentation is oral (*inter praesentes*) or in writing (*inter absentes*) and who the real addressees of such an argumentation are (Jakob, 1987, p. 151ss.). Thus in civil procedure a pleading has four addressees: the judge, the opposing party, the lawyer and finally the own party. The judge should be addressed pertinently, logically and with trust in his authority; whereas the opposing lawyer should have the feeling of loyal solidarity. The aggressive threat has to be applied to the opposing party and it should be formulated in a way that it can be readily recognized by the other. Should all these aspects be accomplished then the modern lawyer had done his job well—at least from the participants' point of view. If he wants to do his job really well, he will also offer to the judge, aside from substantive arguments, possibilities of identification (advertisement).

As far as the oral argumentation is concerned, it will be more aggressive against the opponent than the written one. In contrast to the written word which is always present and can be re-read, the spoken word is a transitory occurrence. Apart from extreme situations, neither the court nor the opponent's lawyer will stand by the attacked person. The custom of mutual professional dependence is stronger than the client's interest in protection who, as a rule, is only a casual client.

The role as plaintiff or defendant, as prosecutor or accused, besides the *onus probandi*, also influences the character of the argumentation. The party who is in the defensive will often not be able to articulate aggressive wishes. He can, however, improve his situation by involving a professional representative who is at least to a certain extent unbiased as far as the procedural issuer is concerned. He will also be able to judge the possibility of attacks better and will be able to respond to them.

A client is well advised to watch the language and the linguistic behavior of his lawyer. After the lawyer has taken the case, he will encourage his possibly insecure client by promising him a good outcome of the matter and will try at the same time to devaluate the opponent. This will be done, for instance, in this way: "Jekyll has no serious chances as far as his claim is concerned . . ." If in the course of the procedure the lawyer speaks of the opponent as "Doctor Jekyll" then the alert client may conclude that in the eyes of his lawyer the procedure is lost already, though the lawyer will inform him to this effect only later.

If we neglect for the moment the problem of the lawyer's fee, this can be even regarded as a positive, psycho-hygienic aspect. By the steady integration into the procedure and by the successive bad news ("the witness X has certified differently than we expected . . ."), the client will be step by step put into the right mood and can thus identify himself with "his procedure" and its unfortunate outcome. The place of aggression is taken over by "harm about the procedure." In the end the party is prepared—more or less peacefully—also to accept an unfavorable outcome.

V. The Troublemaker

Especially obvious aggression is "querulous behavior." The so-called troublemaker is a phenomenon brought about by jurisdiction and administration. Disregarding lunatics, the troublemaker is subject to a disturbance of personality which is due to an abnormal digestion of a key experience, of an experience of injustices. Regarded as a personality, the troublemaker has a strong drive and is characterized by mistrust and malevolence combined with an exaggerated need of justice. Psychoanalytically he can be classified as an anal type of personality. The struggle for securing his right has become the goal of his life (cf. Jakob, 1995, p. 149s.).

He tends to polarize the world (good—evil, just—unjust), and he always holds the opinion that he is the one who has unjustly suffered disadvantages. Therefore he steadily tries to defend in an aggressive manner his "claims." Towards contractors, experts and officials he adds accusation to accusation; incessantly he reproaches someone for bribery, defamation, violation of the duty of supervision etc. Because of a unilateral overestimation of the justice of his claims, his sight for facts is blurred. In relation to his legal problems he loses the sight for reality. The public system for legal protection is accepted by him only so far as it grants him legal claims.

Facing this phenomenon, the judicial system is quite helpless. It is common that in such cases the persons react with instrumentalized aggression. This is so even if the system tries to get rid of the problem by means of guardianship and institutionalization. Such solutions are not lasting as a rule. Moreover, their effect on the troublemaker is counterproductive and thus the vicious circle of aggression and counteraggression is maintained. Admittedly interaction with such personalities is troublesome and the possibilities are limited. As for the rest, the constitutional state has to stand it. It seems that certain chances could be offered by more closeness to the people. Finally infringing social and legal measures, which are not made plausible to the addressees and which can not be understood by the persons concerned, are often a motive for querulous and aggressive behavior.

VI. Hopes and Solutions

Legal procedure is a place of aggressions. This is in its nature and that will also remain so. The question arises how far we are capable to cope with this aggression constructively and thus come closer to the aimed-at interpersona or social peace. The preconditions are not very favorable at the moment. This is due on the one hand to the legal preconditions, which offer little or no space for constructive solutions, and on the other hand to the legal education at the Universities—at least in German speaking countries. The future jurist learns first of all to solve cases in the same manner as is done by the judge who will decide the legal case. Topics like legal counseling, conciliation and mediation as subjects of University studies are unknown.

This leads to the fact that the attempts of alternative forms of procedure are practiced more or less outside of the legal staff's scope. The judicial system limits itself to transfer matters to this scope and to the responsible control of the outcomes of "mediation" and "penal equalization." (Tatausgleich) These alternative procedures are the task of a new professional group, which comes from various professions (social workers, psycho-therapists, psychologists and jurists), who have begun to establish themselves commercially. Such offers are still experimental in Austria and are not to be found in all places. In addition they are limited to certain groups of persons and certain cases. Their acceptance is presently quite small. In the long run we shall observe the tendency towards a two-class-judicature, a "soft" denationalized and an "aggressive" public one. As far as the education of jurists is concerned, there seems little hope for the future.

As far as the civil procedure is concerned, the judicial system has two possibilities to avoid and to master aggressively-settled conflicts. We have already spoken about one, namely more closeness to the people by offering legal counseling. Unnecessary procedures could be avoided in this way and inter-human relations could possibly be maintained.

A classical form of solving conflicts is to reach a compromise. The fundamental idea is to prefer areas of agreement to those that give rise to conflict. Because of the insecurity of the result of a procedure according to juristic means, there is some readiness for compromise. It is the advantage of a compromise—this being its characteristic—that no party to the conflict leaves the arena as a loser. Compromise knows only winners, and offers both parties the possibility of identification with the outcome and the judiciary authority, with the opponent (equally weak) and finally also with its representative (aggressor). In this way all classical varieties of identification can meet (Jakob, 1987, p. 164).

What remains still is the individual personality of the jurist as a source of unconsciously involved aggressive tendencies. In order to uncover and deal with such tendencies, but also other affected scopes, the members of the legal staff should be offered the possibility to participate in groups of such kinds as Balint-groups (cf. Stucke, 1990, pp. 67ss.). Another question in this context is certainly how to motivate the individual members to participate. Such groups could help jurists to clarify and understand their participation in the relations of a legal case. Moreover, their own motivations could be detected and aggressive tendencies could be diminished.

References

Freud, S. (1953 onwards). The Standard Edition of the Complete Psychological Works (ed. by J. Strachey), XXIV vols. London: The Hogarh Press & The Institute of Psycho-analysis.

Gruen, A. (1993). Der Wahnsinn der Normalitaet. Realismus als Krankheit: Eine grundlegende Theorie zur menschlichen Destruktivitaet. 5th ed., Muenchen: Deutscher Taschenbuch-Verlag.

Gruter, M. (1976). Die Bedeutung der Verhaltensforschung für die Rechtswissenschaft, Berlin: Duncker & Humblot.

Jakob, R. (1987). Argumentation und Identifizierung. In: R. Jakob & M. Rehbinder (eds.), Beitraege zur Rechtspsychologie, pp. 151-166, Berlin: Duncker & Humblot.

Jakob, R. (1995). Rechtsberatung und Psychologie: Rechtspsychologische Ueberlegungen zu einem zwischenmenschlichem Prozess. In: R. Jakob & M. Usteri & R. Weimar (eds.), Psyche—Recht—Gesellschaft, pp. 143-153, Bern: Staempfli + Cie.

Jakob, R. (1997). Die alltaegliche Gewalt und die Hilflosigkeit der Juristen. In: M. Gruter & M. Rehbinder (eds.), Gewalt in der Kleingruppe und das Recht, pp. 323-329, Bern: Staempfli + Cie.

Laplanche, L. & Pontalis, J.-B. (1975). Das Vokabular der Psychoanalyse. 2nd ed., Frankfurt/M: Suhrkamp Taschenbuch Verlag.

Rasehorn, Th. (1980). Die Justiz als Theater. In: E. Blankenburg & E. Klausa & H. Rottleuthner (eds.), Alternative Rechtsformen und Alternativen zum Recht, pp. 328-343, Opladen: Westdeutscher Verlag.

Redmount, R. (1973). Law as a Psychological Phenomenon. In: The American Journal of Jurisprudence, vol. 18, pp. 80-104, Notre Dame Law School.

Stucke, W. (1990). Die Balint-Gruppe. 2nd ed., Koeln: Deutscher Aerzte-Verlag.

Law, Emotions, and
Behavioral Biology

Owen D. Jones[*]

Our sentiments on biology, and its role in public affairs, are mixed. The study of life has brought us, for example, both antibiotics and germ warfare. In few contexts, however, is the role of biology more controversial, and less understood, than in the study of biological influences on human behavior. On one hand, this area of research has grown explosively in recent years, offering new insights on why members of our species tend to behave as they do. Some of these insights may be relevant to law. On the other hand, a volatile combination of media sensationalism and the average citizen's thin training in biology has fueled popular misconceptions about behavioral biology. For example, many people mistakenly conclude that invoking behavioral biology in the human context must yield reductionism and genetic determinism, or even foster the

---

[*] Professor of Law, Arizona State University College of Law; Faculty Fellow, Center for the Study of Law, Science, and Technology; Research Fellow, Gruter Institute for Law and Behavioral Research; B.A., Amherst College; J.D., Yale Law School.

proliferation of genetic defenses at trial. Such misconceptions tend to obscure possible benefits. In this essay, I hope to establish two things. First, it is possible to discuss human behavioral biology in a measured voice—without either zealous advocacy or zealous antipathy. And second, such discussions are worthwhile.

It is of course true that biology, like any system of knowledge, can be used for good or ill. But it is also true that understanding even the most fundamental principles of behavioral biology, which are quite accessible,[1] is likely to benefit research, scholarship, and the effective pursuit of policy goals, if one is at all interested in constructing a more robust model of human behavior. This particularly obtains in the context of understanding patterns of human emotions, morals, tastes, and preferences that lead to behaviors relevant to law. Indeed, if studied carefully, and used carefully, increased familiarity with behavioral biology can improve legal thinkers' abilities to make significant contributions in furtherance of our own socially pre-articulated goals.

Behavioral biology is not so much a distinctly boundaried discipline as it is an unbordered and growing interdisciplinary area. It overlaps substantially with such disciplines and topics as sociology, economics, game theory, psychology, genetics, evolutionary biology, ethology, politics, history, anthropology, and the like. Its unifying subject of study is simply the behavior of living organisms.

---

1 For a brief introduction, see Timothy H. Goldsmith & Owen D. Jones, Evolutionary Biology and Behavior: A Brief Overview and Some Important Concepts, 39 Jurimetrics J. 131 (1999). A lengthier overview, prepared especially for lawyers, appears in Part I: A Primer in Law-Relevant Evolutionary Biology of Owen D. Jones, Evolutionary Analysis in Law: An Introduction and Application to Child Abuse, 75 N.C. L. Rev. 1117 (1997).
Treatments of modern behavioral biology for the general audience include: Timothy H. Goldsmith, The Biological Roots of Human Nature: Forging Links Between Evolution and Behavior (1991); Matt Ridley, The Red Queen: Sex and the Evolution of Human Nature (1994); Robert Wright, The Moral Animal: Evolutionary Psychology and Everyday Life (1994). Accessible textbooks, for gaining more technical familiarity, include: John Alcock, Animal Behavior: An Evolutionary Approach (6th ed. 1998); Martin Daly & Margo Wilson, Sex, Evolution, and Behavior (2d ed. 1983); Scott Freeman & Jon C. Herron, Evolutionary Analysis (1998); Douglas J. Futuyma, Evolutionary Biology (3rd ed. 1998); Timothy H. Goldsmith & William F. Zimmerman, Biology, Evolution, and Human Nature (forthcoming 1999); J.R. Krebs & N.B. Davies, An Introduction to Behavioural Ecology (3d ed. 1993); Mark Ridley, Evolution (1993); Robert Trivers, Social Evolution (1985).

Behavioral biology has two very different aspects: 1) behavioral genetics; and 2) evolved or "species-typical" psychology. Behavioral genetics involves efforts to trace the different behaviors of different individuals to different genes. For some behaviors this is an appropriate approach, occasionally law-relevant. And it is this approach that most people have in mind when they consider the relevance of behavioral biology to law. But it is the second aspect of behavioral biology—the evolved psychology aspect—that holds far more promise for legal thinkers.

The evolutionary psychology aspect of behavioral biology, instead of investigating differences between individuals, investigates the sameness of individuals across a species in order to predict and discover which behavioral patterns are most likely to emerge and why. That is, it is an effort to trace the different behaviors of different individuals not to different genes, but rather to different environmental stimuli encountered by neurologically similar brains, sporting similar, evolved, contingent, and highly conditional decisional algorithms. That is, humans bear species-wide (in some cases sex-wide) physical, information-processing commonalities that have evolved to yield predispositions toward certain behaviors, in the face of certain categories and confluences of stimuli, and predispositions toward other behaviors, in other contexts.

I hasten to add three things. First, the fact that a behavioral predisposition has evolved, even if we assume it has, says precisely nothing about whether that predisposition is good to have around today, constructive, defensible, or desirable. Explanation is not justification, and one cannot legitimately reason, without more, from the descriptive to the normative.[2]

Second, a predisposition is not a predetermination. That is, the existence of a species-wide behavioral predisposition enables a

---

2 To do so is to commit the well-known "Naturalistic Fallacy." The term was coined by G.E. Moore in Principia Ethica 62, 89-110 (Thomas Baldwin ed., 2d ed. 1993), but the concept apparently traces to the 1888 edition of David Hume, A Treatise of Human Nature 469-70 (L.A. Selby-Bigge & P.H. Nidditch eds., 2d ed. 1978).

statement about the probability that certain patterns of behaviors will emerge from the accumulated behaviors exhibited by individuals in our society, numbered now in the many millions. With rare exceptions (involving the most fundamental, life-sustaining bodily functions), predispositions of this species-typical sort do not enable confident predictions about how any single person will in fact behave in the future, or why an individual behaved as she did in the past. Yet even uncertain predictions can have tremendous value. (Consider meteorology, for example.[3]) For this reason, this aspect of behavioral biology is likely to illuminate legal issues in the contexts of preventing or encouraging behaviors across society. It is far less likely to provide useful information in a post-act context, such as a trial, or a sentencing hearing.

Third, behavioral biology takes no side in the "Nature versus Nurture" debate. This is principally because, news headlines to the contrary, there is no such debate within relevant scientific communities. Far from being genetically deterministic, biologists are fond of saying that asking whether a given behavior is the product of nature or of nurture is like asking whether the area of a rectangle is the product of its length, on one hand, or of its width, on the other. Nature and nurture are inseparably intertwined. Neither makes any sense without the other. All biological processes, including normal brain development, ultimately depend upon rich environmental inputs. Similarly, all environmental influences can only be perceived, sorted, mentally analyzed, and understood through biological and therefore principally evolved processes.

How is this relevant to law? We start from the premise that law is about regulating behavior. It is a necessary implication of that premise that the effectiveness of various legal approaches to regulating behavior depends on the efficacy of the behavioral models on which law grounds these approaches. Law can therefore be understood, in an important respect, to be a consumer of

---

3   David L. Faigman provides this example in To Have and Have Not: Assessing the Value of Social Science to the Law as Science and Policy, 38 Emory L.J. 1005, 1047 (1989).

behavioral models, which act as the fulcra against which different legal practices attempt to lever. An inaccurate or only partially accurate behavioral model makes for a squishy, sponge-like fulcrum, which provides law with only inefficient leverage against the human behavior it seeks to affect.

Different subdisciplines of law vary along the spectrum from passive to active in how much they help to construct useful behavioral models. The passive approach is simply to adopt an understanding of human behavior that is handed to legal thinkers by one of the many disciplines housed elsewhere in the university. The active approach is to demand that these disciplines be, in the end, consistent with each other, and integrated into one seamless web of knowledge. This ultimately requires efforts to build theoretically and empirically robust behavioral models.

Economics, of course, with its image of *homo economicus*, has one model of human behavior. That model has proven useful to law in many respects, and its success is largely attributable to the large proportion of law-relevant contexts in which it accurately predicts how people's behaviors will change as legal sanctions (interpreted as prices) vary.[4] Yet it is often unable to predict how people will act—as humans seem notoriously prone to irrational outcomes. For example, people consistently use irrelevant information (such as sunk costs), give answers that are highly sensitive to logically irrelevant changes in questions, and make errors in updating probabilities on the basis of new information.[5]

Many have argued that increased predictive power, in the context of such seemingly irrational behavior, requires integrating

---

4 See generally, Robert Cooter & Thomas Ulen, Law and Economics (2d ed. 1995); Richard Posner, Economic Analysis of Law (5th ed. 1998).

5 See John Conlisk, Why Bounded Rationality, 34 J. Econ. Lit. 669, 670 (1996), and sources cited therein. See also Judgment Under Uncertainty: Heuristics and Biases (Daniel Kahneman et al. eds., 1982).

economics with insights from sociology, psychology, and the like.[6] Yet even that constructive and useful effort to integrate a variety of complementary social sciences is insufficiently animated by the pressing need to further integrate the social sciences with the life sciences.

To underscore the significance of that need, consider the obvious. We would laugh incredulously, would we not, if in the course of designing an engine at the Ford Motor Company a team of chemists, in all sincerity, proposed a system thoroughly inconsistent with a robust law of physics. We take completely for granted that chemistry and physics must be integrated with one another.[7] We categorize those disciplines as dealing, at base, with the same sort of things.

But it is today increasingly obvious that future generations would similarly laugh at us, throughout the legal community, if we were to pursue legal strategies premised on ideas about human behavior that are inconsistent with behavioral biology and what is known about the evolution of a species-typical human psychology. In the end, all the social sciences focused on the causes of behavior—and all the life sciences focused on the causes of behavior—need to be integrated as well, just like chemistry and physics.

We could only ignore what the life sciences are learning about biological influences on the human brain and thus on desires and

---

6 See, e.g., Robert C. Ellickson, Bringing Culture and Human Frailty to Rational Actors: A Critique of Classical Law and Economics, 65 Chi.-Kent L. Rev. 23 (1989); Christine Jolls et al., A Behavioral Approach to Law and Economics, 50 Stan. L. Rev. 1471 (1998); Russell Korobkin, The Status Quo Bias and Contract Default Rules, 83 Cornell L. Rev. 608 (1998); Jeffrey J. Rachlinski & Forest Jourden, Remedies and the Psychology of Ownership, 51 Vand. L. Rev. 1541 (1998); Cass R. Sunstein, Behavioral Analysis of Law, 64 U. Chi. L. Rev. 1175 (1997); Thomas S. Ulen, Cognitive Imperfections in the Economic Analysis of Law, 12 Hamline L. Rev. 385 (1989). See also Donald C. Langevoort, Behavioral Theories of Judgment and Decision Making in Legal Scholarship: A Literature Review, 51 Vand. L. Rev. 1499 (1998).

7 See Leda Cosmides, John Tooby, and Jerome H. Barkow, Introduction: Evolutionary Psychology and Conceptual Integration, in The Adapted Mind: Evolutionary Psychology and the Generation of Culture 3, 4 (Jerome H. Barkow et al. eds., 1992); John Tooby & Leda Cosmides, The Psychological Foundations of Culture, in The Adapted Mind: Evolutionary Psychology and the Generation of Culture 19, 23 (Jerome H. Barkow et al. eds., 1992).

behavior at the peril of inaccuracy, avoidable inefficiencies, and behavioral model obsolescence. Just as we presume that biologists interested in a rich understanding of human behavior must attend to the insights of integrative efforts in the social sciences, so too should we conclude that social scientists must attend to behavioral biology. This is the only way: 1) to be true to a holistic approach; 2) to contextualize human behavior within both the facts of human biological and evolutionary history and the facts of modern cultural practices; and 3) to further explore, for example, the evolutionary influences on cooperation, competition, aggression, and sexuality—all of which are the subject of law, and none of which are unique to the human species.

In this enterprise, we legal thinkers would join (albeit more than fashionably late) the exciting cross-disciplinary convergence taking place in many other fields, such as anthropology, psychology, psychiatry, and medicine, which are now making efforts to frame their behavioral work against the larger background of the natural sciences. Behavioral biology is an area of science that can, I have argued elsewhere,[8] provide us with information to help us improve our behavioral models, increase the efficacy of the cost-benefit analyses that underlie many of our policy-making judgments, and suggest ways in which regulatory strategies can be improved, in furtherance of pre-existing goals.

Specifically, a behavioral biology approach (which shares a deep connection to both economic and social/psychological reasoning) invites us to understand some of the complexities of human emotions, desires, and behaviors as influenced by a brain that has evolved to process information—and to correlate information patterns with subjectively perceived psychological states. These, in turn, influence behavior in flexible but non-random ways. Put another way, with the exception of reflexes and

---

8 See, e.g., Jones, Evolutionary Analysis in Law, supra note 2; Owen D. Jones, Law and Biology: Toward an Integrated Model of Human Behavior, 8 J. Contemp. L. Issues 167 (1997); Owen D. Jones, Sex, Culture, and the Biology of Rape: Toward Explanation and Prevention, 87 Cal. L. Rev. 827 (1999); Owen D. Jones, Genes, Behavior, and Law, 15 Politics & The Life Sciences 101 (1996).

the like, all important behavior originates in the brain. Therefore, behavior cannot be fully understood without contemplating the nature of our brain and its non-random information-processing patterns that lead to behavior. The brain, in turn, can be fully understood only if studied as a product of evolution. For like all other aspects of anatomy, the form and function of the human brain has been shaped by evolutionary history. Therefore, if one does not know much about the brain, and does not know much about evolutionary processes, one ultimately can only go so far in understanding—and influencing—human behavior.

The brain is now believed to be a specialized, not generalized, information processor. Sitting behind your eyes, and processing these symbolic ink squiggles, is not your mind per se, but rather your brain (wherein whatever it is we like to call the mind takes up residence). Your peripheral nerves do not just carry stimuli to the entrance of the brain, and dump it on the floor. As a general proposition, different kinds of stimuli are processed by different parts of your brain, dedicated to different tasks. This sort of specialization can only have come about (absent undiscovered or supernatural phenomena) as processes of natural selection operated to shape brain structures and functions—the way it shaped the rest of the human body. Or, as Steven Pinker of MIT describes it in his recent book *How the Mind Works*, the mind is a system of organs of computation, designed by natural selection to solve the problems faced by our evolutionary ancestors.[9]

In other words, the brain is an information processor designed by natural selection to be better at solving certain kinds of problems than others and to yield emotional realities that, on average, led to adaptive behavior for our ancestors, in the environments they faced for most of human evolutionary history. The brain therefore mediates some behaviors by predisposing its owner to correlate certain kinds of emotional states with various kinds of stimuli.

Am I saying that emotions are part of our evolutionary heritage? Of course. Emotions are simply more pliable and environmentally

---

9 Steven Pinker, How the Mind Works (1997).

sensitive than our evolved physical traits—though not infinitely so. Every emotion reflects the internal state of an evolved nervous system. And emotions can be understood as mechanisms that set our brain's highest level goals.

Four things help to make this clear. First, we humans are today fully thirty-five thousand times as far from our first primate ancestor as we are from the year 1 A.D. Second, our ancestors were primates for roughly sixty-two million years before they even began to diverge into what later became the gorillas, orangutans, chimpanzees, bonobos, and early hominids. Third, this same sixty-two million year period is at a minimum six-hundred-and-twenty times as long as the period during which we have existed as our own, distinctly human species. And fourth, during all that time, and longer, our pre-sentient ancestors were motivated by many of the same things that are our most powerful motivators today.[10]

Think, for example, of the following desires: hunger; thirst; a taste for highly caloric sweets and fats; sexual desire; sexual jealousy; psychological and physical pleasure; psychological and physical pain; fear; greed; grief; anger; aggression; affection; sense of family; love of our offspring; moralistic aggression; and desires to cooperate and compete in differing circumstances. We are not the only species to exhibit these emotions, or to have our ensuing behaviors influenced by them.

Emotions exert probabilistic influences on behavior by affecting our tastes and preferences. And these, in turn, affected reproductive success, and hence became subject to natural selection processes. As a species we therefore share an evolved psychology, one that varies at the margin but still clusters around the bulk in the bell-shaped distributional curve. Our brains are living fossils that often lead us to currently maladaptive and irrational outcomes, because we have so quickly and significantly changed our social, legal, penal, and technological environments.

Consequently, for every behavior described by economics or

---

10 This time sequence is described more fully in Jones, Evolutionary Analysis in Law, *supra* note 2, at 1129-1132.

psychology, there are causal processes going on in nerve cells. The most general patterns of processing have in turn been shaped by natural selection[11]—the most ancient systematically economic process in the history of the world. That process incessantly sifts the more successful reproducing organisms from the less successful, and therefore inevitably affects the extent to which various psychological (and therefore behavioral) traits spread and disperse throughout a species' population over ensuing generations. Any theory of behavior not consistent with these aspects of human biology is therefore simply ahistorical—building the human brain not from the ground up, but from above down, using mythical, otherwordly skyhooks that are themselves suspended in nothing.

Law and biology scholars are beginning to incorporate and apply behavioral biology principles to a wide variety of topics of relevance to law.[12] These include, for example: aggression, cooperation, competition, risk assessment, relations between the sexes, emotions, deceptions and self-deceptions, and so on.

If we are to integrate the social and life sciences, in order for us to have a robust model of human behavior, we need to do two things. First, we must admit that dualism is dead, and has been for a long time. Inquiries framed as: Nature v. Nurture; Biological v. Cultural; Biological v. Environmental; Mind v. Body; and Human v. Animal are sterile, distracting, and destructive. Second, we must contextualize human behavior within its evolutionary history. This reveals the relevance, to law, of the evolved human psychology—a shared psychology evident today in our species-typical patterns of preferences, emotions, social bonds, and desires—many of which lead precisely to the behaviors that law attempts to regulate.

There is a vast and useful literature, nearly untapped in law, on the biology of human behavior. Within this literature lie some partial answers to some of the questions that socio-economics, like

---

11 Natural selection is the inevitable result of any system combining three factors: 1) replication; 2) variation, however slight, during replication; and 3) differential replication as a consequence of variation.

12 A bibliography of relevant sources is available on the website of the Society for Evolutionary Analysis in Law (SEAL), at http://www.law.asu.edu/jones/seal/.

law, is attempting to address. For while biology does not dictate behavior in any single individual (for whom the biology is probablistic, not deterministic) the shared components of human psychology nevertheless contribute testably and substantially to the average patterns exhibited across the entire human population and thus within the scope of every legal regime. Understanding the way human brains tend, on average, to perceive environmental events, and understanding the ways in which our brains' evolved and conditional algorithms tend to process those events, can therefore help us to design social and legal systems that more effectively regulate behaviors in ways that further our shared social values and pre-articulated goals.

The Correlation between Psychology and Law—A Few Considerations and Comments on Research and Practice from the Point of View of Legal Psychology and Jurisprudence

Adelheid Kühne* & Martin Usteri**

Introduction

It was at the beginning of this century when psychology found its way into legal practice in Europe. At this time forensic-psychological and criminological issues such as the assessment of criminal responsibility and the analysis of testimonials were central. Since then, the number of psychological issues in research and practice in the field of jurisprudence has expanded; today, the term

* Professor of Psychology, Hannover, Germany.
** Professor of Law, University of Zurich, School of Law, Zurich, Switzerland.

«legal psychology» not only encompasses the practical issues of psycho-diagnostic expert reports in criminal and civil proceedings relating to juveniles and adults—and here especially in family and guardianship proceedings («forensic psychology»)—but also the research results which in the broader sense concern legislation, court proceedings and the administration of justice. In this respect, themes such as the reform and evaluation of laws (Sporen 1983), communication and interaction during trial (Kühne 1983, Ortloff 1995), due process of law (Bierbrauer et al. 1995) and the priority of conflict-resolving over conflict-deciding (Ortloff 1997) have taken on special importance.

Originating in the 1950s as a second branch of legal psychology, juridical legal psychology has come a long way indeed (Jakob & Rehbinder 1987, introduction). It must be noted at this point that all great thinkers have incorporated psychological considerations into all their theories on law and state. This applies especially to the philosophers whom we consider integral humanists: the organicists and the personalists. We can draw up a chronology of ideas here from Socrates, Aristotle and Augustine to Thomas Aquinas, Montesquieu, Goethe, Pestalozzi, Tocqueville, Emil Brunner and Alois Troller. However, it was the results achieved through psychoanalysis that gave the issues of modern juridical legal psychology a tremendous boost. Depending on the problem, the ideas of Freud, Adler or C.G. Jung and their respective (and mostly autonomous) successors proved to be particularly beneficial. Among the more important work and research areas of juridical legal psychology are:

- the psychology of justice and of the humane community (Tammelo 1977, Usteri 1996 and 1999),
- the influence of basic psychological strengths on the constitution (Marti 1958, Imboden 1959, Usteri 1998),
- the sense of justice (Rehbinder 1985, Meier 1985),
- awareness of the law (Würtenberger 1986, Blankenburg 1998),

- anxieties and hopes in environmental law (a systematic examination is not available),
- psychoanalytical fundamentals of ownership and freedom of ownership (Usteri 1999),
- the large area of legal problems regarding culpability (Streng 1980, Schild 1995) and punishment (Neumann 1949, Nägeli 1965),
- the psychological structure of judicial decision-making (Weimar 1996),
- psychoanalytical aspects of legal rhetoric, legal advice and legal practice (Jakob 1995-1998),
- reciprocity, corruption and law (seminar University of Zurich summer term 1998 as well as Gruter Institute conference, Tauberbischofsheim, September 1998).

Finally, juridical legal psychology has made a contribution to methodology as well. In accordance with the demand for interdisciplinary work, the manner of action is primarily synoptical-synthetical. In addition, the introduction to the legal system of the amplificatory method based on the complex psychoanalysis of C. G. Jung proved fruitful. It adds a reference to the unconscious (Usteri & Bauer 1992, Usteri 1995) to the current consciousness-oriented methods utilized in the creation, interpretation and application of laws.

The following considerations deal with the main aspects of psychology in the service of the administration of justice.

Divergent Ways of Thinking and Communication Structures in the Fields of Jurisprudence and Psychology

The problem that arises when jurisprudence and psychology collaborate results from their diverging views on behavior. While psychology tries to describe human experience and behavior, including variables of personality, biology and environment, jurisprudence organizes, regulates and describes the social existence of man as it should be. These differing intellectual approaches leave their mark on the objectives and role concepts of the different areas of science, giving rise to controversies regarding the pursuit of one's profession and differences of opinion on the relevance of research.

Jurisprudence, unlike psychology, acts in a public environment. The legal point of view is legal-normative and dogmatic-assessing, its basis being the Constitution, the laws and their annotations. The norms governing the administration of justice have developed throughout history out of social norms and are committed to the concept of justice as well as to the desire for stability of the law within society. Correspondingly, legal language is abstract and its boundaries of definition clear-cut.

At the center of the court proceedings awaits an unsolved problem around which those involved in the proceedings hold— within the framework of the roles assigned to them, the regulations governing the proceedings (e.g. the Swiss Code of Criminal Procedure and the Swiss Code of Civil Procedure, respectively) and the legal norms—a competition, at the end of which a just solution is found. These proceedings are clearly structured by their role instructions.

Psychology, on the other hand, is orientated towards the needs of the individual. It must be noted, however, that the theoretical approaches to explaining behavior are manifold (e.g. psychoanalytic, cognitive, behaviorist or systemic). Psychological research and practice deals with the description, explanation, assessment, prognosis and control of behavior (Zimbardo 1995). This leads to great complexity and diversity in the examination of human behavior, but also to low predictability as well as to problems regarding retrospective registration of behavior. On the basis of psychoanalytical insights, causal connections can only be established to a limited degree, and in general predictions must remain statements of probability (Kühne & Greuel 1999).

Psychology, judged from the point of view of jurisprudence, is a «complementary science» employed in ongoing legal proceedings to assist the court in finding a decision and to shift part of the burden of responsibility. If the requirements of the psychological experts are met, there is usually no friction between the judges and the psychologists.

Retrospective examination of behavior, as can be required by a judge (e.g. regarding questions of criminal responsibility of the defendant, of the degree of maturity with regard to responsibility of juvenile delinquents at the time of the offense or of plausibility of a statement regarding experienced action) is difficult from a psycho-diagnostic point of view, as the memory of an action is influenced by motives and the constructive process of recalling.

Just as problematic is a prognosis as may be required for the enforcement of social or penal measures for decisions regarding parental custody or the ability to work, because human behavior is always to be considered as dependent on the context and social frame of reference within which a person lives and acts. Behavioral predictions depend on many variables that can not be controlled and whose significance can not be evaluated prospectively.

Schüler-Springorum (1995) refers to the greater acceptance of psychiatrists in comparison with psychologists, e.g. as experts for the assessment of criminal responsibility, and presumes that psychiatry has adapted better to the ideas of order of the judiciary and is less critical of the legal system than psychology. That is why communication between the legal profession and psychiatrists is regarded as seemingly better.

The Current Need for Research Regarding Psychology in the Service of the Administration of Justice

The expectations entertained by jurisprudence are aimed at a psychological examination of theories about everyday life, i.e. about "what constitutes the world" (translation of "wie die Welt beschaffen sei") (Gottwald 1995, page 74), in order to close gaps between legal fictions and psychological findings about human behavior.

Gottwald's (1995) general claim addressed to legal psychology concerns greater clarity and comprehensibility with regard to the presentation of research methods and results, as those working in legal practice are, in his words, either not "curious" enough or too "self-confident" (page 73) to tackle any (legal-)psychological discoveries.

The legal profession is lamenting the "over-criminalization" of legal psychology, as issues of criminal law and criminology (identification, sentencing, prognosis regarding the execution of sentences, research of causes and criminal development) prevail within the framework of the psycho-diagnostic practice (assessment of the credibility of testimonials, criminal responsibility, criminal prognosis etc.), as well as in research. It is evident that so far in this area there has been a very high demand for psychological research results and psycho-diagnostic expertise.

If we examine current literature from the point of view where questions and claims are addressed to psychology, we notice several concurrent claims irrespective of the field of study. Schüler-Springorum (1995) calls for the closing of research gaps in the areas of corruption as well as economic, environmental and organized crime. Furthermore, he urges that social-psychological research be intensified regarding the issue of power (economic, political, police and not least criminal) and the relationship between those who exercise power and those who are subject to it. This assessment is shared from the point of view of administrative law by Ortloff (1995) who raises the question of the consequences of power, expertise and competence of civil servants, and expresses his interest in discoveries regarding methods of manipulation used by and applied to citizens and judges.

However, Schüler-Springorum attaches importance not only to those acting and their motives but also to the victims and their experiences, adding to this circle «imported prostitutes», recipients of blood donations contaminated with HIV and restaurant owners blackmailed for protection money.

Schüler-Springorum (1995) discusses questions of methodology and the appropriateness of (psychological) research efforts, contents and results. To him, deviant behavior is to a large extent found in "normal" people, meaning that psychology has priority over psychiatry.

Gottwald (1995) diagnoses a disorder from the point of view of jurisprudence only if psychology does not answer the questions posed, and thereby fulfills the role of assistant and expert assigned to it by the court while making the law ("psychology of the law") itself the object of research. Nevertheless, as Schüler-Springorum (1995) he calls for self-critical reflection on the part of the judicial system which can be furthered through psychological research, e.g. regarding communication during court proceedings, conflict-resolving through negotiation and due process of law (Lind 1995).

Before every judicial decision all parties involved are to be heard. This requires comprehensible language on the part of the judges (Kühne 1983) but also an understanding of the language, e.g. of plaintiffs and defendants, of the accused and the witnesses. In addition, the judicial decision must be made comprehensible to those involved in the trial in order for them to be able to follow the proceedings and to understand the reasoning leading to the decision and to consider it fair (Ortloff 1995; in full: Bierbrauer et al. 1995).

In order to round out the results of the literary research and the examination (see below), a narrative interview was conducted regarding the general need for research from the juridical point of view—in this case the perspective of an administrative court judge.[1] The results were general demands as well as indications of particular problems of public law.

The general demands refer to the simplification of the legislation procedure; they encompass the psychological aspects of legal action and the communication between the parties involved in the proceedings. Among the measures suggested is the transfer of problem-resolving strategies to all court proceedings, giving priority to conflict-resolving over conflict-deciding. The proceedings should be conducted in accordance with the Harvard Principle.

As special problems regarding public law are considered: intercultural problems involving foreign parties in the proceedings, especially if they depend on the services of an interpreter; the granting of and application for political asylum; the credibility of applicants. In addition, there is the desire for measures to reduce or prevent corruption.

As special problems regarding social security law are considered: the improvement of the advisory procedures and the simplification and clarification of the application procedure.

Special problems concerning the role and position of the attorney refer to his representation of his client in civil proceedings.

Results of a Survey Regarding the Need for Research

As suggested by the discussions of the Special "Relation on Theory and Practice" Committee of the European Association on Psychology and Law (EAP&L), a comparative survey regarding the need for legal-psychological research was conducted among scholars and practitioners of law as well as psychology experts in Germany, the Netherlands, Great Britain, Spain and Hungary. Its purpose is to shed some light on the matters concerned, and it does not claim to be representative.

The main questions concerned the role of psychology in the field of jurisprudence, the future and requested areas of emphasis in research and the improvement of communication and interaction between psychologists and the legal profession.

Legal professionals from various fields of activity as well as psychological experts participated in the survey. The answers were given by:

a. four law professors

b. four public prosecutors

c. three attorneys (male) and one attorney (female)

d. two family judges and two criminal judges

e. three psychologists (psychology experts in court)

All of them worked in the former Federal Republic of Germany (alte Bundesländer). The female attorney interviewed was 40 years of age and had been practicing her profession for 15 years. The men were between 49 and 55 years of age and had been practicing their professions (jurisprudence or psychology) on average for 23 years. All of them worked in cities with populations exceeding 100,000. The somewhat disparate distribution of sexes is partly due to the fact that there are few female scholars in the field of jurisprudence. However, it was (in the other professional areas, at least) rather the men who responded.

(1) What is, in your opinion, the fundamental role of psychology in court today?

Family judges
- Resolution of domestic problems
- Relationship diagnostics
- Parents' child-rearing capabilities

Criminal judges
- Psychological criteria of the assessment of criminal responsibility
- Criteria of testimony

Public prosecutors
- Psychological problems of testimony
- Psychological criteria of criminal responsibility

Defense attorneys
- Psychological assessment should support judge in reaching a verdict and help prevent appeals and corresponding proceedings
- Support in resolving family conflicts

Law professors
- Good presentation of psychological reports in court
- Better acceptance of witness assessment
- Acceptance of psychological reports in traffic law proceedings
- Excessive dependence of psychological reports on psychiatric reports (in questions of criminal responsibility)

Psychological experts
- The court generally has insufficient information on psychological competence in expert question

formulations
-   Exaggerated expectations towards "explanatory models of declaratory effect of an act" ("Erklärungsmodelle") of (criminal) behavior

(2) What areas should research concentrate on in the future?
Family judges
-   Criteria and standards for psychological reports
-   Family therapy

Criminal judges
-   Research on drug abuse and its consequences
-   Research in view of explanation of criminal behavior

Public prosecutors
-   More psychological reports regarding the psychological criteria of criminal responsibility
-   Influence of social and value changes on criminal behavior and criminal responsibility

Defense attorneys
-   Evaluation of family law decisions
-   Consequences of victimization

Law professors
-   Criminal responsibility
-   Legal prognosis
-   Traumatization of victims of violent crimes
-   Transparent standards and criteria for psychological reports
-   Problems regarding sentencing

Psychological experts
-   Research in the field of developmental psychology regarding consequences of divorce for children
-   Research on the motivation to testify
-   Research on the memory capacity of witnesses

(3)   How can communication between psychology and jurisprudence be improved?
Family judges

- Interdisciplinary training
- General fostering of communication between psychologists and legal professionals

Criminal judges
- Improvement of communication and interaction between both professional groups
- Interdisciplinary training
- Information on psychological findings and psycho-diagnostic methods

Public prosecutors
- Interdisciplinary training

Defense attorneys
- Interdisciplinary training

Law professors
- Interdisciplinary training
- Improved and increased communication and interaction between both professional groups
- More information on psychological research and practice in legal journals
- Problem-oriented case discussions

Psychological experts
- Interdisciplinary training
- Training in view of legal-psychological issues

Every professional group named their specific work-related interests—family judges and attorneys in family court proceedings specified those relating to family conflicts and parent-child relationships. Those involved in criminal proceedings (judges, public prosecutors, and defense attorneys) view the problems of criminal responsibility assessment as well as those of the traumatization and victimization of victims as their central matters of concern. However, all professional groups agree on the need for more interdisciplinary training with respect to everyday problems in court. The results presented above coincide with the poll results from Great Britain and Spain (Traverso 1996), which also focus on the demand for interdisciplinary training and more psychological knowledge about experience and behavior of the parties involved in the proceedings.

Summary

The purpose of this short survey was to show the different perspectives and points of view existing in psychological research and practice with respect to their application in legal matters and to psychological reflections on law.

To sum up: There is a need for better understanding between the disciplines in order to increase mutual benefit. Fundamental demands are:

- Improvement of everyday legal actions
- Improvement of communication and interaction between the parties involved in proceedings
- Improvement of communication between the parties involved in proceedings and psychological experts
- More clearly formulated and communicated psychological theories and research results
- Interdisciplinary training
- Fairness and due process of law through clearer and more easily comprehensible juridical decision-making processes
- Simplification of proceedings

Special problem areas are:

- Criminal prosecution
- Decision-making in criminal proceedings
- Decision-making in family and guardianship proceedings.

References

Bierbrauer et al. (1995),
Bierbrauer, B., Gottwald, W., Birnbreier-Stahlberger, B. (Hrsg.),
Verfahrensgerechtigkeit - Rechtspsychologische
Forschungsbeiträge für die Justizpraxis, Köln 1995.

Blankenburg, E. (1998), Situatives Rechtsbewusstsein, in: J. W.
Pichler (Hrsg.), Rechtsakzeptanz und
Handlungsorientierung, Wien 1998, S. 133-141.

Gottwald, W. (1995), Der Beitrag der psychologischen
Verfahrensforschung für die Ziviljustiz - Einige Fragen und
Erwartungen, in: Bierbrauer, B., Gottwald, W., Birnbreier-
Stahlberger, B. (Hrsg.), Verfahrensgerechtigkeit -
Rechtspsychologische Forschungsbeiträge für die
Justizpraxis, Köln 1995, S. 73-83.

Imboden, M. (1959), Die Staatsformen - Versuch einer
psychologischen Deutung staatsrechtlicher Dogmen, Basel,
Stuttgart 1959.

Jakob, R. & Rehbinder, M. (Hrsg.) (1987), Beiträge zur
Rechtspsychologie (Schriftenreihe zur Rechtssoziologie und
Rechtstatsachenforschung Bd. 64), Berlin 1987.

Kühne, A. (1983), Gerichtsverhandlung - Kommunikation und
Interaktion, in: Seitz, W. (Hrsg.), Kriminal- und
Rechtspsychologie - ein Handbuch in Schlüsselbegriffen,
München 1983, S. 78-82.

Kühne, A. & Greuel, L. (1999), Rechtspsychologie in der
Anwendung (im Manuskript).

Lind, E. A. (1995), Verfahrensgerechtigkeit und Akzeptanz
rechtlicher Autorität, in: Bierbrauer, B., Gottwald, W.
Birnbreier-Stahlberger, B. (Hrsg.), Verfahrensgerechtigkeit -
Rechtspsychologische Forschungsbeiträge für die
Justizpraxis, Köln 1995, S. 4-21.

Marti, H. (1958), Urbild und Verfassung, Bern, Stuttgart 1958.

Meier, Ch. (1985), Zur Diskussion über das Rechtsgefühl, Diss,
Zürich 1985.

Nägeli, E. (1965), Das Böse und das Strafrecht, in: St. Galler Festgabe zum Schweizerischen Juristentag 1965, S. 263 ff.

Neumann, E. (1949), Tiefenpsychologie und neue Ethik, 1949.

Ortloff, K.-M. (1995), Rechtspsychologie und Verwaltungsgerichtsbarkeit: Das Rechtsgepräch in der mündlichen Verhandlung, in: Bierbrauer, B., Gottwald, W., Birnbreier-Stahlberger, B. (Hrsg.), Verfahrensgerechtigkeit - Rechtspsychologische Forschungsbeiträge für die Justizpraxis, Köln 1995.

Ortloff, K.-M. (1997), Richterauftrag und Mediation, in: Breidenbach, S., Henssler, M. (Hrsg.), Mediation für Juristen - Konfliktbehandlung ohne gerichtliche Entscheidung, Köln 1997, S. 111-119.

Rehbinder, M. (1985), Rechtsgefühl als Gemeinschaftsgefühl, in: Jakob, R., Rehbinder, M. (Hrsg.), Beiträge zur Rechtspsychologie (Schriftenreihe zur Rechtssoziologie und Rechtstatsachenforschung Bd. 64), Berlin 1987, S. 183-196.

Schüler-Springorum, H. (1995), Zum Stand der Nachbarschaft zwischen Psychologie und Kriminalwissenschaften, in: Pawlik, K. (Hrsg.), Bericht über den 34, Kongress für Psychologie in Hamburg 1994 (Schwerpunkthema: Persönlichkeit und Verhalten), Göttingen 1995.

Seitz, W. (Hrsg.) (1983), Kriminal- und Rechtspsychologie - ein Handbuch in Schlüsselbegriffen, München 1983.

Sporer, S. L. (1983), Gesetzgebung: Psychologische Beiträge zur Reform und Evaluation von Gesetzen, in: Seitz, W. (Hrsg.), Kriminal- und Rechtspsychologie - ein Handbuch in Schlüsselbegriffen, München 1983, S. 82-87.

Schild, W. (1995), Der strafrechtliche Vorsatz zwischen psychischem Sachverhalt und normativem Konstrukt, in: Jakob, R., Usteri, M., Weimar, R. (Hrsg.), Psyche - Recht - Gesellschaft (Schriftenreihe zur Rechtspsychologie Bd. 1), Bern 1995, S. 119-140.

Streng, F. (1980), Schuld, Vergeltung, Generalprävention Eine tiefenpsychologische Rekonstruktion strafreetlicher Zentralbegriffe, in: Jakob, R., Rehbinder, M. (Hrsg.), Beiträge zur Rechtspsychologie (Schriftenreihe zur Rechtssoziologie und Rechstatsachenforschung Bd. 64), Berlin 1987, S. 167-181.

Tammelo, I. (1977), Zur Psychologie der Gerechtigkeit, in: Jakob, R., Rehbinder, M. (Hrsg.), Beiträge zur Rechtspsychologie (Schriftenreihe zur Rechtssoziologie und Rechtstatsachenforschung Bd. 64), Berlin 1987, S. 145-150.

Traverso, G. (1996), Conference of the European Association on Psychology and Law, Siena 1996.

Usteri, M. (1995), Rechtspsychologische Studien in Zürich, in: Jakob, R., Usteri, M., Weimar, R. (Hrsg.), Psyche - Recht - Gesellschaft (Schriftenreihe zur Rechtspsychologie Bd. 1), Bern 1995, S. 227-236.

Usteri, M. (1996), Die Zukunft des modernen menschengerechten Gemeinwesens, in: FS J.-F. Aubert, Basel 1996, S. 191-198.

Usteri, M. (1998), Der Einfluss psychischer Grundkräfte auf die Staatsverfassung, in: FS F. Koja, Wien, New York 1998, S. 201-209.

Usteri, M. (1999), Eigentumsfreiheit (im Manuskript).

Usteri, M. & Baur, G. (1992), Jung's Psychology Adopted in Law, in: Lösel, F., Bender, D., Bliesener, Th. (Hrsg.), Psychology and Law, Berlin/New York 1992, S 500-505.

Weimar, R. (1996), Psychologische Strukturen richterlicher Entscheidung, (Schriftenreihe zur Rechtspsychologie Bd. 2), Bern 1996.

Würtenberg, Th. (1986), Schwankungen und Wandlungen im Rechtsbewusstein der Bevölkerung, in Jakob, R., Rehbinder, M. (Hrsg.), Beiträge zur Rechtspsycholgie (Schriftenreihe zur Rechtssoziologie und Rechtstatsachenforschung Bd. 64), Berlin 1987, S. 197-214.

Zimbardo, P. (1995), Psychologie, Berlin 1995.

1 The interview was conducted with Prof. Dr. Karsten-Michael Ortloff, presiding judge at the Berlin Administrative Court. We hereby once again extend our gratitude to Dr. Ortloff for his kind support.

Evolution in Biology, Economics and Law*

Michael Lehmann[**]

"Ich meinerseits maße mir kein
Urteil über die Richtigkeit der
Darwinschen Theorie an, obschon
gerade die Resultate, zu denen ich
meinerseits in bezug auf die
historische Entwicklung des Rechts
gelangt bin, sie auf meinem Gebiete
im vollstem Maße bestätigen."

R. v. Jhering, Der Zweck im Recht, Vorrede (1877)

* Translated into English by Catriona Thomas, Munich
** Professor of Law, University of Munich, Dr. jur, Dipl.-Kfm.

1. Introduction

I write this in honor of Dr. Margaret Gruter, J.S.M., the "founding mother" who forged the scientific link between biology and law in the U.S., who in her role as an "American ambassador" achieved the breakthrough of this interdisciplinary approach. In Germany in particular,[1] we would therefore like to take up Jhering's theory again and attempt to show that a common foundation, namely evolution, unites us all. Therefore, the research approach pursued by Margaret Gruter at an early point in time, emphasizing the significance of behavioral science for jurisprudence,[2] has in the meantime proceeded to be successful from an academic viewpoint.

2. Long-Term Positive Development Through Evolution?

Like Mark Twain's leap back to King Arthur's Court, let's take a short leap back in the history of mankind and imagine an average natural person in the year 1800. What is the decisive difference in the legal views of that person in comparison with his or her views today?

In my opinion, the decisive difference lies in a considerably higher degree of uncertainty in both legal and existential matters at that time, and, consequently, the lack of a propensity to make legal demands,[3] to be understood in both meanings of the term. If, at

---

[1] In 1997 a "Human science center" was established at the University of Munich which is devoted especially to this interdisciplinary research approach (Humanwissenschaftliches Zentrum, Goethestr. 31, 80036 München).

[2] Cf. for the basics M. Gruter, "Die Bedeutung der Verhaltensforschung für die Rechtswissenschaft," 1976; id., "The Origins of Legal Behavior," 2 J. Social Bio. Struct. 43 et seq. (1979); Gruter & Rehbinder (eds.), "Der Beitrag der Biologie zu Fragen von Recht und Ethik" 1983; F.-H. Schmidt, "Verhaltensforschung und Recht. Ethologische Materialien zu einer Rechtsanthropologie" 1982; W. Schurig, "Überlegungen zum Einfluß biosoziologischer Strukturen auf das Rechtsverhalten" 1983; L. Pospisil, "Anthropologie des Rechts" 1982; R. Zippelius, "Biologische Grundlagen des Sozialverhaltens," in: 12 Rechtstheorie 177 et seq. (1981); E.E. Hirsch, "Die Steuerung des menschlichen Verhaltens," 1982 JZ 41 et seq.; M. Lehmann, "Bürgerliches Recht und Handelsrecht—eine juristische und ökonomische Analyse" VI (1983).

[3] Neither legal concepts in the foundations of claims, cf. e.g. U. Diederichsen, "Die BGB-Klausur" 34 et seq. (8th ed. 1994), nor the demand for a most extensive possible safety net for one's own existence through the welfare state were known; cf. also H. Petir, "Welche Ursachen hat das gesteigerte Sicherheitsbedürfnis des heutigen Menschen?," 1985 Universitas 569 et seq.

that time, a master ran over his servant in a grossly negligent manner, it was an accident, an "act of God;" if a purchaser was cheated or deceived, legal principles such as "a person who does not open his eyes must open his purse" applied; a person who desired an industrial property right, e.g. a patent, had to beg for a privilege qua royal grant. Doctors were expected to provide pain relief, not a cure—the life expectancy was one third of that of today; from lawyers one expected dispute settlement or resolution, not "modern social engineering." Today, doctors and lawyers are frequently sued for "malpractice." There is a marked sense of and demand for increased legality, which is expressed in part in the colorful titles of books written by lawyers, e.g. "I demand more justice." People call for increased certainty, clarity and transparency in all areas, i.e. mankind is attempting to move increasingly from its naturally given quality as an object towards becoming a free individual and the subject of evolutionary developments. The globality of the current explosion in internet information will further enhance this process.

Maslov's famous pyramid of needs[4]—physiological needs, e.g. eating and drinking, certainty, social relations, general appreciation, self-fulfilment—evidently corresponds to reality, since an ever-increasing part of the population strives to satisfy ever-increasing needs; not only do we want to have, we also want to be.[5] In economically developed nations, in any case, the matter at issue is no longer exclusively survival, but the improvement in the quality of life, as exemplified by the still ongoing discussion on protection of the environment.

3. Identical or Analogous Evolutive Mechanisms?

This demonstrates that our overall situation has improved

---

4 Cf. Tietz (Ed.), "Handwörterbuch der Absatzwirtschaft" 953 (1974).

5 Cf. E. Fromm, "Haben oder Sein. Die seelischen Grundlagen einer neuen Gesellschaft" (1979); see also "Lebensziele in den 80er Jahren: Zwischen Haben und Sein," in: 7 Absatzwirtschaft 52 et seq. (1981); Kroeber-Riel, Dichtl, Gümbel, Rafee & Tietz, "Marketing im nächsten Jahrzehnt, Marketing, 1980 ZFP 5 et seq., 81 et seq.; see also E. Noelle-Neumann, "Die Stärkung der Person—die Bedingung einer europäischen politischen Kultur," 1983 Universitas 251 et seq.

drastically within a relatively short period of time. One may pose the question as to what in fact gave rise to this and every preceding improvement; what has been the motivating force behind this societal, ecomonic, social and legal evolution? It is possible to describe this evolution using the catchwords of methodological individualism and the reciprocal altruism deriving therefrom.

Socio-biologists[6] speak of the principle of genetic self-interest in this context,[7] economists since Adam Smith have spoken of self-love,[8] and since the 19th century legal scholars[9] have focussed their attention in research on the subjective right, the individual right or claim.[10] Without doubt, the research approaches taken in this context are not identical, however, the heuristic value of these analogous attempts at explanation should be assessed while taking into account the fact that intentional human conduct is always involved which, within the confines of a certain pre-defined environment, seeks to find a solution to the problem of existence amidst scarce resources.

3.1 Biology

A biologist proceeds on the assumption that the development of human social behavior takes places within certain genetic confines and in accordance with the Darwinistic principle[11] of natural selection, so that there is a closed connection between cause and

---

6 Cf. E.O. Wilson, "Sociobiology, The New Synthesis" (1975); id., "On Human Nature" (1978); cf. also J. Eibl-Eibesfeldt, "Die Biologie des menschlichen Verhaltens. Grundriß der Humanethologie" 121 et seq. (Munich, 1984).

7 Cf. in particular Wickler & Seibt, "Das Prinzip Eigennutz, Ursachen und Konsequenzen sozialen Verhaltens" (1981); W. Wickler, "Die Biologie der Zehn Gebote" 67 et seq. (5th ed. 1981); see also R. Dawkins, "The Selfish Gene" (1976).

8 A. Smith, "The Wealth of Nations" First Book, 2d Chapter; cf. German translation from Recktenwald, 1974, 16 et seq.

9 Cf. in particular v. Jhering and Heck, who developed the theory that subjective private rights serve as a means to satisfy individual interests; F. Wieacker, "Privatrechtsgeschichte der Neuzeit" 574 (2d ed. 1967).

10 As regards this common point of departure cf. M. Lehmann, 1982 BB 1997 et seq.; from a philosophical viewpoint cf. also N. Hoerster, "Utilitaristische Ethik und Verallgemeinerung" 18 et seq. (1971).

11 Cf. on this point, e.g., W. Wickler, "100 Jahre nach Charles Darwin. Wohin führt uns die Evolution" 5 Bild der Wissenschaft 70 et seq. (1982); Darwin on his part was influenced by the economic works of Malthus and Smith, cf. S.S. Schweber, "The Genesis of Natural Selection—1838: Some Further Insights" Bio Science, May 28, 1978.

effect. Where a certain behaviour arises due to certain genes, for example a certain social reaction, and where such behavior enhances the chances in the fight for survival, then these genes will be represented in larger numbers in the next generation. If this natural selection continues through several generations, then these favorable genes will pervade entire populations, and the behavior will become characteristic for a certain species. It is in this sense that human behavior was and is both primarily determined and formed genetically by way of natural selection. Humans also wish to survive and to reproduce, and attempt to fulfill this task in the least expensive manner possible. Consequently, each individual gene and each individual person behaves in principle as a benefit maximizer who has adapted to his or her environment.[12]

Where Jane Goodall[13] discovered direct evidence of imitative behaviour, e.g. as regards the use of tools, during her research into chimpanzees in the Gombe region, this behaviour took place within the tradition of survival techniques, such as defense against leopards, catching termites or "pillaging" of bananas. However, due to our revolutionary cortex layer, the human brain has infinitely more capacity than that of a chimpanzee,[14] so that any indirect equation that goes beyond common basic principles should be regarded critically. Consequently, the success of human life does not depend exclusively on the transfer of genetic information or on external selection; internal selection, i.e. the processing of information and the so-called traditive evolution this entails, as well as the behavior it gives rise to, are of such major significance that some scholars have expressed the opinion that humans have succeeded in "stepping out of biological evolution."[15] At any rate, cultural evolution is able to proceed at a much faster pace than would be possible at a purely biological level. In a pluralistic, open society which offers the best chances for survival and development,

---

12 Cf. Wilson, supra note 6, at 37; see also Wickler, supra note 7.

13 J. van Lawick-Goodall, "Wilde Schimpansen" 80 et seq., 201 (1975).

14 Cf. Wilson, supra note 6, at 30 et seq., 1979.

15 Cf., e.g., H. Zeier, "Evolutionsbedingte Eigenschaften menschlichen Verhaltens," 1984 Universitas 257 et seq.

positive human behaviour and values are able to assert themselves relatively rapidly and stimulate changes in society, which on their part again influence human behaviour.[16] Charles Darwin addressed this process, at least in principle, although he expressed his surprise that during his lifetime people had the audacity to apply his methods to other fields. In the final paragraphs of *The Origin of Species* Darwin emphasizes: "And as natural selection works solely by and for the good of each being, all corporeal and mental endowments will tend to progress towards perfection."[17]

This theory of evolution and the human ability to learn have in the meantime been incorporated within a philosophical meta-theory, the evolutionary theory of knowledge,[18] which according to its own understanding is an evolutionary theory applicable to numerous varied scientific fields. Hence, it is possible to counter the criticism expressed by von Hayek,[19] according to whom biology, in particular socio-biology, limits humankind to primary, genetic and secondary values—i.e. to the products of rational thinking. There can be no doubt that systems frequently arise unintentionally yet as a result of human behavior, and that many aspects of what we call culture are the accidental results of a system that has arisen spontaneously yet which continues to advance evolutively: "Culture is neither natural nor artificial, neither genetically transmitted nor intentionally planned."[20]   However,

---

16 Cf., e.g., the fundamental investigations on family research by Medick & Sabean (Eds.), "Emotionen und materielle Interessen" (1984); e.g. the dicovery of effective contraception methods has decisively influenced our conduct in and around the family in this century, so that family survival strategies and parent-child relationships, as, for example, were common in France during the 19th century (cf. page 412 et seq.) are no longer to be found.

17 Market economists are also familiar with the principle that scant resources strive towards achieving their best possible utilization.

18 Cf. in particular G. Vollmer, "Evolutionäre Erkenntnistheorie" (3d ed 1983); R. Riedl, "Biologie der Erkenntnis. Die stammesgeschichtlichen Grundlagen der Vernunft" (1979); id., "Die Spaltung des Weltbildes. Biologische Grundlagen des Erklärens und Verstehens" (1985).

19 F.A. v. Hayek, "Die drei Quellen der menschlichen Werte" 7 et seq. (1979) ("Die Irrtümer der Soziobiologie"); see also P. Koslowski, "Menschengeschichte als Naturgeschichte?," in: Evolution und Freiheit, Civitas Resultate, Vol. 5, 1984, at 93 et seq.

20 Cf. v. Hayek, supra note 19, at 10; cf. also V. Vanberg, "Evolution und spontane Ordnung," in: Albert (Ed.), FS E. Boettcher, "Ökonomisches Denken und soziale Ordnung," 83 et seq. (1984).

similarly to the field of quantum physics, depending upon the experimental questions posed, the responses provided are disparite and appear to contradict one another. For human behavior is an element within evolution which at the same time was caused by but also stimulates evolution; a human being is both the object and the subject of his or her further development.

3.2. Economics

From the economic viewpoint, one may place at the start of one's considerations on maximation of benefits the famous quote from Adam Smith, *The Wealth of Nations* (1776, Book IV, Chapter II):[21]

> "But the annual revenue of every society is always precisely equal to the exchangeable value of the whole annual produce of its industry, or rather is precisely the same thing with that exchangeable value. As every individual, therefore, endeavors as much as he can both to employ his capital in the support of domestic industry, and so to direct that industry that its produce may be of the greatest value; every individual necessarily labours to render the annual revenue of society as great as he can. He generally, indeed, neither intends to promote the public interest, nor knows how much he is promoting it. By preferring the support of domestic to that of foreign industry, he intends only his own security; and by directing that industry in such a manner as its produce may be of the greatest value, he intends only his own gain, and he is in this, as in many other cases, led by an invisible hand to promote an end which was no part

---

21 Smith, supra note 8, 370-371, 1974 (Book IV, Chapter II).

of his intention. Nor is it always the worse
for the society that it was no part of it. By
pursuing his own interest he frequently
promotes that of the society more effectually
than when he really intends to promote it."

The Nobel prizewinner Buchanan went further to provide an economic foundation for the existence and recognition of the system that is the state:[22] proceeding from the division of human productivity capacities in the battle of all against all into three areas of activity, namely hunting and collecting, pillaging and defense against pillaging. It is productively advantageous to abstain voluntarily from the two latter activities and to pass the responsibility for compliance with this societal agreement on monitoring to a community entity: to the state. All participants profit from such an agreement, although originally this was not appreciated in its profundity by those who concluded the agreement. The evolutive mechanisms of trial and error guided humans towards this path, just as the architects of ancient times observed the laws of falling bodies on the basis of experience and intuition, although it was not until Galilei that the laws were discovered or analyzed scientifically. This applies especially where, as postulated by Adam Smith, one seeks to keep mankind's egoistic striving for progress in check by way of compassion, the state and the law as well as—as emphasized in particular by v. Hayek— through competition.

In the meantime an animated discussion has unfolded between biologists and economists.[23] Some biologists have even proposed a new division of the science of mankind into natural economics

---

22 J.M. Buchanan, "The Limits of Liberty—Between Anarchy and Leviathan" (1975); cf. generally as regards public-choice approach D.C. Mueller, "Public Choice: A Survey," 14 J.E.L. 395 et seq. (1976); B.S. Frey, "Moderne politische Ökonomie" (1977).

23 Cf. M. Tietzel, "Ökonomie und Soziobiolobie oder: Wer kann was von wem lernen?," in: 2 Zeitschrift für Wirtschafts-und Sozialwissenschaften (ZWS) 107 et seq. (1983); B.S. Frey, "Ökonomie als Verhaltenswissenschaft," in: Jahrbuch für Sozialwissenschaft, Vol. 31, at 21 et seq., 1980.

(biology) and political economics (social sciences).[24] In particular, at an early point in time, Hirshleifer[25] pointed out the parallels between biology and economics, e.g. competition, the battle for survival, optimization, selection, reciprocity, adaptation and territorial behavior. In Germany Wickler played a predominant role in research into the suitability of applying the cost/benefit calculation to behavioral research.[26] The economic model considerations in relation to "homo oeconomicus"[27] and his economic selective behavior as both a supplier and a consumer— i.e. as resourceful, evaluative, maximising man (REMM)—appear particularly suitable in order to illustrate the intentional behavior of living creatures. In this respect it is not necessary to take matters as far as the Nobel prizewinner Gary Becker,[28] who viewed the economic approach as being so broad that it was applicable to practically all human behavior. However, in the 18th century Mandeville already attempted to demonstrate on the basis of his bees fable that the vices of one person can benefit all, and that a beautiful building can be constructed of the "most despicable materials."[29] Hence, leading theories in the field of economics, for example the caritative and the balance theory, are directed towards the assumption that situations exist in which egoistic individual

---

24 M.T. Gishelin, "The Economy of the Body," 68 AER May 1978; see also J. Hirschleifer, "Natural Economy Versus Political Economy" (1978); Furubotn & Richter, "Institutions and Economic Theory: An Introduction to and Assessment of the New Institutional Economics" (Ann Arbor, 1997).

25 J. Hirshleifer, "Economics from a Biological Viewpoint," 20 JLE 1 et seq. (1977); id., "Research in Law and Economics, Evolutionary Models in Economics and Law" (1982); id., "Evolution, spontane Ordnung und Marktwirtschaft," in: Evolution und Freiheit, supra note 19, at 77 et seq.

26 Cf. "Der Ursprung der sozialen Abhängigkeit," Speech in Regensburg, MPG-Spiegel 6/76; cf. also "Kindesmord bei Affen" Lanugren, 10 Bild der Wissenschaft 72 et seq. (1984); where the management in a company or ministry changes, the "subordinates" are as a rule also replaced.

27 Cf. M. Tietzel, "Die Rationalitätsannahme in den Wirtschaftswissenschaften oder: Der Homo oeconomicus und seine Verwandten," 1981 Jahrbuch für Sozialwissenschaften 32 et seq.

28 G.S. Becker, "Der ökonomische Ansatz zur Erklärung menschlichen Verhaltens" (1982); see on this point M. Tietzel, "Wirtschaftstheorie also allgemeine Theorie des menschlichen Verhaltens," 1983 Zeitschrift für Wirtschaftspolitik 225 et seq.; id., 1983 ZWS 297 et seq.

29 G.S. Becker, "Der ökonomische Ansatz zur Erklärung menschlichen Verhaltens" (1982); see on this point M. Tietzel, "Wirtschaftstheorie also allgemeine Theorie des menschlichen Verhaltens," 1983 Zeitschrift für Wirtschaftspolitik 225 et seq.; id., 1983 ZWS 297 et seq.

behavior results in a social optimum. Approaches based on game theory are likewise suitable for application in the areas of economics and biology.[30]

In a market economy, a free system in which the dynamic "discovery process competition"[31] is able to function, the functioning of evolutive mechanisms is virtually ensured by nature.[32] Shortages and crisis situations especially demonstrate the extent of the capability to adapt and innovate, in which respect there is an increasingly predominant opinion that cyclic periods can also be observed in economic developments as well. Not only does a product have a cycle of the life starting with its introduction, followed by growth, maturity, saturation and in numerous cases finally degeneration,[33] but there are also innovation cycles and cyclic phases within economic growth. From an agrarian-economic perspective, Kondratjev was apparently the first scholar to develop a theory of long waves, and the theory of changeable economic situations was developed by the German historic school of national economists; both serve as the basis for computer simulation models for global economic development as experimented with during the 1980s at both M.I.T. (Jay W. Forrester) and Yale University (Nelson/Winter).[34] Hence, it would not be surprising if biologists were also able to depict cyclic evolution processes with crisis phases and subsequent recession, which then shifted towards recovery and prosperity. After all, Darwin's concepts served as the basis for the famous equation put forward by the mathematician

---

30 Cf., e.g., J. Maynard Smith, "Game Theory and the Evolution of Fighting," in: id., "On Evolution" (1972); ed., "Evolution and the Theory of Games," 64 Am. Sci. 41 et seq. (1976); Cooter & Uhlen, "Law and Economics" (Glenview, 1988).

31 F.A. v. Hayek, "Der Wettbewerb als Entdeckungsverfahren" (1968); M. Lehmann, "Das Prinzip Wettbewerb," 1990 SZ 61 et seq.

32 G. Hesse, "Die Entstehung industrialisierter Volkswirtschaften" (1982).

33 Cf. Hansen & Leitherer, "Produktgestaltung" (1985).

34 Cf. excellent overview contained in V. Zarnowitz, "Recent Work on Business Cycles in Historical Perspective: A Review of Theories and Evidence," 23 JEL 523 et seq. (1985); from the perspective of the property rights theory cf. North & Thomas, "The Rise of the Western World" (1973); see also "Die Gezeiten der Weltwirtschaft," 2 Bild der Wissenschaft 90 (1982); C. Marchetti, "Die magische Entwicklungskurve," 10 Bild der Wissenschaft 115 (1982); economic practice and theory are also governed by this evolutive process; cf. E. Helmstädter, "Die Geschichte der Nationalökonomie als Geschichte ihres Fortschritts," 1983 WiSt 28.

Vito Volterra, who for his Adriatic fishermen provided an explanation for the periodic increase and decrease in the quantities of fish.[35] There is a cyclic fluctuation betweeen the quantity of prey and predators, so that "crisis situations" are necessary at certain intervals in order to re-establish the natural balance. Any economist is reminded in this context of the pig cycle and the spider's web theory.[36] Indeed this Volterra-equation has been used in order to provide detailed explanations for, e.g., the spreading of disease and for chemical processes. Just as there have been innovative thrusts in economic history between recession and prosperity, biological evolutive thrusts and perhaps long waves also should be capable of being depicted.

Biology and economics may well complement one another so well in their methodological approaches because, at least in part, they both have their roots in natural sciences and, as regards mathematics and micro-economics, have precise investigative instruments available. At any rate, this applies as long as one is able and willing to proceed on the assumption that under certain circumstances economic laws function like natural laws.

3.3. Jurisprudence

In contrast, the degree to which legal science is mathematically structured is so minimal that—at least today—it is not yet possible to depict the pre-requisites of a simple claim basis such as Sec. 985 BGB (German Civil Code) in the form of a computer program.[37] However, even legal science appears to develop in evolutive cycles, whereby crisis situations must be viewed as both a challenge and opportunity.[38] In the year 1877 Rudolf von Jhering[39] remarked as follows:

> "It is with the same necessity with which
> according to Darwin's theory one animal

---

35 Cf. 10 Bild der Wissenschaft 118 (1982).

36 Cf. H.C. Recktenwald, "Wörterbuch der Wirtschaft" (1981) "Schweinezyklus."

37 Cf. on this point the "failed attempt" in 1985 JURA 288; R. Schreiber, "Rechtsanwendung durch Computer."

38 See only E.v. Hippel, "Krisen also Herausforderung und Chance," 1982 ZRP 312.

39 "Der Zweck im Recht" Introduction (1877).

species develops from others, that from one legal purpose the other follows, and if the world were created one thousand times as it once was, after billions of years the world of law would necessarily have the same basic configuration, for the purpose exercises the same irresistible force on the forming of the purpose in law as does the cause on the configuration of matter. Thousands of years can pass by before this compelling force of the purpose becomes visible at a certain individual point in the law—and what are thousands of years compared with billions?— yet the law will be compelled, whether voluntarily or not. Yet it will be compelled step by step. Just as nature, the law does not proceed in leaps and bounds, the previous stage must exist before the higher level can follow. Yet when it exists, the higher level is unavoidable—each previous purpose engenders the subsequent one, and from the aggregate of the individual arises by way of conscious or unconscious abstraction the universal: the legal concepts, the legal opinion, the sense of justice. It is not the sense of justice that has given rise to the law, but the law to the sense of justice—the law only knows one source, and that is the practical one of purpose."

The motor of the individual interests, which of course may be bundled and combined in interest groups and which frequently must be for reasons of efficacy, propels this perpetual development forward. In the meantime there are economic-theoretical approaches which attempt to provide an explanation for the "production of the law."[40] Hence, the law has an evolutive function as regards a certain society and on its part is governed in theory and practice by a continual evolutive development, whereby the ecological context doubltessly plays a decisive role,[41] as Montesquieu had already remarked. The law of Japan, which is temperate and founded on harmony, vis-à-vis the harshness of Germanic legal traditions may serve to illustrate this point precisely.

Civil law will serve as an example, due to its proximity to the market, to prices and to competition; for civil law also has a far-reaching social and economic control function, as Franz Böhm stated with particular clarity:[42]

In order to provide examples, I would not like to focus on explosive areas such as labour law or social law,[43] but, rather, on traditional fields such as tort law and contract law. To be precise, on the developments in manufacturers' liability and in the standard business conditions that took place during the 1980s.[44]

At the end of the 19th century, at the time when the BGB was in preparation, relatively few dangers were ascribed to products, so that the legislature concentrated on regulating the liability of animal owners, animal supervisors and owners or tenants of buildings (cf. Secs. 833 et seq. BGB). Apart from this, modern dangers, for example those relating to railways, were regulated individually in specific laws, e.g. the *Reichshaftpflichtgesetz* (Reich Act on Liability). It was not until continually progressing industrialization gave rise to increasing technically or chemically related general dangers for

---

40 Cf. M. Hutter, "Vom vollständigen zum vollständig produzierten Wettbewerb," in: "Ansprüche, Eigentums-und Verfügungsrechte," M. Neumann (Ed.), at 494 et seq. (1984); this approach was discussed in further detail in his Munich habilitation thesis on macroeconomics, "Die Gestaltung von Property Rights als Mittel gesellschaftlich-wirtschaftlicher Allokation" (Göttingen, 1979).

41 Cf. E. Wahl, "Influences clamatiques sur l'évolution du droit en orient et en occident contribution au régionalisme en droit comparé, 1973 RIDC 261.

42 Cf. "Privatrechtsgesellschaft und Marktwirtschaft," 1966 ORDO 91; cf. also H. Weitnauer, "Der Schutz des Schwächeren im Zivilrecht" 10 (1975): "Civil law is the haute école of justice, since it can nevery give somebody something without taken something away from somebody else."

43 Cf. H.F. Zacher, "Zur Anatomie des Sozialrechts," in: 1983 Schweizerische Zeitschrift für Sozialversicherung und berufliche Vorsorge" 228.

44 Cf. from the viewpoint of economic analysis Lehmann, supra note 1, 118 et seq., 200 et seq.; M. Adams, "Ökonomische Analyse des AGB-Gesetzes," in: Neumann (Ed.), supra note 40, at 655 et seq.

consumers, and until the thalidomide scandal provoked general outrage and displeasure as to the insufficient liability law under the BGB, that legal practice, reacting to demands expressed on the basis of comparative law studies in relation to US law, was in effect compelled to develop laws on manufacturers' liability. Since the legislature failed to act, the development necessarily took place in case law. The German Federal Supreme Court made cautious reference to the rules on the burden of proof as anchored in Secs. 833 et seq. BGB in order to develop a law of manufacturers' liability founded in tort law and based on a violation of occupier's liability.[45] As a result, the dangers emanating from such products were no longer qualified as "accidents," the costs of which had to be borne by the victims without any recourse possibilities or viable insurance options even though the victims were unable to contribute towards mastering or removing these sources of danger. Through manufacturers' liability this negative externality was incorporated into the competitive process so that the "selfish" concept of minimizing costs on the part of suppliers results in a reduction of danger. It must be welcomed that this liability model developed by the Federal Supreme Court was then extended so as to encompass environmental damage as well.[46] This is the best way to guide the various egoistic motives of the participants in a kind of cybernetic regulative circle towards the final result of an efficient defense against dangers which is monitored by competition, although none of the participants intentionally pursues this goal in an individual case. Standard business conditions are also a relatively recent invention of industry and commerce which act to rationalize and simplify the conclusion of contracts, i.e. to reduce the costs of transactions.[47] Although they are capable of furthering the conclusion of contracts, in fact these standard conditions almost

---

45 See fundamental decision of German Federal Supreme Court, 1969 NJW 269, "Hühnerpest," with comment by Diederichsen; on the early developments cf. F.v. Westphalen, "Grundtypen deliktsrechtlicher Produzentenhaftung," 1983 JURA 57; G. Hager, "Zum Schutzbereich der Produzentenhaftung," 184 AcP 413 (1984).

46 See decision of German Federal Supreme Court, 1984 JZ 1106, "Kupolofen"; see also M. Lehmann, "The New German Act on Strict Liability for Environmental Damage: Some Internalization of Negative External Effects," 1991 EWS 202.

47 Cf. on this point Lehmann, supra note 1, at 172 et seq.

caused a crisis in liberal contractual concepts,[48] since they practically prevented the negotiation of contracts and thus the establishment of a guarantee for the correctness of the contractual contents. Consequently, at an early point in time, Ludwig Raiser[49] critisized this wrong turn in private law as moving towards an exclusively "self-made law of commerce." In case law as well, the general clauses of the BGB, Secs. 138, 242, 315(3), and 826, which are the typical normative pitfalls for the equity concepts of legal scholars, were employed to counter this development.[50] However, it was only possible to attack the tip of the iceberg in this manner, so that during the course of the general discussion on consumer protection during the 1970s the legislature finally took action and passed the Act on Standard Business Conditions. At that time nobody realized that the first reform of the law of obligations of the BGB had thus been initiated,[51] which today not only serves to improve the protection of the private end-consumer, but also that of every merchant.[52] At any rate, it was not possible to protect the principle of freedom of contract pursuant to Sec. 305 BGB by law until the point at which it would revoke itself. This is also confirmed by the paradox of freedom which is of course of particular legal significance in competition and antitrust law as well.[53]

4. Natural, Market-Determined and Institutional Evolution

Assuming that there are evolutive processes in jurisprudence as well,[54] the question must be posed as to the fundamental difference vis-à-vis biology and economics. The difference lies in the lack of

---

48 Cf. E.A. Kramer, "Die Krise des liberalen Vertragsdenkens" (1975).

49 L. Raiser, "Das Recht der allgemeinen Geschäftsbedingungen" (1935).

50 Cf. J. Schmidt-Salzer, "Allgemeine Geschäftsbedingungen" (1971).

51 Cf. A. Wolf, "Weiterentwicklung und Überarbeitung des Schuldrechts," 1978 ZRP 249.

52 Cf. Sec. 24 AGBG, and the extensive case law on leasing with outside capital, which also grants protection to merchants, cf. decision of German Federal Supreme Court, 1985 DB 909; decision of German Federal Supreme Court, 1985 WM 573.

53 Cf. in this vein already F. Böhm, "Wettbewerb und Monopolkampf" (1933).

54 See also H. Zemen, "Evolution des Rechts" (1983); cf. from the US perspective E.D. Elliot, "The Evolutionary Tradition in Jurisprudence," 85 Colum. L. Rev. 38 (1985); M. Lehmann, "Cyberlaw: Rechtsevolution durch Globalisierung," in FS Fikentscher, at 943 et seq. (1998).

a selection process which is natural or determined by the market, for in jurisprudence there is no natural science approach to arriving at a decision.[55] Traditionally, a judge renders a decision without applying mathematical or other precise methods deriving from natural sciences. Of course, a judge is involved in the "discovery procedure of practice."[56] He or she is able to rely on extensive experience in trial and error and endeavours in each individual case to deal with the responsibility of natural and legal persons in a manner that maximizes the common benefit of all parties:[57] By taking into account the fact that his or her decisions may be generalized, a judge more or less intuitively ensures that private law is at least interpreted efficiently and further developed from an economic viewpoint.[58]

In addition, in its research approach legal theory should endeavor to take into account expressly the methods of natural science and, at least on an experimental basis, attempt to analyze such methods.[59] Actual experiments would rapidly reach the boundaries resulting from the fact that our research subject-matter is human behavior. However, each and every change of government in democratic societies, such as in Germany in 1998, each and every amendment of the law or case law, can be understood as a new experiment. Comparative legal studies in particular can prevent us from embarking on meaningless and dangerous experiments with the systematic factor that is the law. Corresponding considerations apply to the incorporation of the research results arrived at by our neighboring sciences, and in Germany such an approach is gaining

---

55 Cf. M. Adams, "Ist die Ökonomie eine imperialistische Wissenschaft?," 1984 JURA 337.

56 Cf. Ch. Joerges, "Verbraucherschutz als Rechtsproblem" (1981).

57 Cf. R.A. Posner, "Economic Analysis of Law" 179 (2d ed. 1977); from the German perspect cf. in particular J. Limbach, "Der verständige Rechtsgenosse" 33 (1977); frequently, judges play the role of the "reasonable legal person." In the meantime, the courts frequently deploy the arguments of "subsequent evaluation arguments," cf. Kaufmann & Neumann, "Wie argumentieren Gerichte heute in der Praxis," LMU München, Berichte aus der Forschung, No. 48, 1982, at 7 et seq.

58 Cf. also G.L. Priest, "The Common Law Process and the Selection of Efficient Rules," 6 JLS 65 (1977); Hollander & Mackay, "Are Judges Economists at Heart?," in: C. Ciampi (Ed.), "Artificial Intelligence and Legal Information Systems" 129 et seq. (1982).

59 Cf. R. Zippelius, "Rechtsgewinnung durch experimentierendes Denken, "in: Perelman & Vander (Eds.), "Les notions a contenu variable en droit," 351 et seq. (1984).

ground. On this point the increasing reception of the "economic analysis of the law"[60] and the growing incorporation of the results of behavioral research into the law have equal weight.[61] Consideration of the so-called "nature of the matter"[62] as well as legal factual research[63] also serve to advance the principle of rationality. Questions are posed with increasing frequency to the natural science neighboring disciplines to make available rational arguments in order to improve the monitoring and verification of our sense of justice.[64] Legal sociologists are also starting to examine our biological foundations.[65] In the field of legal anthropology,[66] with a stronger philosophical orientation, this inter-disciplinary scientific approach has a longer tradition.

Therefore, jurisprudence, with the support of its neighboring disciplines, should ensure that there are a sufficient number of institutions in our legal system that enable an evolutive development and improvement of such system, and should also encourage such institutions to the extent desirable. Any dogmatically entrenched enactment of a rule of law is counter-evolutive, although, of course, for reasons of legal certainty it is essential to be able to rely on a certain consistency and continuity of the law. Hence, in legal practice and in legal theory there must be sufficient scope for legal evolution to be engendered by the participating and involved circles. For in contrast to the field of biology and economics, in jurisprudence there are no self-effective mechanisms in this respect. Hence, what legal scholars can learn

---

60 Cf. the overview in H. Hof, "Verhaltensforschung im Recht," in: deutscher Sicht, in: 15 RECHTSTHEORIE 277 (1984); in 1984 the "European Association for Law and Economics" was founded in Lund, Sweden; see also G. Taupitz, "Ökonomische Analyse und Haftungsrecht—Eine Zwischenbilanz," 196 AcP 115 (1996).

61 Cf. the overview in H. Hof, "Verhaltensforschung im Recht, "in: 14 RECHTSTHEORIE 349 (1983); see also supra note 2.

62 Cf. E. Quambusch, "Recht und genetisches Programm. Ansätze zur Neubelebung des Naturrechtsgedankens" 9 (1984).

63 See fundamental work by A. Nußbaum (ed. by M. Rehbinder), "Die Rechtstatsachenforschung. Programmschriften und praktische Beispiele" (1968).

64 Cf. M. Rehbinder, "Fragen an die Naturwissenschaften zum sog. Rechtsgefühl," 1982 JZ 1.

65 Cf. H. Rottleuthner, "Biologie und Recht," in: 1985 Zeitschrift für Rechtssoziologie 104.

66 Cf. in particular A. Gehlen, "Urmensch und Spätkultur" (1964); id., "Moral und Hypermoral" (2d ed. 1970); Fikentscher, "Anthropology and the Law" passim (1997).

from their colleagues in the field of natural sciences, apart from endeavoring to achieve increased inter-subjective rationality, is a certain open-mindedness towards evolutive processes; plurality of methods[67] and tolerance towards inter-disciplinary efforts are the best prerequisites in this respect.

Every society only has as much and as good a law as it deserves. Inter-disciplinary cooperation between biologists, economists and legal scholars and practitioners could have very promising evolutive effects in relation to improving our general living conditions. Margaret Gruter appreciated this at a very early point in time and put it into effect through her academic life's work: Ad multos annos!"

---

[67] Cf. in particular W. Fikentscher, "Methoden des Rechts" Vols. I-V (1975-1977); cf. also K.-H. Fezer, "Die Pluralität des Rechts," 1985 JZ 762.

A Call for Consideration of Human Modes of Behavior when Promoting Environmentally Correct Behavior by means of Information and Force of Law

Thomas M.J. Möllers[*]

I. **Environmental Protection—But How?**

1. **Introduction**

Over the last 20 years, Germany has achieved a fair measure of progress in environmental protection. The rivers are cleaner, smog alarms are generally a thing of the past, and the introduction of catalytic converters and unleaded gasoline has resulted in an overall

---

[*]   Professor Dr. Thomas M.J. Möllers, Faculty of Law, University of Augsburg, Germany; professorial chair in Civil Law, Economic Law, EU-Law, International Private Law and Comparative Law; Chairman of the Institute for European Law Systems and Chairman of the Institute for Environmental Law

decrease in air pollution. Nonetheless, approximately 4% of the population suffer from allergies, particularly children, of whom one in three currently evidence some form of allergic reaction.[1] About half of all residents complain about excessive noise,[2] some 5 million reporting a resulting inability to sleep even with closed windows.[3] The primary noise source is that generated by heavy duty trucks and larger vehicles.[4]

On average about 11 tons of carbon dioxide are produced for each member of the population per year, exceeding the maximum level that the climate can safely withstand by over 500 per cent.[5] This air pollution has resulted in the annual extinction of some 90 different species of animals in Germany alone.[6]

Natural disasters occur increasingly frequently throughout the world,[7] and the ozone hole and global destruction of forests[8]

---

1 Among adults 13% suffer from contact eczema, 12% from allergies, 6% from asthma, and 5% from an allergy to nickel; Vollmer, Allergische Erkrankungen—nehmen sie zu?, Ärztliche Kosmetologie 1990, p. 11; Kretzschmar, Inzidenz allergischer Reaktionen durch kosmetische Mittel, Ärztliche Kosmetologie 1989, p. 254; Aberer, Das allergische Kontaktekzem, Ärztliche Kosmetologie 1991, p. 81; Horak, Neue Trends in der Pollenallergie, Ärztliche Kosmetologie 1991, p. 93; Rakoski, Allergien durch Nahrungsmittel, Jahrestagung der Landeszentrale für Gesundheitsbildung in Bayern 1988, pp. 12/13; Concerning sicknesses common among children view the opinion expressed by the German government in BT-DR (reports of the sessions of the Bundestag, hereafter: BT-DR) 12, p. 2580, concerning children's health and environmental pollution BT-DR 12, p. 4626.

2 Bayerische Staatsregierung (ed.), Der Lärm, third ed. 1988, p. 6; more than 50% of all petitions to the Bundestag concern noise pollution, Jansen, Zeitschrift für Lärmbekämpfung 1986, pp. 2/3

3 Der Fischer Öko—Almanach 91/92, 1991, p. 175; Concerning the impact of aircraft noise on the sleep, instructive: Hermann, Schutz vor Fluglärm bei der Planung von Verkehrsflughäfen im Lichte des Verfassungsrechts, 1994, p. 62.

4 Bundesministerium für Umwelt (hereafter: BMU) (ed.), Umweltbericht 1990, [1990], p. 225; BMU, Umweltbewußtsein in Deutschland 1998, [1998], p. 1.

5 Krägenow, Joint Implementation-Ein Beitrag zum Klimaschutz?, Jahrbuch 1996, [1995], pp. 212/214.

6 Martens, Warten auf Godot, ZRP 1996, p. 44.

7 Berz (chairman of the research group "Geowissenschaften" of the "Münchner Rückversicherung"), Wirtschaftswoche 97/03/27, pp. 110/111 probably caused by the augmentation of the gases responsible for the greenhouse effect.

8 Concerning the historical development in the detection of the destruction of forests: Ell/Luhmann, Von Scham, Schäden und Ursachen—Zur Entdeckung des Waldsterbens in Deutschland, Jahrbuch Ökologie 1996, [1995], p. 310.

highlight the global plight,[9] with the situation in Eastern Europe being particularly devastating. Developments in environmental technology are relentlessly overtaken by accelerating economic growth and the concomitant increase in traffic.[10] The short useful life of many manufactured goods reflects the throwaway mentality of consumers. Consumption of strawberries in the depths of winter is emblematic of our profligate society.

2. Means of Environmental Protection

Environmental protection, then, is matter of extreme necessity. The approach of Germany's federal legislature has been to attempt to guide public awareness of this ongoing need through information and legislative acts.

a) Information: Awareness of the environment and environmentally appropriate behavior

Knowledge and awareness of the environment are prerequisites for environmentally appropriate behavior. Since the 1970s the German government has attempted to accomplish public awareness of the current dilemma by disseminating information. These efforts have been fairly successful and many citizens possess a high degree of environmental awareness.[11] The 1992 Rio Conference agenda also called for an "ethical awareness of the effect on the environment of worldwide daily decisions."[12]

---

9   Further examples to be found in: Hamberger (et al.), Sein oder Nichtsein, Die industrielle Zerstörung der Natur, 1990; exhibition of the Münchner Stadtmuseum with the same topic; Kremers/Kutscher, DIE ZEIT 91/11/08, p. 54.

10   Meadows/Meadows/Randers, Beyond the Limits, 1992; Böhm/Breier, Güterverkehrspolitik und Umweltschutz nach dem EWG-Vertrag, EuZW 1991, p. 523.

11   Many people are convinced that collecting waste-paper, glass, cans and other recyclable products is important, and that something has to be done against the ozone hole and the dying of forests; supra n.4, BMU (ed.), 1998 p. 21; Schluchter/Dahm, Analyse der Bedingungen für die Transformation von Umweltbewußtsein in umweltschonendes Verhalten, UBA-Texte 49/96, p. 181; Dierkes/Fietkau, Umweltbewußtsein und Umweltverhalten, 1988.

12   The agenda is to be found in BMU (ed.), Konferenz der Vereinten Nationen für Umwelt und Entwicklung im Juni 1992 in Rio de Janeiro-Dokumente, Agenda 21; Bayerisches Staatsministerium für Landesentwicklung und Umweltfragen (BaySMLU) (ed.), Umwelt & Entwicklung in Bayern, 1/97; Findley/Farber, Cases and materials on Environmental Law, fourth ed., 1995, p. 22; Töpfer, UN-Kommission für nachhaltige Entwicklung, Jahrbuch Ökologie 1996, 1995, p. 96; concerning the Berlin conference: Müller-Kraenner, Wie geht's weiter nach der Berliner Klimakonferenz?, Jahrbuch Ökologie 1996, [1995], p. 43; Feist, Von Rio nach Berlin—Die Aktivitäten der Vereinten Nationen auf den Gebieten des Umwelt-und Klimaschutzes, JuS 1997, pp. 490/493.

The stance of the present federal government has been to encourage informed and voluntary action. The Rio Conference failed to specify a time by which signatory states should achieve a reduction in CO_2-emissions, but the German federal government itself assumed the obligation to decrease its emission level of 1987 by 25-30 percent by the year 2005 at the latest.[13] In line with this goal, and without being prodded by legal mandates, industries have committed themselves to a 20 percent decrease in the use of energy, while the Verband der Autoindustrie (Automobile Industry Association) has determined to work on a reduction of fuel consumption by some 25 percent.[14]

Nonetheless, the fact is that raising the public's conception of environmental affairs remains dramatically different from an actual translation of awareness into positive action.[15] Often, however, reaching a genuinely clear public comprehension of ecological problems—i.e. the first step—is simply not a reality.[16] Moreover, which types of activity have an obvious negative effect on the surroundings have not been factually proven. There is a wide disparity between the understanding of the typical lay person and the opinions of experts in the field. Many people simply accept the views of those experts whose statements confirm their own

---

13   BT-DR, 12, p. 3380; on that issue: Bender/Sparwasser/Engel, Umweltrecht, third ed., 1995, marginal note (hereafter: MN) p. 36; Kahl (Kahl, Voßkuhle ed.), Grundkurs Umweltrecht, 1995, p. 248.

14   Rengeling, Das Kooperationsprinzip im Umweltrecht, 1988, p. 40; Kloepfer/Elsner, Deutsche Verwaltungsblätter (hereafter: DVBl) 1996, pp. 964/967; creates an obligation for the exploitation of auto-wrecks by the AIA (96/02/21), the corresponding regulation is still under debate in the Bundesrat (the second Chamber), BT-DR.13, p. 5998; further information especially with a comparative aspect can be found at: Rennings (et al.), Nachhaltigkeit, Ordnungspolitik und freiwillige Selbstverpflichtung, 1997, Anhang (appendix) 1.

15   An overview is to be found at: supra n.11, Dierkes/Fietkau p.11; Urban, Was ist Umweltbewußtsein? in: Kursbuch 1984, p. 6; Sparda, Umweltbewußtsein: Einstellung und Verhalten, in: Kurse/Graumann/Lantermann (ed.), Ökologische Psychologie, 1990, p. 623; Schneider (et al.), Zur Ethik des Handelns in Privatrecht und Erwerbswelt, 2nd vol., 1992; Spiegler, Umweltbewußtsein und Umweltrecht, 1990, p. 8; further sources are to be found in: Siebenhüner, Umweltbewußtsein-weiter gedacht!; Wissenschaftszentrum Berlin für Sozialforschung (WZB), paper FS II 96-402, 1996, p. 29.

16   Concerning the tort liability for information: Möllers, Rechtsgüterschutz im Umwelt-und Haftungsrecht, 1996, pp. 250/261.

preconceptions.[17]   Even among those persons who realize and appreciate the causes of destruction, appropriate environmental behavior is not the necessary consequence: thus a wide gulf remains between comprehending the problem and acting accordingly,[18] with environmental awareness leading to correlative behavior in only 10-15 percent of cases.   In fact, the current situation might be described as a syndrome of the proverbial "do-as-I-say-not-as-I-do" attitude.[19]   Only in so-called "low cost" circumstances does the average individual appear to be prepared to accept a duty to preserve his surroundings.[20]   Whereas the separation of household waste with respect to recyclable materials, cans, glass items, general garbage, etc. is routinely performed by everyone, a unilateral refusal to "do one's bit" is apparent when it comes to renouncing present-day general mobility and methods of reaching one's destination.   The automobile is truly the "favorite child" of Germans.[21]

---

17   Supra n.11, Schluchter/Dahm p. 9.

18   Supra n.4 BMU (ed.), 1998 p. 57; UBA (ed.), Umweltbewußtsein als soziales Phänomen 2. Fachgespräch zur sozialen Umweltforschung im Umweltbundesamt, Texte 32/95, 30/71, 25; Kirsch, Umweltbewußtsein und Umweltverhalten, Eine theoretische Skizze eines empirischen Problems, Zeitschrift für Umweltrecht (ZfU) 1991, p. 249; Kloepfer, Umweltrecht, 1989, § 4 RN 152; Michelsen, Der Fischer Öko-Almanach 91/92, 1991, p. 91; the opinion, to reach effective environment protection by mere information, is too simplified, but being of this opinion: Schäuble, Mut zur Zukunft, in: Politische Meinung, 1992, pp. 15/17.

19   Often what is preached is not practiced: Diekmann/Preisendörfer, Persönliches Umweltverhalten, Diskrepanzen zwischen Anspruch und Wirklichkeit, Kölner Zeitschrift für Soziologie und Sozialpsychologie, 1992, pp. 226/227.

20   The majority of the population is aware of the tremendous amount of traffic being one of the major causes of the CO_2-emissions, which itself being the cause for the dying of forests and the ozone hole; but despite that only a very few are willing to renounce their car; Diekmann/Preisendörfer, Kölner Zeitschrift für Soziologie und Sozialpsychologie, 1992, pp. 226/248; supra n.19, Siebenhüner p. 40; Wehrspann, Umweltbewußtsein im Spannungsfeld normativer   Umorientierungen, psychosozialer Belastungen und umweltgerechter Verhaltensweisen, in: UBA (Hrsg.), Umweltbewusstsein als soziales Phaenomen, 2. Fachgespräch zur sozialen Umweltforschung im Umweltbundesamt, Texte 32/95, S. 30, 71; Bauriedl, Wann ändern Menschen ihr Verhalten?, Jahrbuch Ökologie 1996, 1995, p. 11.

21   The most kilometers are driven at leisure times: Schweis, Moderner Naturtourismus und die Beziehung zwischen Mensch und Natur, in: Seel (ed.), Mensch—Natur, 1993, pp. 199/203; according to a study carried out by the BAT Freizeitforschunginstitut ([BAT]-institute for leisure research) in Hamburg, 35% of all car-drivers love to just "cruise": Süddeutsche Zeitung (hereafter: SZ), 95/06/14, 12; supra n.4, BMU (ed.), 1998 p. 59.

Catering for one's own personal needs—not to say desires—clearly take preference over a communal attempt to protect the environment. The individual tends to ignore the crisis.[22] Avoidance of environmental destruction is viewed as meaningless, the rationale being that renouncing a single car-ride would be a minuscule contribution to such an effort,[23] and would have a virtually insignificant effect, if any, on the ozone hole or any impact on climatic factors. Often one will rationalize and insist that the low-cost means he has taken are proof of his consciousness, thereby shifting any additional responsibility, and indeed blame, onto others who make no such efforts at all.[24]

b) Legal Acts and their Control

The laws themselves have been directed toward controlling or monitoring activity.[25] In this way a range of the crassest environmental "sins" could be reduced, but while this approach can normally eradicate a significant degree of the most severely destructive behavior, it results on the other hand in a profusion of laws.[26] Although this myriad of statutes should not be ignored by the relevant authorities, still there is an evident paucity of enforcement.[27]

---

22 Supra n.11 Schluchter/Dahm p. 184.

23 Supra n.20, Wehrspann p.71; supra n.11 Schluchter/Dahm p.181.

24 The idea of the "big ones" being responsible for the environment dilemma might have contributed to the success of the Greenpeace-organized consumer-boycott of Shell in 1995: supra n.11, Schluchter/Dahm, pp 7/185; concerning the legal relevance: Möllers, Zur Zulässigkeit des Verbraucherboykotts—Brent Spar und Mururoa, NJW, 1996, p. 1374.

25 Concerning the means of direct and indirect guidance of behavior by the lawmaker with relation to national and (supra-national) European law: Epiney/Möllers, Freier Warenverkehr und nationaler Umweltschutz, 92, p. 90. Rittner, Umweltschutz zwischen Staat, Markt und Moral, in: Festschrift für Helmrich, 1994, pp. 1003/1007.

26 Gassert, Umweltschutzorientiertes Management, in: Zahn/Gassert (ed.), Umweltschutzorientiertes Management, 1991, pp. 1/9; concerning US-legislation: Ruhl, [45] Complexity Theory as a Paradigm for the Dynamical Law-and-Society System: A Wake-up Call for Legal Reductionism and the Modern Administrative State, Duke Law Journal, 1996, p. 849.

27 The abilities to finance the personnel and technical equipment are limited and there is not much hope for a change in times of limited budgets: BT-DR: 7, p. 2802, 180; Lübbe-Wolff, Modernisierung des Umweltordnungsrechts, 1996; Lübbe-Wolff (ed.), Der Vollzug des europäischen Umweltrechts, 1996; Hansmann, Schwierigkeiten bei der Umsetzung und Durchführung des europäischen Umweltrechts, NVwZ 1995, p. 320; further sources are to be found, supra n.16 in Möllers, p. 7.

In addition, these laws fail to establish the requisite environmental consciousness. Rules of law have always been violated, especially if the rule's addressee lacks understanding of the law or its purposes,[28] as exemplified by the general disregard for the posted speed limit on the Autobahn (major highway).

On the other hand, there are numerous examples of people who are genuinely perturbed about the preservation of the environment and who have tried to prevent the usage of radioactive materials, or as an alternative example, have made efforts to reverse the Shell Company's decision to sink the drilling platform known as Brent Spar. One wonders how behavior can be so contradictory and inexplicable.

3. Ethology and the Law

If the government aspires to improve upon and make more effective its explanation and clarification to the public about the reasons for environmental statutes and regulations in the future, it necessarily follows that the legislature must consider altering or expanding upon those laws which address human behavior.

a) Ethology and Sociobiology

The earliest research comparing human behavioral patterns (i.e. ethology) was conducted by Niko Tinbergen and Konrad Lorenz. Both used a systematic approach to undertake research into the basic principles of behavior.[29]

Sociobiology is a modern branch of ethology,[30] a concept which

---

28 So explicitly Engel, DVBl, 1997, p. 388.

29 Tinbergen, The Study of Instinct, 1952; Tinbergen, On Aims and Methods of Ethology, Zeitschrift für Tierpsychologie 20 (1963), p. 410; Lorenz, Über tierisches und menschliches Verhalten, in: Aus dem Werdegang der Verhaltenslehre (2 vol.), 1974; Lorenz, Vergleichende Verhaltensforschung, Grundlagen der Ethologie, 1978; Eibl-Eibesfeld, Grundriß der vergleichenden Verhaltensforschung, 6th ed., 1980; Eibl-Eibesfeld, Die Biologie des menschlichen Verhaltens—Grundriß der Humanethologie, 1984; Wickler, Die Biologie der Zehn Gebote, 1975; Wickler/Seibt, Das Prinzip des Eigennutz, Ursache und Konsequenzen sozialen Verhaltens, 1977 (updated 1991); Trivers, Social Evolution, 1985.

30 An historical overview is to be found in: supra n.29 Eibl-Eibesfeld p. 121; supra n.29 Wickler/Seibt pp. 17/67; de Waal, Good Natured. The Origins of Right and Wrong in Humans and Other Animals, 1996; Frank, Verhaltensbiologie, 3rd ed., 1997, p. 1; Gruter, Die Bedeutung der Verhaltensforschung für die Rechtswissenschaft, 1976, p. 15; Alexander, The Biology of Moral Systems, 1987, p. 6; Alexander, Recht, Biologie und Sozialverhalten, in: Gruter/Rehbinder (ed.), Ablehnung-Meidung-Ausschluß, 1986, p. 29.

itself subsumes several methodologies.[31]   To date, contributions to sociobiology have not followed the theory of social evolution, which attributes human behavior solely to the fundamental principles of "survival of the fittest."[32]   Rather, sociobiology subcribes to the principle that the greater influence upon one's conduct is what he has learned through culture and exposure, not what he has inherited.[33]   According to this principle, the human being is capable of learning, his ultimate behavior depending not solely upon the need to leave issue, but on an awareness of his own existence and consciousness of his behavior.[34]   From this consciousness spring his values of love, concern for his fellow man, and his altruism.[35]   Generally, sociobiology is based upon a systematic study of both the effect of one's culture in addition to that of his biological characteristics upon his conduct.   This principle is used in the study both of humans and of all forms of animal life.[36]

b) The Role of Biology in the Law: Legal Ethology
Having completed her studies of Law at the University of

---

31   Koslowski, Evolution and Society—A Critique of Sociobiology, in: Ethics of Capitalism and Critique of Sociobiology, 1995, p. 75; supra n.30 Franck p. 7.

32   Evolution is to be understood as a process during which those individuals are selected, who in their behavior have adapted the best to the environment, due to which their genetic fitness and success of reproduction being of the highest standard: Darwin, On The Origin of Species, 1859; Wilson, Sociobiology, The New Synthesis, 1975; Wilson, On Human Nature, 1978; Lumdsen/Wilsen, Genes, Mind, and Culture, The Coevolutionary Process, 1981; Wilson, Naturalist, 1994, 322; similar: Franck, supra n.30, p. 146.

33   Dawkins, The selfish Gene, 1976; Eibl-Eibesfeld, supra n.29, p. 132; supra n.30, Gruter p. 19; Gruter, Rechtstheorie 11 (1980), pp. 96/102; Gruter/Masters, Balancing Altruism and Selfishness: Evolutionary Theory and the Foundation of Morality, Jahrbuch für Recht und Ethik, 4 [1996], p. 561; Hirsch, Zur juristischen Dimension des Gewissens und der Unverletzlichkeit der Gewissensfreiheit des Richters, 1979, p. 52; Hirsch, Die Steuerung menschlichen Verhaltens, JZ 1982, pp. 34/41/42; von Hayek, Die Drei Quellen der menschlichen Werte, 1979, p. 7.

34   This means including the ability of "regarding the other being conscious about yourself."

35   Freedom and subjectivity are explicitly recognized in society: detailed critique is to be found in: Koslowski, supra n.30, pp. 51-66; Alexander, in: supra n.30, Gruter/Rehbinder pp. 29/32; Markl, Biologie und menschliches Verhalten, in: Gruter/Rehbinder (ed.), Der Beitrag der Biologie zu Fragen von Recht und Ethik, 1983, pp. 67/69/75: inborn characteristics supply the stage on which the internalisation by culture and experience is performed, but do not determine what is done and with what degree of success.

36   Gruter, Soziobiologische Grundlagen der Effektivität des Rechts, Rechtstheorie 11 [1980], pp. 96/98; Voland, Grundriß der Soziobiologie, 1993, p. 1.

Heidelberg and of Biology at the University of Stanford, it was of special concern for *Margaret Gruter* to combine those two sciences.[37]

She not only initiated the studies of behavioral research with regard to legal aspects,[38] or as it is usually named, Legal Ethology,[39] but gave it a forum by founding the Gruter Institute for Law and Behavioral research. Various publications,[40] conferences and seminars[41] held at the Institute can only partly reflect its importance for research in that field. Besides that, its significant influence on the Law itself has to be noted.[42]

The reason why ethology has had such an impact on our legal and judicial system is rather simple. The socio-biological approach is most meaningful as a means of clarification for lawmakers and the judiciary when certain rules of law simply do not comport[43] with

---

37 Even further going: supra n.38 Hof p. 7: . . . . not only ethology but the sciences of behavior in general, i.e. sociobiology, sociology, and psychology, [are to be] combined.

38 Supra n.30 Gruter; Origins of Human Behavior, 1991, p. 9; Fikentscher, Rechtstheorie 24 [1993], p. 243; An overview of the historical development towards Eugen Ehrlich's and Arthur Nußbaum's sociological perception in legal affairs as well as that of the US Legal Realism is to be found in: Fikentscher/McGuire, Rechtstheorie 25 [1994], pp. 291/292; Fikentscher, Methoden des Rechts, vol. 1, 1976, pp. 273-325.

39 Hof, Rechtsethologie, Recht im Kontext von Verhalten und außerrechtlicher Verhaltensregelung, 1996.

40 Masters/Gruter (eds.), The Sense of Justice, Biological Foundations of Law, 1992; Gruter/Masters (eds.), Ostracism: A Social and Biological Phenomenon, 1986; Gruter/Bohannan (eds.), Law, Biology and Culture: The Evolution of Law, 1983/2nd ed. 1992; Gruter (ed.), Biology, Law and Human Social Behavior. An Interdisciplinary Reader, 1992; Gruter (ed.), Law and Mind: Biological Origins of Human Behavior, 1991; Gruter/M.T. McGuire (eds.), Human Nature and the New Europe; M.T. McGuire/Rehbinder (eds.), Biology, Law and the Environment, 1993; Fikentscher, Modes of Thought, 1995; Smith/Danilenko (eds.), Law and Democracy in the New Russia, 1993; Masters/M.T. McGuire (eds.), The Neurotransmitter Revolution, 1993; Gruter/Rehbinder (eds.), Gewalt in der Kleingruppe, 1997.

41 I.a. Ethology, Property, Economics, and Growth, March 1990; Biological Perspectives in Law and Social Sciences, June 1991; The Infrastructure and Suprastructure of the European Market: Implications for the next two Decades, August 1991; Void for vagueness, November 1992; Migration and Immigration: Trends and Critical Policy Issues, May 1994; Applications of Biology in the Study of Law, June 1993; Law, Biology, and Human Behavior, June 1994; Biological Perspectives in the Socials Sciences, August 1995; Law, Risk and Risk, Management, September 1996; Frontiers in Law and Biology, June 1997.

42 In the Matter of Baby M, Amicus Curiae Brief, 1988; report from the Gruter Institute, by Fox, in: Politics and the Life Sciences, vol. 7, no.1 August 1988, p. 77.

43 Gruter, supra n.30, p. 81.

inborn, or genetic, behavioral traits.[44]   This even though it is perfect difficult, to discern[45] whether what has been learned, or what has been genetically passed down, is the root cause of a particular behavioral pattern.

Legal research on behavior is based upon two presumptions. The first is that rules of law that contradict and work in opposition to hereditary patterns of behavior will generally have a low acceptance rate among the public.   Thus, human behavior must be considered in the adoption of legal standards in order to predict the likely degree of compliance with these standards.[46] But genetically affected human behavior will not always result in a corresponding legal norm; natural science cannot be the only basis for legal standards.[47] Culture, together with justice, are intended to limit— and also to correct—some behavioral activity which is the result of genetics, such as aggressive responses.[48]   From this foundation comes the second presumption upon which legal behavioral research operates: rules which are contrary to normal patterns of behavior must include clarifying provisions that comport with the culture in order to assure that the general public understands them. The law must present detailed reasons for its enactment.[49] In brief, simple wording will not suffice for environmental laws or regulations that mandate behavior in opposition to what is normal. Ethology therefore must question not only which type of human response is innate, but also by which means culturally learned behavior, in opposition to innate behavior, can be obtained.[50]

---

44   I.e. those not being developed through the process of learning: supra n.30 Franck p. 56; Immelmann/Pöve/Sossinka, Einführung in die Verhaltensforschung, 4th ed., 1995, p. 115; Zippelius, Biologische Grundlagen des Sozialverhaltens, Rechtstheorie 12 [1981], pp. 177/179: inbred or inherited respectively modes of behavior.

45   Markl, Biologie und menschliches Verhalten, in: supra n.30 Gruter/Rehbinder (eds.) pp. 67/77; Alexander, in: supra n.30 Gruter/Rehbinder pp. 29/34.

46   Supra n.30 Gruter p. 19; Gruter, Law and the Mind, 1991, p. 21; Fikentscher, Rechtstheorie 24 [1993], p. 243; Zippelius, supra n.44; Zippelius, Erträge der Soziobiologie für die Rechtswissenschaft, ARSP, 1987, pp. 386/388.

47   Schwartz, Die Bedeutung der Soziobiologie für die Rechtswissenschaft, in: Gruter/Rehbinder (eds.), Der Beitrag der Biologie zu Fragen von Recht und Ethik, 1983, p. 51.

48   Supra n.30 Gruter pp. 16/48; supra n.44 Zippelius.

49   Similar: Wickler, supra n.29 p. 28.

50   In general: Markl, supra n.35 pp. 67/69.

Law corresponding closely to human attributes is the objective of the legal study of behavioral patterns.[51] Hereafter, Environmental Law will be studied in the light of human behavioral research.[52] By examining environmental problems it will be shown which characteristics are hereditary, and which have been developed (II). From this point, the researcher can consider the potentially different directions for environmental law (III). It is essential to determine which kinds of environmentally harmful activity correspond to innate individual characteristics. Then the lawmakers can consider whether and under what circumstances human conduct might be altered by the law in order to attain environmentally appropriate behavior patterns.

The aim should be to ascertain how behavior might be guided effectively[53] by taking into consideration both social and biological factors. Ideally, this will diminish the discrepancy between the public understanding of what activity is ecologically damaging and its actual response in the light of that understanding.

II. Innate Modes of Human Behavior
1. Self-Preservation and Reproduction

The striving for self-preservation is one of the fundamental modes of human behavior.[54] The drive for self-preservation was illustrated by Maslow in his motivation pyramid. This distinguishes between fundamental material human needs for nourishment, physical health, shelter and security and post-material values such as friendship, status and self-expression.[55] An extreme example of

---

51 Literally: Fikentscher, Rechtstheorie 24 (1993), p. 243.

52 This essay is aimed in part at initiating an exchange among various sciences which seems indispensable in the field of environmental protection: Luhmann, Ökologische Kommunikation, 1986; Raiser, Das lebende Recht, 2nd ed., 1995, p. 165; Lehmann, Das Prinzip Eigennutz, JZ 1990, pp. 61/67.

53 Rodgers, Where Environmental Law and Biology Meet: Of Panda's Thumbs, Statutory Sleepers, and Effective Law, 65 (1993) Univ. of Col. Law Rev., pp. 25/27.

54 Gruter, Das Bedürfnis nach Sicherheit und Bereitschaft zum Risiko: eine evolutionsbiologische Perspektive, in: Festschrift Helmrich, 1994, pp. 1083/1084.

55 Maslow, Motivation and Personality, 1954; Inglehart, The Silent Revolution, Chance and Political Styles in Western Publics, 1977; critical on that opinion: Klages, Traditionsbruch als Herausforderung, 1993.

the legal protection of these fundamental human rights, such as the right to life and good health, would be the threat of the death penalty for having taken another's life. This striving for self-preservation might be one of the reasons why a major portion of the daily news concerns catastrophes, where we are especially moved if there have been multiple deaths among the human species.[56]

Secondly, it is important for humans to secure reproductive opportunities so as to promote the survival of the race. This concern is naturally accompanied by the desire to protect one's children and grandchildren.[57] The continuing resistance of a substantial portion of the world's population to the use of atomic energy can be attributed to a general concern about the ultimate storage of radioactive waste. Future generations will probably be required to deal with methods of nuclear waste disposal. The principal concern underlying this resistance would seem to be concern for future generations.[58]

Current demands for cessation of the use of atomic weapons are based upon the belief that a continuation will eventually exterminate the entire human species. The environmental organization Greenpeace certainly owed the success of its call for a boycott of Shell to its convincing argument to the public that the sinking of the Brent Spar drilling platform in the North Sea was intended as a rehearsal for the sinking of a further 100 such platforms in the following decades, and that this form of disposal would be a burden on future generations.[59]

2. Rationality and Capacity Limits of the Human Brain

The conventionally assumed characteristic separating human

---

56   Fikentscher, Wirtschaftliche Gerechtigkeit und kulturelle Gerechtigkeit, 1997.
57   A gene being successful if bearing a characteristic which itself is useful for the gene: supra n.33 Dawkins; this has to be distinguished from self-interest: supra n.33 de Waal p. 25; supra n.29 Trivers p. 20; supra n.55 Gruter p. 1083/1085; supra n.36 Voland p. 2.
58   Letters to the editor in: DIE ZEIT, 97/03/28 p. 67.
59   Of less importance seemed to be the information about the actual polluting consequences of the mud by the oil, which were not true; a description of the circumstances is found in: supra n.24 Möllers pp. 1374/1376; of a different opinion being: Kratz/Piper, DIE ZEIT, 96/06/23 p. 17.

from animal life is the ability of the former to think and comprehend. A human can make certain choices according to his own free will, and he can distinguish between right and wrong according to his system of values. Since he is able to learn which conduct corresponds to the concept of good and which to the concept of evil or negative, he therefore has the ability to form a defined system of values.[60] This is not to infer, however, that this freedom of thought and action is not limited in many ways, these limitations deriving from the capacity limits of the human brain. Therefore the second innate mode of human behavior is: the mind and the limits on its capacity. Three limits may be named.

a) Complexity and Capacity Limits

The usual course of human thought is linear in fashion, i.e. assimilating information in a selective pattern. Often, one's brain capacity makes it impossible for him to absorb complex matters which are inter-related. He cannot think beyond his genetic "network of thought."

Dörner's research reveals almost shocking results: subjects in experiments were expected to indicate that a poor African tribe could be transformed into a prosperous group with the aid of computer technology. However, in spite of the best possible motivators, the decisions of the experiment subjects consistently led to the extinction of the tribe.[61] Because of memory restrictions,[62] an individual also is limited with regard to his capacity to learn, and consequently it is often not feasible to alter the status quo.[63] Numerous individual catastrophes such as the atomic energy disaster in Chernobyl and the tragedy of the Exxon carrier Valdez on the coast of Alaska[64] illustrate how the human is often incapable

---

60   Fikentscher, in: Masters/Gruter pp. 106/113; Fikentscher/McGuire Rechtstheorie 25 (1994) pp. 291, 295; Bilz, Wie frei sind wir wirklich?, 1971.

61   Dörner, Die Logik des Mißlingens, Strategisches Denken in komplexen Situationen, 1989; Dörner et al. (eds.), Vom Umgang mit Unbestimmtheit und Komplexität, 1983; Vester, Leitmotiv vernetztes Denken, Für einen besseren Umgang mit der Umwelt, 1988.

62   Supra n.61, Vester p. 293.

63   Preuss, Umweltkatastrophe Mensch. Über unsere Grenzen und Möglichkeiten ökologisch bewußt zu handeln, 1991, p. 39.

64   Supra n.61 Dörner p. 56; supra n.54 Rodgers p. 66.

of intellectually reacting in a positive manner to difficult situations.

Quite often we insist upon maintaining the status quo simply because it has not been factually proven that our own conduct damages the environment. It often appears that many different causes are destructive to the surroundings (alternative causation). Moreover, with regard to vehicular emissions, one might argue that a single automobile has little impact and that overall emission is to blame for ecological damage, such as destruction of forests (additive causation). Legal scholars have produced no convincing response to these alternative-and-additive causation positions.[65]

b) Loss of Perception due to a Gap in Experience

A second limitation upon an individual's ability to comprehend and appreciate is a gap in his experience. Using mind and logic the human can learn and "imagine" the consequences but that does not necessarily mean, having actually comprehended the content. The German word for comprehension ("Begreifen") is a multi-faceted term. It includes not only a mental comprehension or appreciation, but also the experience of sensations of feeling and taste, and the ability to hold onto a concept through trial and error. So it is semantically close to the English word "grasp."

The human being learns through his senses. Although a child might know that a plate is hot, he nonetheless will grab it. The heat registers on his sensation of feeling and causes him to release it. This same phenomenon works for adults people. So simple mental comprehension will remain without success if it is not accompanied by sensual grasp.

Annual statistics show that young adults, in spite of the exceptional quality of their training, have more driving accidents than do older people. This is because they as yet lack the experience which leads to an appreciation of the potential results of

---

65 Concerning those different possibilities of causation: Hager, in: Landmann/Rohmer, Umweltrecht, lose-leaf collection (1994), § 6 UHG, MN 35/§ 7 UHG, MN 19; Staudinger/Roth, 12th ed. 1995, § 906 MN 10—37/108; Staudinger/Kohler, 12th ed., 1995, Einl. (introduction) UmwHR, MN 209-261; Larenz/Canaris, Schuldrecht II/2, 1994, p. 658.

excessive speed.[66]   Although weather reports regularly include information and warnings about icy road conditions, there are nonetheless countless accidents each year because inexperienced drivers feel secure in their case, and are no longer exposed to the hazards of natural forces.

This lack of perception due to a gap in experience, is directly applicable to the scope of this article. One might not yet appreciate which factors harm the environment. Only occasionally is an individual affected by radioactivity, odors from formaldehyde, or emissions from a single engine. One becomes convinced of these dangers only through artificial means.[67] Thus, one naturally regards the hazards one person causes, but does not sense, as harmless. Because of the complexity of this situation, the "Erfahrungsdistanz,"[68] i.e. gap in *experience*, or the passage of time since one's actual experience in order for him to comprehend and appreciate its significance, is widening. He who buys something made of mahogany spares no thought for the cost to tropical forests, just as he who travels by air is heedless of carbon dioxide emissions or the resulting rise in sea levels.

c) Emotional Reactions: Hysteria and Apathy

Emotions also limit rational thinking. As contrasted with comprehension, emotions are governed by older parts of the brain.[69] Research into risks indicates that knowledge and perception of what is certain sometimes run contrary to each other. Knowledge does not necessarily determine perceptions.[70] Loss of perception and the gap in experience can be increased through human feelings, one of which is fear. Fear is considerably

---

66   The lawmaker reacting by a "license on probation" (§ 2a StVG; introduced by the law of 86/05/15, BGBl I 1986, p. 700), the insurance companies reacting by policies demanding a rate of 260% for drivers of the age 18 to 21.

67   Supra n.63 Preuss p. 47.

68   Supra n.63 Preuss p. 48.

69   Gruter, Die Bedeutung der biologisch orientierten Verhaltensforschung für die Suche nach den Rechtstatsachen, in: Gruter/Rehbinder (eds.), Der Beitrag der Biologie zu Fragen von Recht und Ethik, 1983, pp. 225/229.

70   Wildavsky, Vergleichende Untersuchung zur Risikowahrnehmung, in: Bayerische Rückversicherung (ed.), Risiko ist ein Konstrukt, 1993, pp. 192/194.

augmented through media exaggerations, e.g. television.[71] A single accident which has caused many deaths has a much stronger impact than do several smaller incidents, even though the sum total of casualties may be far greater.[72] An obvious example is provided by airline disasters, which are generally perceived as far more deplorable catastrophes than car accidents, despite the fact that the total numbers of deaths or serious injuries resulting from automobile accidents far outnumber those in airline crashes. Fear, then, is a powerful force,[73] and hysteria is often the consequence. Consumers will react irrationally and exaggerate a danger, despite the fact that objectively all factors prove that there is literally no such danger to either the public or the environment. The dangers of BSE contaminated meat are an example.

Meanwhile, it is submitted that there is a continually increasing number of people who contract illnesses caused by dangerous ecological circumstances, although there is no absolute corroborative medical proof of these causes.[74] And last but not least reports of catastrophes can indeed even result in the opposite of hysteria, i.e., apathy and lethargy; insisting that one's individual contribution to environmental protective efforts are simply too insignificant to make a difference.

3. Self-Interest and Altruism

a) Self-Interest and Possession

To a certain degree, the human's self-interest is governed by what will best facilitate and insure his own existence.[75] One's

---

71   Concerning the relationship of nature and media: Mettler-Maibom, Natur-Mensch-Medien, in: Altner (ed.), Jahrbuch Ökologie 1994, 1993, p. 209.

72   McGuire, Biological factors contributing to risk assessments of products and responses to unsatisfactory products, Paper, distributed during the course of Summer School: Risk and Security; Berkeley 1996, p. 5.

73   Supra n.11 Schluchter/Dahm p. 187.

74   Ring et al., Klinisches-Ökologie-Syndrom, in: Münchner Medizinische Wochenschrift, 91/02/01, 50; supra n.20 Wehrspann p. 79.

75   Supra n.20, Bauriedl p. 11; It's open to discussion if our whole society is built upon and determined by the idea of self-interest as maintained by: Becker, The Economic Approach to Human Behavior, 1976; Tietzel, Ökonomie und Soziobiologie oder: Wer kann was von wem lernen?, ZWS 1983, p. 107; Lehmann, Evolution in Biologie, Ökonomie und Jurisprudenz, Rechtstheorie 17 (1986), pp. 463/470; Kirchgässner, Homo oeconomicus, 1991.

individual needs might lead to overall environmental damage, as the "Dilemma der Allmende" (Dilemma of Mankind) has made clear: Fishermen caught so much fish that there were none left in the lake.[76] There are two aspects in this regard: Firstly, there is simply an inadequate degree of cooperation, i.e., "a deal,"[77] to limit oneself to catching a reasonable number of fish in order to avoid the inevitable shortage. Secondly, in addition to the problem of co-operation, the "Free loader-phenomenon" is also apparent. There is no self-limitation indicating an intent to ensure that the general public will be able to enjoy those natural resources which essentially are not the individual's private property. Research into behavior confirms that borders which were once the object of battles are now respected according to law.[78] In this regard, human conduct corresponds actually to the order and organization which accompanies private ownership. This resulting order and lack of chaos emanating from individual ownership can indeed be useful for the environment.[79] On the other hand it cannot alter the owner's entitlement to damage his own property.[80]

b) Altruism

Scholars of sociobiology have interpreted every form of altruism as being, in a broader sense, motivated by individual self-interest.[81] The individual is prepared to accept disadvantages in order to be

---

76   Hardin, The Tragedy of the Commons, Part Two, 15 (1992) Harv. Jour.Law & Pub. Policy, p. 325; Rodgers, Environmental Law, 2nd ed., 1994, p. 39; Spada/Ernst, Wissen, Ziele und Verhalten in einem ökologisch-sozialen Dilemma, in: Pawlik/Stapf (eds.), Umwelt und Verhalten, 1992, p. 83; supra n.20 Wehrspann p. 76; supra n.11 Dierkes/Fietkau p. 43; Gramm, Nachweltschutz durch kooperative Rechtsstrukturen, JZ 1990, pp. 905/907.

77   The initial thought of this being the "Prisoner's Dilemma": Rapport/Chammah, Prisoner's Dilemma. A Study in Conflict and Cooperation, 1956; Koslowski, Gesellschaft und Staat. Ein unvermeidlicher Dualismus, 1982, pp. 17/152; very illustrative the example of crows mutually stealing twigs for building their nests, so the reproduction achieved being less successful than without such behavior: supra n.29 Wickler/Seibt p. 83.

78   Supra n.36 Voland p. 93; supra n.60 Fikentscher/McGuire pp. 291/302.

79   Hardin, 162 (1968) Science, 1243/1245; supra n.47 Gruter p. 127.

80   As an example of which might be cited the rather careless treatment by the owners of their own cars: supra n.60 Fikentscher/McGuire p. 303.

81   Huxley, Struggle for existence and its bearings upon man, in: Nineteenth Century, Februrary 1888; Hamilton, Selection of selfish and altruistic behavior, in: Eisenberg/Dillon (eds.), Man and Beast: Comparative Social Behavior, 1971, pp. 59/83; supra n.33 Dawkins p. 215; Williams, A sociobiological expansion of "Evolution and Ethics" in: Huxley, Evolution and Ethics, 1989, pp. 179/210; Altruism in that sense standing for mode of behavior which gives advantage to others costs the one who gives.

able to act in the interest of his family.[82]   In one view, a businessman acts in an altruistic manner when he engages in a "tit-for-tat" deal.[83]   Any possible advantage a free loader might glean from acting in what is essentially a hypocritical manner will be limited by what is referred to as the law of moral aggression (a sense of justice and punishment for transgressors of the law).[84]

An individual's system of morals develops accordingly, and is based on categorical imperatives.[85]   The consequence is that one's image and his status are bound together into what is perceived as a social person.[86]   Other researchers in the area of human behavior have strictly opposed a view which reduces all individual actions to taking care of one's own needs.   De Waal has been the first to show that monkeys, too, can be caring and empathetic to one another, exhibiting relationships like friendship, but by the same token enmity.[87]

---

82   Concerning the theory of relative-selection: Hamilton, The Genetical Evolution of Social Behavior, 7 (1964) Journal of Theoretical Biology, p. 1; supra n.29 Wickler/Seibt p. 50; supra n.30 Franck pp. 111/153; supra n.36 Voland p. 4: at the uttermost he might even be willing to sacrifice himself just so that his genes do survive.

83   Called "reciprocal altruism": Trivers, The Evolution of Reciprocal Altruism, 46 (1971) Quarterly Review of Biology, p. 35; supra n.29 Wickler/Seibt p. 89; supra n.30 Franck p. 109; supra n.36 Voland p. 86; with regard to its transformation into legal norms: Axelrod, The Evolution of Cooperation, 1984.

84   Supra n.29 Wickler p. 101; Tietzel, ZWS 1982, pp. 107/119; supra n.33 Gruter/Masters pp. 561/569.

85   Alexander, Biological considerations in the analysis of morality, in: Nitecki/Nitecki (eds.), Evolutionary Ethics, 1993, p. 163.

86   Concerning gain of status: Boyd/Richerson The Evolution of indirect Reciprocity, 11 (1989) Social Networks, p. 213; supra n.33 Gruter/Masters pp. 561/566; supra n.30 de Waal p. 48; supra n.30 Frank p. 153; even without such a gain of status the individual may want to renounce some supposedly chances since he is aware of the advantages offered by the community as there are for example joint hunting, protection against enemies, etc.: supra n.32 Darwin p.119; supra n.30 Gruter pp. 19/28; supra n.29 Wickler/Seibt p. 75; supra n.36 Voland p. 115; supra n.33 Gruter/Masters pp. 559, 570; Frank, Passions Within Reason: The Strategic Role of the Emotions, 1988; supra n.54 Rodgers p. 43.

87   de Waal, Peacemaking among Primates, 1989; The individual being willing to co-operate—to escape the "Prisoner's dilemma": Schüßler, Kooperation unter Egoisten: vier Dilemmata, 1990; supra de Waal n.30 pp. 28/31/57/101/105/112; Schnabel, DIE ZEIT, 96/03/21 p. 27; Boyd/Richerson, Punishment Allows the Evolution of Cooperation (or Anything Else) in Sizeable Groups, 13 (1992), Ethology and Sociobiology, p. 171; supra n.33 Gruter/Masters p. 570; the preference of relatives hereby not being perceived as nepotism, rather affection, acts against the reciprocal altruism, even though usually punished by sanctions and ostracism, won't be related to egoism: supra n.30 de Waal p. 30.

4. Fundamental Human Needs—Back to Nature

a) Nature and Warmth

The fourth mode of human behavior remains to be considered. Our ancestors lived near the Equator, presumably in the Eastern African tropical area.[88] From this origin comes an innate need for warmth and sunshine. Solariums are often provided as therapy for patients who are depressed and suicidal.[89]

b) Mobility and the Urge for Freedom

Our forefathers were also hunters. They were able to pursue this activity unhindered in the savanna, moving from place to place with relative ease. The human being naturally loves his freedom, so that it is essentially human that democratic societies reserve stiff prison sentences for the most heinous crimes. It is correspondingly no wonder that the attempt to enclose a whole people behind a wall, or peoples behind an iron curtain, was doomed to failure. The desire for a Savanna-style region has led to the maintenance of parks. Indeed, homes in areas near parkland command the highest prices, since the buyer is actually purchasing a form of "happiness" in addition to shelter.[90] Although the consumer has less money at his disposal for such an investment, tourism continues to thrive.[91] Generally, people make no attempt at thrift when it comes to expenditure on vacations. When some 20 million northern Europeans annually travel south to the Mediterranean beaches,

---

88 Leakey, Human Origins, 1982; Wainssocat et al., Evolutionary relationship of human populations from an analysis of nuclear DANN polymorphisms, 319 (1986), Nature, p. 491; Jones/Rouhanni, How small was the bottleneck?, 319 (1986) Nature, p. 449; with regard to the findings made by the paleontologist Philip Tobias: Der Spiegel, 38/1996 pp. 190 at 192.

89 With regard to Sweden: Belt, National Geographic, Vol 184, no. 2, August 1993 pp. 2 at 16.

90 Even with regard to people suspicious in the beginning it can provoke a spontaneous feeling of happiness—the happiness to see such a garden and find oneself standing in the middle of it: Baring, with regard to the Wörlitzer Garten; similar Peterich, Oberitalien, 8th ed. 1985, with regard to the Tuskany, cited at Möllers, BayVBl. 1992, p. 587.

91 Air-traffic has only in Germany risen to an amount three times as high between the years 1980 to 1993 and gained about 82% during the last couple years: Roy/Morawa, Zum Konzept eines umweltverträglichen Tourismus, Jahrbuch Ökologie 1997 [1996], pp. 176; Krohn, DIE ZEIT (96/10/18), p. 74; Kiani-Kress/Klesse, in: Wirtschaftswoche, 97/03/27, pp. 72/73

there is a summer population shift. "Everybody wants to go 'back
to nature'—but nobody is willing to walk there."[92]

Many retired persons from northern Europe ultimately relocate
in these warmer climates, e.g. in Mallorca or the Canary Islands. A
similar development is evident in the U.S.A., where there is
continuously a disproportionate number of older residents in the so-
called "Sun Belt" states in the south.[93]

III. Conclusions for the Law

After an introduction to the as-yet unachieved goal of
environmentally appropriate behavior and to typical modes of
human behavior, the next question is how the lawmakers might
govern more effectively with regard to attaining a desirable
response by people to environmental problems. It must be
demonstrated that environmental protection can be achieved with
relative ease if it reflects human behavioral modes (1.), and only
under certain conditions (2., 3.), or perhaps not at all (4.) where it
contradicts human behavior. In the latter case the individual must
be "outwitted."

1. Information and Self-Preservation due to the Force of Law

Information and implementation of legal standards should take
into account the fact that to secure the personal existence and the
protection of one's descendants is one of the strongest of human
impulses. As long as the legislature bears this in mind, enactment
of legally enforceable environmental protection statutes will be
relatively easy. Scarcely anyone would dispute that lasting
development and the provision of adequate resources are critical for
the survival of future generations. People differ only with regard to
which is the best route to achieving this common good.[94] Security
of human existence is one of the most potent of human urges, and
for this reason, the lawmakers could take advantage of the situation

---

92   Cf. supra note 21.
93   In Sun City right next to Phoenix, Arizona, thousands of retired people enjoy themselves.
     Arizona and Nevada being among the fastest growing states : Müller-Moewes, USA—
     Der Westen, 1998, p. 136.
94   Schluchter/Dahm, supra n.11.

following a catastrophe to promptly introduce legislation. Environmental protection mandates, too numerous to mention, were the products of earth-damaging events, for example the promulgation of the EU Seveso-Directive in response to the accident at Seveso,[95] the amendment to section 2 of Germany's Environment Statutes[96] following the reactor incident at Chernobyl, the passing of the Environmental Liability Law after the Sandoz accident,[97] the tightening of the language of section 29 of the Federal Emissions Protection Statute in the aftermath of the Hoechst disaster,[98] and the adoption of the Ozone Regulations after the substantial increase in the 1995 recorded ozone level.[99]

The recently introduced Art. 20a of the Grundgesetz (Basic Law) states: "It is the responsibility of the government to assure, also with regard to future generations, protection of the natural environment."[100] Both the legislature and the courts must take special care to ensure that laws in pursuance of this constitutional mandate are clear and unambiguous. An example of how this might be accomplished is improving legal protection for children by setting down the threshold value (the lowest acceptable maintained value of emissions)[101] and broadening health protection standards

---

95 Directive 82/501/EEC with regard to the danger of severe accidents occuring at certain jobs in the industrial field 1982/06/24 (Seveso-directive), incorporated into German law by the 12. BundesImmissionsSchutzVerordung (Störfall-Verordnung) as amended on 91/09/20; BGBl. I, 1991, p. 1891.

96 Gesetz zur Errichtung des Umweltbundesamtes geändert am 26.11.1986 (Law constituting the federal environmental office as amended on 86/11/26) 1986 BGBl. I 1986, p. 2089; Strahlenschutzvorsorgegesetz vom 19.12.1986, BGBl. I 1986, p. 2610.

97 BGBl. I 1990, p. 2634.

98 § 29a BundesImmissionsSchutzGesetz (BImSchG) amended by the law of 92/08/26, BGBl. I 1992, p. 1564; with regard to the occurences at the Hoechst-company: Möllers, supra n.16.

99 Infra n.145; with regard to US-legislation after the incident of Exxon-Valdez there is to be named the Oil Pollution Act 1990, Pub.L.No. 101-380 Stat.484.

100 Art. 20a GrundGesetz (Basic Law), amendment to the constitution by the law of 94/10/27, BGBl. I 1999, p. 3146.

101 With good cause it was established that today's threshold values protect children in an insufficient way against asthma, pseudocroup, etc., since they only take into consideration the predisposition of the average adult; Böhm, Der Normmensch, 1996, pp. 22; Möllers, DVBl. 1996, pp. 1387; Schultze-Fielitz, JZ 1997, pp. 298, 299; Damarowsky/Stevenson/Wassermann, Größte Gefahr für die Kleinsten, in: Jahrbuch Ökologie 1997 [1996], pp. 56; BT-Dr. 12, p. 4626.

by expanding the concept of what is defined as "health."[102]

As a consequence, the enduring protection of the world should be enshrined as the principal goal of all environmental laws, so that it will have to be taken into consideration by weighing conflicting interests against each other.[103]

2. Complexity and Limits of Capacity—Preconditions for an Informed Environmentally Appropriate Behavior

Although the human being is defined in terms of, and in ideal cases is led by the mind, behavior in the context of environment protection is sometimes schizophrenic. The person knows what he ought to do, but he does not, in fact, act accordingly. A mere explanation of the reasons why a certain conduct is desirable, is not necessarily the means through which change is effected. In order for information to have a cultural effect upon innate human behavior, and thus lead to environmentally correct behavior, the information will have to bypass the brain's capacity limits and make positive use of the subject's feelings, in addition to his thinking. This approach rests upon the following three presumptions.

a) Building up an Information System

Environmentally appropriate conduct demands the communication of which activities create damage. Such an information network will have to be built up in Eastern Europe, while in Western Europe it will have to be perfected.[104] The Government receives insufficient up-to-date factual data concerning the environment because of an inadequate legal basis. Thus, the flow of information between governmental authorities and businesses must be improved. An example may be cited in the lack

---

102 Möllers, supra n.16; assenting: von Bar, DVBl. 1997, pp. 387/388. The conditions so far set forth by the judiciary to comply with the demand of a behavior due diligence have a protecting effect on children exposed to the dangers of traffic, see BGH 52/07/07 = BGHSt 3, p. 49; BGH 92/05/05 = VersR 1992, p. 890; Cramer, in: Schönke/Schröder (eds.), StGB, 25th. Ed.1997, § 15 m.n. 213.

103 Murswiek, in: Sachs, GrundGesetz (GG), 1996 Art. 20a, m.n. 70 with further reading; see, §1 Nr. 1 BWaldG of 75/05/02, BGBl. I 1975, p. 1037; see §1(1) BNatSchG of 87/03/12, BGBl. I 1987, p. 889; Martens, ZRP 1996, pp. 44.

104 Möllers, supra n.16; von Bar, supra n.102.

of duty for enterprises concerned with chemicals or food to communicate data concerning the environment. So far, from a legal point of view, there is a call for a duty on the part of the businesses to communicate information; the simple right for administrative bodies to demand information is not sufficient. That way businesses would have to communicate the information automatically, and thus the flow of information was not dependent upon administrative request for such information.[105]   Complex environmental data should be supported by a monitoring system which records and communicates observations, measurements, and rates of potential damage from particular products.[106]

Moreover, this knowledge of government and business enterprises must be passed on to the general public, so that the desired conduct will follow.[107]   The right of the public to be informed, which has been expanded in recent years[108] cannot be seen as a sufficient means, since the individual will only ask for information when he is aware of the lack of it. In order to perceive this deficit, he already needs to be "suspicious" of his ignorance. In this regard, the flow of information between the government and the people must be improved. Logically, there is a corresponding obligation on the part of the state or the government.[109]

---

105   With regard to that lack: Möllers, supra n.16, pp. 324/347.

106   A legal definition is to be found in: § 46c LMBG of 93/07/08, BGBl. I 1993, p. 1170; Monitoring does exist with regard to forest-damage, food-contaminants, and cancer; lacking a long-term monitoring process, to draw conclusions is rather difficult.

107   Very clear is the Non-smoking campaign during this century. Just after realizing that smoking has a detrimental effect on the risk of cancer and cardiac infarction, one was able to promote Non-smoking as the adequate healthful behavior by the means of information and legal acts: see, Möllers, Rechtsschutz des Passivrauchers, JZ 1996, p. 1050.

108   Directive 90/313 with regard to free access to information concerning the environment 90/06/07 O.J. No. L 158, 56, in Germany incorporated by the Umweltinformationsgesetz of 94/07/07 BGBl. I 1994, p. 1490.

109   Möllers, supra n.16, p. 369; The Robert-Koch-Institut has to evaluate data on cancer, to discover trends in the development and of regional differences, and to publish those information: § 10 KrebsregisterG of 94/11/04 BGBl. I 1994, pp. 3943, 3951; with regard to the obligation of the Bundesinstitut für gesundheitlichen Verbraucherschutz und Veterinärmedizin to publish the results of the food-monitoring: § 46d(5)(5) LMBG; with regard to the forest damage inventory report of the EU: EuZW 1997, p. 2; in general to the research on those risks: Scherzberg, Risiko als Rechtsproblem, Ein neues Paradigma für das technische Sicherheitsrecht, VerwArch 84 [1994], pp. 484/509.

Between business enterprises and consumers there is still a gap between advertisements on the one hand and tort-law duty to warn on the other hand. This gap must be closed by the legislature, so that a company will not only have to inform the consumer of the advantageous aspects of a product, but also of the effects which that product has on the environment. The product does not necessarily have to be an "environmental devil" for this duty to be imposed.[110] It would be a positive step indeed if motor vehicle producers assumed an overall obligation to inform about the environmentally detrimental effects of their vehicles, especially with regard to fuel-consumption, CO_2-emissions, and ultimate disposal.[111]

b) Reduction of Complexity

An explanation is not effective if it is confusing. Excessive detail simply results in maintaining the status quo through inaction.[112] The second presumption, then, is that the complicated nature of the subject matter must be minimized: explaining environmental problems must be simplified in order for the general public to perceive their significance and to instigate environmentally conscious conduct.

In its ecological balance sheet on packing-materials, the Federal Office for Environment attempts to prove that the usage of recyclable bottles as opposed to one-way glass is more beneficial to the environment when the transporting distance of these materials is less than 100 kilometers (about 62 miles). Over this distance, however, the higher fuel consumption outweighs environmental advantages of glass over plastic bottles or Tetra-Packs (boxes out of a non-water absorbing layer).[113]

What, then, is the solution to this conflict? Essentially, the complexity of the explanation must be reduced. The soundest approach would be the application of common sense. Common sense usually helps us to see things clearly and to avoid confusion

---

110 But being of that opinion: Gramm, JZ 1990, pp. 905/910.
111 To guarantee an effect on the awareness of the single car-driver, he has to know which emissions are caused by his car, and in which way it causes detrimental effects on the environment and on humans are provoked.
112 Supra n.63.
113 Umweltbundesamt (ed.), Ökobilanz für Getränkeverpackungen, 2 vol., 1995.

born of complexity.[114]   Instead of deeming specific products environmentally tolerable in all circumstances, common sense tells us that only local products can be environmentally benign in re-usable systems.[115]

The reduction of complexity is the task not only of politicians, but also scientists. The dilemma of understanding, that is citing the desired expert opinion to justify inaction, has to be resolved. Rather than claiming, as may be justifiable, that a particular environmental effect has not been proven beyond doubt, thereby raising environmentally counter-productive issues of causality—scientists should simply have the courage to make choices based upon probabilities of potential destruction. Here, too, the application of common sense might be helpful.[116]

c) Specifying and Localization

This discussion leads us directly to the third condition: efficient information. Since environmentally harmful behavior is frequently not perceived as such, the gap in experience has to be narrowed by providing concrete and local examples. It is not the widely publicized major catastrophes that count, but the "small" numbers, showing what is happening in the immediate locality. Abstract and generalized cancer statistics have no noticeable impact upon the reader or viewer; they have to refer to individual cases in a concrete way. For example, when you realize that every month two people in your own community become ill from fumes from heavy-duty trucks, this has more impact than a report that such illnesses affect some 20.000—or even 200.000—people in all Germany.[117]   This is

---

114 Dörner, supra n.61, pp. 256/307: this including the abolishment of some habits, and to put up schemes about how things are done.

115 Complexity-reduction is also necessary with regard to plans applied in circumstances of a catastrophe: they may not be too complex, because that makes it impossible to plan human behavior: Rodgers, supra n.54; with regard to the responsibility of more people: Möllers, DB 1996, pp. 1455/1459.

116 Very clear on that Gerling, in: Wirtschaftswoche 97/03/27, p. 112; with regard to assumptions in matters of law: Möllers, supra n.16; Kahlert, Alltagstheorien in der Umweltpädagogik, 1990; Wehrspann, supra n.20, pp. 52/78; Schluchter/Dahm, supra n.11, p. 191.

117 Also assumptions have to be sufficient. Warnings with regard to the ozone hole or the increasing temperature in the atmosphere are far more likely to get the individual to think if exposed to results of them at his front door.

the impact of localization. Ecological movements have made considerable strides in west European countries since the 1970s. Citizens in eastern Europe are now required to promote environmental protection in their countries. Positive action can counteract the comprehension dilemma, the experience gap and thereby hysteria and lethargy.[118]   Localization and concrete presentation are also capable of activating the urge to secure the existence of one's family.

3. Self-Interest and Law

   a) Institution of Competition and the Question of the Right Price
   The individual citizen is equally a *homo oeconomicus*. Government action must take the self-interest of people into account in such a way that environmentally appropriate behavior underlies the market and environmental costs are internalized. For this political correction of the market is needed; only in this way can the socio-environmental market advocated by Wolfgang Fikentscher be achieved.   Four measures may be distinguished.[119]   When comparing oil with the far more environmentally friendly gas, for example, we have to remember that special pipelines are needed to transport the latter.   As long as there is a lack of competition, monopolists can dictate the prices.[120]   The state must create competition as a preliminary step.   To this end a second measure would be to cut subsidies for environmentally destructive behavior. That aircraft fuel continues to be subsidized by financial support for state airlines despite its highly environmental destructive effects, distorts transport cost comparisons with rail and the car.   A further example of an area where governmental funding has to be reduced

---

118 Schluchter/Dahm, supra n.11, p. 187; UBA—32/95, p.95
119 Fikentscher, Die umweltsoziale Marktwirtschaft—als Rechtsproblem, 1991, p. 31.
120 Even though there soon will be rights to transportation in the field of energy, one can not yet call this a "market"; the U.S. und the U.K. being much further ahead in that matter; O.J. No. L 161, 147; Stewing, Umsetzung einer allgemeinen Durchleitungsverpflichtung für Elektrizität in das nationale Recht, EWS 1997, pp. 83; with regard to the U.K.: Fischermann, DIE ZEIT, 97/03/07; atomic energy being subsidised since the nuclear-plants operators are not obliged to have an insurance against nuclear risk: Loske, Jahrbuch der Ökologie 1996 [1995], pp. 50; 60.

is the coal-mining industry.[121]   Only by abolishing those subsidies will more environmentally friendly gas be able to compete fairly. In addition, abolishing tax relief for the use of the private car for travel to work would result in fairer competition for public transportation.[122] The third measure is to internalize the currently externally-borne costs of improving ecological conditions, thus reducing the total financial burden.[123] For example, an "Ökosteuer" (environment tax) is to be imposed upon vehicles.[124]   Fourth should be a consideration of subsidizing environmentally appropriate behavior. To name some examples from the past there was financial support for the installing of catalytic converters, or additional compensation for environmentally conscious construction.[125] Internationally, there are many countries with far better incentives aimed at promoting environmentally appropriate conduct than those provided by Germany.[126]

Since caring for and protecting one's own property is central to the self-interest of the individual, environmentally beneficial conduct can obviously be achieved through effective property regulations.[127] Through the partition of plots of land, millions in Germany now have cultivated small gardens, an apparently significant factor in improving upon and maintaining the natural environment. This property ownership factor must be combined with social connections, for example by recognizing that water no longer appertains to an individual piece of land,[128] or that regulations designed to protect trees in the entire community will

---

121 Loske, supra n.120.

122 Suggestions for reforms on the tax-and pensionsystem: NJW 1997, supplement to vol. 13, pp. 1-8.

123 I.a. Lohmann, Umwelthaftungsrecht: Ein Beitrag zur Internalisierung von negativen externen Effekten, in: Schulz (ed.), Ökologie und Recht, 1991, pp. 81/85.

124 Besides a higher VAT on leaded fuel, the Automobile license fee is no longer established with regard to the piston displacement, but according to the emissions: Kraft-StändG 1997, BGBl. I 1997, p. 805.

125 WärmeschutzVO of 94/08/16, BGBl. I, p. 2121, as well as § 9(4) EigenheimzulageG of 96/01/30, BGBl. I 1996, p. 113.

126 Belgium, Denmark, Sweden: see Opschoor/Turner (eds.), Economic Incentives and Environmental Policies: Principles and Practice, 1994.

127 In the U.S. this thought being expressed e.g. by the entrance-fees to National Parks

128 BVerfGE 58, pp. 300/332 of 81/07/15 " Naßauskiesung".

collaterally augment the rights of the individual property owner.[129]

b) Gain in Esteem: Environmental-Audit and Voluntary Self-Obligation

Furthermore self-interest in the form of the desire for respect and esteem can be harnessed to guide individual action. Using this theory to inform the framing of legislation, lawmakers might cause businesses to adopt environmentally relevant measures and thereby to enhance the reputation of their concerns. At the level of communal laws a powerful regulatory process is proceeding.[130] Though there may still be a need for harmonization,[131] product and concern related environmental protection may be introduced by the "blue environment angel," the "european flower[132] "or the "environment audit,"[133] promoting a company ecological ethic.[134] By analogy the state can harness the gain in esteem by individual citizens through environmental education, promoting the use of the bicycle instead of the automobile, for example.[135]

---

129 Art. 12(2) BayNatSchG of 94/04/28, GVBl. 229.

130 "Bio"-LebensmittelVO Nr. 2092/91 of 91/07/22, O.J. No. L 198, 1; concerning that matter: Schüler, "Bio"-Lebensmittel—Der neue EWG-Verordnungsentwurf, EuZW 1990, pp. 279; Lungguth, Die EG-"Bio"-Verordnung, ZLR 1991, pp. 573; Nacken, Werbung in Europa, in: Festschrift Helmrich, 1994 pp. 367; Möllers/Schmid, Der EU-Richtlinienentwurf über irreführende und vergleichende Werbung—neue Chancen für Gesundheits-und Umweltschutz?, EWS 1997, pp. 150.

131 Wimmer, Ein blauer Engel mit rechtlichen Macken, BB 1989, pp. 565; Köhler, Der gerupfte Umweltengel oder Die wettbewerbsrechtlichen Grenzen der umweltbezogenen Produktwerbung, UTR 1990, pp. 343; Möllers, supra n.16, pp. 156; With regard to the proceedings: Epiney/Möllers, supra n.25, pp. 123.

132 UmweltzeichenVO No. 880/92 of 92/04/11 O.J. No. L 99, 5; Roller, Der "Blaue Engel" und die "Europäische Blume", EuZW 1992, pp. 499; UBA (ed.), Das Europäische Umweltzeichen Texte 62/96.

133 Verordnung über die freiwillige Beteiligung gewerblicher Unternehmen an einem Gemeinschaftssystem für das Umweltmanagement und die Umweltbetriebsprüfung No. 1836/93 of 93/06/29 O.J. No. L 168, 1; Möllers, Qualitätsmanagement, Umweltmanagement und Haftung, ISO 9000; Umwelt-AuditVO und die Haftung von Unternehmen, Managern und Mitarbeitern, DB 1996, pp. 1455.

134 Knights, Ethics and Economic Interpretation, 1935; Koslowski, Ethik des Kapitalismus, 5th ed. 1995; Schneider, Unternehmensethik und Gewinnprinzip in der Betriebswirtschaftslehre ZfbF 42 [1990], pp. 869.

135 Mylaeus/Mylaeus Umwelterziehung—allgemeine psychologische Grundlagen, in: Erdmann (ed.), Perspektiven menschlichen Handelns: Umwelt und Ethik, 1992, pp. 148; Faring, Plädoyer für ökologisch orientierte Verbraucherbildung an Schulen, ZFU 1992, pp. 329; Umweltbundesamt (ed.), Umweltbewußt Leben, Ökologie 1997 [1996], p. 267: Up to now the size of the car still seems determining its owner's status; Lorenz, Die Acht Todsünden der zivilisierten Menschheit, 1973, p. 97

The voluntary assumption of obligations can resolve the co-operation-dilemma[136] and prevent the shifting of responsibility mentioned at the outset.[137]　Voluntary assumptions of obligations which have no enforceable binding character[138] are subject to the risk of not being fulfilled.[139]　In such cases additional means are necessary to overcome human self-interest.　One method could be to announce voluntarily assumed obligations publicly, so that non-observance would lead to a corresponding loss of public esteem.

c) Symbolic Law and Explanatory Norms of Law

If a system of simple morality is employed to draw the difficult line between self-interest and regard for others,[140] it is imperative that the law intervenes in order to convert the ordinary human being into one with social concerns, the *homo sociologicus*.[141]　By laws we understand the customary imperatives (You should . . .) which require particular acts or omissions;[142] they compel by means of an actual sanction or legal penalty.　For legal norms at least two requirements should be met in order that citizens observe them.

Norms must initially be desired by the people in general.　Those laws which only feign an activity of the lawmaker, without actually being executed, are generally ignored or are perceived to be confusing.　Statutes can be distinguished from mere information in such a way, that the former contain distinct penalties for violations,

---

136　Axelrod, supra n.83; Schultze-Fielitz, DVBl. 1996, pp. 658/659.
137　A gaining acceptance can be recognized:　BT-Dr. 10/6028; Schmidt, Öffentliches Wirtschaftsrecht, Allgemeiner Teil, 1990, pp. 497; Schmidt, Einführung in das Umweltrecht, 4th ed., 1995, p. 7; von Lersner, Die ökologische Wende, 1991, p. 55; Henneke, NuR 1991, pp. 267/271.
138　Henneke, supra n.137, p. 272; Brohm, DÖV 1992, pp. 1025/1034; Kloepfer/Elsner, DVBl. 1996, pp. 964/972; of dissenting opinion: Schmidt, supra n.137, p. 499.
139　See Klimaschutzbericht (report on the climate-protection) of the german government of 1996, which states that the CO_2-emissions are increasing so that the goal of a 25% reduction by the year 2005 has become uncertain.
140　Gruter, supra n.47, p. 53.
141　Dahrendorf, Homo sociologicus, 15th ed. 1977.
142　Thon, Rechtsnorm und subjektives Recht, 1878; Ihering, Der Zweck im Recht, vol. 1, 1878; Fikentscher, Methoden des Rechts, vol. 4, 1977, p. 150; Engisch, Einführung in die Rechtswissenschaft, 8th ed., 1983, pp. 22/200; Larenz, Methodenlehre der Rechtswissenschaft, 6th ed. 1991, p. 253.

penalties which will actually be imposed and enforced. Otherwise, the general public will view them as non-binding dictates, which carry no legal responsibilities.[143] These so-called symbolic laws[144] include the ozone regulations[145] in so far as either the threshold value for a prohibition of driving is set so high that this margin will hopefully not be reached (so that it will never be applied), or because of numerous exceptions to the regulations.[146] If legal rules are contrary to one's genetic impulses, there must be an additional provision, i.e., an explanatory section. Because of the complexity involved in which and how specific conduct will damage the environment, ecological standards must clarify what makes them necessary. All environmental laws must make regular and frequent references to the principle of causation,[147] and must explain directly the exact principle involved and why certain acts are ecologically destructive.[148]   Similarly, speed limits—which are regularly violated—should be explicit as to the reason for a lower prescribed speed, such as "playground area," or "area sensitive to excessive noise."

---

143 Pospisil, Anthropology of Law: A comparative theory, 1971; Gruter, Rechtstheorie 11(1980), p. 96; Rehbinder, Rechtssoziologie, 3rd ed. 1993, p. 159; The legal duty to buckle up was publically known and certain, as well as it was considered proportional and in accordance with Art. 2 GG (Basic Constitutional Law) by the Bundesverfassungsgericht (Federal Constitutional Court), but still it wasn't followed by a vast majority of drivers until legislature imposed a fine of 40,-DM; BVerG, NJW 1987, p. 180.

144 Hegenbarth, Symbolische und instrumentelle Funktion moderner Gesetze, ZRP 1981, p. 201; Schmehl, Symbolische Gesetzgebung, ZRP 1991, pp. 251; Voß, Symbolische Gesetzgebung, 1989; Sendler, Der Rechtsstaat im Bewußtsein seiner Bürger, NJW 1989, pp. 1761/1763; Deckert, Folgenorientierung in der Rechtsanwendung, 1995, pp. 24/97.

145 BGBl. I 1995, p. 910.

1466 Sendler, Heinrich Böll und das Ozongesetz, NJW 1995, p. 2829; Kutscheidt, Das Ozongesetz—ein Reizthema, NJW 1996, p. 3153; of a different opinion the BVerG (NJW 1996, p. 651): No violation of the duty of protection how it is foreseen by Art. 2(2)(1) GG can be established. This is the same approach taken with regard to the recommended maximum speed of 130km/h on the German freeways (Autobahn).

147 I.a.: § 1UVPG; § 1/§ 5(1) Nr. 2 BImSchG; § 7(2) Nr.3 AtG; § 9UGBE, in: Umweltbundesamt (ed.), Umweltgesetzbuch Allgemeiner Teil 1991; Kirchgässner, Das Verursacherprinzip: Leerformel oder regulative Idee, JZ 1990, pp. 1042; Murswiek, supra n.103.

148 Talking about the general perception of right and wrong: Bauriedl, supra n.20, pp. 11/15.

4. Fundamental Needs—Back to Nature

a) Insufficiency of Price and Prohibition

Flying is cheaper than ever before. Restrictions prohibiting travel either meet with strong opposition[149] or are simply not permitted.[150] To avoid distortion of the international market, internationally binding regulations would be necessary. But as yet such international environmental-taxation is far from realization,[151] not the least because developing countries are up to 90 percent dependent upon tourism. Furthermore, experience shows that travel, even in times of financial shortage, is not avoided. This clearly indicates that even increasing the expense of travel through taxation would fail to reduce tourism; the urge to visit warmer areas persists.

b) Realistic Alternatives by means of a Local Environment Program: Quality of Life- or Vacation at Home

The human need for nature, warmth and sunshine is undeniable, so that there should be alternatives to traveling all the way to Rimini's beaches in order to meet these needs. One way can be seen in developing so-called "soft tourism."[152] A preferable opportunity is offered by the creation of green areas within our cities through skillful regional planning. This would prevent residents from succumbing to the urge to vacate their own communities each weekend.

The environmental politics of a community need not be confined to the "offers" made by the administrative regulations. There should also be a promotion of an environmental community-wide program.[153] For example, parks which were established

---

149 Because of that driving-prohibitions do not find general acceptance: supra n.146.

150 This thought finding its expression in the freedom of movement as it is granted in Art. 11 GG.

151 Suspicious: Loppow, DIE ZEIT, 97/03/21, p. 59.

152 Mose, Sanfter Tourismus—Möglichkeiten und Hindernisse, Jahrbuch Ökologie 1997 [1996], pp. 167; Roy/Morawa, Jahrbuch Ökologie 1997 [1996], p. 176.

153 Hoppe, Umweltschutz durch Gemeinden, DVBl. 1990, p. 609; Bunge, Bauleitplanung, in: Lübbe-Wolff (ed.), Umweltschutz durch kommunales Satzungsrecht, 1993 m.n. 206; Korte, Kommunaler Umweltschutz trotz leerer Kassen, Jahrbuch Ökologie 1997 [1996], pp. 274.

during the last few centuries in New York City or London have been maintained and remain today as they were at their inception.[154] Networks of bicycle trails present the opportunity for relaxation near home. Forests accessible from city centers have provided pleasant places to stop and enjoy scenic views.[155]

The efforts of several of the German Länder deserve commendation. Near Munich and Augsburg for example, forests have been expanded nearer to and even within the cities, with natural and refreshing areas with green landscapes and lakes.

Moreover, the need for warmth can be met even during the long winter months and on rainy weekends during the summer. The so-called adventure pools (Erlebnisbäder) with saunas and palm trees offer many advantages. Anyone who emphasizes[156] the environmental problems caused by those "establishments"—for which there is a strong demand on the market[157]—simply overlooks the resulting satisfaction of the human need for warmth and sunny surroundings. With such options, tourism which advertises travel to milder climates might even become obsolete with many deciding against the typical three-weekend vacation to Mallorca or the four-day Easter or Pfingsten trip to Italy.

Finally, if public transportation is a realistic alternative, the individual's problem of getting to and from work each day will be greatly simplified.[158] Even more sensible would be to completely refrain from using transport to as great an extent as is possible.

It is not necessary that each person owns a motor vehicle, if he works near his residence and if he spends his free time nearby. Dispensing with this daily transportation need would not only relieve the nuisance of noise and other threats to our health that

---

154 E.g. Central Park in New York/Hyde Park in London/Englischer Garten in Munich (having celebrated its 200th anniversary in 1989); with regard to Central Park: Swedlow, National Geographic, vol. 183, No. 5, May 1993, p. 2.
155 As a good example might be cited the viewpoint—"towers" built in many German forests during the last century.
156 Bayerische Staatsregierung (ed.), Umweltpolitik in Bayern '90, 1990, p. 141.
157 Hennig, DIE ZEIT, 96/03/07, p. 73.
158 The throughout Germany supposedly unique subway and suburban-train-system in the greater Munich area is used by 50 percent of all daily commuters in that area.

vehicular traffic poses for those who live near busy streets,[159] but it would also accomplish a greater protection for the environment. With community efforts and programs, the inner cities will surely become more attractive, and there will be a marked reduction in flight from urban areas. Rather than focusing upon raising living standards, the emphasis should be upon an overall increase in the quality of life. Especially the newly-emerging industrial countries are called upon not to repeat the mistakes of their neighbors in the West.[160]

Summary

1 . a) Frequently the lack of unambiguous information prevents meaningful protection of the environment. And even if information exists, environmental awareness does not automatically lead to the corresponding necessary and environmentally appropriate behavior. Legal norms aimed at environmental protection are often not complied with. Informing and legal rules often fail to achieve the wished for environmentally beneficial behavior. On the other hand, countless people are actively engaged in citizens' action groups founded for the protection of the environment—a seemingly contradictory response.

b) Accordingly it would appear useful to examine the extent to which behavioral research may contribute to the apt regulation of behavior in the area of environmental protection. Employing an inter-disciplinary approach legal behavioral research (legal ethology) examines which human behaviors are innate, and which culturally imparted instruments can be used

---

159 Since it is not possible to set down to a greater extend the noise-threshold-value of vehicles, by ways of constructing it has to be assured that the noise is kept out of apartement buildings: Miller, Interdependenzen zwischen Wohnumwelt und Bewohnerverhalten, in: Günther/Winter (Hrsg.), Umweltbewußtsein und persönliches Handeln, 1986, pp. 207; extending the notion of the term "health" might be helpful.

160 With regard to the detrimental effects of noise on people's health, see supra n.3.

to achieve the desirable behavior despite innate dispositions. Instruments are sought which prove effective in the sense that they not only promote environmental awareness, but also trigger desired environmentally beneficial behaviors.

2. Four examples of human behavior are given. First: man is willing to act in order to secure his own survival as well as that of future generations. Second: there are limitations on our freedom to act and think. In general, human beings think only along linear-causal lines, but not in a web-like stuctures. The memory capacity of the human brain is limited. As one does not feel environmental dangers throught the senses, there is a loss of perception leading to a distance in experience between human beings and their environment. Man is guided by emotions such as fear and the feeling of inability to change anything. This causes hysteria or lethargy. Third: the human being acts selfishly. The tragedy of the commons points up problems of cooperation and free-loading. Yet within narrow limits, man does acts altruistically. Fourth: human behavior includes the need for nature and warmth.

3. Given these four human behavior traits, it must be asked what the lawmaker can or should do to protect the environment.

   a) Informing and legal norms should aim more closely at securing survival and progeny. Then it is relatively straightforward to reach the environmentally beneficial behavior. One example is to protect children in a better way; another example is to protect future generations by law (art. 20a German Basic Law).

   b) Second, complexity and the limitations of the human brain cause further problems. In addition, information on environmental data is not sufficient. As a first step, environmentally beneficial behavior demands appropriate information. An improved system of information is necessary within the relationship of state, businesses, and citizens. Information has to simplify and reduce complexity, so that the individual may translate environmental awareness into concrete action. Common sense is required. Scientists and politicians require courage to make probability statements. Finally, informing has to be done in concrete terms and should refer to the environment where the individual lives. The communication dilemma and thereby also hysteria and lethargy might be counteracted by involvement.

c) State action has to take human egoism into account and recognize that environmentally adapted behavior is subject to the market, and that people have to internalize that the environment is not a cost-free good. Ownership might contribute to this process, in so far as it implies social commitment. It is the gain of reputation for businesses that legal frameworks such as the European Environmental Sign or the Environment-Audit employ. Citizen's environment education could take the same direction. In addition, voluntary self-commitments could prevent the cooperation dilemma, and lead to a gain in esteem by way of appropriate publicity. Norms have to be wanted. Token law without sanctions creates no environmental consciousness. Because of the complex effects, laws with explanatory effect are required within the area of environmental protection, which clarify to the general public why they are indispensible for the protection of the environment.

d) Informing and laws have to be sensibly supplemented by alternative methods, for example by a wise communal environmental policy developing possibilities of relaxation close to the city. Adventure beaches and water worlds present alternatives to a short trip to the Mediterranean. This has to be supplemented by a transportation policy which should as far as possible dispense with long transportation distances.

In these ways, innate human behavior might be corrected partly quite simply (a), partly only under certain circumstances (b,c), and partly not at all or only with difficulty (d).

Epilogue

Margaret Gruter:
A Creative Force
For Improvement in Law

William H. Rodgers*

"Creativity, as usually understood," Oliver Sacks reminds us, "entails not only a 'what,' a talent, but a 'who' – strong personal characteristics, a strong identity, personal sensibility, a personal style, which flow into the talent, interfuse it, give it personal body and form."[1] Margaret Gruter is this creative person – with the talent and the personal style to deliver it.

Margaret combines several of the personal traits expected to appear in truly creative people. One is a willingness to take risks.

The propensity for risk-taking varies across the human species, according to Melvin Konner in his book on *Why the Reckless*

---

* Stimson Bullitt Professor of Environmental Law, University of Washington, School of Law, Seattle, WA
1 Oliver Sacks, *An Anthropologist on Mars: Seven Paradoxical Tales* 241 (1995, Alfred A. Knopf, N.Y.).

Survive.[2] Some people are more disposed than others to try new things in art or work or intellectual endeavor. Risk-taking has special opportunity to prosper in an unpromising environment, which is a fair description of the world of "Law and Biology" before Margaret Gruter decided to enter it. Again and again, in her teaching conferences, publishing projects, and workshops, Margaret has been willing to confront nay-sayers, critics, and doubters. Rejection has never silenced Margaret's resilient willingness to take a chance in support of ideas she has committed herself to.

Margaret is also thoroughly imbued with what Lionel Tiger describes as a "ubiquitous, biologically based human propensity to unwarranted optimism."[3] This is the interesting happy side of self-deception. According to Robert Trivers, a new literature has appeared that demonstrates "that there are intrinsic benefits to having a higher perceived ability to affect an outcome, a higher self-perception, and a more optimistic view of the future than the facts would seem to justify."[4] The basic idea is that life is future-oriented and small illusions about the prospects of success are a better framework for confronting contingency than would be a grim, empirical reality. Edward O. Wilson expresses the notion somewhat differently: "Confidence in free will is biologically adaptive. Without it the mind, imprisoned by fatalism, would slow and deteriorate."[5] Incurable optimism is a nice way to describe Margaret's approach to her "Law and Biology" mission. She has been told a thousand times that social scientists will be resistant to her ideas, law teachers resentful, philosophers disdainful, cognitive scientists disinterested. But Margaret heard none of the reasons why it cannot be done. She simply goes on her way, showing that it can be done.

---

2   Why the Reckless Survive: And Other Secrets of Human Nature (1990, Viking Penguin, N.Y., N.Y.).

3   Quoted in *Why the Reckless Survive* at 130.

4   Robert Trivers, "The elements of a scientific theory of self-deception", Annals of the N.Y. Academy of Sciences, 1999, citing S.E. Taylor & D.A. Armor, Positive illusions and coping with adversity, 64 J. Personality 873 (1996).

5   Consilience: The Unity of Knowledge 120 (1998, Alfred A. Knopf, N.Y., N.Y.) [hereinafter cited as 1998 Consilience].

Some might describe Margaret's career as the work of genius. The idea of genius changes the focus of discovery from process to person. James Gleick's excellent book on Richard Feynman [6]puts "genius" back into the pantheon of creative possibilities. "Genius", Gleick reminds us, "is the fire that lights itself."[7] The imagination of genius is a "rambling and volatile power." It is "perpetually attempting to soar." As Hans Bethe said, "an ordinary genius is a fellow that you and I were just as good as, if we were only many times better."[8] Feynman was a genius in method. How did he work? "You write down the problem. You think very hard...then you write down the answer."[9] He was a genius in reputation. "Someone with a new idea always risked finding, as one colleague said, 'that Feynman had signed the guest book and already left.'"[10] It was "unnerving to learn", another added, "that one's potentially career-advancing discovery had been, to Feynman, below the threshold of publishability."[11] He was a genius in his bearing. He had "showboating in his character." He was like the guy that climbs Mount Blanc barefoot "just to show that it can be done."[12]

Defining genius is no easy thing. Cesar Lombroso got off to a bad start in 1891, identifying the "symptoms of genius": "Degeneration. Rickets. Pallor. Emaciation. Left-handedness."[13] A somewhat better indicator is an enemies' list. Jonathan Swift said, "When a true genius appears in the world, you may know him by this sign, that the dunces are all in confederacy against him."[14] Freud insisted that

---

6   James Gleick, The Genius: The Life and Science of Richard Feynman (1992, Pantheon Books, N.Y.).

7   Id. at 323 ("Originality; imagination, the self-driving ability to set one's mind free from the worn channels of tradition").

8   Id. at 322.

9   Id. at 315.

10   Id. at 316.

11   Ibid.

12   Id. at 323.

13   Id. at 318.

14   Quoted in Dean Keith Simonton, *Greatness: Who Make History and Why 201* (1994, Guilford Press, N.Y., N.Y.) [hereinafter cited as 1994 Who Makes History].

"creative genius is a sign of neurosis."[15] Keith Simonton tells us, reassuringly, that the findings fall short of establishing that "the creative genius is outright mad."[16] They seem to possess "just the right amount of weirdness."[17]

Margaret lacks some of these indicators of genius. She is not left-handed, as far as I know. She seems disinterested in climbing Mt. Blanc. But the dunces are in strong confederacy against her. And every day of her life, she has conformed to the metaphor of the fire that lights itself.

Dean Keith Simonton has argued that major innovators "often hail from the periphery of a discipline, culture, society or political system."[18] There are hidden benefits, it seems, from being self-taught or a latecomer or a field-switcher. Why the outsider might hold the creative edge over the insider is worthy of speculation. One notion, developed by Donald Campbell, is that people of two cultures have a broader range of hypotheses to draw upon.[19] Put somewhat differently, the nonexpert or amateur might be free of the stifling particulars of specialization.[20] The outsider has no heavy investment in the status quo, no sunk costs in settled patterns. The outsider must learn how to overcome rejection, go around obstacles, and find unconventional ways.

Margaret's career fits closely this pattern of the creative outsider. She grew up in Germany – coming to America only after World War II. She was female. She had no scientific discipline to speak of – unless law counts as a science, and this one was picked up later in life. She lacked all necessary connections to academia.

Each and every one of these barriers was but fuel to Margaret's fire. Lacking knowledge of the formidable difficulties that stood in

---

15   Id. at 285 (in a chapter called "The Significance of Psychopathology").

16   Id. at 293 ("Geniuses are fantastic risk takers").

17   Id. at 294.

18   1994 Who Makes History at 166.

19   Ibid.

20   1998 Consilience at 126 (on the "overspecialization of the educated elite").

her way, she simply went around them and through them and over them.

Margaret Gruter shows a number of other traits that are linked to creativity. She is opportunistic in being able to build large enterprises from small pieces. John H. Holland is a writer who describes this form of leveraging,[21]which has "the hallmark of emergence," in the sense of "much coming from little. The ability to build "much from little" is one of Margaret's hallmarks.

Margaret is a paradigm-shifter, as the term is understood in the great work of Thomas S. Kuhn. [22] With her law and biology movement , she has sought to rearrange "the scaffolding of ideas" that are found in the law schools.

Last but not least, Margaret Gruter has shown by example that sheer hard work is a greatly underrated component of creativity. Dean Keith Simonton's study of the one hundred most influential people in history[23]shows the two sides of hard work: these people work around the clock but their "monomaniacal preoccupation" was not work to them but enjoyment.[24] Those who created more failed more. Creativity leading to recognition is "far from a one-shot affair."[25] It is a cumulative process with more gains than setbacks.

By her hard work and eager creativity, Margaret Gruter has done much in the service of the understanding of law and human being. It has been a personal pleasure to be exposed to her example.

---

[21] John H. Holland, Emergence: From Chaos to Order 2(1998, Helix Books, Addison-Wesley, Reading, Mass.).

[22] T.S. Kuhn, The Structure of Scientific Revolutions (1962, Un. Chicago Press).

List of Authors

Susan Low Bloch – Professor of Law, Georgetown University Law Center, Washington, DC.

Paul Bohannan – Professor Emeritus of Anthropology and Law, University of Southern California, Los Angeles, CA

Kingsley Browne – Professor of Law, Wayne State University Law School, Detroit, MI

Robert D. Cooter – Professor of Law and Economics, University of California at Berkeley, School of Law, Berkeley, CA

E. Donald Elliott –Professor (Adjunct) of Law, Yale Law School and Georgetown University Law Center. Partner, Paul, Hastings, Janolsky & Walker, Washington, DC

Wolfgang Fikentscher – Professor of Law, University of Munich, Law School, Munich, Germany

Robert Frank – Professor of Economics, Cornell University, Graduate School of Economics, Ithaca, NY

Lawrence A. Frolik – Professor of Law, University of Pittsburgh, School of Law, Pittsburgh, PA

Timothy H. Goldsmith – Professor of Biology, Yale University, Biology Department, New Haven, CT

Oliver Goodenough – Professor of Law, Vermont Law School, South Royalton, VT

Monika Gruter Morhenn – Attorney at Law, Thelen, Reid et.al., San Francisco, CA

Herbert Helmrich – Member, Legislature, State of Mecklenberg - Vorpommern, Schwerin, Germany

Hagen Hof – Dr. iur., Ahornweg 5, Barsinghausen, Germany

Raimund Jakob – Lecturer of Law, University of Salzburg, Institut fuer Grundlagenwissenschaften, Salzburg, Austria

Owen Jones – Professor of Law, Arizona State University, College of Law, Tempe, AZ

Adelheid Kühne – Professor of Psychology, Hannover, Germany

Michael Lehmann – Professor of Law, University of Munich, Munich, Germany

Michael T. McGuire – Professor of Psychiatry, University of California at Los Angeles, Medical School, Los Angeles, CA

Thomas M.J. Möllers – Professor of Law, University of Augsburg, School of Law, Augsburg, Germany

William Rodgers – Professor of Law, University of Washington, School of Law, Seattle, WA

Robert Trivers – Professor of Anthropology and Biological Sciences, Rutgers University, Department of Anthropology, New Brunswick, NJ

Martin Usteri – Professor of Law, University of Zurich, School of Law, Zurich, Switzerland

Kathleen Wermke – Humboldt University, Charitè, Anthropology, Berlin, Germany

Publications

by Margaret Gruter

1944

1. *Die Stellung der Ehefrau im englischen Scheidungssrecht.* (1944). Unpublished doctoral dissertation. Heidelberg University School of Law.

1973

2. *Legal Behavior and Family Stability.* (1973). J.S.M. Report. Stanford CA: Stanford University.

1976

3. *Die Bedeutung der Verhaltensforschung für die Rechtswissenschaft.* Schriftenreihe zur Rechtssoziologie und Rechtstatsachenforschung. Band 36 (1976). Berlin: Duncker & Humblot.

1977

4. "Law in Sociobiological Perspective." (1977). Florida State University Law Review 5, No. 2: 181-218.

1979

5. "The Origins of Legal Behavior." (1979). Journal of Social and Biological Structures 2: 43-51.

1980

6. "Soziobiologische Grundlagen der Effektivität des Rechts," in Rechtstheorie, Zeitschrift für Logik, Methodenlehre, Kybernetik und Soziologie des Rechts, Band 11 (1980) Heft 1: 96-109. Berlin: Duncker & Humblot.

1982

7. "Biologically Based Behavioral Research and the Facts of Law." (1982). Journal of Social and Biological Structures, 5, No. 4: 315-323.

1983

8. *Law, Biology and Culture: The Evolution of Law.* (1983).Santa Barbara, CA: Ross-Erikson (with Paul Bohannan); available through Gruter Institute, Portola Valley, CA.

9. "Introduction" to: *Law, Biology and Culture: The Evolution of Law.* (see No 8, supra): XI-XVIII

10. "Biologically Based Behavioral Research and the Facts of Law." In: *Law, Biology and Culture: The Evolution of Law.* (see No. 8, supra): 2-15.

11. "The Foundation in Law and Morality." In: *Law, Biology and Culture: The Evolution of Law.* (see No. 8, supra): 1-2 (with Paul Bohannan).

12. "The Search for the Missing Pieces: In Biology." In: *Law, Biology and Culture: The Evolution of Law.* (see No. 8, supra): 47-50 (with Paul Bohannan).

13. "The Search for the Missing Pieces: In Social Science." In: *Law, Biology and Culture: The Evolution of Law.* (see No. 8, supra): 129-133 (with Paul Bohannan).

14. "Epilog." In: *Law, Biology and Culture: The Evolution of Law.* (see No. 8, supra): 191-194 (with Paul Bohannan).

15. *Der Beitrag der Biologie zu Fragen von Recht und Ethik.* Schriftenreihe zur Rechtssoziologie und Rechtstatsachenforschung, Band 54 (1983) (ed.) Berlin: Duncker & Humblot (with Manfred Rehbinder).

16. "Einleitung" zu *Der Beitrag der Biologie zu Fragen von Recht und Ethik.* (see supra No. 15): 11-12 (with Manfred Rehbinder).

17. "Die Bedeutung der biologisch orientierten Verhaltensforschung für die Suche nach den Rechtstatsachen." In *Der Beitrag der Biologie zu Fragen von Recht und Ethik* (see supra No. 15): 225-241.

1986

18. *Ostracism: A Social and Biological Phenomenon* (1986) (ed.) New York: Elsevier: (with R. Masters) available through Gruter Institute, Portola Valley, CA.

19. "Ostracism as a Social and Biological Phenomenon: An Introduction." In *Ostracism: A Social and Biological Phenomenon* (see No. 18, supra): 1-10 (with Roger D. Masters).

20. "Ostracism on Trial: The Limits of Individual Rights." (1986). Ethology and Sociobiology 7:315-323.

21. "Ostracism on Trial." In: *Ostracism: A Social and Biological Phenomenon.* (1986). (see No. 18, supra): 123-137.

22. *Ablehnung - Meidung - Ausschluß*, Schriftenreihe zur Rechtssoziologie und Rechtstatsachenforschung. Band 60. (1986) (ed). Berlin: Dunckers & Humbolt (with Manfred Rehbinder).

23. "Vorwort der Herausgeber." In: *Ablehnung - Meidung - Ausschluß*, (see No. 22, supra): 7-8.

24. "Meidung vor Gericht. Über die Grenzen der Freiheitsrechte."
In: *Ablehnung - Meidung - Ausschluß*, (see No. 22, supra):
203-213.

1987

25. *The Baby M Case: New Technology Testing the Limits of Biology,
Law, and Policy.* (1987). Paper presented at the American
Political Science Association Meeting, Chicago, IL, Sept. 1-4,
1987.

1988

26. *Ethology as a Point of Departure for Basic Legal Research.*
(1988) Working Paper, Febr. 1988

27. Introduction to the First Newsletter of the Gruter Institute,
Summer 1988, Vol. I, No. 1:2.

1989

28. Update in Gruter Institute for Law and Behavioral Research
Newsletter, Summer 1989, Vol. II, No. 1:2.

1990

29. Update in Gruter Institute for Law and Behavioral Research
Newsletter, Spring 1990, Vol. III, No. 1:2.

30. Update in Gruter Institute for Law and Behavioral Research
Newsletter, Fall 1990, Vol. III, No. 2:2.

1991

31. *Law and the Mind: Biological Origins of Human Behavior.*
(1991). Sage Library of Social Research No. 184. Newbury
Park, CA: Sage Publications. Available through the Gruter
Institute for Law and Behavioral Research.

32. *Behavior, Evolution and the Sense of Justice.* (ed.). American Behavioral Scientist (Vol. 34, Jan./Feb.1991) Newbury Park, CA: Sage Publications.

33. Introduction to *Behavior, Evolution and the Sense of Justice.* (see No. 32 supra): 286-288.

34. Update in Gruter Institute for Law and Behavioral Research Newsletter, Summer 1991, Vol. IV, No. 1:2.

35. Update in Gruter Institute for Law and Behavioral Research Newsletter, Winter 1991/92, Vol. IV, No. 2:2.

1992

36. *The Sense of Justice: An Inquiry into the Biological Foundations of Law.* (1992 (ed.) Newbury Park, CA: Sage Publications (with Roger D. Masters).

37. "Preface" to: *The Sense of Justice: An Inquiry into the Biological Foundations of Law.* (see No. 36 supra): vii-ix

38. Update in Gruter Institute for Law and Behavioral Research Newsletter, Spring 1992, Vol. V, No. 1:2.

39. "An Ethological Perspective on Law and Biology." In: *The Sense of Justice: An Inquiry into the Biological Foundations of Law.* (see No. 36, supra): 95-105

40. *Law, Biology and Culture: The Evolution of Law*, 2nd ed. (1992). (ed.) New York: McGraw-Hill Primis (with Paul Bohannan).

41. "Introduction" to: *Law, Biology and Culture: The Evolution of Law*, 2nd ed. (see No. 40, supra): 4-10.

42. "The Foundation in Law and Morality" in: *Law, Biology and Culture: The Evolution of Law*, 2nd ed. (see No. 40 supra): 11-12.

43. "Biologically Based Behaviorial Research and the Facts of Law." In: *Law, Biology and Culture: The Evolution of Law*, 2nd ed. (see No. 40 supra): 13-25

44. "The Search for the Missing Pieces: In Biology." In: *Law, Biology and Culture: The Evolution of Law*, 2nd ed. (see No. 40, supra): 56-59 (with Paul Bohannan).

45. "The Search for the Missing Pieces: In Social Science." In: *Law, Biology and Culture: The Evolution of Law*, 2nd ed. (see No. 40, supra): 136-140 (with Paul Bohannan).

46. "Epilog." In: *Law, Biology and Culture: The Evolution of Law*, 2nd ed. (see No. 40 supra): 195-197 (with Paul Bohannan).

47. "New Lines of Research." In: *Law, Biology and Culture: The Evolution of Law*, 2nd ed. (see No. 40, supra): 198-199 (with Paul Bohannan & Roger D. Masters)

48. "Ostracism on Trial: The Limits of Individual Rights." In: *Law, Biology and Culture: The Evolution of Law*, 2nd ed. (see No. 40, supra): 208-216 (see also No. 18 supra).

49. Update in Gruter Institute for Law and Behavioral Research Newsletter, Fall 1992, Vol. V, No. 2:2.

1993

50. *Rechtsverhalten - Biologische Grundlagen mit Beispielen aus dem Familien- und Umweltrecht.*(1993). Köln: Verlag Dr. Otto Schmidt.

51. Update in Gruter Institute for Law and Behavioral Research Newsletter, Spring 1993, Vol. VI, No. 1:2.

52. "Preface." In: *Biology, Culture and the Environment* (1993) Michael T. McGuire & Manfred Rehbinder (eds). Berlin: Duncker & HumblotVerlag: 7-8

53. Update in Gruter Institute for Law and Behavioral Research Newsletter, Fall 1993, Vol. VI, No. 2:2.

54. "Preface." In: *Human Nature and the New Europe.* (1993) Michael T. McGuire & Gruter Institute (eds.), Boulder, CO: Westview Press Inc. xiii-xiv

1994

55. "Foreword." To: *The Neurotransmitter Revolution; Serotonin, Social Behavior, and the Law,* (1994). Roger D. Masters and Michael T. McGuire, (eds.). Carbondale, IL: Southern Illinois University Press: x-xii.

56. "Das Bedürfnis nach Sicherheit und die Bereitschaft zum Risiko: Eine evolutionsbiologische Perspektive." *Festschrift für Herbert Helmrich* (1994). München:. C.H. Beck'sche Verlagsbuchhandlung: 1083-1092

57. Update in Gruter Institute for Law and Behavioral Research Newsletter, Spring 1994, Vol. VII, No. 1:2.

58. Update in Gruter Institute for Law and Behavioral Research Newsletter, Fall 1994, Vol. VII, No. 2:2.

1995

59. *Where Ethology of Law and Legal Psychology Meet.* Festschrift für Manfred Rehbinder. (1995). Bern: Verlag Stämpfli + Cie AG.: 99-106

60. Update in Gruter Institute for Law and Behavioral Research Newsletter, Spring 1995, Vol. VIII, No. 1:2.

61. Update in Gruter Institute for Law and Behavioral Research Newsletter, Fall 1995, Vol. VIII, No. 2:2.

1996

62. "Balancing Altruism and Selfishness: Evolutionary Theory and the Foundation of Morality." *Annual Review of Law and Ethics.* (1996), Berlin: Duncker & Humblot. Vol 4:561-573 (with Roger D. Masters).

63. Update in Gruter Institute for Law and Behavioral Research Newsletter, Spring 1996, Vol. IX, No. 1:2

64. "Where Law and Biology Meet" (Part I) Gruter Institute for Law and Behavioral Research Newsletter, Spring 1996, Vol. IX, No. 1:1,3.

65. Update in Gruter Institute for Law and Behavioral Research Newsletter, Fall 1996, Vol. IX, No. 2:2.

66. "Where Law and Biology Meet" (Part II) Gruter Institute for Law and Behavioral Research Newsletter, Fall 1996, Vol. IX, No. 2:1, 4.

67. Update in Gruter Institute for Law and Behavioral Research Newsletter, Winter 1996/97, Vol. X, No. 1:2.

1997

68. *Gewalt in der Kleingruppe und das Recht.* Festschrift für Martin Usteri, (ed.) Bern: Verlag Stämpfli + Cie AG Bern (with Manfred Rehbinder).

69. Update in Gruter Institute for Law and Behavioral Research Newsletter, Fall 1997, Vol. X, No. 2:2.

1998

70. Update in Gruter Institute for Law and Behavioral Research Newsletter, Spring 1998, Vol. XI, No. 1:2.

71. *Compassion, Common Sense, and Deception: Social Skills and the Evolution of Law,* Festschrift für Wolfgang Fikentscher (1998) Tübingen, Germany: Mohr Siebeck Verlag, P 91-113 (with Lawrence A. Frolik).

72. "Genetic Knowledge, Deception and Self-Deception - The Human Analyzed," *Annual Review of Law and Ethics.* (1998) Berlin: Duncker & Humblot, Vol 6, (with Lawrence A. Frolik).

73. Update in Gruter Institute for Law and Behavioral Research Newsletter, Fall 1998, Vol. XI, No. 2:2.

1999

74. *Searching for Justice and Living Without It.* An Autobiography (1999). Portola Valley, CA: Gruter Institute for Law and Behavioral Research

75. "Hard Cases in Genetics; Answers to Hypotheticals." To be published *in Annual Review of Law and Ethics* (1999), Vol. 7. Berlin: Duncker & Humblot. (with Lawrence A. Frolik).

76. Update in Gruter Institute for Law and Behavioral Research Newsletter, Spring 1999, Vol. XII, No. 1:2.